Selling Jerusalem

Selling Jerusalem

Relics, Replicas, Theme Parks

ANNABEL JANE WHARTON

The University of Chicago Press CHICAGO AND LONDON

ANNABEL JANE WHARTON is the William B. Hamilton Professor of Art and Art History at Duke University. The editor of the *Journal of Medieval and Early Modern Studies*, her most recent books include *Refiguring the Post Classical City: Dura Europos, Jerash, Jerusalem and Ravenna* and *Building the Cold War: Hilton International Hotels and Modern Architecture*, the latter published by the University of Chicago Press.

The University of Chicago Press, Chicago 60637
The University of Chicago Press, Ltd., London

Printed in the United States of America

15 14 13 12 11 10 09 08 07 06 1 2 3 4 5

ISBN: 0-226-89421-5 (cloth)

ISBN: 0-226-89422-3 (paper)

Library of Congress Cataloging-in-Publication Data

Wharton, Annabel Jane.
Selling Jerusalem : relics, replicas, theme parks / Annabel Jane Wharton.
p. cm.
Includes bibliographical references and index.
ISBN 0-226-89421-5 (hardcover : alk. paper)—ISBN 0-226-89422-3 (pbk. : alk. paper)
1. Jerusalem—In popular culture. 2. Jerusalem—Foreign public opinion—History.
3. Popular culture—Religious aspects—Christianity. 4. Popular culture—Economic aspects.
5. Relics—Jerusalem. 6. Templars. 7. Franciscans. I. Title.
DS109.9.W53 2006
263′.042569442—dc22

2005025599

∞ The paper used in this publication meets the minimum requirements of the American National Standard for Information Sciences—Permanence of Paper for Printed Library Materials, ANSI Z39.48-1992.

For my daughters, Nicole and Andrea,
and all the others of the next generation
who work for the greater social good.

CONTENTS

ILLUSTRATIONS

Introduction: Project, Keywords, Debts

The view of Jerusalem is the history of the world; it is more, it is the history of earth and of heaven. * BENJAMIN DISRAELI, *TANCRED* (1847)

I am not seeking to convince anyone; I am simply investigating the uniformities of phenomena. Those who have another objective will have no trouble finding an infinity of works which will give them complete satisfaction; they need not read this one. * VINFREDO PARETO, *MANUAL OF POLITICAL ECONOMY* (1906)

PROJECT

Jerusalem stands at the center of a violent controversy that destroys the political stability of the Middle East and undermines the security of the world. The city's current volatility is only the most recent expression of the obsessive desires to possess the city and its monuments that have modeled the last two millennia of its history. Brutal military usurpation is the most dramatic demonstration of the longing for Jerusalem. Less destructive and more pervasive is the pilgrim's passion to possess the city through the immediate experience of its landscape. A great deal of serious scholarship has been devoted to the histories of these two modes of spatial control. Systematic attention has not, however, been accorded to the less ambitious, more expedient possession of Jerusalem in the form of its proxies—relics, replicas, reproductions. The forms by which Jerusalem has been procured in the West have changed over time. This book describes a chronological sequence of selected simulations of the Holy Land as a means of better understanding the reception of the historical city and its power in the West.

The first chapter identifies Jerusalem as the primary source for the numinous gift, the relic. Certainly Jerusalem was known in the early Christian West through texts and, a little later, by its rituals. But the Holy Land was also powerfully experienced in more material forms. Pilgrims' "blessings" (*eulogía*)—such as ampullae filled with holy oil or boxes containing bits of the landscape—were produced in Palestine for export. The discovery or "invention" (*inventio*) of the True Cross and of a succession of saints in Jerusalem provided even more potent fragments of the Holy City for distribution in the West. Relics could be stolen or gifted; they could not legitimately be sold. In the early Medieval economy, goods circulated more by gift, barter, and theft than by trade. The materiality of Jerusalem's most familiar embodiment was perfectly paralleled in the personal and physical character of contemporary economic exchange.

Chapter 2 considers Jerusalem in the High Middle Ages as the generator of the Crusades, the great stimulant of Western markets as well as Western piety. Crusader Jerusalem was the nursery of the Templars, the church's first military order and the West's protobankers. The Templars' Temples of London and Paris presented replicas of the Church of the Holy Sepulchre; they rendered Jerusalem's most holy Christian site present in the capitals of important emerging European nation-states. The Temples were an index of both a new monastic and a new economic order. These great churches operated as trophies demonstrating Western control of the East; they equally identified the Templars themselves as exotically Eastern. Templar wealth and the order's esoteric inclinations led to its brutal dismemberment. The Temples of London and Paris record the savage force of monetization and its attendant anxieties.

Chapter 3 describes Jerusalem-surrogates in the late Middle Ages and early modernity. During Mamluk and Ottoman rule of the Holy Land, the Franciscans replaced the Templars as the protectors of both the Christian sacred sites of Jerusalem and their visitors. Franciscan assets in the Holy Land became the order's cultural capital at home. The Franciscans reconstructed Jerusalem, complete with sculptural faux-*tableaux vivants* of the Passion narrative, as *sacri monti* (sacred mountains) in northern Italy. These Jerusalems performed as alternative pilgrimage destinations and as utopian images of urban perfection—perfectly Christian cities where the pious were unmolested by the religious Other, Jew or Muslim. The same anxieties about urban pollution provoked Franciscan efforts to legalize Christian usury as a necessary step to ridding Italian cities of their Jewish inhabitants. The Franciscan-led establishment of a *monte di pietà* (a pious heap of money, that is, a publicly owned pawnshop) in an Italian city was typically followed by the expulsion of the Jews. The poverty-embracing Franciscans were the great economists of the late Middle Ages and early modernity. That it is no coincidence that Franciscans thought so productively about other people's money is the argument of chapter 3.

The new authority of rationalism in modernity not only raised suspicions about the efficacy of the relic but also provided an alternative means of possession. Chapter 4 posits that the material object was displaced by its abstraction. Just as wealth was increasingly both held and circulated in paper form rather than as bullion or coin, so sites were both possessed and exchanged in the form of their mass-produced images. The nineteenth-century invention and perfection of lithographic color printing allowed David Roberts's renderings of Egypt and the Holy Land to circulate as credible proxies for an actual experience of the sacred terrain. The trompe l'oeil presentations of Jerusalem in the popular European and American panoramas of the Holy City served as even more powerful surrogates for the real thing.

The last chapter describes the latest Western constructions of the city. Now, in the globalized economy of the turn of the millennium, Jerusalem is experienced as the violent spectacle of suicide bombers on CNN and of torture in Mel Gibson's *The Passion of the Christ*. It may also be experienced as the "safe" spectacle of the theme park. The devout creator of The Holy Land Experience in Orlando promoted his theme park as a means of reconfirming spiritual values that are threatened by the progressive materialism of a commodity culture. This chapter contends that, contrary to the expectations of their pious producers, theme park and filmic spectacles of Jerusalem are themselves products of an economy that inevitably erodes the aura of their spiritual archetype.

Chapter 5 has one further task: it argues that Jerusalem performs as a prototype for Colonial Williamsburg. The West has episodically remade Jerusalem to resemble its Western images. From the construction of the city as Christian in the fourth century through the Franciscan reproduction of the Stations of the Cross in the Via Dolorosa in the seventeenth century, the West has continuously shaped Jerusalem to meet its own economic and aesthetic expectations.[1] The hypertropic growth of the tourist industry in modernity accelerated this tendency: the touristic desire for a view of a particular historical city precipitated Jerusalem's transformation. Perhaps most remarkably, under the British Mandate in the early twentieth century, Jerusalem was reworked to conform to a Western imaginary dependent on the reproductions of the city that had circulated in the West since the nineteenth century. By making a case for the role of Western images in the shaping of Jerusalem, I hope that my project will reveal some less familiar ways in which the West has contributed to Jerusalem's unbearable place in world politics now.

KEYWORDS

The chapter headings reveal not only the subject matter of the book and its chronological arrangement but also its economic argument.[2] The keywords used in the headings are—as Kalman Bland, a scholar of medieval Jewish thought, observes—ostensive, but not capricious. Both the adjectives describing Jerusalem in the chapter titles and the economic terms in the subtitles require further explanation. *Spectacle* is defined in its place in chapter 5. Here I suggest how I distinguish *replica, reproduction,* and *fabrication.*

A replica and a reproduction are both surrogates for an archetype.[3] The terms *replica/replicate* and *reproduction/reproduce* do not here indicate distinctions in a surrogate's form or even in its making. Rather, they suggest a difference in the strength of the claim made for the relation between the surrogate and its referent. That disparity is suggested by the following sentence: A couple that reproduces has children; a couple that is replicated has been genetically recon-

1. The remaking of Jerusalem since 1967 lies outside the scope of this volume. For an introduction to the subject, see R. Segal and Weizman, *A Civilian Occupation*.

2. Raymond Williams provides a model for the use of language in *Keywords*.

3. *Replica* is discussed further in relation to *souvenir* in chapter 2.

stituted through cloning. Reproduction insists on the possibility of a continuing sequence that can be natural (organic and social), but can also be industrial. Adam Smith combined the two, claiming that industrious people "reproduce, with a profit, the value of their annual consumption."[4] In contrast, a replica, though artificial, retains something of the particularity of its archetype. Some things are more readily replicated then others. Language, for example, lends itself to replication. The Vulgate, the pre-Reformation Bible of record, provides an example: "There was not a word of all that Moses had commanded that Joshua did not replicate [*replicavit*] for the whole assembly of Israel, including the women and children, and the aliens who lived among them" (Josh. 8:35). Though a material replica typically offers a messier version of its prototype than does a reproduction, it participates more fully in its prototype's uniqueness or authenticity.

A fabrication shares some of a replica's qualities, although it is altogether different. Like the replica, a fabrication is a unique construction. However, while a replica has a clear relation to a prototype, a fabrication either has no referent or its relationship to its referent is problematic. In English, as in ancient and medieval Latin, a fabrication is a work that might also be a trick. In the Vulgate version of the book of Exodus, Moses directs his people: "You shall not *make* [*non facies*] for yourself a graven image" (20:4). In Deuteronomy, he threatens disobedient Israelites: "the Lord will scatter you among the peoples" and "you will serve gods of wood and stone, *fabrications* [*fabricati*] of men's hands" (4:27–28). Now, in the postindustrial West, a fabrication is almost always a lie, a language thing. In early modernity and even into the nineteenth century, however, a fabric might well be a factory, and a fabrication more often than not was a crafting or making. So it appears in Gerolamo Morone's early sixteenth-century celebration of the *sacro monte* of Varallo: "This new and most pious work repeats [*refert*] everything [in Jerusalem], and by the very simplicity of the craft [*fabricae*] and the artless architecture [*structura*], the ingenious site surpasses all antiquity."[5] In chapter 3, I use *fabrication* in that same positive sense as Morone—craft with only a faint hint of prevarication.

Also in need of some explanation are two terms derived from economics or from economic history which appear prominently in the text. *Commodity* is one of them. According to the *Oxford Dictionary of Economics*, a commodity is "a standardized good, which is traded in bulk and whose units are interchangeable."[6] *Commodity* does not signal in this text, as it once did in economics and still does commonly in the humanities, any vendible "object, substance, action,

4. A. Smith, *Wealth of Nations*, 401.

5. Morone, *Lettere ed orazioni latine di Girolamo Morone*, 148–49. I want to thank Bart Huelsenbeck for the corrections he made to my translation of this text.

6. Black, *Oxford Dictionary of Economics*, 67. For a review of the use of the term in the social sciences, see D. Miller, "Consumption and Commodities." For a very compelling Marxian reading of the commodity, see Baudrillard, *For a Critique of the Political Economy of the Sign*. Marx's famous analysis of the commodity uncannily supports the term's very different usages in the social sciences and the humanities. Marx, *Capital*, 35–83.

or service which can afford pleasure or ward off pain."[7] I am anxious to retain the word's particular frankness about the invisibility of a thing's history. Pork bellies and crude oil are commodities. Each pork belly and each drop of crude oil certainly has a history, but that history leaves no mark on the economic object. I will call an icon a commodity only when it is treated like a pork belly.

Another expression that comes to history from economics is *primitive accumulation*. That capital accumulation had to precede the division of labor was a notion described by Adam Smith and developed by Karl Marx:[8]

Capitalistic production presupposes the pre-existence of considerable masses of capital and of labor-power in the hands of producers of commodities. The whole movement, therefore, seems to turn in a vicious circle, out of which we can only get by supposing a primitive accumulation preceding capitalistic accumulation; an accumulation not the result of the capitalistic mode of production, but its starting point.

This primitive accumulation plays in Political Economy about the same part as original sin in theology. . . . The so-called primitive accumulation, therefore, is nothing else than the historical process of divorcing the producer from the means of production. . . . The economic structure of capitalist society has grown out of the economic structure of feudal society.[9]

Adam Smith, Karl Marx, and other economists recognized that the ever-growing expansion of industry that they witnessed in the eighteenth and nineteenth centuries depended on the reinvestment of surplus value or profit. Profit could not simply be consumed, it had to be put back to work as capital. But if capitalism depended on surplus value and its reinvestment, how did it get started? The initiating process, as described by theoreticians like Rosa Luxemburg or historians like E. P. Thompson, was violent.[10] Primitive accumulation is commonly identified with early modernity; I suggest that the economic practices enabling "primitive accumulation" begin earlier.[11]

One last term—*the West*—needs some explanation, not so much to avoid the charge of essentialism, but to warn readers that its referent changes from the beginning to the end of the text. In the early chapters, *the West* is shorthand for Catholic western Europe. In the later chapters, *the West* refers to the industrialized societies of northern Europe and of North America: it is a topographic sign for a cultural climate shaped by capitalism and Protestantism. I myself am one of its products. And this book, like the objects that I discuss in it, is one of the ways in which Jerusalem has been circulated in the West.

---

7. Jevons, *The Theory of Political Economy*, 38.

8. A. Smith, *Wealth of Nations*, 221–23.

9. Marx, *Capital*, 713.

10. Luxemburg, *The Accumulation of Capital*. For the brutality of land enclosure, Thompson, *The Making of the English Working Class*, 213–33.

11. For a more recent analysis of primitive accumulation, see Perelman, *The Invention of Capitalism*. For a thoughtful theorization of primitive accumulation and its application to literary history, see Halpern, *The Poetics of Primitive Accumulation*.

DEBTS

As is evident from a summary of its chapters, economics is central to this book. It forced its attention on me while I was working on my previous study, *Building the Cold War: Hilton International Hotels and Modern Architecture.* As the first generation of international Hiltons was shaped quite literally by politics, ideology, and economics, the *Building the Cold War* project made me very aware of my ignorance of the dismal science. Through a Randall and Barbara Smith Faculty Award for Interdisciplinary Study, Duke University provided me with time off from teaching so that I could take courses in microeconomics with Professor Roy Weintraub and the history of economics with Professor Craufurd Goodwin. Later, to my great benefit, I also attended a course on the history and economics of globalization offered by Professor Gianni Toniolo. In addition, I collaborated with another art historian, Professor Hans Van Miegroet, and two colleagues in economics, Professors Craufurd Goodwin and Neil De Marchi, in a successful grant application to the Luce Foundation for the study of the relation between economics and visual culture. I organized a year-long working group treating space and the market which, appropriately, met first in Colonial Williamsburg and then in Disney World, Orlando. The full participants of that seminar—Professors Daniel Monk, Peter McIsaac, Jordan Sand, Ken Surin, and Roberto Dainotto, in addition to Craufurd Goodwin and Neil De Marchi—provided a critical forum for early parts of this study. In fact, I learned a great deal from all my colleagues. I can now read economic texts with some understanding, though economic theory of whatever century remains for me, like theology, an alien and uncomfortable procedure.

My work has benefited greatly from the support of a variety of institutions. For travel and research costs I received a major grant from the Graham Foundation and awards from the Research Council of Duke University. The National Humanities Center, which appointed me Allen W. Clowes Fellow, and the American Council of Learned Societies generously supported my writing and research during the 2002–3 academic year. The Medieval and Early Modern Reading Group at the National Humanities Center provided a perfect intellectual and social setting for the production of chapters 2 and 3. Its members included Professors Kalman Bland, Kathryn Burns, Ed Craun, Gail Gibson, Paul Griffiths, Paulina Kewes, Paula Sanders, Moshe Sluhovsky, and Helen Solterer.

The graduate students of a Jerusalem Seminar, which I offered in spring 2004, helped me work toward coherence. The art historians were Meagan Green, a medievalist; Allison Bienkowski and Kevin Kornegay, both early modernists; and Mitali Routh, a modernist. Cara Hersh and James Knowles are students of medieval English. Rami Dajani came to the course as a Soros Fellow at the Duke University School of Law. We planned a reunion in Jerusalem.

Presenting parts of this book to various groups has worked out at least a few of its many intellectual kinks. I am grateful to those colleagues and institutions that made such conversations possible. Elizabeth Rappaport at the University of New Mexico, Albuquerque, and Ed Craun at Washington and Lee University generously invited me for public lectures on *Selling Jerusalem*. Sarah Iles Johnston, who chaired the Seeing the Gods session at the American Academy of Religion, and Lisa Bitel, who organized the Religion and Material Culture Seminar at the University of Southern California, provided helpful forums for other sections of the work. Sandy Isenstadt, Kishwar Rizvi, and Eeva-Lisa Pelkonen, who asked me to speak on Hilton Hotels in their Yale University Conference on the West in the East, graciously accepted a talk on Ronald Storrs in Jerusalem instead. Two colleagues have provided me with occasions to discuss my project in convivial settings: Professor Elizabeth Clark at Duke, under the auspices of the Theory and the Study of Premodernity Seminar funded by the Mellon Foundation, and Professor Stan Abe at the Research Centre of Kings College in Cambridge. I am indebted also to those experts who have been willing to read various segments of this study; I have acknowledged them in the appropriate chapter.

No conversations or readings have contributed more to the rethinking of my assumptions than those I have had with my beloved partner and colleague Professor Kalman Bland.

CHAPTER ONE

Fragmented Jerusalem: City as Gift

Passing centuries have successively reduced our precious treasure [the True Cross], lost to the winds of revolutions and to the blasts of impiety. There remain few, and their rarity makes each of these relics more precious. Therefore I have taken the liberty of appealing to the Catholic world, and the information that I have received has allowed me to describe those relics that still exist and to chart them. . . . The result of this table is that the total volume of the relics that are known to us is about five million [cubic] millimeters. . . . If one considers also the small fragments that are found in churches, convents, and private collections, it is possible to triple that volume. One arrives then at fifteen million millimeters, which is not even a tenth of the 180 million millimeters that we have shown made up the volume of the cross of Our Lord Jesus Christ. * CHARLES ROHAULT DE FLEURY, *MÉMOIRE SUR LES INSTRUMENTS DE LA PASSION DE N.-S. J.-C.* (1870)

The sum total of these precious things constitutes the magical dower. . . . All these things are always, in every tribe, spiritual in origin and of a spiritual nature. Moreover, they are contained in a box, or rather in a large emblazoned case that is itself endowed with a powerful personality, that can talk, that clings to its owner, that holds his soul. * MARCEL MAUSS, *THE GIFT* (1924)

RELIC

A relic is the remnant of a history that is threatened by forgetting.[1] It records duration and postpones oblivion. It offers reassurance that the past retains its authority. It collapses time. A relic is a sign of previous power, real or imagined. It promises to put that power back to work. A relic is a fragment that evokes a lost fullness. It is a part that allows the embrace of an absent whole. It is the living piece of a dead object. It is an intensely material sign entangled in a

I am grateful to Dr. Kimberly Dennis for her comments on this chapter and to Dr. Jan Drijvers for our discussions of Saints Cyril and Helena.

1. *Relic* is derived from the Latin, *reliquiae* (remains, relics, remnant). For beautifully reproduced relics and a discussion of relics and memory, see van Os, *Der Weg zum Himmel.*

Fig. 1. *Pegasus Motor Oils.* Original modified by Todd Sanders, Roadhouse Relics, Austin, Texas. Author's collection.

spiritual significance. A relic avoids intrinsically valuable materials. It works in part through the uniqueness of its survival.

Pegasus Motor Oils is a sign of a demolished gasoline station that reveals its own history (fig. 1). The bullet holes index its poignant prominence at an abandoned site. It suffered through target practice. The rust stains that run like blood from its punctures attest to the duration of its survival. Its deco figuration suggests commerce before commercialism. The sign is a remnant of a more authentic America, an America before Jiffy-Lube, an America where men changed their own oil. *Pegasus Motor Oils* is now possessed by a man who still changes his own oil or wishes that he did. The sign acts a relic.

But *Pegasus Motor Oils* is not a sign/relic but an artwork.[2] It was produced in 1999, then artificially aged by artist Todd Sanders at his Austin, Texas, Roadhouse Relics studio. There was no gasoline station; Pegasus Motor Oils Company never existed. The concept was derived from the early signage of Mobil Oil Corporation (fig. 2). No doubt, reference to a once familiar image of mythological speed and power contributes to the persuasiveness of the work. In 1995, Mobil Corporation itself returned to Pegasus, not as an emblem of mobility but as a means of deploying memory to promote sales.

To underscore the historical tenor of the campaign, Mobil is returning Pegasus, its venerable flying horse trademark, to a place of prominence on the packaging for Mobil Motor Oil. . . . "If we're going to use a heritage approach, Pegasus is a very valuable symbol," said Jim Taverna, retail marketing manager for the lubricant business. . . . "There is the potential to use Pegasus more heavily," he added, beyond the Mobil Motor Oil packaging and small signs affixed to service stations selling Mobil gasoline. "Our employees responded very, very positively" to the winged horse, he said. Centering the campaign on history stems from research . . . [that] indicated that "people

2. "People don't call it art in other places," Sanders laments. "What I do is art, not because I say so, but because Austin considers it art." D'Amico, "South Austin's Neon Transformers Light Up Life South of the River."

Fig. 2. Mobilgas sign. Author's collection.

have a need for trust in their brand" of motor oils. . . . The heritage campaign was selected as a way to show consumers "we have a lot of reasons to be trusted."[3]

Pegasus Motor Oils is an artwork that passes as a found object, a deception much harder to enact than the Dadaists' found objects that pose as art.[4] When the artifice of the object is recognized and *Pegasus Motor Oils* is identified as art, it ceases to function as relic. This object is no duck/rabbit, an image that continuously oscillates in meaning.[5] Once an observer identifies the work as a contemporary invention, she can never again see it as a unique report of a particular history. It may still serve as a source of satisfaction and pleasure; it certainly may be admired; it can accrue value. But its life is no longer a mystery; it is a product of the market. It reveals newly our peculiarly nostalgic present, but it has lost its magical power to conjure the past. *Pegasus Motor Oils* demonstrates how an artwork can function as a relic until its deception is discovered. Deeply implicated in that deception is the artwork's participation in the market. Prepared by an artist in the expectation of a financial return and bought over the Internet, *Pegasus Motor Oils* may not be a commodity, but it certainly is an economic good.[6]

Pegasus Motor Oils indicates some of the ways in which medieval relics worked like modern ones. Their agency did not depend on their authenticity, but on the perception that they were authentic. So long as a medieval relic was regarded as real, its pious observer might reexperience the historical whole of which the relic was a part. When its authenticity was doubted, as in the case of Henry III's relic of the blood of Jesus, it did not perform.[7]

More obviously, *Pegasus Motor Oils* suggests some of the significant differences between medieval and modern relics. *Pegasus Motor Oils* never healed the

3. Elliott, "Advertising."

4. As Slavoj Žižek reminds us, "While animals can deceive by presenting what is false as true, only humans . . . can deceive by presenting what is true as false." Žižek, *Welcome to the Desert of the Real!* 19.

5. Jastrow, *Fact and Fable in Psychology*, 295.

6. For discussion of the term *commodity*, see the introduction.

7. Vincent, *The Holy Blood*.

blind. The Pegasus of even the most authentic Mobilgas sign never came to life during a hurricane to spread its wings protectively over its hometown. Modern relics might, like medieval relics, evoke a nostalgically idealized past, but they perpetuate it less powerfully. *Pegasus Motor Oils* is a sign of the modern, secularized diminution of the term *relic*. For me to identify it initially as a "relic" was a customary use of the English language. But the value of *Pegasus Motor Oils* is more familiarly expressed in dollars. Now a "relic" can be bought and sold. In contrast, the medieval relic scorned money. Its value had no monetary equivalent. It was possible to steal relics, but it was illicit to sell them. Jerusalem, in the form of relics, was possessed in late antiquity and the early Middle Ages not as an economic good but as a gift.

The greatest of Christian relics was the True Cross. The relic was found in many forms—immured in altars, displayed in reliquaries, worn in pendants and rings. An altar table found near Kherbet-oum-el-Ahdam, Algeria, claims possession of a fragment of the True Cross in an inscription of around 360.[8] Saint Macrina the Younger (d. 397) wore around her neck an iron crucifix and an iron ring that contained a particle of the True Cross.[9] In a sermon given in Antioch in 387, John Chrysostom comments that many women in his congregation sought fragments of the cross to wear as jewelry. Any of these manifestations of the cross might be remarkably efficacious.[10] Even a robe in which the True Cross was wrapped might perform miracles, as the sixth-century bishop and historian Gregory of Tours relates:

The nature of the power of this wood became apparent to me in this way. A man arrived who showed me a small robe that was made entirely of silk and that was very old. He claimed that the Lord's cross had been wrapped in this robe at Jerusalem. Because of my ignorance this claim seemed outrageous. . . . [In response to Gregory's skepticism, the man explained:] "As I was leaving Jerusalem, I met the abbot Futes, who had great favor with the empress Sophia [wife of Justin II]; for they had entrusted the entire East to this man as if it were his prefecture. I attached myself to this man, and when I was returning from the East I received from him both these relics of saints and this robe in which the holy cross was then always wrapped." After this man told me this story . . . I dared to wash the robe and allow people with fevers to drink [the water]. But soon, as the divine power brought aid, they were healed. Then I even cut off some pieces and gave them to monks as a blessing. I gave one piece to an abbot who returned two years later and claimed under oath that it had healed twelve possessed people, three blind people, and two paralytics. He had placed [his piece of] the robe in the mouth of a mute man, and as soon as it touched his teeth and tongue, it restored his voice and speech.[11]

8. These examples all come from the magisterial list of pieces of the True Cross known from both archaeological and literary contexts compiled by Frolow, *La relique de la Vraie Croix*. The list is chronological. Cited are Frolow's earliest examples outside Jerusalem: 3–5, 158–59.

9. Gregory of Nyssa, *The Life of Saint Macrina*, 45–46; Gregory of Nyssa, "Vita Macrinae Junioris."

10. John Chrysostom, "Homilia quod Christus sit Deus."

11. Gregory of Tours, *Miracula*, 41.33–42.14. For the translation: Gregory of Tours, *Glory of the Martyrs*, 26.

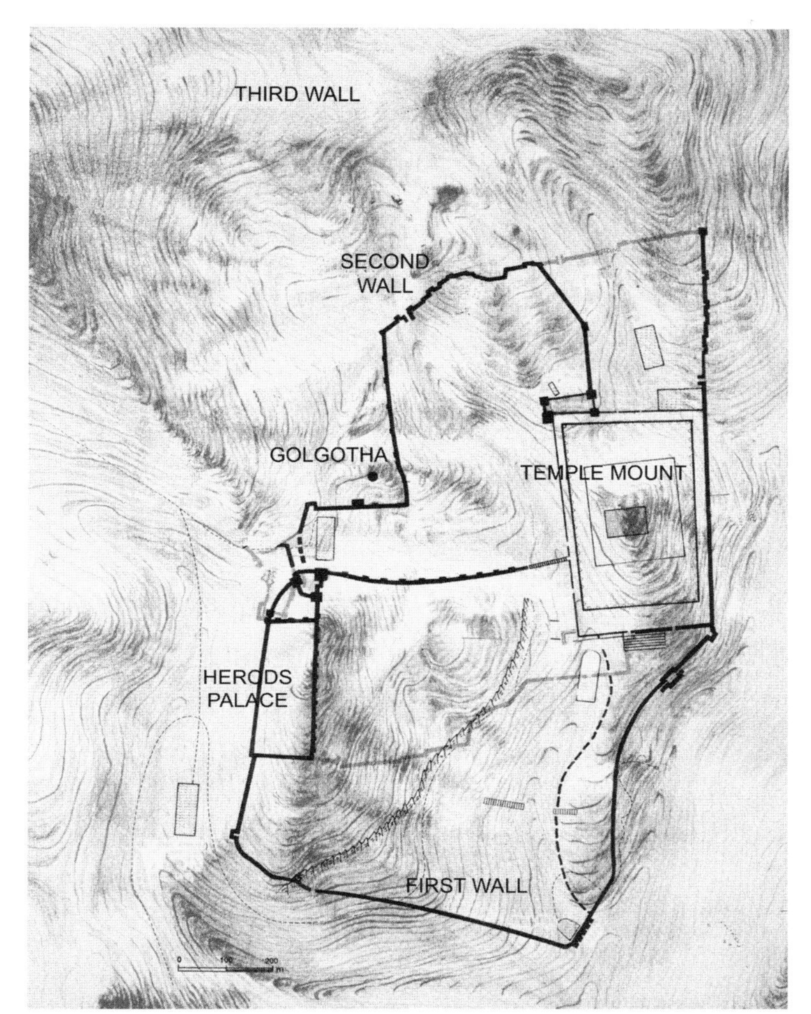

Fig. 3. Herod's Jerusalem, plan. Author's modification of a plan from F. E. Peters, *Jerusalem*.

Fig. 4. (*bottom*) Model of Herod's Jerusalem, view of the "city" from the southwest. Holy Land Hotel, Jerusalem. Author photo.

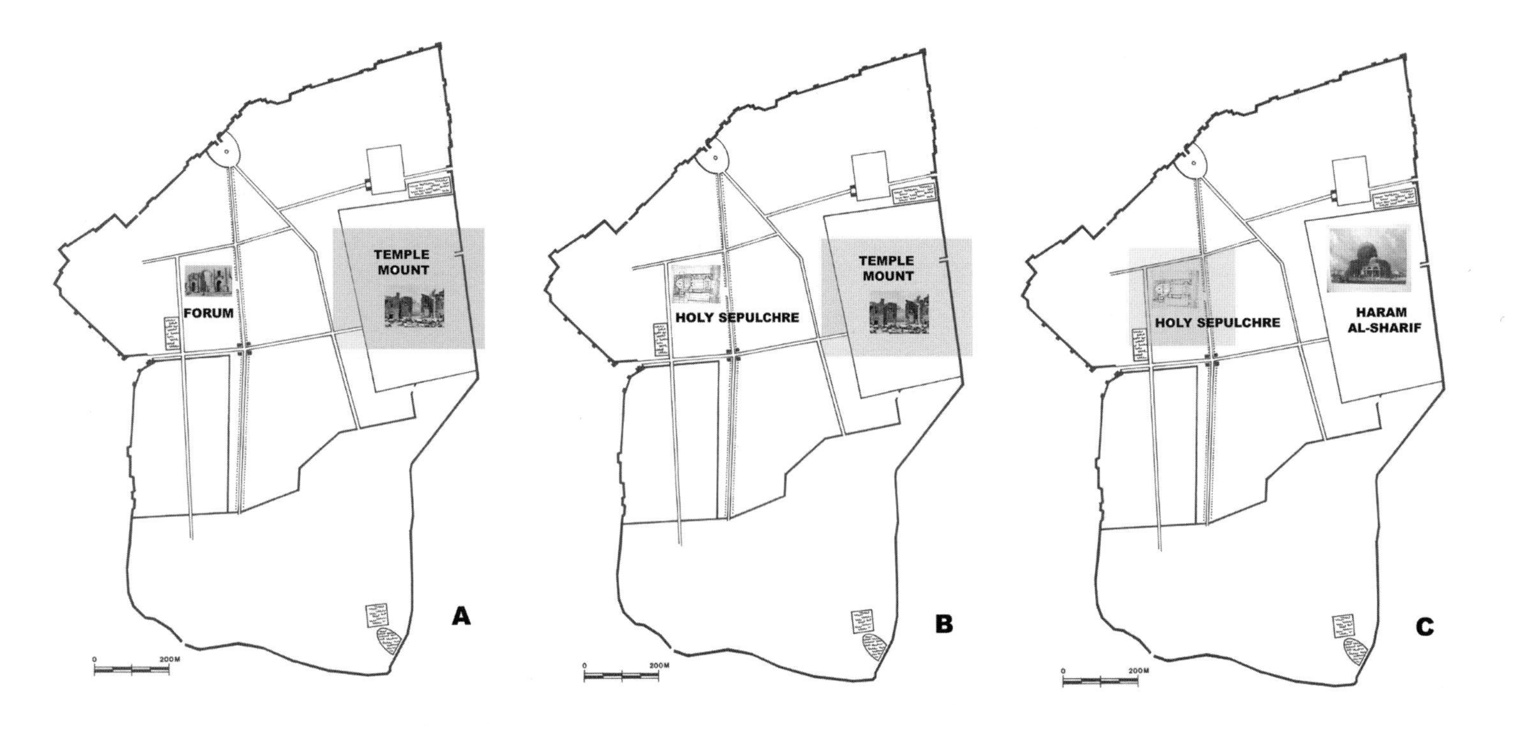

Fig. 5. Comparative sketch plans of Jerusalem. *A*, Jerusalem at the time of Hadrian, with added icons of a forum and ruins (both from Jerash); *B*, Jerusalem at the time of Constantine, with an added plan of the Holy Sepulchre and ruins of the Temple (from Jerash); *C*, Jerusalem under Muslim control, with an added plan of the Holy Sepulchre and an icon of the Dome of the Rock. Shading represents erasure. Author's drawing based on a plan by Yoram Tsafrir.

The True Cross raised the dead, gave sight to the blind, healed the sick, protected its possessor from evil, and presented a transcendent vision that attracted pilgrims.

The True Cross absorbed its power through its intense contact with the physical body of the Divine. It was the vehicle of Jesus's sacrifice and, consequently, the instrument of the pious Christian's salvation. Few parts of Jesus remained behind after his Ascension.[12] The wood of the cross acted as a substitute for the absent body of Christ. The True Cross also had material attributes that contributed to its efficacy. It was readily divisible; its particles were as effective as the whole. It could not be mistaken for worldly wealth. Its substance—small pieces of common wood—had virtually no monetary value. Its particles had only spiritual worth; they resisted vending. The True Cross was made in Jerusalem. Those who venerated its pieces were aware of their origins, if not of their history. The Holy City itself was circulated in the distribution of its fragments.

JERUSALEM

Jerusalem was the sacred center of a Jewish state in the first century CE. Herod the Great (r. 37–4 BCE) had made the city into a showplace (figs. 3, 4). Pliny the Elder identified this Jerusalem as "by far the most brilliant city of the East, not just of Judea alone."[13] Herod's greatest work was a massive new temple, begun in 19 BCE and finished sometime between 62 and 64 CE. The Temple, controlled by the Jewish religious elite, was the spectacular center of Jerusalem. The Temple's spatial and social antithesis was the place of execution, at the periphery of the city, just outside its walls. At that site, imagined as Golgotha, the Place of the Skull, criminals of the lowest sort were crucified. According to tradition, Jesus was executed on the hill of Golgotha in 29 CE, then buried nearby in a cave-tomb.[14]

Judea's later history as a discontented part of the Roman Empire had disastrous consequences for Jerusalem. Herod's recently completed Temple was destroyed in Titus's suppression of the First Jewish Revolt of 66–73 CE. The Second Revolt of 132–35 CE ended with Hadrian's elimination of Jerusalem itself. The Roman emperor replaced Herod's magnificent metropolis with a provincial outpost set to the west of the old city (fig. 5A). Jews were banished from the city; it was repopulated with gentiles. This new town was dedicated to its imperial begetters, the emperor himself (Publius Aelias Hadrianus) and his god, Jupiter Capitolanus, and named Colonia Aelia Capitolina.[15] A military camp was installed on the most elevated area on the site of the new settlement. The new forum was located outside the walls of the old city, on the adjacent hill. It deter-

12. Bodily excesses and fluids were left behind: Jesus's blood from the Passion and his foreskin from the circumcision. Part of the latter remains in the papal collection of relics in Rome.

13. Pliny, *Natural History*, 2:5.15.70.

14. For the tomb's proximity to Golgotha, John 19:41–42; for the tomb's preparation for his own burial by Joseph of Arimathea, see Matt. 47:59–60 and Mark 15:4.

15. Avigad, *Discovering Jerusalem*, 205–7; Tsafrir, "Jerusalem." For an excellent assessment of the nearly two centuries of Jerusalem as a city of Roman cults, see Belayche, *Iudaea-Palaestina*, 108–70.

mined the intersection of Aelia's principal avenues, the new *cardo maximus* and the *decumanus,* and acquired the traditional Roman trappings of a community center, including a marketplace, a temple precinct, and a monumental arched entrance. Hadrian radically recentered the city, as well as renaming it. The old core became the desolate periphery: the ruins of the Jerusalem Temple were retained as the material witness of Roman military and political supremacy.

Despite its conversion from the Jewish capital to a Roman garrison town, Jerusalem retained its sacred aura for both Jews and Christians. By the fourth century, Christians venerated the city, not only as the principal site of Jesus's earthly existence, but also as the setting of the Hebrew Bible, transformed into the Old Testament and reread as a prophecy of the new order. Nearly two centuries after Hadrian's establishment of Aelia, the emperor Constantine stimulated Christianity's craving for Jerusalem. Constantine, who reigned between 312–32 CE, was the first openly Christian emperor. Under the protection of a cross (the ☧ chi rho, the first two letters of *Christ* in Greek) that he had seen in a vision, Constantine famously defeated Maxentius, his rival in the West, at the Milvian Bridge in 312 and consequently occupied Rome. After he defeated Licinius, his rival in the East, in 324, Constantine was the sole ruler of the Roman Empire. The emperor reasserted the imperial presence in Aelia Capitolina/Jerusalem and monumentalized the Christian cult in the city.[16] Christian triumph over Greco-Roman cults was celebrated with a new cathedral that displaced Hadrian's temples in the great forum at Aelia's core (fig. 5B). Foundations for the new church complex required considerable excavation. In book 3 of his *Life of Constantine,* Eusebius (d. 339), bishop of nearby Caesarea at the time, describes the dramatic results:

> *At a word of command those contrivances of fraud [pagan temples] were demolished from top to bottom, and the houses of error were dismantled and destroyed along with their idols and demons. His efforts however did not stop there, but the Emperor gave further orders that all the rubble of stones and timbers from the demolitions should be taken and dumped a long way from the site. This command also was soon effected. But not even this progress was by itself enough, but* under divine inspiration *once more the Emperor gave instructions that the site should be excavated to a great depth and the pavement should be carried away with the rubble a long distance outside, because it was stained with demonic bloodshed [of animal sacrifices]. This also was completed straightaway. As stage by stage the underground site was exposed, at last* against all expectation *the revered and all-hallowed Testimony* [martyrion] *of the Savior's resurrection was itself revealed, and the cave, the holy of holies, took on the appearance of a representation of the Savior's return to life. Thus after its descent into darkness it came forth again to the light, and it enabled those who came as visitors to see plainly the story of wonders wrought there, testifying by facts louder than any voice to the resurrection of the Savior.*[17]

16. For a recent sketch of Jerusalem in the fourth century, see Drijvers, *Cyril of Jerusalem,* 1–30.
17. Eusebius, *Life of Constantine,* 133; emphasis added.

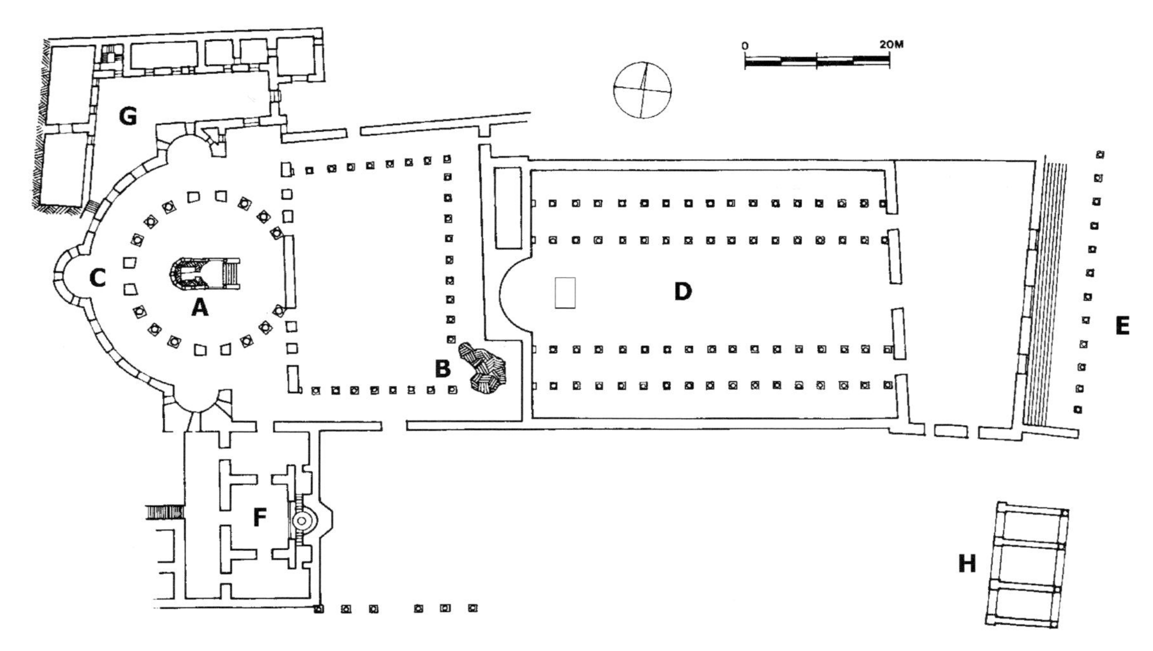

Fig. 6. Church of the Holy Sepulchre, Jerusalem, reconstructed plan of the church from the fourth century. *A*, tomb of Jesus; *B*, Golgotha, or Calvary; *C*, Rotunda, or Anastasis; *D*, Basilica, or Martyrium; *E*, Cardo Maximus; *F*, Baptistery; *G*, bishop's palace. Author's drawing based on plans by Robert Ousterhaut and Virgilio C. Corbo.

Thus, according to Eusebius, our most detailed contemporary source, the site of Jesus's burial was miraculously revealed during construction of the new cathedral.[18]

Constantine's patronage was centered in Hadrian's Aelia; his city continued to be called either Aelia or the new Jerusalem. The cult center of the old Herodian city was not reincorporated into the new Christian metropolis; the ruins of the desecrated Temple remained untouched, a reminder of Jewish defeat. The commemorative force of the site lay in its desolation. Jesus had predicted of the Temple that "not one stone here will be left on another; every one will be thrown down" (Matt. 24:2; also see Luke 19:42–44). Its destruction was preserved as proof both of Jesus's prophecy and of Christian dominance. The ancient opposition between the Jerusalem Temple as the privileged center of sacrificial ritual and Golgotha as a peripheral and polluted site of torture and death was curiously inverted. Under Constantine, the locus of Golgotha and the tomb became the privileged center of ritual sacrifice standing in opposition to the Temple as the place of death and shame.

18. Modern scholars have attempted to rationalize this miracle, arguing that this site must have been known as the place of the burial of Jesus before excavations began. For a critique of such a position, see Wharton, *Refiguring the Post Classical City*, 85–92.

Constantine's cathedral in Jerusalem was, like many of the other churches that he patronized, a Roman civil basilica modified for liturgical use: a large structure, internally divided by rows of columns which processed from the entrance in the east toward the altar, framed by a grand apse, in the west (fig. 6, *D*). The basilica was commonly referred to in contemporary texts as the Martyrium (testimony). The tomb of Jesus (*A*) was apparently discovered when the high ground behind the cathedral was leveled to accommodate the bishop's palace (*G*) and the grand baptistery (*F*).[19] Constantine's engineers left the burial cave as an isolated, cone-shaped stone outcrop. The rock-cut tomb, provided with a marble veneer, became the focus of a great rotunda, identified as the Anastasis (Resurrection). Soon, too, an outcrop behind the south nave of the basilica was identified as Golgotha, and marked with a cross (*B*).[20] The two sites intimately associated with Jesus's body at its most human (death) and its most divine (resurrection) made the space numinous. A single complex, known as the Church of the Holy Sepulchre, incorporated them both. For Christians, this was the most privileged of all pilgrimage destinations.

The saturated sanctity of the Holy Sepulchre was remarkably generative. It bred a superabundance of relics: pilgrims of the fourth century saw there such wonders as the *titulus* identifying Jesus as the King of the Jews, the ring of Solomon, and a phial of oil used in the anointment of Old Testament kings.[21] By the sixth century the inventory was greater: the plate on which the head of John the Baptist was presented to Salome, the horn used to anoint David, the altar stained with the blood of the murdered Zacharias, the reed and sponge from the Crucifixion, and the chalice used at the Last Supper.[22] Here, too, was the altar on which Abraham had offered Isaac and at which Melchisedek officiated.[23] But the most valuable of the relics produced by the site was the True Cross. References to the cross first occur in Saint Cyril of Jerusalem's lectures for Christian initiates delivered around 350. In one of these lectures (Catechesis X), the prelate points to the True Cross as material proof that Jerusalem was distinguished from all other cities by the special presence of the Divine:

Many, my beloved, are the true testimonies concerning Christ. The Father bears witness from heaven of his Son . . . the blessed place of the manger [in the Church of the Nativity in Bethlehem] bears witness. . . . The holy wood of the Cross bears witness, seen among us to this day, and from this place now almost filling the whole world, by means of those who in faith take portions from it. . . . Golgotha, the holy hill standing above us here, bears witness to our sight; the Holy Sepulchre bears witness, and the stone that lies there to this day.[24]

19. For a thorough review of the archaeological and literary evidence, see Biddle, *The Tomb of Christ.*

20. For a discussion of the texts, see Barag, "Glass Pilgrim Vessels from Jerusalem," (1970) 39–40.

21. Egeria, *Egeria: Diary of a Pilgrimage,* 111; Egeria, *Itinerarium Egeriae,* 37.24–26.

22. "Breviarius de Hierosolyma," 110.50–73.

23. Antoninus Placentinus, *Itinerarium,* 172.2–5.

24. Cyril of Jerusalem, "Catechetical Lectures," *33*:331–1128; translation from Cyril of Jerusalem, "Catechetical Lectures," in *A Select Library of the Nicene and Post-Nicene Fathers,* 62–63.

In his sermon, Saint Cyril presented the True Cross in the context of the tomb of Jesus and the site of Jesus's Crucifixion on Golgotha. These material presences provided his local audience with the immediate and physical proof of the divine mysteries that occurred in Jerusalem. By circulating fragments of the True Cross, Jerusalem itself was rendered present to pious believers in distant parts of the Christian Empire. Pieces of the cross provided palpable evidence of Jesus's sacrifice for the salvation of mankind. Those particles also testified to Jerusalem's distinctive spiritual fecundity.

The distribution of fragments of the True Cross—"from this place now almost filling the whole world"—mentioned by Saint Cyril had, however, occurred only very recently. The earliest archaeological and literary references to cross relics occur only in the eastern part of the empire and only after Saint Cyril gave his lecture. The first documented appearances of pieces of the True Cross in the West date from the very end of the fourth century and the beginning of the fifth century.[25] An early reference suggests how they circulated. John, bishop of Jerusalem, gave Melania the Elder, a pious wealthy aristocrat and generous donor to the church, a piece of the True Cross. Upon her return to Italy from Jerusalem in 402, she gave a fragment of her fragment to her friend Bishop Paulinus of Nola (354–431); he in turn, in 403, sent "an atom" of his treasure on to his colleague Sulpicius Severus.

I have found . . . a fragment of a sliver of the wood of the holy Cross to send you as a worthy gift. . . . This goodly gift was brought to me from Jerusalem by the blessed Melania, a gift of the holy bishop John there. . . . So from your loving brethren, who long to associate with you in every good, receive this gift, which is great in small compass. In this almost indivisible particle of a small sliver take up the protection of your immediate safety, and the guarantee of your eternal salvation. Let not your faith shrink because the eyes of the body behold evidence so small; let it look with the inner eye on the whole power of the cross in this tiny segment. . . .

[Be impressed by the cross, not by] the arrangement by which I have enclosed this relic, which imparts a great blessing, in a golden casing. Rather in this adornment I have imitated your faith. I sent you your own exemplar clothed with gold, for I know that you have within you, like gold tried in the fire, the kingdom of God—in other words, faith in the cross, by which we enter the kingdom of heaven. . . .

[There follows a history of the discovery of the Cross by Saint Helena, then the way it is displayed in Jerusalem.] Only on the day when we celebrate the mystery of the cross itself is that source of mysteries brought out to mark the holy and solemn occasion; but occasionally devout pilgrims who have come there merely for that purpose beg that it be shown them as a reward for their long journeying. It is said that this request is granted only by the kindness of the bishop and it is likewise by his gift alone that these tiny fragments of sacred wood from the same cross are made available to win great graces of faith and blessing.

---

25. See the enumeration of references to relics of the True Cross mentioned above, note 8.

Indeed this cross of inanimate wood has living power, and ever since its discovery it has lent its wood to the countless, almost daily, prayers of men. Yet it suffers no diminution; though daily divided, it seems to remain whole to those who lift it, and always entire to those who venerate it. Assuredly it draws this power of incorruptibility, this undiminishing integrity, from the Blood of that Flesh which endured death yet did not see corruption.[26]

Paulinus's letter reveals a good bit about the late ancient reception of a relic of the True Cross. It expresses anxiety about the fragment's size and humble materiality by insisting that its small scale doesn't detract from its power and that its gold encasement doesn't increase its effectiveness. The text also illuminates the remarkable capacities of a tiny particle of the True Cross to render Jerusalem present in the West through the contemplation of contemporary ritual in the Holy City. The letter further indicates how the fragment of the cross acts like the body that endured it, having the power to save and to regenerate. Paulinus also suggests here how pieces of the True Cross circulated as gifts—multiplying in number without reducing the size or power of the originating source.[27] Paulinus's letter, finally, indicates that the mounting number of fragments of the True Cross required a fuller narrative of their sacred history.[28]

The familiar story of Helena's discovery of the True Cross first appears where the story was most needed: in the West. In 395, Saint Ambrose of Milan told the earliest recorded version of the narrative of Helena's discovery of the three crosses near Golgotha.[29] The dowager empress Helena, Constantine's mother, traveled to Jerusalem in 325; Bishop Eusebius of Caesarea provides a rich account of her journey and pious activities.[30] He indicates that she was involved in the dedication and endowment of the Church of the Nativity in Bethlehem and a church on the Mount of Olives. He makes no mention of the cross. Only at the very end of the fourth century, nearly four hundred years after the Crucifixion

26. Paulinus of Nola, *Epistulae,* 36:125–33; Paulinus of Nola, *Sancti Pontii Meropii Paulini Nolani,* 31:267–75.

27. Later, at the end of the fifth century, Saint Avitus, bishop of Vienne, requested a fragment of the True Cross from the pope, Symmachus. He insisted that the relic come directly from Jerusalem, indicating that a secondary particle from Rome was not what he wanted. His letters to Symmachus and Elias I of Jerusalem register the True Cross as "a not unworthy measure" of Jerusalem. Sanctus Avitus episcopus Viennensis, "Epistolae," 59:240B.

28. Josef Engemann theorizes that supply-and-demand explains the legend: the popularization of the use of splinters of the cross in phylacteries required a narrative to explain their power. Engemann, "Der 'corna'-Gestus," 486–87.

29. Ambrose, "De obitu Theodosii," 393–95; Drijvers, *Helena Augusta,* 109–13. "Helena is of course mainly known for her discovery of the True Cross. This discovery is definitely not a historical event and was only ascribed to Helena in the second half of the fourth century. The legend of the *inventio crucis* had its origin in Jerusalem. Cyril, bishop of Jerusalem (349/50–386/7), almost certainly exerted great influence on the composition of the story about Helena's discovery of the Cross and may have been its *auctor intellectualis.*" So writes Drijvers, "Marutha of Maipherqat on Helena Augusta, Jerusalem and the Council of Nicaea," 57.

30. Eusebius, *Life of Constantine,* 3.42–47; Eusebius, "*Vita Constantini,*" 3.42–47.

and some seventy years after Helena's pilgrimage, did a remote Latin bishop first associate the empress with the discovery of the True Cross. The tradition of Helena's excavations was generally accepted by ecclesiastics and laymen as historical reality in the Middle Ages and, more surprisingly, by some scholars in modernity.[31] The story is perhaps most compellingly presented as a novel, as in Evelyn Waugh's *Helena*. Even there, however, it takes a *deus ex machina* to explain the reappearance of a wooden cross after its long absence. The wandering Jew—an unsympathetic witness to the Passion who is doomed by Jesus to roam the earth until the Second Coming—steps out of one legend into another in order to direct Helena to the relic. Although highly regarded by its author, the book was generally dismissed by literary critics as sectarian apologetics.[32]

Constantine banned crucifixion as a means of execution in the Roman Empire.[33] Before the proscription, crosses had appeared in Christian texts and monuments as abstract signs of victory. On sarcophagi and in wall paintings, the cross was most commonly rendered as a simple + or X or as a ☧ (chi rho).[34] The earliest known representation of the Crucifixion is an insult. A third-century graffito from Rome depicts a crucifixion with a witness. The crucified figure, seen from the rear, has a man's body and an ass's head. The accompanying Greek inscription reads: "Alexamenos worships [his] god."[35] Only after crucifixion was no longer familiar as the despicable means of punishing slaves and lowlife could the cross of Jesus's Crucifixion become a prominent object of veneration in the life of the church. The earliest known Christian representation of the Crucifixion dates only to the fifth century.[36] Even then, Jesus is displayed wide-eyed and erect—triumphing over death rather than suffering through it.

Relics of the True Cross became popular at about the same time. The origins of the cross from which the fragments came are unclear. Perhaps it was discovered, like Jesus's tomb, miraculously.[37] Or perhaps, as the liturgist Heinrich

---

31. For the legend's reception in the Middle Ages, see Schreiner, "'Discrimen veri ac falsi' Ansätze und Formen der Kritik in der Heiligen- und Reliquieverehrung des Mittelalters," esp. 17–20. For an insightful discussion of the art of the legend, see Bann, *The True Vine*, 216–43.

32. "*Helena* . . . fails badly because it is obviously a work of Christian apologetics. Waugh believes that only in spiritual values can people find ultimate hope, salvation, and eternal life. The problem with *Helena*, then, is that Waugh is using this novel essentially as a vehicle for moral instruction." Doyle, "Waugh, Evelyn," 580.

33. Sozomenus, "Church History," 19. For a discussion, see Barnes, *Constantine and Eusebius*, 51.

34. For the distinction between the relic of the True Cross and its symbolic renderings, see Frolow, "The Veneration of the Relic of the True Cross at the End of the Sixth and the Beginning of the Seventh Centuries."

35. Solin and Itkonen-Kaila, "Graffiti del Palatino," 209–12. For a color reproduction and the counterintuitive claim that this representation is "proof that believers in Christ proclaimed the Cross as the central symbol of their faith—even in public—long before the time of Helena and Constantine," see Thiede and D'Ancona, *The Quest for the True Cross;* plate follows p. 114.

36. The Crucifixion is represented on one of four ivory plaques that originally decorated a small box. All four plaques show scenes from the Passion and are in the collection of the British Museum. Weitzmann, *Age of Spirituality*, 502–4.

37. Modern scholars are remarkably anxious to establish the rationality of the recovery of the tomb and cross. For example, Biddle, *The Tomb of Christ*.

Goussen suggested as early as 1923, the fragments began as souvenirs from a wooden cross placed on Golgotha when it was identified as the site of the Crucifixion, and only later were venerated as relics of the True Cross.[38] With the disappearance of crucifixion as a form of execution and with the political and social ascendancy of Christianity under Constantine, the popularity of the cross steadily increased, as did the number of its miracles.[39] Hymns to the cross appear in the West in the sixth century.[40] The story of its discovery by Saint Helena ensured that it had imperial associations as well as divine ones. The early discovery narratives acknowledge that a substantial part of the True Cross was immediately appropriated for the empire and sent to its capital, Constantinople.[41] Indeed, Constantinople soon became an important center for the distribution of its fragments. But though the True Cross collected triumphal imperial connotations, it never lost its primary identification with Jerusalem and the events of the Passion.

MATERIALITY

The True Cross shows how a part of a thing might come to represent the whole, assume its power, and distribute its reputation. Jerusalem produced other objects that were put to the same use. Even the ground of the city and its neighborhoods was numinous.[42] A common stone from Jerusalem was uncommon; it might even perform as a relic.[43] An early medieval collection of such stones, labeled with their places of origin ("from Bethlehem," "from the Mount of Olives," "from Zion," and "from the Life-Giving Anastasis"), was dis-

38. Goussen, *Über georgische Drucke und Handschriften,* 9.

39. Frolow's impressive catalogue of nearly 1200 literary and archaeological references to the True Cross provides a crude, but not-altogether-arbitrary means of grasping the chronological and territorial spread of the Cross. The catalogue proceeds from the earliest known sources in the fourth century through the nineteenth century. Jerusalem dominates the fourth-century sources; there are no fourth-century references to works in the West. Nola and Rome appear in the fifth century, but the East still outnumbers the West. Balance begins to shift to the West in the sixth century, and by the eighth through tenth century, the West is completely dominant. By that time, too, Jerusalem was under Muslim control, and Constantinople, which was always a center of the cult of the cross in the East, became its most prominent locus. Frolow, *Les reliquaires de la Vraie Croix,* 155–661.

40. Szövérffy, "Venantius Fortunatus and the Earliest Hymns to the Holy Cross," 107. Also, see below.

41. For example, Socrates, "Church History," 21.

42. For the relationship of text to land, see W. D. Davis, *The Gospel and the Land.* A number of important relics were uncovered in the city and then exported. See discussion of Saint Stephen and John the Baptist later in this chapter.

43. An early sixteenth-century pilgrim's account suggests that stones from some sites might have particular properties of healing: "And in a vault underneath [the church of St. Anne] is the very same place where our blessed Lady was born; and there is a plenary remission. The Saracens will suffer no man to come into this place but privately or for bribes, because it is their mosque. Note that relics of the stones of the place where our Lady was born is remedy and consolation to women that travail of child." Chaplain of Sir Richard Guylforde, *Pylgrymage of Sir Richard Guylforde to the Holy Land,* 29–30.

Fig. 7. Relic box from the Sancta Sanctorum, c. 600; view of the box open, showing the painted underside of its lid. Museo Sacro, Vatican. Photograph copyright © Biblioteca Apostolica Vaticana. By permission of Biblioteca Apostolica Vaticana.

Fig. 8. Relic box from the Sancta Sanctorum, c. 600; detail of the painting on the underside of the lid. Museo Sacro, Vatican. Photograph copyright © Biblioteca Apostolica Vaticana. By permission of Biblioteca Apostolica Vaticana.

covered within the greatest of Western spiritual treasuries, the altar of the Sancta Sanctorum—the Holy of Holies—in Rome.[44] According to a tradition recorded in the twelfth century, Pope Leo III (r. 795–816) placed a number of important relics in a cedar ark within the altar. The grill that sealed the altar had been locked in the early sixteenth century and was opened again only in 1903.[45] Relic

44. Lauer, *Le Trésor du Sancta Sanctorum,* 93–95. Lauer introduces his book with the complex and wonderful story of how he gained access to the altar and its contents.

45. During the pontificate of Leo X (r. 1513–21). See ibid., 3–4. Also see Grisar, *Die römische Kapelle Sancta Sanctorum und ihr Schatz.* For the twelfth-century tradition, see John the Deacon, "Liber de ecclesia lateranensi," 194:1549.

fragments of wood and stone are preserved in an ancient wooden box, which has been dated to around 600 (figs. 7, 8).[46] Labels on some of these bits claim that they came from holy sites in Palestine. These claims of association with places of epiphany are reinforced by paintings of scenes from Jesus's life (Crucifixion, center panel; Marys addressed by the angel at the empty tomb of Jesus and the Ascension, above; the Nativity and the Baptism, below) on the inside of the box's lid. As scholars have noted, the extrabiblical props of these narrative miniatures, such as the dome over Jesus's tomb and the manger as altar in the Nativity, assert the work's topographic contemporary association with the Holy Land.

The great sociologist Émile Durkheim wrote of a similar set of sacred objects: "In themselves *churingas* [sacred artifacts of Australian aborigines] are objects of wood and stone like so many others; they are distinct from profane things of the same kind in only one respect: they are engraved or painted with the totemic mark. This mark, and this mark alone, confers their sacred character."[47] The language-signs on the fragments from Jerusalem were not enough. Their sacredness was authenticated by representation. Images reinforced in a material, visual mode the claim for the common objects' uncommon sacrality. Further, the images indicated which of the pieces were most important: the nonchronological arrangement of the scenes, which emphasizes Golgotha by its centrality and the Marys at the tomb by its primacy in the narrative sequence, affirms the preeminence of the Church of the Holy Sepulchre.

The extraordinarily privileged place of these fragments from the Holy Land in the altar of the Sancta Sanctorum, as well as their storage in a richly painted box, indicates that they were valued possessions of the social elite.[48] Objects of this same sort were, however, available also to the humblest of pilgrims. A mundane bit of nature sacralized by association with divinity and by the pious attention of a pilgrim was familiarly called a blessing (*eulogia*).[49] The Piacenza Pilgrim, in his account of a journey to Jerusalem in the later sixth century, observes that "earth is brought to the Tomb and put inside, and those who go in take some as a blessing."[50] A similar action happens now at the pilgrimage center of Chimayó, west of Santa Fe, New Mexico. Chimayó is an unpretentious village; its church is rustic. It is a simple, wooden-roofed, single-nave structure; instead of side altars there are wardrobes flanking the nave, holding images of saints. A

46. The earliest and most extensive considerations of this piece by art historians were largely concerned with establishing its provenance as Palestinian through iconographic analysis. See Morey, "The Painted Panel from Sancta Sanctorum"; Weitzmann, "*Loca sancta* and the Representational Arts of Palestine."

47. Durkheim, *The Elementary Forms of Religious Life*, 98.

48. For a thought-provoking, but not unproblematic discussion of relic collections, see Elsner, "Replicating Palestine and Reversing the Reformation."

49. For excellent, accessible introductions to the materialities of pilgrimage, see Coleman and Elsner, *Pilgrimage;* Vikan, *Byzantine Pilgrimage Art*. Also see Vikan, "Two Unpublished Pilgrim Tokens in the Benaki Museum and the Group to Which They Belong."

50. Antoninus Placentinus, *Itinerarium*, 171.4–10; translation in Wilkinson, *Jerusalem Pilgrims before the Crusades*, 83.

Fig. 9. Altar, Pilgrimage Church, Chimayó, New Mexico. Author photo.

dramatic, locally carved Crucifixion in an elaborate and brightly painted frame occupies the sanctuary. Below that cross is a trough filled with dirt—dried mud from a miraculous spring (fig. 9). Pilgrims line up to enter the church; they file down the nave to its east end, where plastic bags and children's sand shovels are provided so that believers might each take a share of dirt. The line exits through the side chapel. The walls of the chapel are lined with neatly ordered ex-votos—most numerously crutches—left behind by those healed at the shrine. The similarities between Chimayó and Jerusalem are, of course, superficial: the CEO of Halliburton is not interested in possessing dirt from Chimayó; in the sixth century, great lords sought the dust of the Holy Sepulchre.

The Piacenza Pilgrim describes another form of blessing that took place in the Church of the Holy Sepulchre: "At the moment when the Cross is brought out of this small room for veneration and arrives in the court to be venerated, a star appears in the sky and comes over the place where they lay the Cross. It stays overhead whilst they are venerating the Cross, and they offer oil to be blessed in little flasks. When the mouth of one of the little flasks touches the Wood of the Cross, the oil instantly bubbles over, and unless it is closed

Fig. 10. Pilgrim's ampulla from Jerusalem, c. 600, 4.6 cm in diameter. *A*, obverse, with the Crucifixion; *B*, reverse, with the Marys at the tomb; *C*, author's reconstruction of the original form of the ampulla. Photograph courtesy of Dumbarton Oaks, Byzantine Collection, Washington, DC.

very quickly, it all spills out."[51] Some of these pilgrim flasks (ampullae) survive.[52] Usually made from base metal alloys, sometimes of glass or ceramic and more rarely from silver, the meanings of these small vessels are often articulated with images. Like the painting of the Sancta Sanctorum box, the decorations of these objects emphasize the cross. Again, pictures and inscriptions insist on the oil's association with Jesus's Jerusalem.

One example: the flask in the Dumbarton Oaks Collection in Washington, D.C., has lost its neck but not its figural decoration. On one side, a heraldic version of the Crucifixion is encircled with a neat inscription in Greek that reads: "Oil of the Wood of Life [True Cross] of the Holy Places of Christ" (fig. 10).[53] At the center of the medallion is a small, equal-armed cross that is raised on a pole above a mound of stones from which, apparently, flow the four rivers of Paradise. Above the cross, dominating the miniature work, floats a large bust of Jesus, cross-nimbused, cloaked, bearded, and very much alive. The two criminals flanking the central section refer to the historical Crucifixion. The two pilgrims adoring the cross at the bottom of the medallion refer to the contemporary veneration of the cross on Golgotha. The present and the past similarly collapse together on the ampulla's reverse. In the center is the tomb, not as a cave as described in the Gospels, but as the architectural reliquary at the cen-

51. Antoninus Placentinus, *Itinerarium,* 172.12–73.2; translation in Wilkinson, *Jerusalem Pilgrims before the Crusades,* 83.

52. Barag, "Glass Pilgrim Vessels from Jerusalem"; Engemann, "Palästinensische Pilgerampullen im F. J. Dölger-Insitutut in Bonn"; A. Grabar, *Ampoules de Terre Sainte (Monza, Bobbio);* C. Lambert and Demeglio, "Ampolle devozionali ed itinerari di pellegrinaggio tra IV e VII secolo."

53. Lesley, "An Echo of Early Christianity"; M. Ross, *Catalogue of the Byzantine and Early Mediaeval Antiquities in the Dumbarton Oaks Collection,* 1:71–72; Vikan, *Byzantine Pilgrimage Art,* 20–23.

ter of Constantine's Holy Sepulchre. The historical narrative is relegated to the edges: the Marys arrive on the scene from the left and are greeted by an angel on the right. The angel's consoling salutation, "The Lord has risen," appears as an inscription connecting the interlocutors.[54]

A number of holy shrines in the East produced "blessings" that are now found in Western collections—the pilgrimage center of Saint Menas outside Alexandria in Egypt and that of Saint Symeon at Kalat Siman in Syria are among the most famous. Ampullae were also produced in Jerusalem to carry oil or dirt from the Temple Mount for Jewish pilgrims.[55] But no site is so well represented among the surviving containers as the Holy Sepulchre in Jerusalem. Although these small, standardized vessels may have been sold to the pilgrims, the holy oil that filled them must have been, like the mud of Chimayó, the gift of the holy site itself. In the early Middle Ages, the Holy Land circulated as gift-fragments in the West, not just among the very wealthy but also among the more modest.

GIFT

The power of Jerusalem was available to the nonelites as well as elites through its stones and its oils. Its more rarefied fragments—pieces of the True Cross and parts of the saints—were less readily acquired. They might be stolen.[56] Egeria, a pilgrim to Jerusalem in the late fourth century, alludes to such a theft in her well-known description of the display of the True Cross in the Church of the Holy Sepulchre on Good Friday:

The bishop sits on his throne, a table covered with a linen cloth is set before him, and the deacons stand around the table. The gilded silver box containing the sacred wood of the cross is brought in and opened. Both the wood of the cross and the inscription are taken out and placed on the table. As soon as they have been placed on the table, the bishop, remaining seated, grips the ends of the sacred wood with his hands, while the deacons, who are standing about, keep watch over it. There is a reason why it is guarded in this manner. It is the practice here for all the people to come forth one by one, the faithful as well as the catechumens, to bow down before the table, kiss the holy wood, and then move on. It is said that someone took a bite and stole a piece of the holy cross. Therefore, it is now guarded by the deacons.[57]

Relics were certainly also sold, as the laws passed against such practices indicate. The Theodosian Code stipulates that "no person shall sell the relics of a

54. For an analysis and review of the literature, see Vikan, "Early Byzantine Pilgrimage *Devotionalia* as Evidence of the Appearance of Pilgrimage Shrines." Also see Kötsche-Breitenbruch, "Pilgerandenken aus dem Heiligen Land."

55. Barag, "Glass Pilgrim Vessels from Jerusalem."

56. The classic work on the theft of relics deals with a somewhat later time period. See Geary, *Furta Sacra*.

57. Egeria, *Egeria: Diary of a Pilgrimage*, 110–11.

martyr; no person shall traffic in them."[58] Those who offered relics for sale were called swindlers and their merchandise denounced as fake.[59] Theft and fraud might meet the desire of a small number of those who wished to possess a share in the power of relics. More commonly as well as more legitimately, relics were obtained as gifts.

Europe was poor in the Early Middle Ages.[60] Though trade and money exchange never ceased after the Gothic invasions, declines in population through war and pandemics significantly reduced the volume of both.[61] From the sixth through the tenth centuries the small available surplus in goods and wealth was redistributed in the West both symmetrically and asymmetrically. On a local and even regional level, goods were commonly exchanged by barter. Barter may be defined as a freely undertaken exchange of goods or services agreed upon by two parties. Notionally, the parties engaged in barter are, at least in that particular act, equal. Unequal exchange was also essential to the early medieval economy. From the local to the supraregional, assets were commonly redistributed by coercive acts—plunder and plunder's legal double, taxation. Gifts were another important means of dispersing wealth between those who were not equal in power, wealth, or status.[62]

Gifting is as complex as barter is simple.[63] Gift giving *appears* to be an unsolicited act of unselfish generosity.[64] However, as anthropologists have documented and as we all know from personal experience, gift giving is familiarly a display of power.[65] A gift implies of its giver an undiminished substance; that which is held back is not reduced by what is given.[66] The lavish gift inscribes a difference in social status between the giver and receiver, at least until the gift

58. *Codex Theodosianus*, 9.17.7.

59. Augustine, "De opere monachorum," 40:576.

60. For an accessible survey, see Cipolla, *Before the Industrial Revolution*.

61. Lopez, "The Trade of Medieval Europe," 257–354.

62. Grierson, "Commerce in the Dark Ages," 131. For a sophisticated discussion of the gift in the medieval economy, see Duby, *The Early Growth of the European Economy*, 53–55.

63. A great deal of useful work has been done on the gift. The classic text on the subject is Mauss, *The Gift*. For other important contributors, see Bourdieu, *Algeria, 1960;* Cheal, *The Gift Economy;* N. Davis, *The Gift in Sixteenth Century France;* Godelier, *The Enigma of the Gift;* Gregory, *Gifts and Commodities;* Thomas, *Entangled Objects*.

64. Or, as Bourdieu posits, "Gift exchange is an exchange in and by which the agents strive to conceal the objective truth of the exchange." Bourdieu, *Algeria, 1960*, 22.

65. For a darkly humorous consideration of asymmetrical gift-giving practices now, consider reading the novel by Flusfeder, *The Gift*.

66. Older anthropological notions of necessary reciprocity have been powerfully criticized, perhaps most persuasively by Titmuss, *The Gift Relationship*. Titmuss investigates the theoretical implications of the fact that blood donors give freely of their blood, while resisting reciprocity. This example also has important consequences for a newer anthropological concern with keeping-while-giving. Nevertheless, the greatest significance of Titmuss's book lies in its critique of the place of self-interest in modern economic thought. "All exchange is predicated on a universal paradox—how to keep-while-giving." See also Weiner, *Inalienable Possessions*, 5. The author offers a compelling feminist-revisionist perspective on deeply embedded anthropological notions of reciprocity as the means of maintaining stability in "primitive" cultures.

is reciprocated. A gift imposes a debt that must be settled. There is another significant aspect of the gift as it functioned in precapitalist economies, and which we can still appreciate today: the gift's identification with its giver. A standard commodity (a box of cereal, a pair of Nike shoes) erases evidence of the human contribution to its production. The gift exceeds a commodity because it absorbs and evidences something of its genesis. The gift bears with it its giver, if not its producer. Memory slips by the commodity, but clings to the gift. A commodity has no numinousness; the gift has an aura.

The aura of a gift of relics was particularly numinous. Its sanctity issued from the gift-act that produced it (martyrdom) as well as from the gift-act that transferred it. A Christian relic of the Middle Ages was itself a sign of a sacrifice, a special category of gift. Obviously, the greater the sacrifice, the greater the gift, death being its ultimate exemplar.[67] A fragment of the True Cross was among the most prized of relics because it so effectively evoked the memory of God's gift of himself to humanity. (Of course, like most gifts, the gift of God's sacrifice required reciprocation. Faithfulness, pious acts, and alms were the required exchange for the salvation that the cross enabled. The relic was part of an economy of retributive justice.)[68] The status of the giver also informed the status of the gift. Just as the power of the relic was an index of the power of the giver, the eminence of the giver might well supplement the power of the relic. The effectiveness of this mutual reinforcement of authority was revealed in the exchange relations that they produced as well as in the miracles that they wrought.

Perhaps most obviously, pieces of the True Cross participated in the circulation of gifts as diplomacy. Along with silks, ivories, purple codices, giraffes, and princesses, relic-gifts contributed to alliances among rulers and to distinctions between the powerful and the more powerful.[69] A gift to a social superior might now look like a questionable inducement. Saint Cyril and later Juvenal, bishop of Jerusalem between 422 and 458, were engaged in the vicious ecclesiastical politics of the period in their struggle to raise the status of their church. In the fourth century the bishop of Aelia/Jerusalem remained merely the suffragan, or subordinate bishop, of the metropolitan archbishop of Caesarea, the prosperous port of Palestine. By the end of the fifth century, Jerusalem was one of four great patriarchates of the East along with Antioch, Alexandria, and Constantinople. Constantinople gained admission to this league of ancient bishoprics by its exalted economic and political position as capital of the late Roman Empire. Jerusalem's pretensions to authority depended entirely on its control of sites made holy through association with the divine.

---

67. For a general discussion of this exchange, see Derrida, *The Gift of Death*.

68. For the phrase "economy of retributive justice," see Caputo, "The Time of Giving, the Time of Forgiving," 117.

69. For discussions of medieval gifts as diplomacy, see Buettner, "Past Presents"; Cutler, "Gifts and Gift Exchange as Aspects of the Byzantine, Arab, and Related Economies"; Cutler, "Les échanges de dons entre Byzance et l'Islam (IXe–XIe siècles)"; O. Grabar, "The Shared Culture of Objects"; Michalowski, "Le don d'amitié dans la société carolingienne et les 'translationes sanctorum.'"

If Cyril did not "invent" the True Cross, he certainly brought it to prominence with remarkable political effect. He reinforced the cult of the cross and further promoted the sense of Jerusalem's special sanctity with an account of a heavenly vision of the cross that appeared over the city.[70] Juvenal finally succeeded in obtaining a rank above his former metropolitan, the bishop of Caesarea, becoming the powerful rival of his arch competitor, the bishop of Antioch.[71] Pope Leo the Great of Rome (r. 440–61) was one of Juvenal's severest critics, but nevertheless acknowledged the power that Jerusalem's holy shrines might exert in the doctrinal disputes that enmeshed Juvenal's metropolitan pretensions. His appreciation of Jerusalem's case may have been enhanced by the gift of a relic of the True Cross.[72] One of Leo's letters to Juvenal ends with this note: "I received with veneration a small fragment of the Lord's cross together with the *eulogia* [blessing] of your Charity."[73] Cyril and Juvenal's ambitions advanced the reputation of the True Cross, and relics of the True Cross arguably contributed to the bishops' ultimate success. At the Council of Chalcedon, control of the three parts of Palestine was claimed by Juvenal specifically in the name of the Church of the Anastasis (Holy Sepulchre) rather than of Jerusalem.[74] A fragment of the True Cross successfully represented the numinousness of Jerusalem to the pope. Jesus's historical presence in the city, rendered immediate in the form of relics, persuaded church authorities to recognize an otherwise unimportant provincial town as one of the great patriarchates in the formidable ecclesiastical hierarchy of the Roman Empire. Juvenal's gift seems to a modern observer suspiciously like a bribe.

The drama of a later exchange of another fragment of the True Cross offers a more complex sense of the relic's potential social and political significance. The tale concerns Queen Radegund (ca. 525–87). The story, set in early medieval France against a background of bloody tribal struggles, is best told by Radegund and three of her contemporaries: Gregory, bishop of Tours; Venantius Fortunatus, poet and Radegund's confessor; and Baudonivia, a nun in Radegund's convent.[75] Radegund herself tells the tale of how (in 531) she, a child-princess of

70. Drijvers, *Cyril of Jerusalem*, 51–53.

71. Honigmann, "Juvenal of Jerusalem."

72. For the cult of the cross in Rome, see de Blaauw, "Jerusalem in Rome and the Cult of the Cross." The author does not include the fragment of the cross sent by Juvenal to Leo I in her discussion.

73. This sentence is included in three of the nine main manuscripts. See *Leonis papae epistole*, 139, *Patrologia Latina* 54:1107, note j. Letters 109 and 113 also allude to the didactic value of the holy sites of Palestine.

74. In *Concilium universale Chalcedonense*, 5.22–25.

75. For the poem describing Radegund's abduction that is ascribed to Radegund herself, see Fortunatus, *Fortunatus: Poésies mêlées*, appendix 3. For references to Baudinovia's, Fortunatus's, and Gregory of Tour's accounts of Radegund's life as well as good translations of these texts, see McNamara and Halborg, *Sainted Women of the Dark Ages*, 86–105. Martha Jenks is preparing a political biography of Radegund equating her actions to those of powerful bishops. In the meantime, see M. Jenks, "From Queen to Bishop." For an evocative account of Radegund's life, read O'Faolain, *Women in the Wall*. This novel is both literarily and historically more compelling than Evelyn Waugh's tale of the Empress Helena, mentioned above.

the Thuringian ruling house, was abducted by the Franks after they had slaughtered the rest of her family.[76] Her friends continue her story. The sons of Clovis gambled for Radegund; Clothar won the prize. Clothar sent her to his villa at Athies until about 540, when he forcibly married her. In 550, after Clothar murdered her surviving brother, Radegund fled from him to Noyon, where Saint Medardus consecrated her as deaconess, despite threats from the king. Radegund subsequently established a monastery at Poitiers. Baudonivia describes Radegund's relic collection:

After she had entered into the monastery, she assembled a great multitude of the saints through her most faithful prayers, as the East bears witness and North, South and West acknowledge. From all sides, she managed to obtain those precious gems that Paradise has and Heaven hoards and as many came freely to her as gifts as came in response to her pleas.[77]

Radegund's greatest desire was to obtain a fragment of the True Cross. She "repeatedly sent servants to Jerusalem" in search of the relic.[78] Finally, she received the gift that she so desired not from Jerusalem but from Constantinople. As Baudonivia attests, Radegund's piece of the True Cross came directly from the emperor and empress, Justin II and Sophia:

Like Saint Helena, imbued with wisdom, full of the fear of God, glorious with good works, she eagerly sought to salute the wood where the ransom of the world was hung for our salvation. . . . When she had found it, she clapped both hands. When she recognized that it was truly the Lord's cross that had raised the dead to life with its touch, she knelt on the ground adoring the Lord. . . . What Helena did in oriental lands, Radegund the blessed did in Gaul! Since she wished to do nothing without counsel while she lived in the world, she sent letters to the most excellent King Sigebert who held this land in his power asking that, for the welfare of the whole fatherland and the stability of his kingdom, he would permit her to ask the emperor for wood from the Lord's cross. Most graciously, he consented to the blessed queen's petition.[79]

Gregory of Tours describes how the cross, once it was placed in the sanctuary at Poitiers, worked: "Often I heard how even the lamps that were lit in front of these relics bubbled up because of the divine power and dripped so much oil that frequently they filled a vessel underneath." But the author was skeptical until, after praying at the altar, he witnesses the miracle himself:

---

76. The account of the massacre of her family was written in the first person by Radegund, or in her voice by her learned friend Venantius Fortunatus, more than thirty years after the event. For a discussion of the poem "The Thuringian War," see McNamara and Halborg, *Sainted Women of the Dark Ages,* 65–70.

77. Baudonivia, "Life of Radegund," 95.

78. Gregory of Tours, *Miracula,* 40.1; Gregory of Tours, *Glory of the Martyrs,* 22.

79. Baudonivia, "Life of Radegund," 96–99.

To my right was a burning lamp that I saw was overflowing with frequent drips. I call God as my witness, I thought that its container was broken, because placed beneath it was a vessel into which the overflowing oil dripped. I turned to the abbess [Agnes] and said: "Is your thinking so irresponsible that you cannot provide an unbroken lamp in which oil can be burned, but instead use a cracked lamp from which the oil drips?" She replied: "My lord, such is not the case; it is the power of the holy cross you are watching." Then I reconsidered and remembered what I had heard earlier. I turned back to the lamp that was now heaving great waves like a boiling pot, overflowing in swelling surges throughout that hour. . . . Stunned, I was silent, and finally I proclaimed the power of the venerable cross.[80]

Three of early Christianity's most distinguished modern scholars have offered persuasive interpretations of the historical significance of Radegund's relics. Averil Cameron considers how the imperial donors benefited from their gift: "There must have been a strongly political slant to the gift. The Franks after all were catholic, unlike most of the Germanic world [who were Arians]; they stood out from the rest of the barbarian peoples as obvious potential allies for Byzantium. . . . [Even through the Italian wars of Justinian] Byzantine interest in the Franks never waned. . . . The Poitiers relic demonstrated that both sides were alive to the possibilities."[81] Peter Brown and Raymond Van Dam emphasize the relic's importance in local politics. Van Dam argues that relics were as critical a force in the power politics of Poitiers as the strong personalities with whom they were associated. He suggests that Radegund's relics, particularly that of the True Cross, offered unwonted competition with the cult of Hilary, the local saint. Radegund antagonized Maroveus, the bishop of Poitiers, by its acquisition to such a degree that he refused to attend the translation of the relic into the Chapel of the Holy Cross in Radegund's monastery.[82] Brown suggests that bishops were not as socially secure as historians once assumed; relics were a foundation on which they might construct their status. In sixth-century Gaul, a saint's festival, focused on the saint's relics, was "a ceremony of *adventus* [arrival] and *consensus* [concord]. The saint arrives at a shrine, and this arrival is the occasion for the community to show itself as a united whole, embracing its otherwise conflicting parts, in welcoming him [or her]." Brown describes miracles as a physical consensus, whereby those marginalized by blindness, lunacy, illness were reunited with the healthy body of the community.[83]

These perceptive assessments emphasize the critical play of relics in supraregional, local, and even personal relations. But relics were the stuff not only

---

80. Gregory of Tours, *Miracula*, 40.16–30; Gregory of Tours, *Glory of the Martyrs*, 23–24.

81. Cameron, "The Early Religious Policies of Justin II," 58–62. Also see Cameron, "The Artistic Patronage of Justin II."

82. Van Dam, *Saints and Their Miracles in Late Antique Gaul*, 28–41.

83. P. Brown, "Relics and Social Status in the Age of Gregory of Tours," 244–46.

of politics but also of economics. As Baudonivia relates, Justin and Sophia sent a relic of the True Cross to Radegund, along with a Gospel book adorned with gold and jewels and other relics:

She who had made herself a pauper for God, full of devotion and inflamed with desire, sent no gifts to the emperor. Instead she sent her messengers bearing nothing but prayers and the support of the saints whom she invoked incessantly. She got what she had prayed for: that she might glory in having the blessed wood of the Lord's cross enshrined in gold and gems and many of the relics of the saints that had been kept in the east living in that one place. At the saint's petition, the emperor sent legates with gospels ornamented in gold and gems. And the wood where once hung the salvation of the world came with a congregation of saints to the city of Poitiers. . . . After receiving this celestial gift, the blessed woman sent the aforementioned priest and other messengers to the emperor with a simple garment as a gift of thanks.[84]

The texts make it clear that Radegund's reciprocation was not the material equal of the gift. In return for the rich assortment of reliquaries and illuminated manuscripts, she sent to the emperor and empress a "simple garment" and a poem. About the garment one can only speculate. The poem, written by Venantius Fortunatus, has, however, survived:

May the highest glory be to You, Creator and Redeemer of the world, who in your justice establish Justin on high in the world. Of equal merit to him, marrying him in blessed years, noble Sophia, gains august rank. The holy places she tends with devotion, she adorns with love, and by this offering she causes herself to draw near to heaven. Her abundant faith, shining in splendor from the eastern skies, sent resplendent gifts to God as far as the setting of the sun; when Thuringian Queen Radegund asked, she bestowed the sacred gift of the Cross she desired, on which Christ, thinking it worthy, hung in the flesh He had taken on and bathed our wounds in his blood. . . . Behold, Augusti, you rival each other with like offerings; you ennoble your sex, as he does his; the man brings back Constantine, the godly woman Helena; as the honor is alike, so is the very love of the Cross. She found the means, you scatter salvation everywhere, and what was first the Rising fills the Setting too. . . . Through you the Cross of the Lord claims power over the whole world; where it was unknown now it is manifest and offers protection. Greater faith has reached Christ's people, when hope, with eyes to see, perceives the power of salvation, and faith is doubled through the senses, when through your gifts, souls believe all the more in what they verify with the Cross as witness. . . . Radegund, prostrate on the ground in supplication, adores this, and prays for long years for your rule, and, joined with her sisters in outpourings of tears, wishes that your faith will garner great joy from this.[85]

84. Baudonivia, "Life of Radegund," 96–99.
85. Fortunatus, *Personal and Political Poems*, 111–15.

Venantius Fortunatus also wrote a hymn to the cross sent by Justin II and Sophia to Radegund that became a standard part of the Western liturgy.[86]

By the material inequity of the exchange, Radegund presented herself not as the queen of the Franks but rather as a pious and supplicant nun. The imbalance of the exchange left the superior position of the Byzantine imperial couple unchallenged.[87] The disparity in the gifts sent between Constantinople and Poitiers may be contrasted with the competitive extravagance of those exchanged between Constantinople and Baghdad by emperors and caliphs.[88] Equally powerful rulers could not allow themselves to appear to be outdone in an exchange. In addition, the narrative's emphasis on the immateriality of Radegund's offerings absolves the queen of any accusations of bribery of the sort that I leveled against Juvenal. It also protects her from charges of illicitly buying the relic. A eulogistic poem is the appropriate expression of gratitude for a gift valued above worldly wealth and given by a social superior.

Baudonivia's text acknowledges, nevertheless, the material lavishness as well as the spiritual value of the gifts that were sent from Constantinople to Poitiers. "She got what she had prayed for . . . the blessed wood of the Lord's cross enshrined in gold and gems." In addition, she received "gospels ornamented in gold and gems." A veritable treasure seems to have been transferred from the East to the West. Both the supraworldly worth of the gift and the earthly power of the giver were enhanced by its valuable adornment. Though the relic was the principal object of desire, jewels and precious metals were an important testament not only to the power of their imperial donors but also to the authenticity of the fragment of the True Cross that they enclosed.

By the twentieth century, the reliquary of the True Cross delivered to Poitiers from Constantinople had become the subject of a different sort of assertion of authenticity. In the *Antiquaries Journal* of 1932, William Martin Conway (later Lord Conway of Allington), antiquarian, collector, mountain climber, and Tory politician, wrote,[89]

The Reliquary of the True Cross which is preserved at Poitiers in the convent of Saint-Croix is the earliest existing authentically *dated object decorated with enamel in a Byzantine workshop. It has never before been reproduced in any accurate form, and no living expert has had the opportunity of examining it. Its history is complete and fully* authenticated.[90]

Conway makes several dramatic truth claims in these three sentences—the last being the most remarkable. No one now would dare declare that an ancient

86. Fortunatus, "Vexilla Regis."

87. My reading here differs from that offered by Hahn, "Collector and Saint." The author was kind enough to let me read her article in typescript.

88. O. Grabar, "The Shared Culture of Objects."

89. Sutton, "Discoveries," 122. For a remarkable reflection on collecting art at the beginning of the end of the nineteenth and the beginning of the twentieth century, see Conway, *The Sport of Collecting*.

90. Conway, "St. Radegund's Reliquary at Poitiers," 1; my emphasis.

Fig 11. Fieschi-Morgan Reliquary of the True Cross, front of cover. The Metropolitan Museum of Art, New York, Gift of P. Morgan, 1917 (17.190.715ab). Photograph courtesy of The Metropolitan Museum of Art, New York.

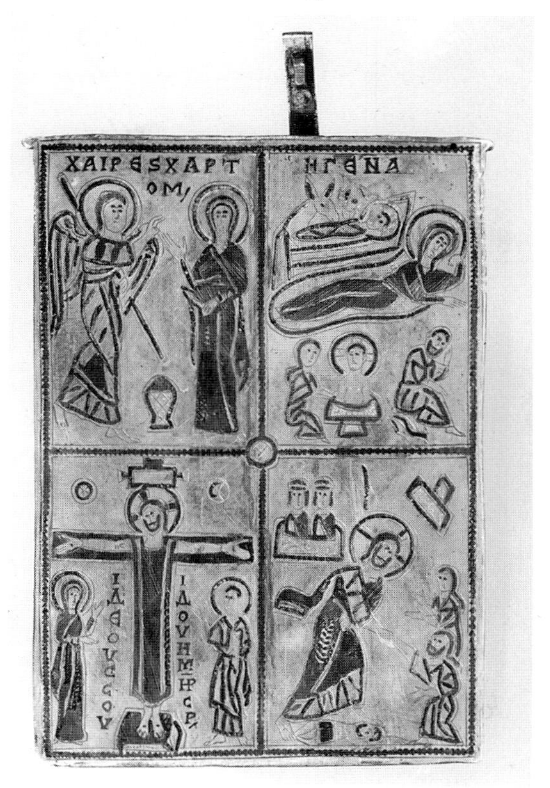

Fig. 12. Fieschi-Morgan Reliquary of the True Cross, back of cover. The Metropolitan Museum of Art, New York, Gift of P. Morgan, 1917 (17.190.715ab). Photograph courtesy of The Metropolitan Museum of Art, New York.

artifact's history was ever complete, much less that its narrative was incontrovertibly documented. The unusually rich literary sources for the imperial gift to Radegund tempted Conway into his declaration. "Radegund's reliquary" is now dated by specialists to the eleventh century.[91] Conway's article and the art-historical discussion of the cloisonné object that survived in Poitiers indicate how the value of the relic had shifted from the Middle Ages to modernity. Virtually no mention is made of the wood of the cross; art-historical interest lies entirely with its gift wrapping.

OBJECT

The Fieschi-Morgan reliquary in the collection of the Metropolitan Museum of Art in New York supplements the stories of Radegund's relic and its gift wrapping (fig. 11). It is a small box (4″ × 2 7/8″ or 10.2 × 7.4 cm); it rests comfortably in an adult's open hand. The container is closed by a sliding lid. The exterior of the box is brilliantly decorated. Cloisonné, from the French *cloison* (chamber or compartment), describes the enameling technique used to ornament its top and sides. Ribbons of gold wire were attached to a gold plate to form an intricate design of miniature cells. After these segments were filled with ground glass of various colors and transparencies, the piece was fired, causing the glass

91. For a review of the scholarship on the reliquary, see Cormack, "Reflections on Early Byzantine Cloisonné Enamels." For a full bibliography, see Skubiszewski, "La staurothèque de Poitiers."

to vitrify and fill the tiny chambers with jewel-like color. The surfaces were then polished to brilliance. The box is figured with the Crucifixion and busts of assorted saints and apostles identified by Greek inscriptions. In its presence, the work looks fragile and delicate; enlarged or projected, the workmanship appears crude. On the bottom of the box is a chased cross against a punched ground. The underside of the lid is decorated in niello, a technique in which an opaque black paste (silver sulfide) is rubbed into the recessed design etched into the surface of the silver panel. It is divided into four compartments and figured with epigrammatic renderings of the Annunciation, Nativity, Crucifixion, and Anastasis (fig. 12).

This precious box is difficult to *place*. Scholarly discussion has focused almost exclusively on where and when it was produced. Arguments have been made for an early date (ca. 700) and a Syro-Palestinian provenance.[92] Now the box has been generally accepted as a work of the early ninth century, produced either in the West for a Greek-speaking patron or, more likely, in the East.[93] Helen Evans, curator of the Department of Medieval Art at the Metropolitan Museum, identifies the box as having been made around 800 in Constantinople.[94] Only authoritative claims, not absolute ones, can made about the box's date and provenance.

Scholarly debate about the origins of the Fieschi-Morgan reliquary is licensed in part by the abstraction of the decoration. The images that adorn the box include no referents that might help to localize their settings. Consider the scene that represents Jesus's triumph over death, commemorated annually on Easter Sunday, Christianity's greatest festival. On the ampulla at Dumbarton Oaks and on the painted box in the Sancta Sanctorum, the event is signified by the scene of the Marys witnessing the empty tomb of Jesus as it was then found in the Anastasis or Rotunda of the Church of the Holy Sepulchre in Jerusalem. In contrast, on the Fieschi-Morgan reliquary Jesus's triumph over death is more literally figured: Jesus breaks down the gates of hell (upper right corner), tramples on Death, and liberates Adam and Eve, while Kings David and Solomon act as witnesses. There is no doubt that this image represents the Anastasis ("awakening," usually translated as "Resurrection"), as it is so labeled in other, near-contemporary examples.[95] Commemoration of the most crucial moment in Christian history has shifted its location from a familiar Jerusalem to an unknowable hell, from the biblical narrative of the Passion to an apocry-

92. Lucchesi Palli, "Der syrisch-palästinensische Darstellungstypus der Höllenfahrt Christi," 250–67; Rosenberg, *Niello bis zum Jahre 1000*, 61–67; Rosenberg, *Zellenschmelz*, 31–38; Wessel and Gibbons, *Byzantine Enamels from the Fifth to the Thirteenth Century*, 42–43.

93. Buckton, "Byzantine Enamel and the West," 236–42. Buckton contends that the reliquary originated in the West in the ninth century. For a date of the first quarter of the ninth century and an ascription to Constantinople, see Kartsonis, *Anastasis*, 102–21. The debate is summarized by Cormack, "Reflections on Early Byzantine Cloisonné Enamels."

94. Evans, Holcomb, and Hallman, *The Arts of Byzantium*, 39.

95. For a discussion of the texts and the emergence and development of the image, see Kartsonis, *Anastasis*, 94–125.

Fig. 13. Fieschi-Morgan Reliquary of the True Cross, interior view. The Metropolitan Museum of Art, New York, Gift of P. Morgan, 1917 (17.190.715ab). Photograph courtesy of The Metropolitan Museum of Art, New York.

phal account.[96] The scenes and saints on the Fieschi-Morgan reliquary have lost their ties to the Holy City as it was experienced contemporaneously. The sites of Jesus's earthly suffering are abstracted from a specific geography. The images represent a doctrinal truth rather than a material history.

The problems of localization extend from the relic's production to its reception. It is difficult to identify the object's medieval use. The box was apparently not designed for permanent public display. It lacks fittings for hanging or for attachment to a support for exhibition. Its small scale and delicate design may suggest an individual viewer, if not a private possessor, rather than a large audience. Or possibly the figuration was not meant to be seen at all, but to act as a magical reinforcement of the power of the relic it enclosed and of its donor. In any case, it must have been secured in an altar or treasury, as it shows few signs of wear. The box has lost only its most important part: the gift it enclosed. The box is empty. The reliquary does, however, retain an expression of its former contents (fig. 13). Metal strips describe the absent object as a patriarchal or double-transverse cross about 3.2 inches tall with a long cross-arm of about 2 inches and a depth of less than a half inch. That which has been lost has left its trace.

Art historians have largely neglected the question of the Fieschi-Morgan reliquary's original function.[97] The box's initial use seems to be of little interest and its original contents of no value. In modernity the box acts not as a reliquary but like an artwork. The way that the work is discussed in academic literature

96. For a convenient English version of the text, see "Gospel of Nicodemus or Acts of Pilate."

97. Still the best survey of reliquaries is Leclercq, "Reliques et reliquaires," 2294–359. For a more recent discussion of reliquaries and bibliography, see Dierkens, "Du bon (et du mauvais) usage des reliquaires au Moyen Âge."

certainly, as intended, informs its function as a historical document; less obviously and often unintentionally, scholarship also adds to its product value. The history of the Fieschi-Morgan reliquary reverses that of *Pegasus Motor Oils*. The sign functioned like a commodity that had become a relic until it was revealed as an artwork. The Fieschi-Morgan box performs now as an art object, but it was originally made to function as a relic-receptacle and then later was treated as a commodity. "Commodity" is defined in the introduction as "a standardized good, which is traded in bulk and whose units are interchangeable." That the Fieschi-Morgan reliquary might ever behave as a commodity seems so unlikely that some explanation is required.

COMMODITY

In Henry James's novel *Outcry*, the hero of the tale is an art historian, Hugh Crimble, who is deeply concerned about the American consumption of the English artistic heritage. One morning Crimble expresses his anxiety about the wealthy American entrepreneur collector Breckenridge Bender to his patroness, Lady Grace: "[The *Journal* has] a leader this morning about Lady Lappington and her Longhi, and on Bender and his hauls, and on the certainty—if we don't do something energetic—of more and more Benders to come: such a conquering horde as invaded the old civilization, only armed now with huge cheque-books instead of with spears and battle-axes."[98] James, the great expatriate American writer, might well represent the American millionaire as a marauder. After all, Bender presumably conquered his corporate competitors at home before he looted the art treasures of Europe. CEO pillaging is certainly still a familiar phenomenon. The Enron and WorldCom scandals may have contributed as much to destabilizing the stock market as the terrorist attacks of September 11, 2001, on the World Trade Center and the Pentagon. One of the two investment banking firms most committed to Enron was J. P. Morgan Chase, which had about three billion dollars in loan exposure to the company.[99]

From the third quarter of the nineteenth century, J. P. Morgan and Company, like its successor J. P. Morgan Chase, offered exclusive commercial banking and investment services, including asset management, for institutions, corporations, and the very wealthy. J. Pierpont Morgan furnished capital to states and corporations desperately in need of money; in exchange he extracted earnings for investors and power for himself. Morgan embodied the capitalist mogul of the era before antitrust laws. He disliked the messiness of competition; he profitably disciplined the market by establishing monopolies in the production and flow of commodities.[100]

J. Pierpont Morgan turned his attention from railroads to art during the last two decades of his life.[101] If the object of his desire shifted, his mode of

98. James, *The Outcry*, 131.

99. Berger, "Enron Gets $250 Million Credit Line."

100. Chernow, *The House of Morgan*, 108–11.

101. For a general discussion of Morgan's collecting, see Allen, *The Great Pierpont Morgan*, 136–51.

acquisition did not. Roger Fry, the English connoisseur and critic, describes him in a letter to his wife: "*Entre nous* he's a brigand like all these great businessmen. They don't have any ties of honesty or decency whatever. 'Business is warfare' is their acknowledged motto."[102] For Wilhelm von Bode, art historian, connoisseur, and founder of the Kaiser Friedrich Museum in Berlin, the new political and industrial power of the United States was wreaking havoc in the European art markets during the first years of the twentieth century.[103] Traditional patronage—the purchase of works of art by those with the wealth to afford them and the taste to appreciate them—was under threat. Just as American millionaires "seek to create their monopolies in industry and the market through power and through powerful institutions, so they also wish to dominate the art market and to seek to make theirs into something great in a single blow: they buy whole collections and make their deals through agents, underlings and middle men of various kinds. They desire to bring together their art collections like they do their trusts; they understand only business, but from art little or nothing. . . . These men of the iron trust have in fact entered into the art market with iron feet, crushing the old and making a strange new market. The art market, changed with a single blow, seems to be dominated entirely by Americans."[104] Bode identified the worst of the predators: "The most dreaded and—by sellers and middle men—most sought out man in today's market, and at the same time the greatest and most successful speculator in business trusts . . . [is] Pierpont Morgan."[105]

Morgan apparently enjoyed acquiring works of art. In a description of his trip with Morgan to Italy, Fry wrote: "I persuaded Morgan to go round by the old ladies' Castello and see the Majolica service. It was a lovely place up in the hills and Morgan was always pleased by the idea of buying family heirlooms from the family itself, the object seemed to convey with it some of the distinction of impoverished nobility."[106] It is less apparent that Morgan fully appreciated the works once he possessed them. Morgan's sympathetic biographer, Jean Strouse, allows that the collector "was not a scholarly connoisseur who studied and fell in love with each object he acquired." She also provides a compelling example of Morgan's lack of familiarity with the objects in his collection: "One day at the end of 1909, he came across a receipt for a bust of the infant Hercules by Michelangelo, for which he had paid £10,000 (about $50,000). He sent the bill to his librarian, Belle da Costa Greene, with a note asking where the sculpture was. 'This bronze Bust is in your library,' she wrote across the receipt, 'and

102. Fry, *Letters of Roger Fry,* 1:251. Fry was offered the directorship of the Metropolitan; after negotiation he was appointed its European adviser on paintings, a post that he held between 1906 and 1910. This position allowed him to live in England for most of the year, spending only three or four months annually in New York.

103. For a general assessment of Bode, see McIsaac, "Wilhelm (von) Bode, the Public Museum, and the Case for Public Support of the Arts in Second Empire Germany."

104. Bode, *Kunst und Künstler* 1:7. The rough translations in the text are my own.

105. Ibid., 1:8.

106. Woolf, *Roger Fry,* 143.

faces you when sitting in your chair. It has been there about a year.'"[107] Indeed, the extent of Morgan's collection and the means by which it was acquired make it likely that he never even saw many of his possessions.

Morgan gathered his European treasures in London. Many of his possessions were on loan to the Victoria and Albert Museum. In 1910, after successfully lobbying Washington to abolish its twenty-percent import duty on works of art and antiques over one hundred years old, Morgan arranged for his collections' shipment to the United States. He hired Jacques Seligmann, a French art dealer, to supervise the packing. He even imported a U.S. customs official to London to approve the crates as they were loaded in order to avoid damaging artworks upon their arrival in New York.[108] Morgan's removal en masse of his collections from England precipitated a furor and perhaps also Henry James's novel *Outcry*. Morgan seems the prototype for James's rapacious American collector, Breckenridge Bender, who strikes fear in those who wish to keep Britain's cultural inheritance of Italian paintings safe in the homes of the British aristocracy where it belonged. After the collection was packed and shipped from England to the United States in 1909–10, a great part of it remained crated in storage until after Morgan's death in 1913.[109] In 1917, his son, J. P. Morgan Jr., gave part of his father's collection—some seven thousand pieces—to the Metropolitan Museum. Among those thousands of artworks was the Fieschi-Morgan reliquary.

How exactly Morgan added the Fieschi-Morgan reliquary to his collection is not yet clear, though information about its acquisition may someday be discovered in the Morgan Library archive.[110] It had been part of the collection amassed by the banker and sportsman Freiherr Albert von Oppenheim (1834–1912). It seems to have gone to Germany from Genoa, where a dealer acquired it from the Countess Thellung, a scion of the Fieschi family, in 1887. It is claimed that the reliquary had been in that family at least since the time of Sinibaldo de' Fieschi, the Count of Lavagna, Pope Innocent IV (r. 1243–54). The pope apparently gave the relic to the church San Salvatore Nuovo in Lavagna, near Genoa, at the time that he founded it. According to an inscription still extant in the church, it received the relic in 1245 as a gift from its founder. San Salvatore still possesses a relic of the True Cross, encased in a small cross-shaped crystal and displayed in a sixteenth-century, Cellini-esque reliquary.[111] The crystal was originally designed as

---

107. Strouse, "J. Pierpont Morgan," 21–22. For Belle da Costa Greene, her ethnicity, and her affair with Bernard Berenson, also see Strouse, "The Unknown J. P. Morgan"; Wixom, "Morgan."

108. Strouse, "J. Pierpont Morgan," 51.

109. Ibid., 581.

110. Receipts and notes for the objects purchased by Morgan are arranged according to the dealers through whom they were acquired. As the dealer involved in the Fieschi-Morgan acquisition is unknown, finding the receipt presents difficulties. I want to thank Christine Nelson, Curator of Literary and Historical Manuscripts, The Pierpont Morgan Library, for undertaking an initial search for such material and offering suggestions as to how I might pursue the question further. For some sense of how medieval pieces were collected by Morgan, see K. Brown, Kid, and Little, "From Attila to Charlemagne." For a perfect example of the kind of art-historical detective work that can be done on enamels, see Buckton, "Bogus Byzantine Enamels in Baltimore and Washington, D.C."

111. Algeri, *Il Museo diocesano di Chiavari*, 39–40.

a patriarchal-cross pendant to be worn around the neck; its measurements would allow it to fit neatly into the empty cruciform of the Fieschi-Morgan box.[112]

Morgan was a devout Episcopalian. He piously supported the Salvation Army and prudishly arranged the cancellation of the New York staging of Richard Strauss's opera, *Salome*.[113] He attended religious services regularly; he gave money to the church; he made a pilgrimage to Jerusalem. He describes his experience of the Holy City in his journal entry of February 18, 1882:

We had no time to look about Jaffa, in fact I judge there is little of any great interest except the house of Simon, the tanner, and that we had already seen very well from the yacht. . . . Just outside of the city we stopped at a small prayer station, built upon the site of the house of Dorcas, where Peter stopped, and then continued our route over the plains of Sharon. . . . In the distance we saw Zorah, where Samson was born, and various other points of historical interest, either biblical or of the times of the Crusaders. . . . Just before dark we stopped to water the horses at an inn on the bank of the brook near which David fought Goliath of Gath and from which he picked the pebble with which he slew him. . . . I must leave you to imagine for I cannot describe the sensations with which I entered that gate [Jaffa Gate]. I shall not soon forget it. We were lighted by a lantern to our hotel "Mediterranean," there being no lights whatever in the streets. Fortunately it was close to the gate and here we were only too glad to avail ourselves of poor beds and cold rooms after a most fatiguing ride. This morning we were up bright and early, none the worse for our journey, and naturally turned our first steps to the Church of the Holy Sepulchre. It is a rambling structure, built upon the site of the crucifixion and the burial place of our Savior. The whole thing was so different, so entirely different, from what I had preconceived, that I can hardly yet realize that I have really been on a spot, which has been held for so many centuries to be sacred. The street leading to it is very narrow, down a steep incline, too narrow for any wheeled vehicle to go, in fact there is no street in Jerusalem wide enough for a wagon. The Church was begun in the fourth century, but little remains of the original structure, which has been rebuilt, repaired and added to, as years have elapsed. As you enter the door, directly in front of you is a slab of marble covering the stone, said to be the one upon which the Savior was anointed for burial, after the crucifixion. Turning to your left, you ascend stairs and you find yourself in a vaulted Chapel, built upon what is supposed to be the summit of Calvary, a death-like stillness pervades, the distant sounds of an organ in a distant part of the Church are heard, awestruck and impressed you stand almost breathless upon what must always be the most sacred spot on earth. I cannot attempt to describe my feelings, words fail me entirely. I could only say to myself, it is good to be here. While we stood there pilgrims came in one after the other, in rapid succession and thus, I suppose, it has been for centuries. Descending the stairs to the Church, we wandered

112. The crystal enclosing the cross is 3.15 inches high and .40 inches wide; the upper arm is 1.20 inches long and the lower one is nearly 2 inches in length. The fit was claimed to be perfect by the countess Thellung. G. Williamson, "The Oppenheim Reliquary and Its Contents," 296n3.

113. Chernow, *The House of Morgan*, 114.

through chapel after chapel, built by different creeds, Greeks, Catholic, Copts, Armenians, etc., until we found ourselves under the large dome; in the center was a small chapel, built up like those one sees in our countries. Entering through a door about four feet high into a vestibule [of the aedicula of the Holy Sepulchre] you pass through another door and you are in the Sepulchre of our Lord. There is the slab on which He was laid. Impelled by an impulse impossible to resist you fall on your knees before that shrine.[114]

From his description, Morgan's experience at the Holy Sepulchre was apparently not so different from those of earlier pilgrims. In the fourth century, Jerome recounts how Paula prostrated herself on Calvary before the cross, "as if she saw the Savior crucified."[115] Margery Kempe is even more expressive in the early fifteenth century.[116] Morgan's journey to Jerusalem was, however, different. The trip, undertaken as a private voyage on the steam yacht *Pandora*, was a test drive for the purchase of his own ship, the *Corsair*.[117] After her encounter with the holy in the Holy Sepulchre, Paula retired to a monastery in Bethlehem. Margery left Jerusalem to continue her pilgrimage to Rome, taking with her many relics as proof of the power of the holy sites. The religious emotion that Morgan felt in the Church of the Holy Sepulchre was apparently not translated into a desire to possess a part of the True Cross.

The emptiness of the enamel box identified as the Fieschi-Morgan reliquary did not matter to Morgan, who may not have seen its outside, much less its inside. Nor has it much mattered to the scholars who have studied the object in the later twentieth century.[118] Whatever Morgan thought about the objects that he acquired, he seems to have treated them in a manner similar to the other commodities by which he represented his power. In a way common in modernity but most perfectly exemplified by Morgan's remarkable mode of collection, the artwork assumed the attributes of a commodity. By the time the box was acquired by Morgan, it had been uninhabited for at least two centuries, and perhaps for as long as six. The functions of the enamel box had changed well before it became one of Morgan's commodities: its metamorphosis from treasure box to treasure was not precipitous but protracted.

What eroded the relic's aura? Relics certainly remained an essential element of Western cultural identity throughout the Middle Ages, though after the ninth century Rome displaced Jerusalem and even Constantinople as their major source.[119] The Crusades reopened for the West the great Eastern depots of relics. The crusaders' conquest of Jerusalem in 1099 led to the discovery or rediscov-

---

114. Quoted from Satterlee, *J. Pierpont Morgan*, 202–4.

115. Jerome, "Letter 108 to Eustochium," 9.2; Wilkinson, *Jerusalem Pilgrims before the Crusades*, 49.

116. See chapter 3 of the present text.

117. Satterlee, *J. Pierpont Morgan*, 204–5.

118. In the early twentieth century, G. C. Williamson concerned himself with what was contained in the reliquary. See Williamson, "The Oppenheim Reliquary and Its Contents."

119. Geary, "The Ninth Century Relic Trade," 8–19; Geary, "Sacred Commodities," 169–91.

ery of many sacred artifacts. The looting of holy objects at a previously unimagined scale accompanied the capture of Constantinople in 1204.[120] In their new abundance, relics participated in the progressively monetized economy of the West in the High Middle Ages. Indeed, relics began acting like money. As early as the late eleventh century, the rollicking *Tractatus Garsiae; or, The Translation of the Relics of SS. Gold and Silver* bitterly satirized the treatment of relics as wealth: "Then the Archbishop [of Toledo] offered [Pope Urban] an immense weight of relics, namely: innards of Silver, ribs of Gold, and his heart, arms and left shoulder, which the Roman pontiff bore to the shrine of S. Cupidity next to the chapel of her sister S. Greedyguts, not far from the basilica of their mother, S. Avarice."[121] In the thirteenth century, relics were notoriously used to pay off cash debts: most infamously, Baldwin II of Constantinople pawned the great Constantinopolitan relic of the True Cross.[122] In 1241, the True Cross was sold by the Venetians to Louis IX (Saint Louis), king of France, who created for it and the other relics he acquired from the looting of the Christian capital of the East perhaps the most impressive of all reliquaries, Saint-Chapelle, in Paris.[123]

By the time of the Reformation, relics had been contaminated by commerce. Still venerated by Catholics, relics were despised by Protestants. A broadside entitled *Religious reliques, or, the sale at the Savoy; upon the Jesuits breaking up their school and chappel,* published in London in 1688, suggests how relics were sterilized and destroyed in the sixteenth and seventeenth centuries:

Last Saturday, by chance,
I Encountered with France [a Jesuit],
That Man of Upright Conversation,
Who told me such News,
That I cou'd not chuse
But Laugh at his sad Declaration.
Says he [the Jesuit], if you'l go,
You shall see such a Show
Of Reliques Expos'd to be Sold,
Which from Sin and Disease
Will Purge all that please
To lay out their Silver and Gold
[Says the priest crossing himself multiple times] You see our sad State,
'Tis a folly to prate,
Our Church and our Cause is a-ground;
So in short, if you've Gold,

120. For an excellent and disturbing analysis of the sale of relics after the fall of Constantinople, see Riant, *Dépouilles religieuses à Constantinople au XIIIe siècle.*

121. Garcia Canon of Toledo, *Tractatus Garsiae*, chap. 3.

122. Piquet, *Des banquiers au moyen âge*, 54.

123. D. Weiss, *Art and Crusade in the Age of Saint Louis*, 6.

Here is to be Sold
For a Guinny the worth of Ten Pound.
[St. James' scollop shell in a bottle]
Here's a piece of the Bag,
By Age turn'd to a Rag,
In which Judas the Money did bear;
With a part of his Rope,
Bequeath'd to the Pope,
As an Antidote 'gainst all despair.
[Rib of St. Lawrence]
[Joseph's cloak in which he was married and his breaches]
[Gall of a saint]
Heres a Bottle of Tears,
Preserv'd many years,
Of Mary's that once was a Sinner;
Some o'the Fish and the Bread
That the Five thousand fed,
Which our Saviour invited to Dinner.
[St. Francis's cord]
[The beard of Pope Joan]
[St. Christopher's boot]
Here's infinite more,
I have by me in store,
All which lye conceal'd in this Hamper;
Either buy 'em today,
Or I'll throw 'em away,
For to morrow, by Heaven, I'll scamper.[124]

Despite the Protestant assault, some Catholic relics continue to work: the dirt from Chimayó, the bones of St. Anne at Sainte-Anne-de-Beaupré, the bed of Padre Pio in San Giovanni Rotondo. Nevertheless, Protestantism apparently compromised the power of Catholic relics even for Catholics, especially in predominantly Protestant countries. The reassembled and embalmed body of John Southworth, a Catholic priest drawn and quartered in London by order of Cromwell in 1564, worked miracles in France until the Revolution. In 1929 his body was rediscovered during roadwork at Douai; now he is the only saint displayed in the Catholic Cathedral of Westminster. No miracles have been attributed to him since his return to England.[125] Even in largely Catholic countries, the great pilgrimage destinations of the later nineteenth and twentieth centuries have been places of incorporeal appearances—LaSallette, Lourdes, Medjugorje—rather than sites of physical relics.

124. "Religious Reliques."
125. Wharton, "Westminster Cathedral."

CONCLUSION

Jerusalem first circulated in the West in the form of its physical fragments—pieces of stone, drops of oil, bits of bone, particles of wood. The city proved a productive source of sacred debris by which the divine might be possessed. A series of miraculous discoveries, which began in the fourth century with the revelation of the Holy Sepulchre and continued in the fifth with the *inventiones* of the protomartyr Stephen and John the Baptist, maintained the stock of credible witnesses to the city's holiness.[126] These and other pieces of the city and its blessed inhabitants were distributed as gifts in the West, reminding their recipients of the giver's access to holiness as well as celebrating Jerusalem's sacrality and power.

The dispersal of pieces of Jerusalem followed the economic pattern of the period. In the impoverished conditions of Europe in the early Middle Ages, gifting was one of the principal noncoercive means of exchanging surplus goods. Gifts were often lavish. The fragments of the True Cross that are followed in this chapter were presented by their donors in sumptuous parcels often worked with great artistry in gold, silver, and jewels. The wealth involved in such packaging signified the importance of both the gift and its giver. The reliquary was subject to pillage. It could be melted down and recirculated. But so long as the gift was a gift and not loot, it resisted commodification. Emphasis in scholarly literature has been on the mobility of relics.[127] In practice, relics, once in place, are remarkably stable; the aura of the great gift inhibited its migration. It resisted moving through society; rather, society tended to move around it. The great gift is a noncirculating fortune. Modern economists might identify it as unproductive treasure, because the initial investment made in it did not breed further wealth. But, of course, in the Middle Ages the great gift was prolific. A relic of the True Cross, like that Radegund received from Emperor Justin II and Empress Sophia, promoted local power and community identity. It worked miracles, healing the pious and protecting its possessors. As an object of local and regional veneration, it stimulated pilgrimage, which in turn induced exchange. Finally, the gift of the

126. The unearthing of the Holy Sepulchre in the fourth century was followed by further revelations in the fifth. In 415, the body of the protomartyr Stephen was miraculously revealed. Constantinople received a piece of Stephen in 421, in reciprocation for imperial largess. For the date of the translation of relics, see Holum, "Pulcheria's Crusade a.d. 421–22 and the Ideology of Imperial Victory," 163. The discovery is described in some detail: "In this year the pious Theodosios, in imitation of the blessed Pulcheria, sent much money to the archbishop of Jerusalem for distribution among those in need. He also sent a golden cross, set with precious stones to be fixed on the holy site of Calvary. The archbishop sent as a return gift the relics of the right hand of the first martyr Stephen, by means of Passarion, one of the holy men. In the very night that he reached Chalcedon the blessed Pulcheria saw St. Stephen saying to her in a vision, 'Behold your prayer has been heard, your request is fulfilled, and I have come to Chalcedon.' She arose and, taking her brother, went out to meet the holy relics and, taking them into the palace, she built a wonderful church for the holy First Martyr and deposited his holy relics there." Theophanes, *The Chronicle of Theophanes Confessor,* 135–36; Theophanes, *Chronographia,* 1.86.25–87.5; Vanderlinder, "Revelatio Sancti Stephani," 179–80. The *inventio* of John the Baptist occurred in 452. See Peeters, *L'Orient et Byzance,* 53–61.

127. For example, Geary, "Sacred Commodities."

True Cross often produced further gifts—the fragment of the cross given as a gift by Bishop John of Jerusalem to Melania the Elder generated further gifts to Paulinus of Nola and Sulpicius Severus. The particles of Jerusalem that came to lodge in the West as relics provided proximity to the city from which they came. They also described the early medieval economy of which they were a part.

Relics no longer fit comfortably in the Western economy. Two examples of the contemporary sale of relics suggest something of the dissonance caused by the circulation of the sacred in the modern market. The first is an eBay advertisement:

eBay auction, Document Item # 1080381927. Collectibles: Cultures & Religions: Religions, Spirituality: Christianity: Relics. Auction currently $610.00 (reserve met). First bid $85.00. Description: Relic True Cross & Crown of Thorns. This 19th century French silver reliquary or theca is most exceptional. Fully documented and authenticated, it bears two quite substantial relics of Our Lord's Passion—one of the True Cross, another of the Crown of Thorns. The reliquary, relics, wax seal and authenticating document have all been carefully preserved since they were assembled in 1879 and are in superb condition. Shipped by Priority Air, it should arrive anywhere in the world by Easter. Individual relics of the True Cross and of the Crown of Thorns are seen from time to time in European collections, but they are not always properly documented. In this instance we have been fortunate enough to find an antique reliquary containing both precious relics, authenticated by the Bishop of Langres more than 120 years ago. The seal on the authentic matches perfectly the wax seal set in place to preserve the integrity of the relics. . . . The relics are seated on a very sober field of burgundy-colored fabric, probably silk. The cruciform True Cross relic is placed above a label reading "vera Crux." . . . The Crown of Thorns relic is seated just below, above a label reading "ss, coron. sp." . . . When the back is opened, the red wax seal and red sealing strings are revealed to be in perfect condition. The authentic (document) measures about 13 by 8 inches. It bears both the printed and inked seals of Bishop Bouange of Langres and is dated February 24, 1879. The Latin manuscript text describing the relics reads as follows: "sacras Particulas Sanctissimo Ligno Crucis in quo Salvor Mundi Pependit——et S. Smae Coronae Spinae D.N.J.C. quas reverenter deposimus in theca argentae formae rotundae." This is the only time we have been able to offer a reliquary of this importance, and we doubt that we will ever have the opportunity to do so again. Personal Checks welcome and are deposited to our US bank account. Payment by credit card is welcome. We make international payment easy by using PayPal; just click the PayPal button below. For purchases of under $500, you can also automatically send us a money order using BidPay.[128]

In the age of HurryDate and Halliburton, you can buy a relic of the True Cross over the Internet.

The second example reverses the first. Rather than a suspiciously authenticated ancient relic, you are offered a truly authentic modern one. A *New York Times* article from 1992 explains how this works:

128. eBay, "Auction."

Perhaps the most innovative merger of DNA technology and free enterprise is occurring in California, where Kary Mullis, a biotechnologist, recently founded a company to sell pieces of DNA cloned from rock stars and other cultural heroes. Dr. Mullis is best known as the inventor of a gene amplification technique called the polymerase chain reaction, which can take a single bit of DNA and within hours make millions of identical copies. The technique has revolutionized the field of molecular biology, but Dr. Mullis wants to use it to become the Henry Ford of celebrity DNA. "Originally we were thinking about jewelry," said Dr. Mullis, who considered making bracelets containing DNA cloned from Mick Jagger's lips. "But now we're thinking more about cards. Something a little classier than a baseball card, with the person's picture and some of their DNA worked right into the card, and some sequence information printed on the back. . . . People could use the cards as totems or relics."[129]

But in the years since the *New York Times* article was published, Kary Mullis has not become the Henry Ford of celebrity DNA; there are no DNA cards of Mick Jagger now on auction at eBay. The power of a relic depends on its uniquely intimate relationship with its originating source. When an object begins life as one of an identical series of clones, it struggles to become a relic. When a real relic enters the modern market, it struggles to retain its identity as something other than an economic good. EBay erodes the relic's originality. As in the case of the Fieschi-Morgan reliquary, the object gives up something when it is treated like a commodity. That something is the subject of the rest of this volume.

---

129. R. Weiss, "Techy to Trendy: Products Hum DNA's Tune."

CHAPTER TWO

Replicated Jerusalem: Temple, Templars, and Primitive Accumulation

How blessed to die there as a martyr! Rejoice, brave athlete, if you live and conquer in the Lord; but glory and exult even more if you die and join your Lord. Life indeed is a fruitful thing and victory is glorious, but a holy death is more important than either. If they are blessed who die in the Lord, how much more are they who die for the Lord! To be sure, precious in the eyes of the Lord is the death of his holy ones, whether they die in battle or in bed, but death in battle is more precious as it is more glorious. * BERNARD OF CLAIRVAUX, "IN PRAISE OF THE NEW KNIGHTHOOD"

Clement Attlee
James Boswell
Geoffrey Chaucer
Sir Francis Drake
Mohandas Gandhi
William Gilbert
James II
John Maynard Keynes
Jawaharlal Nehru
Cecil John Rhodes
Abraham Stoker
MEMBERS OF THE INNER TEMPLE

Edmund Burke
Edward VII
Diana, Princess of Wales
Charles Dickens
Elizabeth II
Henry Fielding
John Pym
Richard Sheridan
William Thackeray
Five signatories of the American Declaration of Independence
MEMBERS OF THE MIDDLE TEMPLE

REPLICA

Through the Middle Ages, Jerusalem continued to generate relics that circulated in the West as political as well as spiritual agents.[1] But devotion to holy fragments was increasingly complemented by a veneration of sacred spaces. The West's chronic desire for the experience of Jerusalem was idiosyncratically expressed in the replication of sites from the Holy Land. In compensation for

I want to thank Jaroslav Folda for his comments on this chapter.

1. For example, for the rediscovery and gifting of fragments of the True Cross during the Crusades, see Cadei, "Gli Ordini di Terrasancta e il culto per la Vera Croce"; Ligato, "The Political Meanings of the Relic of the Holy Cross among the Crusades and in the Latin Kingdom of Jerusalem."

Table 1. Relic, souvenir, replica

	RELIC	SOUVENIR	REPLICA
RELATION TO JERUSALEM	Means of possessing Jerusalem	Means of possessing Jerusalem	Means of possessing Jerusalem
RELATION TO PLACE	Travels well	Must travel	Represents displacement
RELATION TO ORIGINAL	Identical to what it represents	Is a sign of what it represents	Recognizably a reproduction of what it represents
RELATIVE MATERIALITY/ SPIRITUALITY	Perfectly integrates material and spiritual	Accommodates material and spiritual	Imperfectly separates the material and the spiritual
ACTION	Acts magically	Acts mnemonically	Acts practically

not seeing Jerusalem or as a means of maintaining the memory of having seen the city, replicas of the Holy Sepulchre were constructed in Western Europe. Although there are early examples of such replicas, most were built from the end of the eleventh through the thirteenth centuries.[2] The highest demand for replications of the Holy Sepulchre coincided with the Crusades—the period of the medieval West's most aggressive attempts to possess the site itself. Simultaneously, the European economy expanded and the West was progressively monetized.[3]

Like relics and souvenirs, replicas of the Holy Sepulchre represented the East in the West. But the distinct ways in which these various forms of consumption work should not be confused (table 1). The relic perfectly integrates the material and the spiritual. The relic's capacity to travel well is a proof of its integrity. The holy and its fragments remain potent wherever they go. A piece of the True Cross is usually as efficacious in one location as it is in another. Relics may travel, but their power doesn't depend on it. Souvenirs, in contrast, are designed to travel. The souvenir functions as a mnemonic device. It is the personal repository of a special memory. The souvenir only fully realizes its purpose through dislocation. A souvenir may remind its possessor of a meeting with the sacred, but it does not ordinarily act as the substitute for such an encounter or as the vehicle by which its experience might be reenacted. A souvenir that works a miracle cannot be intelligibly named a souvenir. A postcard of the Virgin that begins to weep like the miraculous image it represents is not a normal postcard.[4] Like souvenirs, monu-

2. The still magisterial study of the forms of these structures is Krautheimer, "Introduction to an 'Iconography of Medieval Architecture.'" For a general discussion of realizing Jerusalem in material form, see Jaspert, "Vergegenwaertigungen Jerusalem in Architektur und Reliquienkult."

3. For a social-science parody of an understanding of the Crusades, see Anderson et al., "An Economic Interpretation of the Medieval Crusades."

4. "The Newest Weeping Icons."

mental replicas work by displacement. They function properly only when they are removed from their archetype. They may also act as repositories for memory.

If the relic perfectly integrates the material and the spiritual, the replica imperfectly separates them. Sacred spaces are very hard to move, though angels can occasionally accomplish the task.[5] In the absence of heavenly intervention, holy sites are relocated only by reproduction. In their dislocation, the metaphysical and the physical components of a sacred space become distinguishable, though never entirely disentangled. However powerful the referents of a particular architectural form might be, the successful replica of a sacred space is inevitably marked as a reproduction.[6] It is not the original thing but a copy, and copies are not as reliably efficacious as originals. The notion of "copy" bears with it a sense of being secondary to its archetype, subscribing to the original's reality without itself being real. Inevitably present is the acknowledgment of its fictive character. The replica of the Holy Sepulchre appropriated something of the aura of the original, but no one in the Middle Ages seems to have mistaken the copy for the actual tomb of Jesus.[7]

If architectural replicas do not have the same force as relics, they are more potent than souvenirs. Bishops never awarded indulgences for experiencing a souvenir, but an annual visit to the Temple Church in London saved a soul from sixty days in purgatory.[8] Generally, souvenirs are personal things; monumental replicas have communal as well as private functions. A replica of the Holy Sepulchre performed as a place of worship; at the same time it might also act both as a built icon, rendering present a distant archetype, and as a monumental index—a marker or pointer—of local power. Prominent buildings are also enduring incitements in the landscape, continually clamoring for some explanation of their presence. A replica of the Holy Sepulchre provoked stories not only of Jesus's Passion but also of the status and authority of its patrons.

Most medieval duplications of the Holy Sepulchre were built by individual donors. Only one institution has consistently been associated with its replication in the West: the Knights Templar. The military Order of the Knights Templar—officially the Poor Knights of Christ and of the Temple of Solomon—was itself the progeny of Jerusalem, having been established there during crusader rule.[9] The order in turn reproduced Jerusalem. Monastic orders were commonly

5. As in the case the Sancta Casa in Loreto, Italy, which, at the end of the thirteenth century, was transported by angels from Nazareth via Tersato in Illyria to the site near Ancona. For a discussion of the Sancta Casa and of rich remains of crusader sculpture left behind in Nazareth, see Folda, *The Nazareth Capitals and the Crusader Shrine of the Annunciation*.

6. Of course, an unsuccessful replica is not marked as a reproduction, whatever the intentions of its producer.

7. The number of claims made in the Middle Ages concerning the originality of icons suggests that the idea of a "copy" as derivative is not exclusively modern. A painting of the Virgin done by Saint Luke or an image of Jesus not made by human hands but, rather, appearing miraculously tended to be more privileged than their copies.

8. For a more detailed discussion of indulgences, see chapter 3 of the present text.

9. Pauperes commilitiones Christi templique Salomonici.

Fig. 14. Arch of Titus, relief panel of the spoils from the Temple of Jerusalem. Forum Romanum, Rome. Author photo.

named for the men whose rules they followed—Benedictines, Augustinians, Dominicans, Franciscans.[10] In the high Middle Ages, orders might also bear the name of the location of their motherhouse—Cluniacs, Cisterians. Only the Order of the Knights Templar was named for a famous building.[11] This chapter investigates how a temple of the military order, constructed in the West, acted as an imposing index not only of the knights' esoteric Eastern-ness but also of their economic effects.

SITE

Solomon constructed the Jerusalem Temple at the beginning of the first millennium BCE. It was destroyed by the Babylonians in 586 BCE. Zorobabel constructed a modest replacement within two generations. Herod the Great began another, rebuilding the Temple in 19 BCE on a scale that gave it the status in the Roman world that its Solomonic predecessor had enjoyed in the early Iron Age (fig. 3). Mount Moriah, site of Solomon's Temple, was transformed by Herod's engineers, who created one of the largest platforms in the Roman Empire as the base for the new sanctuary—a space equivalent to about

10. In the West, monastic communities in the East are commonly referred to as Basilian, as they followed the rule of Saint Basil. Byzantine monastic communities, however, were regulated according to *typika*, charters established by their founders which only broadly, never rigidly, followed Basil's "rule."

11. The Hospitallers—Hospitallers of Saint John of Jerusalem—were named for their function rather than their site. The great hospital near the Holy Sepulchre that served as the headquarters of the order was built only after its foundation. For a good introduction, see Forey, *The Military Orders*.

twenty-three American football fields.[12] Surviving parts of the podium's retaining wall, constructed of skillfully dressed stones, some as long as thirty-six feet and weighing as much as four hundred tons, still witness the magnitude of Herod's undertaking. The Temple was finished between 62 and 64 CE, well after Herod's death. It was destroyed less than a decade after its completion during the First Jewish Revolt of 66–73 CE.

After suppressing the uprising, Titus, son of the emperor Vespasian, returned to Rome with his booty. The spoils of the Temple—the golden menorah, the Ark of the Covenant, and other Temple vessels—were displayed ephemerally in Titus's triumphal procession and permanently in the sculptured panels of his great triumphal arch on the Via Sacra in Rome (fig. 14). The remarkable trophies of the destruction of the Temple still survive in their monumental representation, reminding modern tourists of the ancient Roman suppression of the Jews.[13] In the fourth century, the Christian emperor Constantine reportedly deposited the censer of Aaron and the Ark of the Covenant in his new cathedral in Rome, the Lateran Basilica. Through the seventeenth century, they served there to mark not the Roman defeat of Jewish revolutionaries but rather the Christian triumph over Judaism.[14] They have now disappeared. Some Israeli government officials seem to believe that the pope still has the great golden menorah hidden in the catacombs.[15]

The residual aura of the Temple Mount was put back to work only in the seventh century. Christian Jerusalem bloodlessly capitulated to the Muslim caliph Omar ibn al-Khattab in 638. The patriarch Sophronios identified the Temple Mount for the caliph. According to tradition, Omar himself began the clearance of the site from the waste that had obscured it by filling his cloak with rubbish.[16] The Temple Mount, left desolate by Christians for five hundred years, thus became a locus of Muslim holiness.[17] In the late seventh century, the Umayyad caliph Abd al-Malik enshrined the outcrop of rock identified with

12. The ancient platform corresponds to Jerusalem's Temple Mount, al-Haram al-Sharif, the dimensions of which are 1,070 feet (north), 920 feet (south), 1,540 feet (east), 1,630 feet (west). An American football field is 160 feet wide and 360 feet long, with a 30-foot end zone designated at each end of the field.

13. It is ironic that Israel depended on this representation of Roman triumph over the Jews and of the Roman destruction of Jerusalem for its coat of arms. The great menorah from the panel is used now as the state's emblem. For an archaeological analysis of the panel, see Yarden, *The Spoils of Jerusalem on the Arch of Titus*.

14. Freiberg, *The Lateran in 1600*, n110.

15. Shimon Shetreet, Israel's religious affairs minister, "claimed that recent research at the University of Florence indicated the menorah might be among the hidden treasures in the Vatican's catacombs. 'I don't say it's there for sure,' he said, 'but I asked the pope to help in the search as a goodwill gesture in recognition of the improved relations between Catholics and Jews.'" Palmieri-Billig, "Shetreet." I want to thank Steve Fine for bringing this article to my attention.

16. "According to Raja' b. Haywah. . . . 'Umar made the front part of the masjid [the southern end of the Haram] its qiblah [determining the direction of prayer]. Then he stood up from his place of prayer and went to the rubbish in which the Romans buried the temple. . . . He said, 'O people, do what I am doing.' He knelt in the midst of the rubbish and put it by the handful into the lower part of his mantle. . . . By the time it was evening nothing remained of the rubbish." Al-Tabari, *The History of al-Tabari*, 194–96.

17. For an excellent introduction to Islamic Jerusalem, see O. Grabar, *The Shape of the Holy*.

Fig. 15. Al-Haram al-Sharif, Dome of the Rock, Jerusalem. Author photo.

Abraham's sacrifice and Muhammad's ascension to heaven in the Dome of the Rock. Muslims had briefly prayed in the direction of this rock before turning toward the Ka'bah in Mecca, and it is the rock's shrine that is now Islam's most ancient surviving monument.[18] The building, with its gilded dome raised above a lavishly tiled octagon, adorns the covers of guidebooks and travel brochures. Since its construction, the Dome of the Rock has identified Jerusalem to all those attracted to the city.

It is not the scale of the Dome of the Rock that impresses but its simplicity. Whether standing before the building or seeing it from a distance, the observer finds the structure compelling in its conceptual effortlessness. The building's isolation on its grand podium dramatically stages its chaste volumes (fig. 15). Its base is a broad octagon; rising from the octagon's center is a cylindrical drum crowned by an exuberant dome. The fine marbles, mosaics, tiles, and gilding that adorn the structure confirm its authority. Its interior displays the same profound integration of rational geometry and spiritual energy. Two low, dimly lit annular aisles circle the high, brilliantly lit center. The polished columns and the marble-revetted piers of the aisle arcades frame the building's core. The reflective gold-ground mosaic of the walls and spandrels enlivens the movement of light through the structure. These glass, gold, silver, and mother-of-pearl mosaic decorations, produced by Byzantine craftsmen using imported Byzantine tesserae, emphasize the surface they cover. Vessels and vegetation, heraldically flattened and symmetrical like the inscriptions that occupy the

18. The Ka'bah, the holiest shrine in Islam, has been subject to multiple reconstructions. For a lively fictional account of the Jerusalem site, see Makiya, *The Rock*.

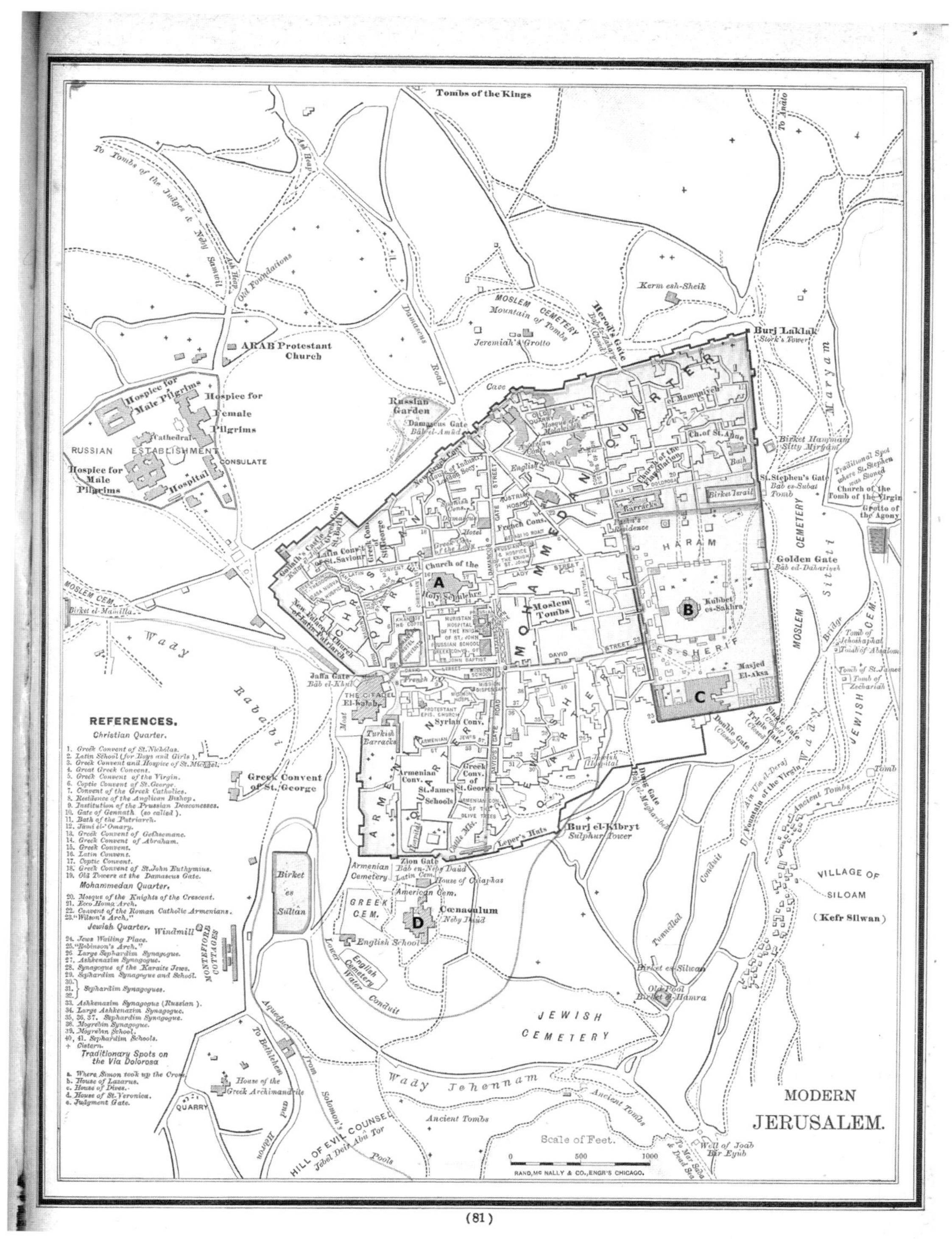

Fig. 16. Jerusalem, showing the Holy Sepulchre and al-Haram al-Sharif. *A*, Holy Sepulchre; *B*, Dome of the Rock; *C*, al-Aksa Mosque; *D*, Cenacle. From Hurlebut, *Manual of Biblical Geography* (1884). Modified by the author.

cornice, enhance the spatial geometries of the building. The controlled splendor of the structure makes it sublime. The Dome of the Rock has endured many and varied restorations, but it has always served the function for which it was designed: the commemoration of a holy site. It remains a perfect building.

Like the Rotunda of the Holy Sepulchre, the Dome of the Rock was a pilgrimage destination, not a place of conventional public worship. Prayer was accommodated on the Temple Mount to the south of the rock, in al-Aksa Mosque (fig. 16). Al-Aksa originated, it seems, as a large but simple structure. Arculf, a bishop from an unidentified see in France who made a pilgrimage to Jerusalem around 675, describes the Muslim construction on the Temple Mount: "The Saracens now have a quadrangular prayer house. They built it roughly by erecting upright boards and great beams on some ruined remains. The building, it is said, can accommodate three thousand people at once."[19] The mosque seems to have been rebuilt in a grander fashion by the Umayyad caliph al-Walid (r. 705–15) as a great rectangular space with a grand central aisle flanked on either side by seven narrower ones. The central aisle culminated in the *mihrab,* or niche, in the *kibla,* the wall facing Mecca. The *mihrab*'s importance is further emphasized by a dome raised in front of it over the last bay of the nave. In directing their prayers toward the *kibla,* worshippers turned their backs on the Dome of the Rock. Al-Aksa, in contrast with the Dome of the Rock, has suffered not only significant rebuildings and additions but also violent shifts in function. It is experienced now as a monumental palimpsest.

The Temple Mount was reconsecrated by the Muslims as al-Haram al-Sharif, "the Noble Sanctuary." The new building complex on the Temple Mount superseded its spatial competitors. As display, it replaced (literally) the Jewish Temple and displaced (figuratively) the Church of the Holy Sepulchre. Al-Mukaddasi, an Arab traveler and geographer writing at the end of the tenth century, describes the contest: "This mosque [al-Aksa] is even more beautiful than that of Damascus, for during the building of it they had for a rival and as a comparison the great church [of the Holy Sepulchre] . . . and they built this to be even more magnificent than the other."[20] As in the competition among the great cathedrals of Europe, preeminence was expressed by outdoing the rival on its own terms. Like the Church of the Holy Sepulchre, the new sacred space was made up of a great rotunda enshrining a stone outcrop aligned with a massive basilica.

It was to the Noble Sanctuary that the Muslim inhabitants of Jerusalem fled for refuge when the crusaders breached the walls of the city in 1099—to no avail, as Fulcher of Chartres describes:

Then some, both Arabs and Ethiopians, fled into the Tower of David; others shut themselves up in the Temple of the Lord and of Solomon, where in the halls a very great attack was made on them. Nowhere was there a place where the Saracens could

---

19. Arculf, *The Pilgrimage of Arculfus in the Holy Land about the Year A.D. 670,* 1.1.

20. Mukaddasi, *Descriptio imperii moslemici,* 178.5, note h; al-Mukaddasi, *Description of Syria Including Palestine,* 3:41. I want to thank Kalman Bland for checking the Arabic source for this translation.

escape the swordsmen. On the top of Solomon's Temple, to which they had climbed in fleeing, many were shot to death with arrows and cast down headlong from the roof. Within this Temple about ten thousand were beheaded. If you had been there, your feet would have been stained up to the ankles with the blood of the slain. What more shall I tell? Not one of them was allowed to live. They did not spare the women and children.[21]

The structures identified by Fulcher as the Temples of the Lord and of Solomon were, respectively, the Dome of the Rock and al-Aksa Mosque. Al-Haram al-Sharif became the administrative center of the crusader city. The Temple of Solomon, al-Aksa Mosque, was appropriated as the palace of the first three rulers of Jerusalem, Godfrey of Bouillon (1099–1100), Baldwin I (1100–18), and for the early part of his reign, Baldwin II (1118–31). Baldwin II later moved his residence to the citadel, the traditional residence of the rulers of Jerusalem.[22] By then, the small new monastic order of knights that Baldwin had earlier installed in part of his palace had so expanded in numbers and power that they inherited the entire structure. The great basilica, once a mosque, then a palace, became the seat of one of the most wealthy and powerful religious and military organizations of the twelfth and thirteenth centuries—the Knights Templar.[23]

TEMPLARS

The establishment of the Templars and their early history is described by William of Tyre (d. 1185), one of the most respected chroniclers of the Latin Kingdom of Jerusalem:

In this same year [1118], certain pious and God-fearing nobles of knightly rank, devoted to the Lord, professed the wish to live perpetually in poverty, chastity, and obedience. In the hands of the patriarch they vowed themselves to the service of God as regular canons. Foremost and most distinguished among these men were the venerable Hugh de Payens and Godfrey de St. Omer. Since they had neither a church nor a fixed place of abode, the king granted them a temporary dwelling place in his own palace, on the north side of the Temple of the Lord. . . . The king and his nobles, as well as the patriarch and the prelates of the churches, also provided from their own holdings certain benefices, the income of which was to provide these knights with food and clothing. . . . The main duty of this order—that which was enjoined upon them by the patriarch and the other bishops for the remission of sins—was "that, as far as their strength permitted, they should keep the roads and highways safe from the menace of robbers and highwaymen, with special regard for the protection of pilgrims." . . . It was in the time of Pope Eugenius, it is said, that they began to sew on their mantles crosses of red cloth, that they might be distinguished from others. Not only the knights, but also the infe-

21. Fulcher of Chartres, *The Chronicle of Fulcher of Chartres*, 77.

22. Schein, "Between Mount Moriah and the Holy Sepulchre," 180–81.

23. For two documents materially linking the Templars with the Haram, see Abel, "Lettre d'un templier"; Pringle, "A Templar Inscription from the Haram al-Sharif in Jerusalem."

rior brothers called sergeants, wore this sign. The Templars prospered so greatly that today there are in the order about three hundred knights who wear the white mantle and, in addition, an almost countless number of lesser brothers. They are said to have vast possessions, both on this side of the sea and beyond. There is not a province in the Christian world today that does not bestow some part of its possessions upon these brethren, and their property is reported to be equal to the riches of kings.[24]

William of Tyre's characterization of the Templars is that of a good historian and a jealous bishop.

The Templars were recognized as an order at the Council of Troyes in 1129. There the formidable church reformer, Saint Bernard of Clairvaux, was one of the Templars' principal advocates and the assumed author of their first official rule. The Templars represented an innovation in Christian tradition: a monastic order with a military function. Righteous killing rather than spiritual contemplation was its primary objective. "How blessed to die . . . as a martyr!"[25] Saint Bernard's powerful celebration of fighting for God's sake and his glorification of death in combat in his *In Praise of the New Knighthood* is uncannily similar to current religiously inspired terrorist rhetoric. Warrior monks seemed as unnatural in the twelfth century as they do now. A text ascribed to Hugh de Payns, founder of the order, unconvincingly rationalizes the Templars' military function. Is their labor as soldiers an obstacle to contemplation? No. Does not the hermit have to attend to eating and clothing? Instead of weaving baskets or growing vegetables like a holy recluse, the Templar safeguards the pious visitors of the holy shrines.[26]

The ascetic obedience required of monasticism enhanced both the authority and discipline of the knights of the order. The Old French Rule of the Templars—a thirteenth-century compilation of earlier foundation documents—indicates the community's strict control of their members' military and social lives.[27] Before aspirants were admitted, they were both tested for their appropriateness and warned of the privations that they would have to endure.[28] If no objections were raised to a candidate in discussion with the brothers of the house, two or three of the senior members of the community met with the petitioner to describe the "sufferings" he would endure as a Templar. If he indicated

24. William of Tyre, *A History of Deeds Done beyond the Sea*, 1:524–26. Jacques de Vitry and Michael the Syrian also provide descriptions of the foundation of the Templars. A translation of Michael the Syrian's very useful text is provided in an appendix to this chapter. Michael the Syrian, *Chronique de Michel le Syrien*, 3:iii.201–3; iv.595–97. For Michael the Syrian's historical and literary importance, see Kiraz, "Special Issue: Michael the Syrian"; Weltecke, *Die "Beschreibung der Zeiten" von Mor Michael dem Grossen (1126–1199)*. Also see Weltecke, "Contacts between Syriac Orthodox and Latin Military Orders."

25. Bernard of Clairvaux, "In Praise of the New Knighthood," 130.

26. Leclercq, "Un document sur les débuts des Templiers."

27. For the Old French text, Bernard of Clairvaux, "La Règle du Temple." Upton-Ward provides a good translation of the text, as well as a clear introduction to the history of the order, in Bernard of Clairvaux, *The Rule of the Templars*, 1–17. Rules, as ideal formulations, are particularly problematic historical documents, suggesting what should be rather than what is. Nevertheless, the Rule provides an appreciation of Templar practices that is confirmed by other sources.

28. "Reception into the Order," in Bernard of Clairvaux, *The Rule of the Templars*, 168–74.

that he would "willingly suffer all for God," and that he wished "to be a serf and slave of the house forever," he was asked a set of questions: Did he have a wife or fiancée? Had he ever made a vow to another order? Did he owe a debt to any man that he could not pay? Was he healthy and free from any secret illness? If he answered each of these questions appropriately, the interrogators returned to the assembly of brothers and reported on the supplicant's suitability for admission to the order. Subsequently he was introduced to the chapter, where he made a formal petition for admission. There he received a final warning:

Good brother, you ask a very great thing, for of our Order you see only the outer appearance. For the appearance is that you see us having fine horses, and good equipment, and good food and drink, and fine robes, and thus it seems to you that you would be well at ease. But you do not know the harsh commandments that lie beneath: for it is a painful thing for you, who are your own master, to make yourself a serf to others. For with great difficulty will you ever do anything that you wish: for if you wish to be in the land this side of the sea, you will be sent to the other side; or if you wish to be in Acre, you will be sent to the land of Tripoli or Antioch, or Armenia. . . . And if you wish to sleep, you will be awoken; and if you sometimes wish to stay awake, you will be ordered to rest in your bed.[29]

At his final reception, the man seeking admission as a Templar knight was also asked "if he is the son of a knight and a lady, and if his father is of knightly lineage; and if he was born in legal wedlock."[30] Only members of the social elite could become knights of the Temple; the young aristocrats who entered the order embraced a life of abstinence. The Rule imposed strict limits on diet, dress, communication, appropriation of horses, movement, and even the degree to which asceticism might be practiced. Possessions were limited. The knights wore a white cloak devoid of fur or other ornament; they were given a linen shirt if they desired it because of the heat of the East. They were forbidden to wear pointed shoes or shoes with laces, "for it is manifest . . . that these abominable things belong to pagans" (32–33/25). "And they will at all times sleep dressed in shirt and breeches and shoes and belts, and where they sleep shall be lit until morning" (ibid.). Eating was equally regulated. Meat, for example, should be eaten only three times a week, and wine should be well mixed with water. Money was forbidden. "None may carry or keep money without permission." The punishment for being found with money was severe: "For if it happens that a brother dies, and money is found on him . . . it will be considered his and stolen. And these wicked brothers should not be buried with the other good brothers . . . but they should have him buried like a slave" (190–91/92–93).

---

29. Ibid., 168–69.

30. Ibid., 171. When it was found out that a nonaristocrat had been given the mantle of a Templar, it was taken away from him, and he was given in its place the brown mantle of a chaplain brother. Had the master who ordered his induction still been alive, his mantle would also have been taken away. Bernard of Clairvaux, "La Règle du Temple," 304–5/The Rule of the Templars, 151–52; references hereafter cited in the text and notes, with the Old French–language reference preceding that of the English source.

The Rule included a list of infractions and their punishments. For example, "The third [thing for which the brothers lose their habits is striking] a Christian man or woman with a sharp weapon . . . or anything which could kill or wound him. . . . It happened in Acre that Brother Hermant was commander of the livestock and two clerks took some *doreiz* doves that belonged to the dovecote of the house. And the commander told them to do it no more. [But when they did it again] the commander with the brothers beat them hard and wounded one on the head. And the clerks appealed to the legate, and the legate informed the Master . . . [who] made them plead for mercy in chapter, and their habits were taken from them, and they were put in irons and sent to Cyprus, because the blow was very serious" (307/153). Or again, "The eighth [thing for which a brother is expelled from the house] is if a brother does anything against nature and against the law of Our Lord. . . . At Château Pèlerin there were brothers who practiced wicked sin and caressed each other in their chambers at night. . . . And the Master took the advice that this thing should not come to chapter, because the deed was so offensive. . . . One of the brothers, who was named Brother Lucas, escaped by night and went to the Saracens. . . . [A second] thought to escape, but he died, and the other remained in prison for a long time" (297–98/148).

The Rule attempted not only to impose ascetic practice but also to ensure that asceticism was not carried to an extreme. It limited overindulgence in ascetic practice through admonitions like that directed to "Brothers who stand too long in chapel" (26/23). Directives for moderation in self-mortification are also included. "Because of the shortage of bowls, the brothers will eat in pairs, so that one may study the other more closely, and so that neither austerity nor secret abstinence is introduced into the common meal" (35/26). Reference to the immoderate asceticism of the Templars is even found in popular literature. In his collection of anecdotes, or *exempla,* for sermons, Stephanus de Borbone teaches that asceticism that hinders useful labor is false pride by citing the story of a Templar (Master Bread and Water) who fasts so assiduously that he lacks the strength to stay on his horse during a battle with the Saracens.[31]

The discipline of the Templars' social life transferred directly to their military actions. According to the Rule, the brothers mount and ride only on command; the line of march is orderly and silent; ranks may not be broken without permission; an unfurled banner is carried into battle along with the furled one, so that if the marshal bearing the banner is struck down, the second might be used to rally the troops. "If it happens that the Christians are defeated, from which God save them, no brother should leave the field to return to the garrison while there is a piebald banner [the Bauceant, the black and white banner of the Templars] raised aloft, for if he leaves he will be expelled from the house forever" (125/59–60). Even those hostile to the order recognized that along with their fraternal and sometimes rival monastic-military organization, the Hospitallers, the Templars provided the crusader states with their strongest and most

31. Stephanus de Borbone, *Anecdotes historiques, legends et apologues,* 163–64.

dependable military presence.[32] Acknowledged as the best-disciplined forces in the Christian army, knights of the two orders were often assigned to take the two flanks of the battle line or to form the first line of attack.

In this land there are two religious houses, to wit, the Temple and the Hospital. They have an exceeding great abundance of riches, for they have property in and draw revenues from every part of Europe. When they go to the wars, the Templars fight on the right wing and the Hospitalers on the left. The Templars are most excellent soldiers. They wear white mantles with a red cross, and when they go to wars a standard of two colors called balzaus [Bauceant] is borne before them. They go in silence. Their first attack is the most terrible. In going they are the first, in returning the last. . . . Should any one of them for any reason turn his back to the enemy, or come forth alive [from a defeat], or bear arms against the Christians, he is severely punished: the white mantle with the red cross, which is the sign of his knighthood, is taken away with ignominy, he is cast out from the society of the brethren, and eats his food on the floor without a napkin for the space of one year. If the dogs molest him, he does not dare to drive them away.[33]

A Templar's courage was literally proverbial. In Jacques de Vitry's collection of sermon-stories, a Templar exemplifies the rewards of extraordinary faith. Surrounded on all sides by Saracens, a Templar spurs his horse over a precipice rather than surrender to the infidels the alms that he is carrying. God saves both horse and man.[34]

The Rule repressed the arrogance of individuals within the community: "If any brother out of a feeling of pride . . . wishes to have as his due a better or finer habit, let him be given the worst" (30/24). However, the Rule itself confirms its institutional arrogance by revealing the Templars' concern with external appearances. "For it happened in Antioch that a brother who was named Brother Paris, and two other brothers who were in his company, killed some Christian merchants. . . . And they were sentenced to be expelled from the house and flogged throughout Antioch, Tripoli, Tyre and Acre. Thus they were flogged and cried, 'See here the justice which the house exacts from its wicked men,' and they were put in perpetual imprisonment at Château Pèlegrin, and died there" (289–90/144). Or again, "Those wicked brothers who left the house and took their habits, and wore them among the taverns and prostitutes in wicked places . . . brought to the house great shame, dishonor and scandal: and for this reason the convent . . . established that mantles are worth more than shoes" (291–92/145). Arrogance, along with military discipline and wealth, became synonymous with the order. The English chronicler Matthew Paris describes a meeting between King Richard the Lion Heart (r. 1189–99) and Fulk, a

32. The Hospitallers, though founded earlier than the Templars, were only militarized later, on the model of the Templars. See Riley-Smith, *Hospitallers*.

33. Anonymous Pilgrim V, 29–30.

34. Jacques de Vitry, *Exempla*, 41.

formidable French preacher and prophet. Fulk accuses Richard of having three wicked daughters, which he must marry off as soon as possible or else meet disaster. King Richard replies:

"Thou hypocrite, thou hast lied, because I have no daughter at all." To which Fulk replied, "Certainly I do not lie, because, as I have said, you have three most infamous daughters, one of which is pride, the second covetousness, and the third luxury." Accordingly, the king having summoned the counts, and many others who were at hand to appear before him, said to them, "Hear all of you the prompting of this hypocrite, who says that I have three very wicked daughters, namely, pride, covetousness, and luxury, and he has enjoined me to give them in marriage; I therefore give my pride to the pride of the Templars, my covetousness to the monks of the Cistercian order, and my luxury to the prelates of the church."[35]

But perhaps the most persuasive description of Templar arrogance is fictive. It is offered by the Templar Brian de Bois-Guilbert as an excuse to Rebecca for her impending rape in Sir Walter Scott's extraordinarily popular nineteenth-century novel, *Ivanhoe*:

I have separated myself from life and its ties. My manhood must know no domestic home, must be soothed by no affectionate wife. My age must know no kindly hearth. My grave must be solitary, and no offspring must outlive me, to bear the ancient name of Bois-Guilbert. At the feet of my Superior I have laid down the right of self-action, the privilege of independence. The Templar, a serf in all but the name, can possess neither lands nor goods, and lives, moves, and breathes, but at the will and pleasure of another. . . . The Templar loses . . . his social rights, his power of free agency, but he becomes a member and a limb of a mighty body, before which thrones already tremble, even as the single drop of rain which mixes with the sea becomes an individual part of that resistless ocean, which undermines rocks and engulfs royal armadas.[36]

PRIMITIVE ACCUMULATION

Disproportional wealth has elicited censure in most cultures, if not our own. After arrogance, the second, virtually universal complaint made by commentators about the Templars concerned the order's riches.[37] Indeed, the stridency of the protests against Templar wealth might be ascribed in part to the particularly problematic place of money in the High Middle Ages. During the twelfth and thirteenth centuries, money's increased presence, fluidity, and power were sources of anxiety. Suspicions focused particularly on money's dangerous tendency to self-generate—that is, anxiety concentrated on profit, which

35. Matthew Paris (Matthew of Westminster), *The Flowers of History*, 2:90–91.

36. Scott, *Ivanhoe*, 254–56.

37. Although the Templar's Rule itself offers support for allegations of pride, the text provides little *positive* reflection on the order's finances. Negative considerations of money are certainly in place in the text. Prominent in the rule are sanctions against personal wealth and its misuse. Indeed, simony—the selling of admission into the order—is listed first among its penances. Bernard of Clairvaux, 153/73.

was, in the Middle Ages, identified as usury. Usury then was any profit, not just unreasonable profit.[38] Thomas Aquinas, the great thirteenth-century theologian, provides some sense of the contemporary uneasiness about how money acts. Aquinas depends heavily on Aristotle, who wrote,

There are two sorts of wealth-getting, as I have said; one is a part of household management, the other is retail trade: the former necessary and honorable, while that which consists in exchange is justly censured; for it is unnatural, and a mode by which men gain from one another. The most hated sort, and with the greatest reason, is usury, which makes a gain out of money itself, and not from the natural object of it. For money was intended to be used in exchange, but not to increase at interest. And this term interest, which means the birth of money from money, is applied to the breeding of money because the offspring resembles the parent. Wherefore of all modes of getting wealth this is the most unnatural.[39]

Aquinas refines the ancient argument against usury by introducing new economic terms. Fungible things (*res fungibiles*) are goods which are interchangeable and commonly traded in quantity; they are exchanged as a class according to measure, like grain or oil. Consumable things (*res quae minuuntur vel consumuntur*) are things diminished or eliminated in their appropriate use, like a bottle of fine wine.[40] Aquinas identifies money as a consumable thing:

To take usury for money lent is unjust in itself, because this is to sell what does not exist, and this evidently leads to inequality which is contrary to justice. In order to make this evident, we must observe that there are certain things the use of which consists in their consumption: thus we consume wine when we use it for drink and we consume wheat when we use it for food. Wherefore in such like things the use of the thing must not be reckoned apart from the thing itself, and whoever is granted the use of the thing, is granted the thing itself and for this reason, to lend things of this kind is to transfer the ownership. Accordingly if a man wanted to sell wine separately from the use of the wine, he would be selling the same thing twice, or he would be selling what does not exist, wherefore he would evidently commit a sin of injustice. On like manner he commits an injustice who lends wine or wheat, and asks for double payment, viz. one, the return of the thing in equal measure, the other, the price of the use, which is called usury.

On the other hand, there are things the use of which does not consist in their consumption: thus to use a house is to dwell in it, not to destroy it. Wherefore in such things both may be granted: for instance, one man may hand over to another the

38. There is a vast literature on the subject of usury and the historical development of its understanding. For a sampling, see Kaye, *Economy and Nature in the Fourteenth Century;* Langholm, *Economics in the Medieval Schools;* LeGoff, *Your Money or Your Life;* Little, *Religious Poverty and the Profit Economy in Medieval Europe;* J. Noonan, *The Scholastic Analysis of Usury;* Polanyi, "Aristotle Discovers the Economy."

39. Aristotle, *Politics,* 1141.

40. Kelly, *Aquinas and Modern Practices of Interest Taking,* 25–26.

ownership of his house while reserving to himself the use of it for a time, or vice versa, he may grant the use of the house, while retaining the ownership. For this reason a man may lawfully make a charge for the use of his house, and, besides this, revendicate the house from the person to whom he has granted its use, as happens in renting and letting a house.

Now money, according to the Philosopher [Aristotle] was invented chiefly for the purpose of exchange: and consequently the proper and principal use of money is its consumption or alienation whereby it is sunk in exchange. Hence it is by its very nature unlawful to take payment for the use of money lent, which payment is known as usury: and just as a man is bound to restore other stolen goods, so is he bound to restore the money which he has taken in usury.[41]

Money is licit though suspect; it is a man-made thing that functions lawfully so long as it is consumed in a fair exchange. Justice requires full reciprocity. Receiving more money than was lent, as happens when interest is charged, is unjust. More critically, having been made by man, not God, money is not a natural thing; as an unnatural thing, money should not reproduce. If money begets money, as happens when interest is charged, it is a deviant act. Money's offspring, profit, is born unnaturally; like the issue of sodomy or bestiality, it is illegitimate and unlawful. The accomplice in money's self-generation is like a pimp or procurer. In the medieval West, doing that which was unjust, particularly if it also was unnatural, was a sin. Lending money on interest was an affront to God.

The horror of profit was not limited to theologians.[42] Stephanus de Bourbone devotes a section of his book of examples for preachers to the divine punishment of usurers. As an art historian, my favorite story in the collection gives the artwork an active role in retribution:

It happened in Dijon, toward the year of Our Lord 1240, that a certain usurer wanted to celebrate his wedding with great pomp. As he was led to the accompaniment of musical instruments to the parish church of the Blessed Virgin and stood beneath the church porch so that his fiancée could state her words of consent, and so that the marriage would be ratified, as was customary, by the "words of present," and thus the marriage could be crowned by the celebration of the Mass and by other rituals inside the church—as these things were being carried out there [under the portico] and the bride and groom were supposed to be introduced into the church with joyous celebration, a stone statue of a usurer (which had been fashioned on top of the portico with a sculpture of a devil bearing him to hell) fell, money pouch and all, upon the head of the living usurer, who was about to be wed, and crushed and killed him. The wedding

41. Thomas Aquinas, Second Part of the Second Part, Question 78, Article 1, in Thomas Aquinas, *Summa Theologica*.

42. For a thorough analysis of scholastic understanding of the economy, see Langholm, *Economics in the Medieval Schools*.

was changed into mourning, joy into sorrow. The stone usurer excluded the living usurer from the church and from the sacraments, although the local priests, instead of excluding him from the church [as they should have], had been on the contrary willing to admit him. The other usurers of the city gave money to have the other sculptures on the outer front side of the porch destroyed, so that similar events, by some accident like this, would not occur. I myself have seen these destroyed statues.[43]

Such an anecdote shows, of course, that the practice of usury was commonplace. It also vividly demonstrates the high level of social anxiety caused by the practice.

The Roman Catholic Church embedded Thomas Aquinas's arguments against usury in canon law. As late as 1917, the Pio-Benedictine Code of Canon Law still reveals anxieties about profit, though the church's fears had been allayed by several centuries of familiarity:

Canon 1543: If a fungible thing is given to another so that it becomes his, and later it must be restored in the same sort, no profit can be made by reason of the contract; but in the loan of a fungible thing, it is not by itself illicit to reap a legal profit, unless it can be shown to be immoderate of itself, and even greater profit [can be made] if there is a just and proportionate title so supporting.[44]

The residual Catholic concern over profit is also explicitly articulated by Aquinas's twentieth-century apologists:[45]

Note on the fertility of money. The Rev. Januarius Bucceroni, S. J. . . . puts this objection to himself: Considering the present increase in commerce, continuous and ever progressing in modern society, precisely on account of money and the incredible facility in its transmittance and change, money can really no longer be called today barren and unfruitful, but fertile and particularly fruitful. He answers: It is as true that modern commerce does not make money fruitful as it is true that modern commerce rests rather on credit, as it is called, than on material money (coin); and credit comes from one's own industry, genius, labor, confidence with public merchants, and especially honesty of life. Besides it is particularly noticeable in these days that poor workmen, laborious and industrious, gather great wealth in a short time; the nobility on the other hand, who are very rich, through want of work and due industry, are reduced to extreme poverty. Therefore it is not money which is fruitful, but one's own labor and industry.[46]

---

43. Stephanus de Borbone, *Anecdotes historiques, legends et apologues*, 421. I want to thank Bart Huelsenbeck for the corrections he made to my translation of this text.

44. Roman Catholic Church, *The 1917 or Pio-Benedictine Code of Canon Law*, 516. Concerns over profit predictably disappear in the 1983 code.

45. For example, Kelly, *Aquinas and Modern Practices of Interest Taking*.

46. *Theologia Moralis*, 1908, 1.511–12; reprinted in Thomas Aquinas, *Commerce*, 21–22.

In all of these medieval discussions—even those written in modernity—money is a hazardous thing; but like the dinosaurs of *Jurassic Park,* it becomes lethal when it is allowed to reproduce by itself. The ever-increasing fecundity of money threatened the established social and moral order. It transferred wealth increasingly to the emergent entrepreneurial classes. It also undermined the traditional ethics of individual interaction by its abstraction of human relations. An individual's moral responsibility was no longer to his partner in exchange but rather to a depersonalized market.[47] Individual ethical behavior, on which medieval thinking concentrated, is entirely absent in modern "rational choice" theory.

The Templars participated fully in the monetization of Europe. Evidence of the order's finances is found in its cartularies, or property registers; in papal bulls; and in anecdotal accounts in historical writings. William of Tyre, in the passage quoted earlier, observes that the Templars "are said to have vast possessions, both on this side of the sea and beyond. . . . Their property is reported to be equal to the riches of kings." William neglects to cite his sources, but admits their hearsay character. By the twentieth century, the Templars' wealth and their function as bankers were commonly presented as facts.[48]

In addition to vast European possessions, they became one of the great bankers of the period. With houses all over Europe, inspiring confidence because of their religious standing and the permanent presence of armed guardians, the Templars were quick to enter the field of high finance. Deposits, transfers, the movement and exchange of money, issuance of credit instruments and, finally, money lending, must all have included, dissimulated and decried usury. By the thirteenth century the Templars were familiar figures among the fiscal advisers of Western royalty, as they had long been in the financial councils of the papacy. Their economic activities embraced the whole of Western Europe and the Levant.[49]

So writes Joshua Prawer, one of the great modern historians of the Crusades. His lack of footnotes here suggests just how familiar is the representation of the Templars as bankers. Indeed, the bulk of a very bulky popular literature on the Templars assumes them to be adept entrepreneurs with a vast investment portfolio. In a recent popular historical work, for example, Alan Butler and Stephen Dafoe argue that the Templars, being good bankers, established themselves clandestinely in Switzerland, where they originated both Protestantism and capitalism.[50] William of Tyre's attribution of great wealth, Prawer's accusation

47. For perhaps the clearest statement of this shift, see the quote from Weber in the conclusion of the present work. Weber, *Economy and Society,* 636–37.

48. Naming the Templars bankers is misleading even etymologically. *Bank* comes from *banco*—the bench at which money changers sat. See de Roover, "New Interpretations of the History of Banking," 200. There is little evidence that the Templars functioned as money changers except that they transferred money in different currencies.

49. Prawer, *The Latin Kingdom of Jerusalem,* 263.

50. Alan Butler and Dafoe, *The Warriors and the Bankers.*

of usury, and Butler and Dafoe's assumption that the Templars invented the modern market may be exaggerated. They are also suggestive.

The Crusades, begun in response to Urban II's sermon in Clermont of November 1096, required the mobilization of money as well as men. Raising and maintaining armies is always expensive; the costs involved in moving armies over great distances are exorbitant. The Crusades stimulated the production of money, increased its fluidity, and contributed to the slow erosion of the suspicion that money occasioned. The Templars were both the product and producers of militant Christianity. The order was instituted in response to the Western need for fighting men loosed from feudal obligations at home and committed to the occupation of Palestine. By attracting both wealth and warriors, the Templars contributed significantly to the human and material resources available for war in the East. Their construction of massive fortifications and their maintenance of a large number of outposts in Syria and Palestine required continuous fund-raising. The scale of their financial needs necessitated the constant collection of money in the West and its transport to the East. Under the pressure of necessity, the Templars, along with Italian merchants, refined the means by which resources were relocated.

It is tempting to claim that what war bonds were to World War II, the Templars were to the Crusades.[51] Giving alms to the Templars was a means of supporting the war effort without participating in it. Contributors received papal indulgences for their contributions—that is, they invested for the future, though their treasures accrued value for them in heaven rather than on earth.[52] In addition to money, gold, and jewelry, benefactors endowed the Templars with land. By the end of the thirteenth century, the order held a vast number of estates in France, England, Spain, Germany, and Italy, as well as in the eastern Mediterranean. To support their military operations, the Templars liquefied land wealth through rents. A survey of Templar land holdings in England, carried out between 1185 and 1195, indicates the remarkable number and extent of their properties relatively early in the order's history. The survey also reveals the Templars' central concern with fixed money rents.[53] The Templars seem to be participants in an early stage of alienating labor from the land: free labor generating money is substituted for serfs producing foodstuffs.

Templar economic practices also participated in the modification of the urban landscape. Medieval cities tended to be ordered according to social allegiances—guilds, religious affiliations, political and state alliances—rather than by rent price.[54] The treatment of urban space as a source of income presages modernity. Templar holdings in urban areas were typically let for a monetary rent; tenants were entirely free from labor obligations. In London, Templar properties were

---

51. For the war psychology of bonds, see Samuel, *Pledging Allegiance*.

52. Indulgences are offered in the *Milites Templi* bull of 1144. Roman Catholic Church, *Cartulaire général de l'Ordre du Temple, 1119?–1150*, 381.

53. Lees, *Records of the Templars in England in the Twelfth Century*; see particularly xv–xxvii, lxii. Also see Lord, *The Knights Templar in Britain*.

54. Vance, "Land Assignment in the Precapitalist, Capitalist, and Postcapitalist City."

rented by the well-to-do. Even churches generated income: a priest paid seventy shillings a year to the Templars for St. Clement Danes.[55] In Paris, rents in the Templar domain, the *villeneuve,* nearly doubled in the second quarter of the thirteenth century.[56] Rent increases may reflect the relatively efficient administration by the order as well as inflation. The royal sections of Paris did not fare so well. According to Jean de Joinville in his *History of St. Louis*: "By the great perjuries and great robberies that were made within the jurisdiction of the provost, the lesser folk dared not stay on the King's land, but went to dwell in other jurisdictions and other lordships."[57] Association with the Templars was sought not only because of their administrative efficiency but also, no doubt, because the order benefited from remarkable fiscal rights.[58] Papal bulls not only provided ecclesiastical protection to the order but also presented it with both tax (tithe) exemptions and rights to collect alms in interdicted churches.[59] Like multinational corporations now, the Templars had the advantage of being locally unregulated.[60]

The wealth that accrued to the Templars through alms and rents was certainly great. The wealth ascribed to them by their contemporaries and by our own commentators is even greater. Assumptions of vast Templar wealth may arise from a confusion between their own monies and those treasures of others held in trust by the order. Templar houses were important depositories. It was recognized that the Templars offered security. Their commanderies were well defended. Traditional taboos against violating sacred space protected them—monasteries had functioned as depositories since the early Middle Ages. In the case of the Templars, spiritual power was supplemented by a reputation for martial force. The great Temples of London and Paris served as royal treasuries—Paris for the kings of France from at least the reign of Philip Augustus, and London for the kings of England from the time of Stephen.[61] The Temple was the medieval equivalent of Fort Knox. There is, however, no evidence that the Templars put the wealth that they held in trust to work. Their treasuries certainly contained an accumulation of wealth, but that wealth apparently remained inert.

The Templars appear often in Jean de Joinville's retelling of his crusade in the company of Saint Louis (1248–50). The king and many in his retinue were taken prisoner in Egypt. One passage describes how Joinville managed to get money from the Templars to make up an unexpected shortfall of fifteen thousand crowns in the king's ransom:

Said I to the King that it were well that he should send to fetch the Commander and the Marshal of the Templars (for the Master was dead) and that he should make

---

55. Lees, *Records of the Templars in England in the Twelfth Century,* xcii–xciii.

56. Etienne, "Étude topographique sur les possessions de la maison du Temple à Paris," 88.

57. Joinville, *The History of St. Louis,* 217 [bk. 2.141].

58. Curzon, *La maison du temple de Paris, histoire et description,* 283–84.

59. See particularly the bulls *Omne datum optimum* (1139), *Milites Templi* (1144), and *Militia dei* (1145). Roman Catholic Church, *Cartulaire général de l'Ordre du Temple, 1119?–1150,* 375–79, 381, and 382.

60. Piquet, *Des banquiers au moyen âge,* 4–5.

61. Forey, *The Military Orders,* 115–16.

request to them that they should lend him the fifteen thousand crowns. . . . The King sent for them, and the King told me what I was to say to them. When I had said it, Brother Stephen of Otricourt, who was the Commander of the Temple, said to me: "Lord of Joinville, this counsel that you give the King is neither good nor reasonable; for you know that we receive what is entrusted to us in such wise that by our oath we may not hand it over but to them who entrusted it to us." There was then hard words and anger between him and me. And then spoke Brother Reynold of Vichiers, who was Marshal of the Temple, saying: "Sire, let be the dispute betwixt the Lord of Joinville and our Commander; for, even as our Commander says, we can hand over nothing but by breaking our oath. And as for what the Seneschal counsels you, that, if we will not lend, you should take, he says nothing that is strange, and you shall do what you will therein; and if you take of our goods, we have fully enough of yours in Acre wherefrom you may make restitution to us. I told the King that I would go, and he would; and he bade me go. I went into one of the galleys of the Temple, into the master galley, and when I would go down into the hold of the galley, there where the treasure was, I asked the Commander of the Temple to come to see what I took; and he never deigned to come. The Marshal said that he would come to see the violence I did him. So soon as I had got down there where the treasure was, I asked the Treasurer of the Temple, who was there if he would hand over to me the keys of a chest which was before me; and he, that saw me thin and fleshless from my sickness and in the habit that I had worn in prison, said that he would not give them to me. And I saw a hatchet lying there, so I picked it up and said that I would make it the King's key. When the Marshal saw this, he took me by the hand and said, "Sir, we see well that you would do us violence, and we will hand over the keys." And when the Marshal told the Treasurer who I was, he was much abashed.[62]

Even for a king's ransom, when an equal amount of the king's wealth was held nearby, the treasure of another depositor is appropriated only under "duress." Personal treasure left in the London Temple was locked with two keys—one held by the depositor and one by the Templars.[63] Another, less familiar episode recounted by Joinville also suggests the Templars' fiscal and fiduciary conservatism:

I told the King that my lord Peter of Courtenay owed me two hundred crowns of my pay, which he would not pay me. And the King answered that he would have me paid out of the money that he owed the Lord Courtenay; and thus he did. By the counsel of my lord Peter of Bourbonne, we took twenty crowns for our expenses and the remainder we entrusted for keeping to the Commander of the Palace of the Templars. When the time came that I had spent the twenty crowns, I sent the father of John Caym of Sainte Menehould, whom I had as retainer overseas, to fetch another twenty crowns. The commander answered him that he had not a penny of mine and knew me not. I went to Brother

62. Joinville, *The History of St. Louis*, 113–14 [bk. 1.75].

63. For other forced usurpations of Templar deposits and for the comment on keys, see Piquet, *Des banquiers au moyen âge*, 30–31.

Reynold of Nichiers, that was Master of the Temple . . . and made the accusation to him against the Commander of the Palace, who would not give me back my money. . . . When he heard this, he was sore dismayed and said to me, "Lord of Joinville, I love you well; but be you sure that if you will not abstain from this claim, I will love you no more; for you would have men understand that our brethren are thieves!" And I told him that God willing I would not abstain. In this disquiet of heart was I for four days, like a man who hath no more money at all to spend. After these four days the Master came to me laughing, and told me that he had found my money again. The manner in which it was found was this, that he had changed the Commander of the Palace and had sent him to a village that is called as-Safiriyya; and this man gave me back my monies.[64]

Deposits were apparently tied not only to those individuals who made them but also to those who received them. It appears that depositing money with the Templars was like putting it under the mattress (albeit a very secure mattress)—it did not reproduce itself there. Money is congealed in both episodes.

Such anecdotes challenge claims that the Templars lent their deposits on interest.[65] They certainly lent money. Perhaps most famously, they lent King Baldwin of Constantinople large sums on the security of a relic of the True Cross.[66] But in contrast with the Italian merchant houses, most of the Templars' loans tended to be small.[67] And, more important, it seems likely that the money they lent was their own, collected from rents and alms, not that of their depositors. Further, how they benefited from those loans is undocumented. If there was interest, it was well masked. Most significantly, in contrast with the Italian bankers and the Jews, the Templars were not accused of usury so much by contemporaries as by modern historians.[68]

Other banking activities have been quite reasonably attributed to the Templars. They acted as the trustworthy financial agents of untrustworthy kings, particularly those of England and France.[69] In 1214, John, the unreliable king of

64. Joinville, *The History of St. Louis,* 123 [bk. 2.80].

65. "Perhaps the Templars went into banking, in Jerusalem, not precisely because they had cash to spare and wondered what to do with it, but rather because they saw the opportunity of securing a much higher return on their capital in that way, and thus of increasing their wealth." Metcalf, "The Templars as Bankers and Monetary Transfers between West and East in the Twelfth Century," 12. Léopold Delisle, whose collection of documents is indispensable to the study of Templar finances, also appears to slip from deposits to usurious investments. Delisle, *Mémoire sur les opérations financières des Templiers,* 15–16.

66. Piquet, *Des banquiers au moyen âge,* 54.

67. Ibid., 92.

68. In Phillip the Fair's Articles of Accusation of August 12, 1308 (*Procès,* 1, 89–96), economic matters are only briefly mentioned: "Item, that charitable gifts in the said Order were not made as they ought, nor was hospitality offered. Item, that they did not reckon [it] a sin in the said Order to acquire properties belonging to another by legal or illegal means. Item, that it was authorized by them that they should procure increase and profit to the said Order in whatever way they could by legal or illegal means. Item, that it was not reckoned a sin to commit perjury on this account." Cited in Barber, *The Trial of the Templars,* 250–51.

69. For the economic and political relations between the kings of France and the Templars, see Delisle, *Mémoire sur les opérations financières des Templiers,* 40–73. For the economic and political relations between the kings of England and the Templars, see Parker, *The Knights Templars in England,* 43–50.

England, deposited monies with the Templars for pensions (bribes) that were to be paid out over time to his equally unreliable French barons.[70] Indeed, during the entire course of the thirteenth century, kings and princes commonly treated the Temples of London and Paris as their exchequers. Henri de Curzon, a distinguished nineteenth-century historian, identified the Paris Temple as the royal treasury.[71] Besides acting as depositories and lenders, the order was given more complex fiscal responsibilities. Kings entrusted it, for example, with the transfer of funds and with funds consigned for later payment. Léopold Delisle argues that these Templar transactions are primitive forms of modern public contracts and contracts of private interest.[72] The Templars also seem to have functioned as estate executors for the elite. Delisle provides a list of the aristocrats for whom they administered properties.[73] More radically, the Templars apparently transferred credit without the transfer of specie. The invention of bank checks is even attributed to them: "One might even be able to say that those mandates of which the Temple perfected the employment and technique constituted a primitive form of check. The evolution followed toward the creation of the *clause à ordre* with the facility of endorsement, born of the necessity of commerce."[74] In all of these actions there is no evidence that the Templars employed the money in their care to generate interest or profit for themselves. Whatever reward they received for their stewardship, it seems to have been external to the funds they administered.

Templar disdain for tainted treasure is evidenced in an apparently unbiased source, the chronicle of Michael the Syrian. The author describes a raid on the Syrian Orthodox monastery of Mor Barsawmo by the crusader leader Count Jocelyn II. The Latin priests immediately began robbing the church, and the soldiers were ordered "to inspect the cells and to collect everything to be found in gold, and silver, and brass, and iron, and garments, and carpets. . . . [But when the Templars who were part of the count's Latin forces realized what was taking place, they said to Jocelyn]: 'We come with you for the battle with the Turks, and for the relief of Christians—not for the plundering of churches and monasteries!' And as they went away from him, they would not even eat bread nor drink water."[75] It seems that money was not the object of Templar desire; for the Templars, as for medieval theologians, money was tolerable only if it was employed for a just cause.

On August 14, 1291, the Templars evacuated Château Pèlerin—the last crusader stronghold in the Holy Land—and escaped to Cyprus.[76] In 1307 the Grand Master of the order, Jacques de Molay, returned to Europe to plan a new Crusade

70. Delisle, *Mémoire sur les opérations financières des Templiers,* 10.

71. Curzon, *La maison du temple de Paris, histoire et description,* 246–58.

72. Delisle, *Mémoire sur les opérations financières des Templiers,* 14.

73. Ibid., 32–40; also see Piquet, *Des banquiers au moyen âge,* 36–46.

74. Piquet, *Des banquiers au moyen âge,* 50–51. My rough translation.

75. Michael the Syrian, *World Chronicle,* quoted by Weltecke, "Contacts between Syriac Orthodox and Latin Military Orders," 66. I am grateful to Professor Lucas Van Rompay for this reference.

76. Prawer, *The Latin Kingdom of Jerusalem,* 33.

and perhaps to oppose King Phillip the Fair's attempts to merge the Templars and Hospitallers and then to assume headship of the new order.[77] At dawn on Friday, October 13, 1307, Phillip's agents broke into Templar houses throughout France with warrants for the arrest of all Templars.[78] The king charged them with heinous heresies:

Phillip, by the grace of God, king of the French, to our highly esteemed and faithful lord of Onival, Sir John of Tourville, and the bailiffs of Rouen, greeting and love. A bitter thing, a wretched thing, a thing which is horrible to know, terrible to hear, a detestable crime, an execrable impiety, an abominable act, a detestable disgrace, a thing thoroughly inhuman, indeed alien to all humankind, a little while ago sounded in our ears, related by many of good faith, and not without being seized by astonishment and shouting in horror. . . . Now the report is conveyed to us by numerous men of good faith that the brothers of the order of the Knights Templar are wolves wearing the appearance of lambs and behind the religious habit dreadfully insult our religious faith, our Lord Jesus Christ . . . when, at their entrance into the order, that is when they make their profession, one presents them His image and then, indeed it is miserable to say, thrice they renounce [Him] then with horrible crudity thrice spit in His face. And after that, stripped of the clothes worn in their secular life, naked they are taken to the witness who received their profession or alternatively to his substitute, and they are kissed by him first on the lower part of the spine, second on the navel, and finally on the mouth, in a scandal to human dignity.[79]

They were also accused of worshipping an idol—a bearded, wooden head.[80]

Templar knights taken into custody outside the jurisdiction of Phillip the Fair's prosecutors denied the charges of heresy brought against them. Most of those directly subject to the king's interrogation admitted their guilt only after torture or under its threat. Nearly forty Templars died during torture; many others were maimed for life. When those who confessed under duress recanted, they were burned. Fifty-four brothers were burned at the stake in 1310; Jacques de Molay, the last Master of the Templars, was burned with three other brothers in 1314, after attempting publicly to defend the order.[81] The evidence brought against the Templars was patently fabricated; the proceedings were illegal.[82] In

77. For the extraordinary document from 1306 making this proposition, see Pierre Dubois, *De recuperatione Terre Sancte.*

78. For a thorough examination of the documents, see Barber, *The Trial of the Templars.* Also consult Burrows, "The Templars' Case for Their Defence in 1310." For a close analysis of a trial of the Templars outside France, see Gilmour-Bryson, *The Trial of the Templars in Cyprus.*

79. Lizerand, *Le dossier de l'affaire des Templiers,* 16–18.

80. Ibid., 24. Ian Wilson takes the king's accusations seriously, postulating that the image worshipped by the Templars was the Turin Shroud. Wilson, *The Turin Shroud.* Wilson's arguments have been compellingly refuted. See Barber, "The Templars and the Turin Shroud."

81. For a translation of Jacques de Molay's last words and a reference to the original source, see Nicholson, *The Knights Templar,* 223. For a recently translated account of the affair, see Templar of Tyre, *The Templar of Tyre,* 180–81.

82. Early in 1308, at the king's request, the masters of theology at the University of Paris commented on the proceedings taken against the Templars. They indicate that the king was legally required to

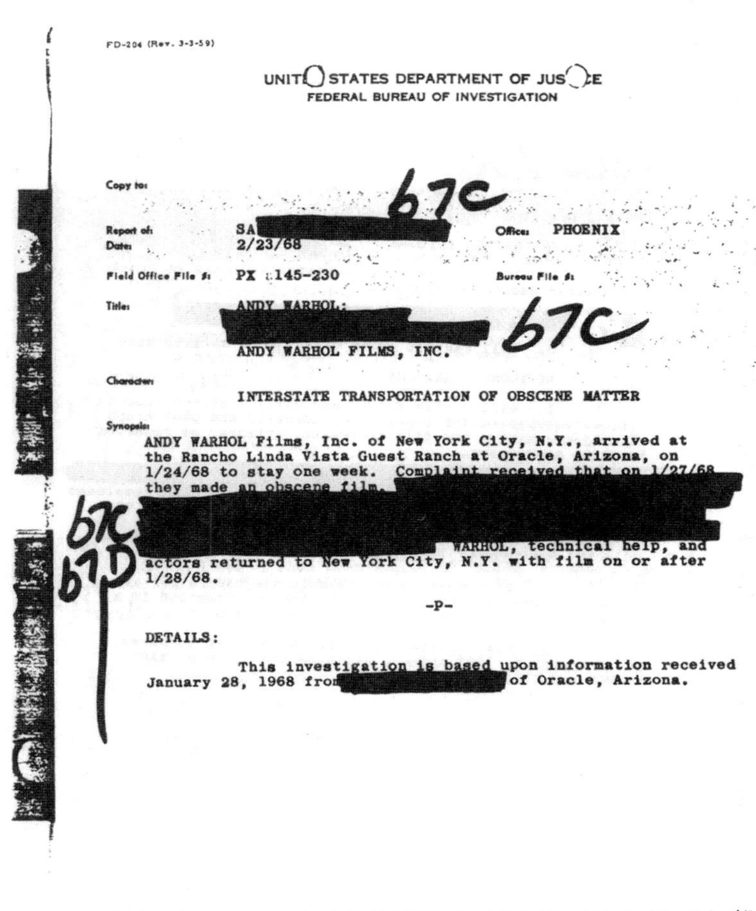

FD-204 (Rev. 3-3-59)

UNIT[illegible] STATES DEPARTMENT OF JUS[illegible]E
FEDERAL BUREAU OF INVESTIGATION

Copy to:

67C

Report of: SA [redacted] Office: PHOENIX
Date: 2/23/68

Field Office File #: PX 145-230 Bureau File #:

Title: ANDY WARHOL; [redacted] 67C
ANDY WARHOL FILMS, INC.

Character:
INTERSTATE TRANSPORTATION OF OBSCENE MATTER

Synopsis:
ANDY WARHOL Films, Inc. of New York City, N.Y., arrived at the Rancho Linda Vista Guest Ranch at Oracle, Arizona, on 1/24/68 to stay one week. Complaint received that on 1/27/68 they made an obscene film. [redacted] WARHOL, technical help, and actors returned to New York City, N.Y. with film on or after 1/28/68.

67C 67D

-P-

DETAILS:

This investigation is based upon information received January 28, 1968 from [redacted] of Oracle, Arizona.

This document contains neither recommendations nor conclusions of the FBI. It is the property of the FBI and is loaned to your agency; it and its contents are not to be distributed outside your agency.

Fig. 17. Margia Kramer, *Andy Warhol et al: The FBI File on Andy*. By permission of the artist. (Ref. in bibliography)

fourteenth-century France, as in twenty-first-century Iraq, torture reveals only what the torturers seek.

The Templars were cruelly undone by the king's greed. To meet his need for money, Phillip identified three communities to plunder: Jews, "Lombards" (Italian merchants and moneylenders), and Templars. All three groups were recognized as wealthy outsiders for whom there would be limited local sympathy. The Jews and Lombards were represented as usurious aliens.[83] They were harassed and finally, in 1306 and 1311, respectively, they were arrested and expelled, their properties confiscated. The Templars, the third body to be savaged by the king, were othered by their suspicious eastern associations and by

remand the heretics to the church for interrogation and sentencing—as a religious order, the Templars were exempt from secular jurisdiction. They also point out that the Templars' possessions could only be used for the defense of the faith. Lizerand, *Le dossier de l'affaire des Templiers,* 62–83. Also see Burrows, "The Templars' Case for Their Defence in 1310."

83. For the development of anti-Semitism and more generally the evolution of a persecuting society, see, respectively, Chazan, *Medieval Stereotypes and Modern Antisemitism;* R. Moore, *The Formation of a Persecuting Society.*

their true arrogance.[84] But it was their real and imagined wealth that precipitated their brutal evisceration.[85] The Templars did not, like certain present-day corporations, self-destruct through executive greed and poor management. The order was a victim of economic change.[86] Fiscal transformation inevitably involves violence. The brutal suppression of the Templars serves as a sign of their identification with money. The Templars were the victims of both the covetousness and the anxiety generated by the new profligacy of money's breeding.[87]

TEMPLE

The Poor Knights of Christ and of the Temple of Solomon were viciously erased. But erasure is not a simple act. Most obviously, the act establishes the eraser's authority to suppress. Its object is scraped away, rubbed out, removed. Nevertheless, as demonstrated by the illustrations from Margia Kramer's *Andy Warhol et al: The FBI File on Andy,* erasure leaves a mark (fig. 17). That mark may well frustrate the gesture and reverse its effect. The mark of erasure preserves an emptiness that was once full. It is an absence that demands restitution. It is a void that generates possible meanings. What is lost through erasure from the Warhol document is restored by its reader. Although whatever is imagined into the lacuna never has the same stability as the original, the mark of erasure records and confirms the persistence of that which was once present. Erasure may even be said to witness the initiating power of that which is now absent. Andy Warhol's social and political practices may have seemed dangerous to the FBI, but those dangers are exaggerated by the erasure that they elicited. In any case, in erasure two forces, however unequal, remain in play.[88] Human communities mark the landscape; when they are eliminated, their trace remains.

The Templars inscribed themselves and their interests in the topography of Europe as well as in the territories of the Latin kingdoms in the Middle East. The physical effects of their precincts perpetuate memories of their social and economic actions. Panoramas of Paris and London, the cities in which their greatest houses were located, reference the Templars' absence. In *The Hunchback of Notre Dame* (1831), Victor Hugo celebrates the urbanism of the nineteenth century in his reconstruction of 1482 Paris as a view from a tower of the city's great cathedral:

For the spectator who arrived, panting, upon that pinnacle, it was first a dazzling confusing view of roofs, chimneys, streets, bridges, places, spires, bell towers. Everything struck your eye at once: the carved gable, the pointed roof, the turrets suspended at

84. For a fuller discussion of the Templars' eastern associations, see Kluncker, "Die Templer."

85. Barber, *The Trial of the Templars,* 40–41.

86. Norman Cohn discusses the trial of the Templars in relation to the European fantasy of a satanic cult bent on the destruction of society. Cohn, *Europe's Inner Demons,* 75–98. He concentrates on King Phillip's charges of idolatry.

87. For the dissolution of the Templars in England and the redistribution of their wealth, see Perkins, "The Wealth of the Knights Templars in England."

88. For a fuller examination this notion of erasure, see Wharton, "Erasure."

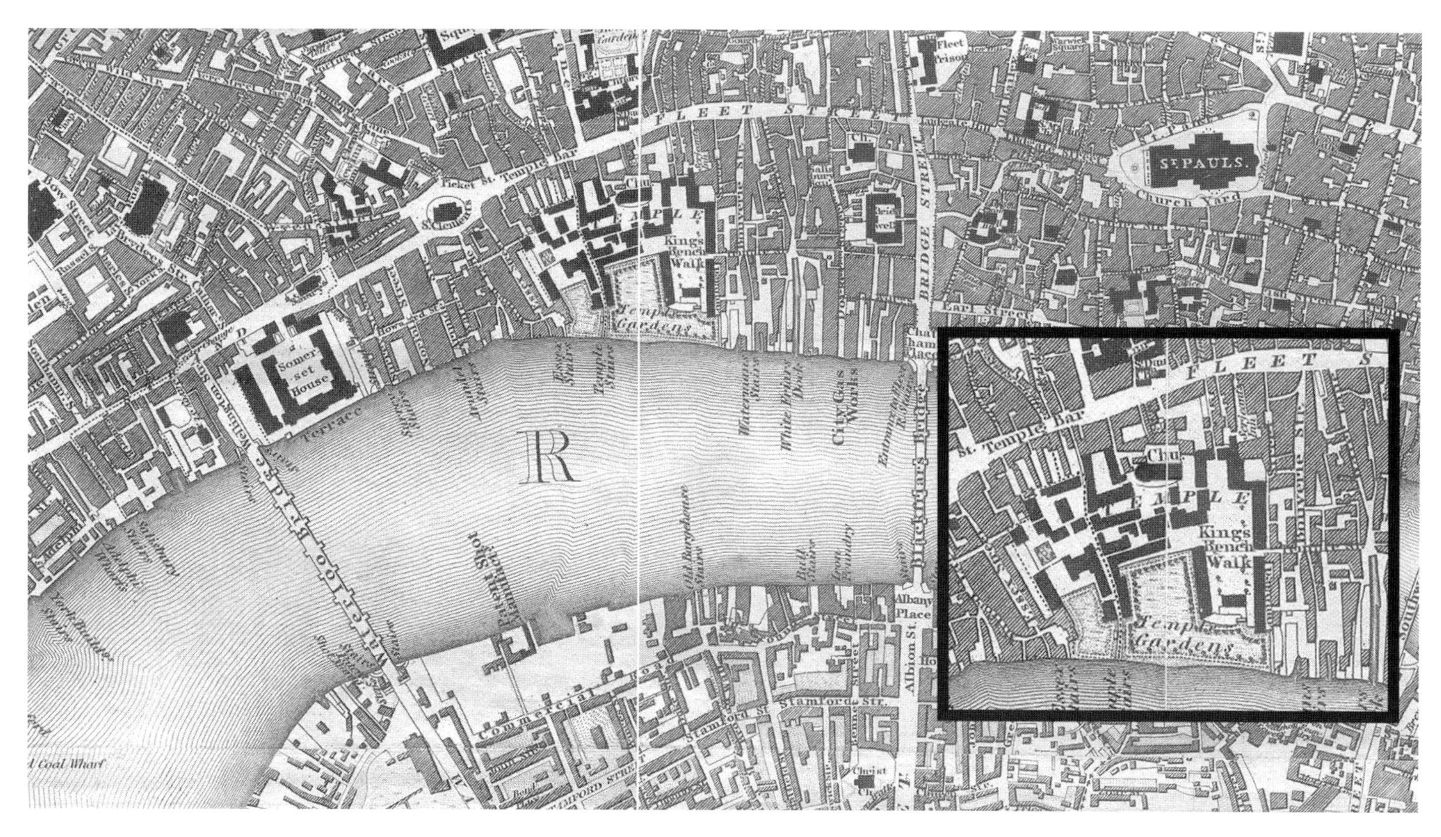

Fig. 18. Greenwood's map of London, section along the Thames from Somerset House (the Courtauld Institute) to St. Paul's Cathedral, with the Temple Precinct enlarged in an inset. From C. and J. Greenwood, *Map of London* (London: Greenwood, 1830). Modified by the author.

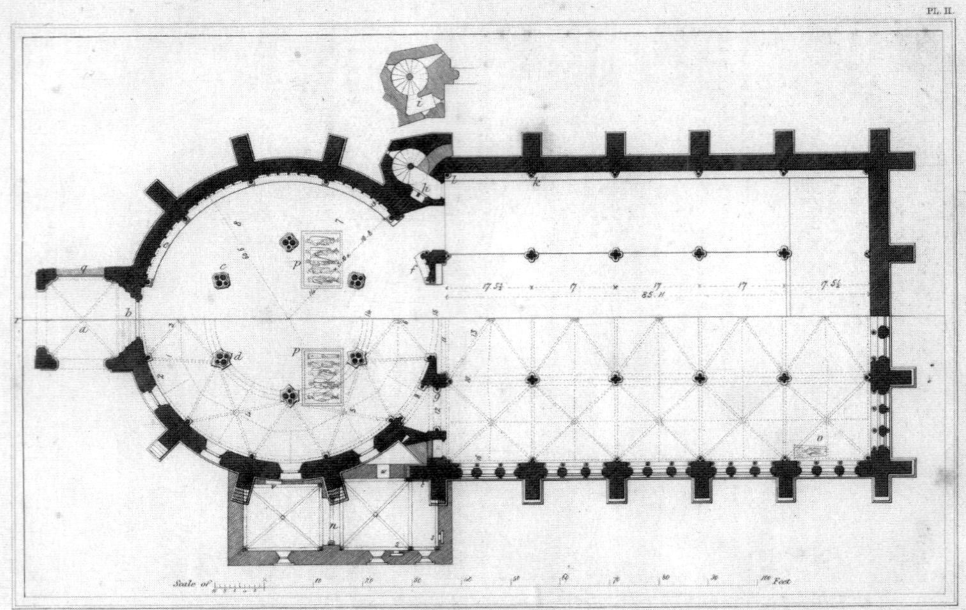

Drawn & Engraved by R. W. Billings.

TEMPLE CHURCH, LONDON.

GROUND PLAN, & PLAN OF WINDOWS, &c.

London, Published by T. & W. Boone 1838.

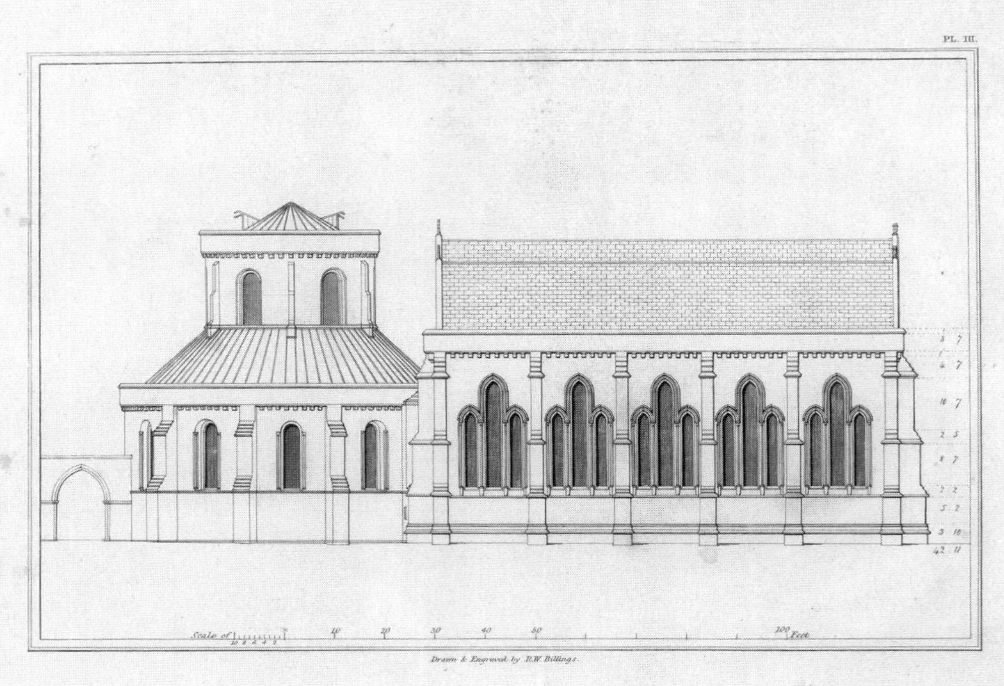

Drawn & Engraved by R.W. Billings.

TEMPLE CHURCH, LONDON.

SOUTH ELEVATION.

London, Published by T. & W. Boone, 1838.

Fig. 19. (*facing top*) Temple Church, London, plan. From Billings and Clarkson, *Architectural Illustrations and Account of the Temple Church, London*.

Fig. 20. (*facing bottom*) Temple Church, London, south elevation. From Billings and Clarkson, *Architectural Illustrations and Account of the Temple Church, London*.

Fig. 21. Temple Church, London, exterior of the Round from the south. Author photo.

the angles of the walls; the stone pyramids of the eleventh century, the slate obelisks of the fifteenth; the round, bare tower of the donjon keep; the square and fretted tower of the church; the great and the little, the massive and the aerial. The eye was, for a long time, wholly lost in this labyrinth, where there was nothing which did not possess its originality, its reason, its genius, its beauty—nothing which did not proceed from art; beginning with the smallest house, with its painted and carved front, with external beams, elliptical door, with projecting stories, to the royal Louvre.[89]

Gazing to the north from Notre Dame, the hunchback Quasimodo might see the Temple: "Between the old and the new Rue du Temple, there was the Temple, a sinister group of towers, lofty, erect, and isolated in the middle of a vast, battlemented enclosure."[90]

Hugo's nineteenth-century representation of the Temple enclosure in Paris was archaeological. The church had been destroyed during the French Revolution.[91]

89. Hugo, *The Hunchback of Notre-Dame*, 120–21.

90. Ibid., 130.

91. For the details of its demolition, see Curzon, *La maison du temple de Paris, histoire et description*, 74n1.

The great square tower with its round corner turrets, the principal landmark of the Paris Temple, was, in contrast, privileged by the revolutionaries: King Louis XVI and Marie Antoinette were imprisoned there before they were guillotined. Ironically, the tower that held the treasure for which one French king murdered the Templars enclosed the death cell of another. After the prison was suppressed in 1808, the tower became a popular pilgrimage site. Furniture, bits of clothing, and other debris were sold as souvenirs of its royal victims. It was shortly thereafter demolished.[92] At present, the ancient street names remain, a historical marker has replaced the church and fortified towers of the Templars' precinct, and a boutique hotel reminds the visitor of its martyred Master.[93]

The London Temple also left a literary residue. In the late sixteenth century, Edmund Spenser described his swans' progress down the Thames by what they passed on its banks:

. . . those bricky towers
The which on Thames' broad aged back do ride,
Where now the studious lawyers have their bowers,
There whilom wont the Templar Knights to bide,
Till they decay'd through pride.[94]

The precinct in London survived, and nearly three hundred years after the dissolution of the order, it was read by Spenser as Templar.

In the nineteenth century, the Templars' enclosure was still named the Temple and still haunted by its knights.

There are . . . worse places than the Temple, on a sultry day, for basking in the sun, or resting idly in the shade. There is yet a drowsiness in its courts, and a dreamy dullness in its trees and gardens; those who pace its lanes and squares may yet hear the echoes of their footsteps on the sounding stones, and read upon its gates, in passing from the tumult of the Strand or Fleet Street, "Who enters here leaves noise behind." There is still the plash of falling water in fair Fountain Court, and there are yet nooks and corners where dun-haunted students may look down from their dusty garrets, on a vagrant ray of sunlight patching the shade of the tall houses, and seldom troubled to reflect a passing stranger's form. There is yet, in the Temple, something of a clerkly monkish atmosphere, which public offices of law have not disturbed, and even legal firms have failed to scare away.[95]

Even now the visitor may experience the London Temple as Charles Dickens did. It is an enclave separated from the modern commercial confusion of the City by its walls and gates, the quiet of its grounds, the domestic scale of its

92. The tower was about fifty meters high. Ibid., 115–25.
93. Hotel Jacques de Molay, 94 rue des Archives, 75003 Paris.
94. Spenser, *Prothalamion*.
95. Dickens, *Barnaby Rudge*, 113–14.

buildings, the presence of a carefully tended nature, and its vague antiquity (fig. 18). It is a complex of gardens and lawns segueing with moderately sized stone or brick buildings. Apart from its inhabitants, nothing looks modern. The precinct retains its politically independent status (as an extraparochial liberty), thus maintaining its legal as well as atmospheric separateness; it is a self-governing, self-policing domain.[96] Like Dickens, the modern observer might even imagine that the Templars live on in the space that they created and occupied, particularly upon discovering the Temple Church concealed at the quarter's core. The structure reveals how the Templars reproduced Jerusalem in the West. It also suggests how that reproduction initially presented its knightly patrons and later perpetuated their authority.

The Temple Church is made up of two discrete parts (figs. 19, 20). To the west is a twelfth-century rotunda that has its own name, "the Round." In the mid-thirteenth century, a basilica was added to the east. Both halves of the building maintain their integrity and distinct character. The Gothic east end is a well-proportioned rectilinear structure. Triple-lancet windows open its walls and reduce their weight; buttresses provide an anatomical rhythm. The Round is more muscular. Its proportions are broad; its arched windows emphasize the substance of the walls by puncturing them; its buttresses add to its mass (fig. 21). The rotunda controls the attention of the observer more by its circularity than by its scale. Round buildings are not so common; round churches—in which the eucharistic liturgy fits rather badly—are relatively rare. The distinct figuration of the Round not only attracts notice, it also elicits its reading as special, indeed as symbolic. The name given to the church attached that symbolism specifically to Jerusalem. Though dedicated to Mary, like many Templar sanctuaries, this church has been identified from the Middle Ages to the present as the Temple.[97] The building's association with the Holy City was reinforced at its dedication by the officiant—Heraclius, the patriarch of Jerusalem. Once located over the south entrance, the dedicatory inscription was destroyed during restorations in 1695 after having been repeatedly defaced by righteous Protestants. A transcription was preserved, and a copy appears on the west wall of the church, around the entrance arch:

On the 10th of February in the year from the Incarnation of our Lord 1185, this Church was consecrated in honor of the Blessed Mary by the Lord Heraclius, by the grace of God Patriarch of the Church of the Holy Resurrection, who, to those visiting it annually, granted an indulgence of sixty days off the penance enjoined upon them.[98]

---

96. On the precinct and its exemption, see Honeybourne, "The Temple Precinct in the Days of the Knights Templar."

97. In the Middle Ages, it was sometimes referred to as the New Temple because it replaced the earlier, smaller Templar church in its first London enclosure at Holborn. That church was not demolished until 1595. Lewer and Dark, *The Temple Church in London*, 18–20.

98. J. Williamson, *The History of the Temple, London*, 11. The translation here is a slightly modified version of that which appears in note 2.

Fig. 22. Temple Church, London, interior view from the Round toward the altar in the east. Author photo.

The reference to Jerusalem is played out on the inside of the Temple Church. In the Round, six piers of dark Purbeck-marble clustered-columns separate the lower, vaulted ambulatory from the brighter, higher central space of the structure. Above, the core is ringed by a spacious triforium and covered by a wooden vault supported on the high drum of the clerestory. The central focus of the Round gives this section of the Temple Church a dramatic vertical axis. The thirteenth-century supplement takes the un-English form of a "hall church"—its aisles are the same height as the nave (fig. 22).[99] It adds a powerful horizontal axis to the building. Light fills both vessels and erodes their differences. Further, the two sections are laced together by the dark stone colonnettes and ribs that play against the interior's pale walls. Even the furniture is subordinate to the integration of the volumes. After World War II, collegiate-style pews—two sets of pews running parallel to the long walls of the aisles and facing one another across the nave—replaced the familiar transverse arrangement of pews facing the altar that dated from the mid-nineteenth century.[100] The space is open; it is uninterrupted by liturgical screens or religious images; there is only one altar, located at the east end. The appearance of the church is now responsibly Protestant.

The building's "style" is considered an eccentric confusion of Romanesque and Gothic, with pointed arches and rib vaults in the annular aisle combined with old-fashioned, round-headed windows. The Temple does not fit the established

99. Webb, *Architecture in Britain,* 96.

100. Dove, "The Temple Church and Its Restoration," 168. There is no way of establishing how the liturgical furnishings of the Temple were arranged in the Middle Ages.

Fig. 23. Church of the Holy Sepulchre, Jerusalem, section showing the inclusion of both pointed and round-headed arches. Drawing by Louis-Hugues Vincent. From Vincent and Abel, *Jérusalem: Recherches de topographie, d'archéologie et d'histoire*.

pattern of the evolution of medieval building; it is provincially unfashionable. The Temple Church is absent from canonical surveys of Gothic architecture.[101] One excuse for the church's neglect is its lack of historical integrity. The Temple was often remodeled and twice thoroughly rebuilt: it was restored with classicizing details after a major fire in 1678; Sir Christopher Wren added new paving and wainscoting in 1682–83; Robert Smirke refaced much of the structure in 1825–27; in 1840–46, Sidney Smirke and James Savage reconstructed the outer walls, introduced a new conical roof on the Round, replaced the Wren floor with medievalizing tiles, and removed Wren's altar, reredos, pulpit, and pews; finally, after the bombing of World War II, between 1948 and 1954, the Temple Church was rebuilt with careful attention to archaeological evidence.[102] But art historians have never been put off publishing French Gothic churches because of their multiple restorations. Rather, the Temple Church is probably ignored because of its stylistic dissonance, which is understood by traditional architectural his-

101. The ones that I checked include Bony, *The English Decorated Style;* Branner, *Gothic Architecture;* Frankl and Crossley, *Gothic Architecture;* Grodecki, Prache, and Recht, *Gothic Architecture*. Even in a survey book exclusively devoted to the medieval architecture of England, the Temple Church gets little notice: it is included in a list of churches using Purbeck marble, and there is a brief speculation concerning the source of the choir's elevation. See Webb, *Architecture in Britain,* 73, 96.

102. Godfrey, "Recent Discoveries at the Temple, London, and Notes on the Topography of the Site"; Lewer, "The Anniversary Address." Of the Gothic Revival restorations, W. J. Loftie commented, "The work carried out in 1845 at this place would alone justify a recent suggestion, namely, that in writing or speaking of modern, or mock, Gothic, as distinguished from the real thing, the term Vandal or Vandalic might be used." Loftie, *The Inns of Court and Chancery,* 5.

Fig. 24. Duke University Chapel, Durham, North Carolina, view down the nave toward the altar. Author photo.

torians as inconsistency and dismissed as incompetence.[103] In consequence, the building has been studied and published almost exclusively by antiquarians who loved it.[104]

Less traditional architectural historians, reading incoherence as heterogeneity, make style a social document.[105] The odd combination of round and pointed in the Temple Church might then be interpreted more imaginatively

103. Historians interested in sculpture have attended to the west portal. See P. Williamson, "The West Doorway of the Temple Church, London"; Zarnecki, "The West Doorway of the Temple Church in London."

104. For example, Baylis, *The Temple Church and Chapel of St. Ann;* Billings and Clarkson, *Architectural Illustrations and Account of the Temple Church, London;* Dove, "The Temple Church and Its Restoration," 164–72; J. Williamson, *The History of the Temple, London*. The latest of these quite wonderful works provides a thorough introduction to the church and its history as well as a complete bibliography. See Lewer and Dark, *The Temple Church in London*. Lewer writes in the preface: "During my chorister days at the Temple church before the war, I grew to love the building as well as the music and wanted to find out more about its history. Encouraged by the late Captain Alred Dewar, noted historian at the Admiralty, a member of the congregation and a supporter of the Temple Choir, it led me during my architectural training to think of writing a book about the church" (p. 8).

105. Trachtenberg, "Qu'est-ce que 'le gothique'?"; Trachtenberg, "Suger's Miracles, Branner's Bourges."

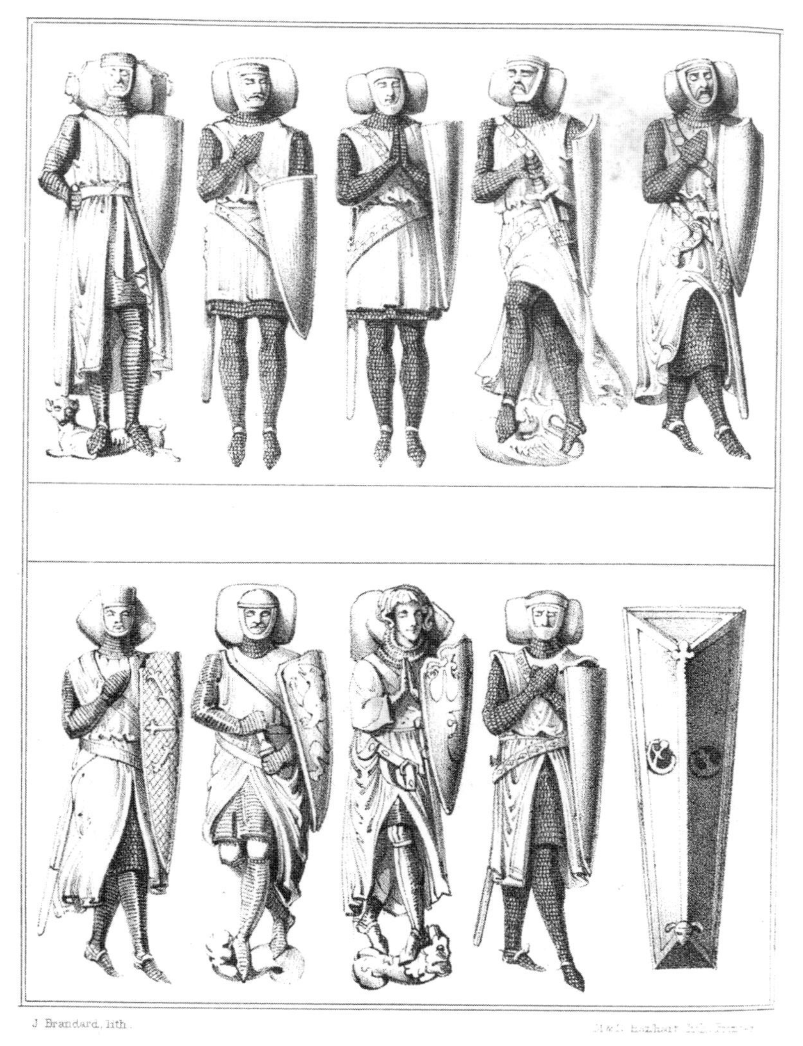

Fig. 25. Temple Church, London, funerary effigies. Etching from Addison, *The Temple Church*.

as reauthorizing the same mixture of forms found in the Holy Sepulchre in Jerusalem. By the twelfth century, the Holy Sepulchre was already a historical hodgepodge. Over the centuries, the Constantinian complex was subjected to repeated destructions. The worst was its conscientious dismantling in 1009 by the fanatic Fatimid caliph al-Hakim. By the mid-eleventh century the Anastasis and its tomb had been rebuilt by the Byzantine emperor Constantine Monomachus.[106] The crusaders expanded the building; their most notable addition was a great choir with a new high altar to the east of the Rotunda. The new church was dedicated in 1149.[107] The crusader building incorporated the round-headed forms of the older structure in their fashionably French-Gothic extension. The section of the building drawn by one of its great early twentieth-century

106. Ousterhout, "Rebuilding the Temple."

107. Folda, *The Art of the Crusaders in the Holy Land, 1098–1187*, 175–245.

students, the Dominican archaeologist Louis-Hugues Vincent, demonstrates its combination of old and new features (fig. 23).[108]

The architectural program of the Temple Church is just as unconventional as its style. Its spatial order is ambivalent and therefore a cause of indecision. In traditional churches, like Duke University Chapel, the spatial hierarchy processes unambiguously from the entrance toward the high altar, the locus of Jesus's perpetually reenacted sacrifice (fig. 24). The axis is unequivocal. The sanctuary is the most important part of the church. In contrast, in the Temple Church, the Round at the west competes with the altar in the east for the attention of the pious beholder. The Round is the visually most dramatic part of the structure. The lively effigies of dead knights staged in the central space of the Round reinforce its demand for the viewer's attention (fig. 25). In contrast, a flat wall provides a simple backdrop to the altar in the east. When observers attend to the Eucharist, they must turn their backs on the most compelling space of the building.

Perhaps this building equivocates in its liturgical arrangements, as in its style, because its archetype equivocates. The London Temple's combination of basilica and rotunda revisits the arrangement of both of Jerusalem's great sanctuary complexes. The Holy Sepulchre is cited almost universally as the Temple's model, though the Templum Domini (the Dome of the Rock) has also been claimed as a prototype.[109] The Templars were, after all, established on Mount Moriah in Solomon's Temple (al-Aksa Mosque), in close proximity to the Templum Domini. But the knights also had a special relationship with the Holy Sepulchre. According to their rule, if a Templar left the house in Jerusalem at night, it could be only to go to the Holy Sepulchre.[110] Along with the Hospitallers, they held the keys of the treasury in the Holy Sepulchre in which the True Cross was kept. Most critically, the Holy Sepulchre was the principal object of veneration of the pilgrims whom the Templars were sworn to protect. Architecture lacks DNA; its two possible progenitors are not readily distinguishable either in the Temple's forms or its written sources. The confusion can, in any case, only be generative: two references, rather than one, give greater resonance to the building's meaning; it imports more of Jerusalem to London.

The Holy Sepulchre does, however, offer certain attributes that reverberate in the Temple Church and assist in its interpretation. The Temple Church is linked to the Holy Sepulchre not only by its form but also by practices that occurred within its space. The sacredness of the Rotunda in Jerusalem proceeds from the vacant tomb at its center. The building provides a monumental frame for the material proof of Jesus's Resurrection—the body-less sepulcher carved into the living rock. The Round seems to have had a special attraction for those who

108. Vincent and Abel, *Jérusalem*, 2:114.

109. For example, see Pardi, "L'architettura sacra degli ordini militari." The earliest reference to the Temple Church as a replica of the Holy Sepulchre that I have found is in Howell and Stow, *Londinopolis* of 1657. For a discussion of the history of this association, see Lambert, *L'architecture des templiers*, 96–99. For a compendium of copies of the Holy Sepulchre in the West, A. Grabar, *Martyrium*. For a theory of the copy, Krautheimer, "Introduction to an 'Iconography of Medieval Architecture.'"

110. Bernard of Clairvaux, *The Rule of the Templars*, 29.

hoped to be resurrected to new life on Judgment Day in emulation of Jesus's own triumph over death. Many were buried in the Round. The high relief stone effigies of knights, now arranged in an orderly fashion on either side of the axis in the central space, mark the site as a cemetery, although they do not mark graves. The effigies are now independent of the bodies they were intended to commemorate—most have lost their names as well as their mortal remains. The animation of the sculptures, with their oddly crossed legs, seems to have anticipated their sporadic rearrangement. They have been in their present locations only since 1842. Indeed, the history of the dead bodies of the Round suggests why the Temple might still be haunted. In the mid-nineteenth century the church was subjected to consolidation, restoration, and the introduction of a heating system. The floor of the Round was excavated and the remains of numerous burials recorded. "In the enthusiasm for restoration . . . thirteenth-century relics were subjected to what can only be described as vandalism. The 'decayed and decaying remains of coffins and human bodies' below the pavement were replaced by 'a stratum of lime rubbish and concrete . . . to keep down the damp and prevent all noxious exhalation.' The decomposing remains were visited by curious thousands before being 'heterogeneously thrown into a vaulted grave dug in the reconstructed Round.'"[111] The indecent treatment of the Templars persisted, from the torture of their living bodies to the desecration of their dead ones.

The function of the Round as a tomb associates it with the Holy Sepulchre. Analogous ritual performance reinforces the correlation. The crusaders constructed a new choir to the east of Constantine's rotunda in such a way that the main altar of the new church stood in the east, opposite the sacred site of Jesus's entombment in the west. Similarly, the Templars in London extended the choir to the east of the Round. The practice of worshipping toward the east, turned away from the magical space of the Round, may feel odd to a modern worshipper, but perhaps it felt familiar to a Templar newly returned from Palestine. The possibility that the Temple was recognized as similar to the Holy Sepulchre is sustained by its inversion. In 1506, an English pilgrim to Jerusalem understood the Holy Sepulchre through its copy:

The disposition and making of the Temple of the Holy Sepulchre is round at the west end and eastward formed after the making of a [normal, basilican] church, much after the form and making of the Temple at London, save it is far exceeding in greatness.[112]

The Temple Church's identification with the Holy Sepulchre is further supported by what is known of the destroyed Templar church in Paris.[113] It, too, was a rotunda with an added nave to the east (fig. 26). The functional association of

111. Crook, "The Restoration of the Temple Church," 43.

112. "The disposycion and makynge of the sayd Temple of the Holy Sepulcre is rounde at the west ende, and estwarde fourmyd after the makynge of a churche, moche what after the fourme and makynge of the Temple at London, safe it is fer excedynge in gretenesse." Chaplain of Sir Richard Guylforde, *Pylgrymage of Sir Richard Guylforde to the Holy Land*, 24.

113. For the fullest discussion of the Temple in Paris, see Curzon, *La maison du temple de Paris, histoire et description*, 74–91. Curzon comments that "this church [like others built by the Templars] was

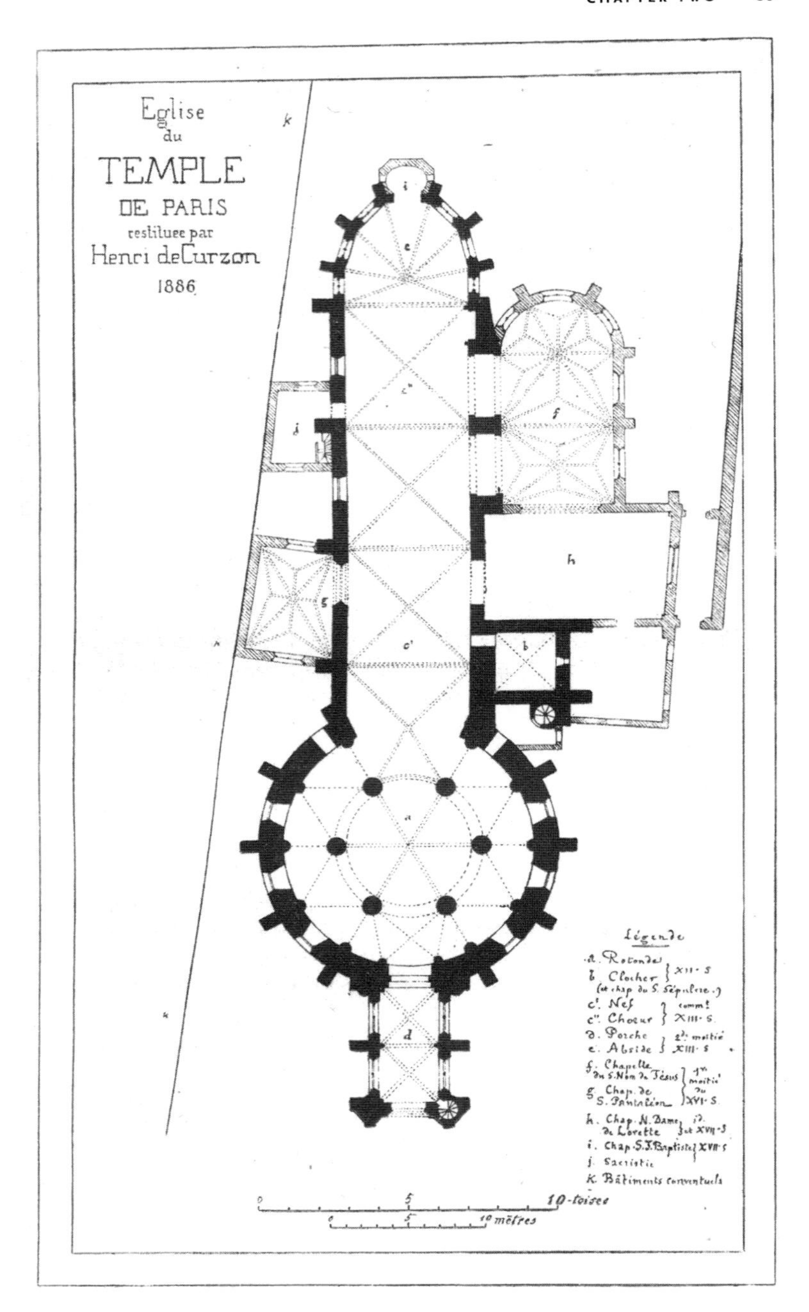

Fig. 26. Temple Church, Paris, plan. From Curzon, *La maison du temple de Paris*.

the Templars with the Holy Sepulchre, reinforced by the two churches at their most powerful centers, was so strong that it was mythologized. Round churches with no Templar connections have been ascribed to the order. Indeed, historians have tended to assume that all Templar churches were conventionally modeled after the Holy Sepulchre. The claim was established by the great French archi-

constructed in the image of the Holy Sepulchre, but on a plan in proportions that are only rarely found elsewhere." The author also provides a detailed discussion of the relationship between the Temple Churches in London and Paris and the Holy Sepulchre.

Fig. 27. Templar chapel, Laon, France. Author photo.

Fig. 28. (*below*) Templar church, Rampillon, France. Author photo.

tectural historian, theorist, and practitioner Eugène Viollet-le-Duc: "One gave the name of Temples, during the Middle Ages, to chapels of the commanderies of the Templars; these chapels were habitually built on a circular plan, as a reminder [*souvenir*] of the Holy Sepulchre. . . . The earliest of these chapels date only to about the middle of the twelfth century, and they were nearly all built at that time."[114] It seems, however, that with the exception of a few round funerary chapels like the intimate sanctuary at Laon (fig. 27), Templar churches were conventional basilicas, like the handsome thirteenth-century church at Rampillon, near Nanglis, to the southeast of Paris (fig. 28).[115]

Viollet-le-Duc's assumption that most Templar churches were round (and that most round churches were Templar) was naive, but it was not groundless. The two most prominent and familiar Templar churches, those of London and Paris, were, it seems, replicas of the Holy Sepulchre. It might easily be assumed that those great cities performed in the twelfth and thirteenth centuries in the same way that they did in the nineteenth and twentieth—providing models for their culturally dependent provinces. Already in the late twelfth century, London and Paris acted as prescient centers of European modernity, concentrating state and commercial power. The Templars established their headquarters within the domains of two of the greatest contemporary secular authorities in the West. The order might depend on rents and alms from the countryside, but its power had an urban base. Both the London and Paris Temples were intimately tied to their respective monarchs, even serving, at least occasionally, as their treasury. The Temples provocatively contributed to the new order in the urban fabric, realizing both the sacrality of Jerusalem and the institutional force of the Templars. Each building was a monumental metaphor of the Holy Sepulchre and its keepers—a volatile fusion of abstract ideas of spiritual power with physical presence. The Holy Sepulchre was a potent referent. The Templars persuasively deployed its signs—the Temples of London and Paris—as a means of confirming the order's privileged place within the city. The Temples performed as totems, marking the territory of a clan (the Templars), claiming a special relationship with its archetype (the Holy Sepulchre) and assuming its authority. The Temples also operated as trophies. No less than the Arch of Titus in Rome, the Temples demonstrated the Templars' military ability to occupy the East and appropriate its forms. The persuasiveness of that architectural sign in the past is confirmed by its continued power in the present.

AFTERLIFE

The articulate reference to the sacred topography of Jerusalem once made by the Temple Church is now obscure. It no longer functions as a replica of the Holy

114. Viollet-le-Duc, *Dictionnaire raisonné de l'architecture française*, 9:13. My rough translation.

115. Andrault-Schmitt, "Les églises des templiers de la Creuse et l'architecture religieuse au XIIIe siècle en Limousin"; E. Lambert, *L'architecture des templiers;* Voltz, "La chapelle des Templiers de Metz." For the architecture of the Templars in England, see Ritoók, "The Architecture of the Knights Templars in England."

Sepulchre. Nevertheless, the building retains something of the authority of its origins, though its force is differently expressed. After the suppression of the Templars, Edward II ignored the pope's order to deliver the precinct to the Hospitallers and presented it instead to a series of his favored nobles.[116] The Prior of the Hospitallers succeeded in a suit for possession of the property only in 1337. Within seventy years of the eviction of the Templars, their buildings were being leased from the Hospitallers by a new order: secular lawyers. Charles Addison, a nineteenth-century historian of the Templars, provides a patriotic history of the circumstances. In the early Middle Ages, churchmen controlled the practice of law, just as they did other areas of learning. However:

In the reign of King Stephen, the foreign clergy attempted to introduce the ancient civil law of Rome into this country [England], as calculated to promote the power and advantage of their order, but were resolutely resisted by the king and the barons, who clung to their old customs and usages. . . . [Later] Pope Innocent IV forbade the reading of the common law by the clergy in the English universities and seminaries of learning, because its decrees were not founded on the imperial constitutions, but merely on the customs of the laity.

As the common law ceased to be studied and taught by the clergy . . . it became necessary to educate and train up a body of laymen to transact the judicial business of the country; and Edward I, in the twentieth year of his reign (1292), in order to promote and encourage the study by laymen of the ancient municipal law of England, authorized the chief justice and other justices of the court of Common Pleas, to confer the exclusive privilege of pleading causes upon a certain number of persons learned in the laws, who were to be selected from every county in England, the king and his council deeming the number of one hundred and forty to be sufficient; but it was left to the discretion of the said justices to add to that number or to diminish it, as they should think fit.

At this period the Court of Common Pleas, which then had exclusive jurisdiction over all civil causes, had been fixed at Westminster, which brought together the students and professors of the common law at London, and about the period of the imprisonment of the Knights Templars (1307), the advocates of that court and the students who were candidates for the privilege of pleading therein, appear to have fallen into a sort of collegiate order, and to have formed themselves into a society under the sanction of the judges, for the study and advancement of the science of the law. The deserted convent of the Temple, seated in the suburb of London, away from the noise and bustle of the city, and presenting a ready and easy access by water to Westminster, appeared a desirable retreat for the learned members of this infant legal society. . . . From the time of Chaucer to the present day, the professors of the law have dined together in the ancient hall of the knights, as the military monks did before them; and the rule of their order requiring "two and two to eat together," and

116. First to the Earl of Pembroke, then to the Earl of Lancaster, and after Lancaster was executed for treason, back to Pembroke, then, in 1324, to Hugh le Despencer. Lewer and Dark, *The Temple Church in London*, 54.

"all the fragments to be given in brotherly charity to the domestics," is observed to this day.[117]

Addison goes on to enumerate the habits established by the Templars that continued to inform the practice of the lawyers who occupied their space: "In the sixth year of the reign of Edward the Third (1333) . . . the judges of the Court of Common Pleas were made knights, being the earliest instance on record of the grant of the honor of knighthood for services purely civil, and the professors of the common law, who had the exclusive privilege of practicing in the court, assumed the title or degree of Freres Serjens or Fratres Servientes, so that knights and serving brethren, similar to those of the ancient order of the Temple, were most curiously revived and introduced into the profession of law."[118] But perhaps most telling is the effect of the Templars' accommodations on the formation of two societies within its ancient precincts. The Inner and Middle Temples, apparently divided according to the dining and living space (hence the term "*Inns* of Court" applied to them) offered within the enclosure, became separate institutions, with distinctive rules and procedures. The lawyers "came as tenants of the Order of St. John [the Hospitallers], and there were already two halls in existence, probably the separate refectories of the Templar priests and knights. It is in the use of these halls by the lawyers that we may possibly find the origin of the Inner and Middle Temples."[119] After the Hospitallers were suppressed by Henry VIII in 1540, the Crown became the lawyers' landlord. Rent was extinguished in 1705. Now the properties of the Inner and Middle Temples are again their greatest revenue-producing asset.[120] The Crown retains control only over the appointment of the Master of the Temple, and that authority is purely formal.[121]

The Inner and Middle Temples are two of the four Inns of Court.[122] Only members of these four Inns may be called to the bar and admitted to the ancient and honorable degree of barrister of law. Until recently, only barristers had the rights of audience in every court in England and Wales. The effect of the

117. Addison, *The Temple Church,* 1–11. For a more recent and scholarly assessment of early legal education in England, see Brand, "Legal Education in England before the Inns of Court." For this and other references on the English legal system, I'd like to thank Paul Griffith.

118. Addison, *The Temple Church,* 13.

119. Lewer and Dark, *The Temple Church in London,* 55.

120. Southwell QC, "Challenges to the Inns," 6.

121. The Temple Master, Robin Griffith-Jones, related to me the following story: "The Master of the Temple is independent of the barristers; he takes care of the church, its offices, and its music. The Inns are obligated to pay the Master of the Temple. Officially he and his successors are due £17 6s. 8d. per annum. The Benchers [senior members of the Temple Inns] generously make some allowance for inflation. The Master's appointment is formally made by the Crown on the advice of the prime minister. In 1935, the prime minister, Ramsay Macdonald, wanted to ignore the Inns' candidate and appoint his own. He was, of course, quite within his rights to recommend to the king whomsoever he wanted. And the Inns—as they made clear—would be within *their* rights to pay such an incumbent exactly £17 6s. 8d. In the end, the prime minister backed down." Robin Griffith-Jones, interview by the author, May 6, 2003. Also see Griffith-Jones, "'Hearty and unanimous sentiment.'"

122. The others are Lincoln's Inn and Gray's Inn.

architecture of the Temple on the English legal profession was not limited to the definition of its institutional origins. Lawyers are now called to the bar in the Temple Church.[123] Thus the societies that occupy the Templars' quarters continue the order's close ties to secular power. The list of members of the Inner Temple that appears as the chapter's epigraph suggests the cultural and political power of the institution. Five of the signatories to the United States' Declaration of Independence were Middle Templars. The Templar enclosure continues to nurture state power. With their appropriation of the Templars' space, the lawyers assumed the order's signs—their heraldry and their church—as well as their privileged status, with their power sustained first by the monarchy and later by the secular state. In the pomp and prerogative of the barrister are the reverberations of the Templar knight.

If the quite real institutional afterlife of the Templars in the English legal system goes generally unnoticed, the mythological presence of the order in the clandestine exercise of world power is always on view. Modern myths and fictions of the Templars perpetuate the order's medieval associations with economic power and esoteric understanding. In the eighteenth and early nineteenth centuries, the association of the order with the East was commonly rendered as a form of deviation from religious and social orthodoxy. In Protestant contexts, this orientalism was apparently aggravated by anti-Catholic prejudice. The writing of Anglican scholar Rev. George Oliver, D.D., the vicar of Scopwick, is typical. Oliver represented the Templars as scions of Catholic fanaticism and depravity. His account of the Templars' church at Temple Bruer, published in 1837, reveals how bias frames science: "Beneath the church and tower was a perfect labyrinth of vaults and dungeons, and intricate passages, arched over with stone." He adds in a note:

Some of these vaults were appropriated to purposes that it is revolting to allude to. In one of them a niche or cell was discovered, which had been carefully walled up; and within it the skeleton of a man, who appears to have died in a sitting posture. . . . Immuring was not an uncommon punishment in these places. . . . In a corner of one of these vaults, many plain indications of burning exists. The wall stones have assumed the color of brick, and great quantities of cinders mixed with human skulls and bones. . . . Several large square stones were taken up with iron rings attached; and altogether the ruins exhibit woeful symptoms of crime and unfair dealing. We can scarcely forbear entertaining the opinion that these are the crumbling remains of unhappy persons, who had been confined in the dungeons of the preceptory.[124]

Later excavations by W. H. St. John Hope revealed Oliver's evidence of Templar perversity to be a complete fiction.[125]

---

123. Lawyers were at one time also required to take communion twice a year in the Temple Church as proof against Roman Catholicism. J. Williamson, *The History of the Temple, London*, 287.

124. Oliver, *History of the Holy Trinity Guild at Sleaford*, 28–29.

125. St. John Hope, "The Round Church of the Knights Templars at Temple Bruer, Lincolnshire," 188–90.

As his footnotes indicate, Rev. Oliver's understanding of the Templars depended on novelistic versions of the knights as religious and social heretics infected by eastern perversions and obsessions. The best known of these fictions is Sir Walter Scott's *Ivanhoe*, from which Sir Brian de Bois-Guilbert's description of the Templars has been quoted.[126] In film versions and TV miniseries, if no longer as part of the canon of English literature, *Ivanhoe* continues to popularize the image of the Templars as depraved and schismatic.[127] But noticeably from the mid-nineteenth century onward, the Templar was increasingly redefined as a heroic agent of the West in its attempt to take control of the East. In *Tancred; or, the New Crusade*, a novel published in 1847 by Benjamin Disraeli before he became the prime minister of Great Britain, the Crusades provide a model for British imperial interests in the Middle East.[128]

In his introduction to Jesse Lyman Hurlebert's popular *Manual of Biblical Geography: A Text-Book on the Bible History especially prepared for the use of Students and Teachers of the Bible, and for Sunday School Instruction* (1884), the Reverend John Heyl Vincent names the Templar as the West's consummate authority on the East:

During ten years of my pastoral life, wherever the itinerant system of my church placed me, I held on every Saturday afternoon, in the lecture-room of my church, a class to which old and young, and the representatives of all denominations, were admitted. It was called "The Palestine Class," and was devoted to the study of Bible history and geography. An outline of facts, prepared in catechetical form, was printed, and committed to memory by every pupil. Difficult old Hebrew names of lands, cities and mountains, were arranged in a rhythmic way, and chanted after the manner of the old-time "singing geography" classes. Answers were given in concert to help the memory, and personal examinations were afterward conducted to test it. The class constituted an "ideal company of tourists to the far East." The course of lessons was divided into five sections, covering the whole of Bible history. As each member, passing a personal examination, gave proof that he had thoroughly mastered "Section One," he was constituted a PILGRIM *to the Holy Land, and given a certificate to that effect. Having studied "Section Two," and passed a satisfactory examination, he was made a* RESIDENT *in Palestine, and his name was associated with one town or mountain. In that way every principal place on the map was associated with the name of some member, who was held responsible to the class for information concerning its history and present condition. An examination in "Section Three" made our "pilgrim" and "resident" a* DWELLER IN JERUSALEM. *Having been examined in "Section Four," he was made an* EXPLORER *of other Bible lands, and was located on some mountain, or city of Egypt, Arabia, Chaldea, Asia Minor, etc. A final examination made him a* TEMPLAR.[129]

126. Almost as popular in the nineteenth century, though less familiar now, was Scott, *Talisman*.

127. Still the most powerful adaptation is MGM's 1952 release, with Elizabeth Taylor as Rebecca and George Sanders as Sir Brian de Bois-Guilbert.

128. Disraeli, *Tancred*. This text is discussed in chapter 4.

129. J. Vincent, introduction to Hurlebut, *Manual of Biblical Geography*, vii.

Rev. Vincent's positive use of *Templar* in creating hierarchies had precedents and antecedents in the various ranks of "Templar" in Masonic and Masonic-related societies. More recently, in the first script of George Lucas's immensely successful *Star Wars*, the Jedi Knights were Templars. Now even the Templars' alleged heterodoxy has morphed from a liability into a lure. They are celebrated as anti-Catholic protofeminists in Dan Brown's best-selling novel, *The Da Vinci Code*.[130] Similarly, their association with wealth, once an embarrassment, is now an attraction. Novels and films, even some scholarship, inflate Templar treasure. Roy Lewis's *The Cross Bearer* (1994) enmeshes the ancient order in local graft.[131] On a larger stage, *National Treasure* (2004), a Walt Disney production, connects the Templars to the modern economy of the United States—with the East providing the entrepreneurial accumulation essential to the establishment of a new Western empire.

CONCLUSION

The economic and military traumas of the twelfth and thirteenth centuries were curiously figured in the Templars. Their rise to prominence coincided with a dramatic expansion of the European economy, the thorough monetization of Europe, and the invention of capital.[132] This correspondence was not coincidental. The Order of the Knights Templar was the product of the Crusades—the great stimulus of the economic reshaping of the West. The order was, in turn, among the Crusades' greatest producers. The Templars' engagement with the transfer of wealth and human resources between the East and the West was as profound as their military commitment to defend the West's claims on the East.

The Templars' power depended on their familiarity with the East. Their knowledge of Muslim social and tactical habits gave them diplomatic and military skills essential to the project of the Crusades. Texts reveal their intimacy with the enemy: in rules against wearing pointed shoes, in references to the kinds of horses they possessed, and in the stories of the refuges sought by knights charged with crimes. That the Templars understood the religious practices of Muslim friends is witnessed by a remarkable anecdote found in the autobiography of Usama ibn Munqidh (1095–1188):

When I was in Jerusalem I used to go to the Masjid al-Aqsa, beside which is a small oratory which the Franks have made into a church. Whenever I went into the mosque, which was in the hands of Templars who were friends of mine, they would put the little oratory at my disposal, so that I could say my prayers there. One day I had gone in, said the Allah akhbar, and risen to begin my prayers, when a Frank threw himself on me from behind, lifted me up and turned me so that I was facing east. "That is the way to pray!" he said. Some Templars at once intervened, seized the man and

---

130. D. Brown, *The Da Vinci Code*.

131. R. Lewis, *The Cross Bearer*.

132. *Capital* defined as money invested in a business venture is found in notarial and business records from the twelfth century onward. De Roover, "Scholastic Economics," 165n4.

took him out of my way, while I resumed my prayer. But the moment they stopped watching him he seized me again and forced me to face east, repeating that this was the way to pray. Again the Templars intervened and took him away. They apologized to me and said: "He is a foreigner who has just arrived today from his homeland in the north, and he has never seen anyone pray facing any other direction than east." "I have finished my prayers," I said, and left, stupefied by the fanatic who had been so perturbed and upset to see someone praying facing the qibla![133]

The Templars' construction of the two principal churches of their European headquarters on a plan recognizably imported from Jerusalem is emblematic of their political and economic role: they embraced the East and made it available for consumption in the West.

Architecture is deeply implicated in an irony: in the aftermath of the collapse of the crusader empire, the Templars' attachment to the East was no longer an asset but a serious liability. The strengths of the Templars—from their agility in financial matters to their facility with foreign languages—became fatal weaknesses. The order may have been marked for destruction because of its wealth, but its associations with the East made it an easy target. The charges of heresy brought against the knights by Phillip the Fair no less than the ascription of esoteric practices to the order by modern writers depend on the Templars' identity with the East. The suspicions provoked by Templars' ties with the East supplemented the anxieties caused by their wealth. Their Temples' inscription of an eastern presence into the western urban landscape uncannily corresponded to the Templars' role in the West's increasing familiarity with money and its abstractions. The order collected alms, rents, and treasures and contributed to an unlanded labor force. But its source of wealth—its association with the East—caused its destruction before its wealth could be converted into capital. The Templars may be counted among the earliest victims of primitive accumulation.

Appendix: Michael the Syrian, History of the Frer, Frankish Brothers, from his *Chronicle,* ed. Chabot, 595–97, translated by Lucas Van Rompay

At the commencement of the reign of Baldwin the Second, a Frankish brother[1] came from Rome in order to pray in Jerusalem. And he had on himself a vow not to return to his country, but after assisting the king in warfare for three years—he himself and thirty knights (who were) with him—subsequently to become a monk and in Jerusalem to end his life. And after the king and his nobles had seen that they excelled in the war and that they were extremely useful to the city by their service those three years, they advised him that instead of becoming a monk and save his soul (in this way), he would serve in the military along with those who were following him and they (together) would guard these (holy) places [*596c*] against robbers.

---

133. Usama ibn Munqidh, "Autobiography," 79–80.

1. The copyist hesitated between *'nsh* "a man" and *'h* "a brother," but the result clearly is the latter.

And after that man—whose name was Hugh de Payens—had accepted this advice and also these thirty knights had followed and joined him, the king gave them the house of Solomon for their habitation and villages for their subsistence. Similarly also the patriarch gave them (some) of the villages of the church.

And they defined for themselves these canons that they would live monastically, not having women and not entering the bathhouse, and that they would not have individual possessions at all, but (that) all their property would be in common. And through such a lifestyle they began to excel and their fame spread in all countries. There were coming kings' sons and kings, nobles and humble ones, joining them in such a spiritual brotherhood. And every one who became a brother with them gave to the community whatever he possessed, be it villages or cities or something small. They became numerous and big and lands came into their (possession) not only in the countries of Palestine but particularly in the vast countries of Italy and Rome.

Now, their code and their canons are written and (well) defined. And every one who comes to become a brother with them, they admonish for one year, while the canons are being read to him seven times and each time it is said to him: "Look if perhaps you have regrets; perhaps you will not be able to observe[2] until the end these canons. Admit (it), go home." And at the end of the year, for the one who accepts and promises to carry the yoke they say prayers while they vest him in their habit. And after that, the one who turns away from his promise dies by the sword, without mercy and without any persuasion.[3]

Their code is: that it is not permitted to anyone to possess anything individually, not a house, not gold, not any property; and (that it is) not (permitted) to go (anywhere) without the order of the superior; and (that it is) not (permitted) to sleep anywhere but in their house; and (that it is) not (permitted) to eat bread at the public table; and neither is it permitted to some one, when he is ordered to go somewhere and to die, to say: "I will not go." But (it is their code) that, according to his promise, one works in this service until (his) death with faith. And for every one who dies, they perform forty masses[4] and they give food to the poor on his behalf forty days, every day (to) forty souls. And his commemoration is in the liturgy of the masses[4] of their churches until eternity. And those who die in combat are regarded by them as martyrs. And the one who is found to have kept something hidden from the community or who at his death is found to possess something without having given it to the community, they do not even deem him[5] worthy of burial.

Their garments (consist of) one white simple habit and apart from that they are not permitted to wear (anything else) and when they sleep they are not permitted to take off their [*597a*] habit, nor to ungird[6] their loins.

---

2. I am uncertain about the reading here.

3. That is, "without any attempt to persuade him to come back" (?).

4. Literally: "offerings."

5. The manuscript incorrectly has the pronoun *l-hên* instead of *leh*. The copyist seems to have made a link to the following sentence.

6. I read *l-meshrâ*. The *shin* is a bit unclear.

Their food is as follows: on Sunday and Tuesday and Thursday they eat meat and on the remaining days milk and eggs and cheese. Wine, however, only the priests who serve in their churches drink (it) every day with bread,[7] as well as the soldiers, or knights, during their activity; and similarly the foot soldiers during combat. (As for) the craftsmen, each one works in his one craft; and likewise the workers of the land. And in each town and village in which they have a house there is a superior and a manager and on their orders all who (are) there serve, each one in his task.

The general superior of them all is in Jerusalem. (He is) the one who gives orders to all of them, while absolutely no individual has any authority over anything at all. And all that is gathered in from the harvest, of wheat and wine and the rest, one tenth (of it) they distribute to the poor. And all the bread which is baked in any house, one tenth (of it) is provided to the poor. And every day that the table is set up and that the brothers eat bread, all that is left over is given to the poor. In addition, twice in a week they distribute separately to the poor bread and wine.

And while their beginning[8] was because of the pilgrims,[9] in order to protect them on the roads, later on they also went out with the kings to (wage) war with the Turks. And they became numerous until they numbered one hundred thousand. And they acquired fortresses and also they themselves built fortified places in all the countries under the authority of the Christians. And their property increased in gold and in all kinds of things, and weapons of all sorts, and herds of sheep, and cows, and pigs, and camels, and horses, more than all the kings. (At the same time) they all were detached, not bound by anything, and friendly and loving towards all the worshippers of the Cross. They established in all their places, and particularly in Jerusalem, houses for the sick, so that any stranger who falls ill finds a place and (people) who serve (him) and take care (of him) until either he recovers—and then they give him provisions and let him go in peace—or when he dies, they take care of his burial. It is finished.

---

7. The text seems not to be in order. It would be more natural to see this sentence as the conclusion of the section on the food of the brothers: "Wine, however, they drink every day with (their) bread." One might speculate that the copyist has made a wrong combination with the following section, in which the different functions are listed (?).

8. That is, "the beginning of their presence in the Holy Land."

9. Literally: "prayers."

CHAPTER THREE

Fabricated Jerusalem: Franciscans and Pious Mountains

There is not in it a mountain, a valley, a plain, a field, a fountain, a river, a torrent, a castle, a village, not even a stone, which the Savior of the world did not touch, either with his most holy feet in walking . . . or with his holy body. . . . . When ascending into heaven he left the print of his most holy feet impressed on the mount. Besides this, with his sweat . . . he bathed this most holy land. . . . Also you cannot deny but that many times he bathed it abundantly with his precious blood. . . . This blessed land above all parts of the world had the greatest contact with him, and therefore it is all full of divine virtues and it is become a most holy habitation. * FRANCESCO SURIANO, FRANCISCAN CUSTODIAN OF JERUSALEM, *TREATISE ON THE HOLY LAND* (1524)

The Franciscan order has asked Israel to allow some of the two hundred or so armed Palestinians sheltering in Bethlehem's Church of Nativity to leave unharmed. The Roman Catholic order in the Holy Land also called for water and electricity to be urgently supplied to its monks inside the complex, which has been blockaded since 2 April. Israel, whose army has sealed off the complex in pursuit of suspected militants among the Palestinians, reportedly rejected the appeals immediately. * BBC REPORT, APRIL 22, 2002

DESIRE

And after we settled the boundaries . . . I decided to turn aside to the mountain that lies next to Varallo and faces east. On this mountain I had noticed that there was a shrine being built by the Franciscans, in imitation of that on Mount Calvary [in Jerusalem], where our lord and savior Jesus Christ suffered, which is commonly visited with the greatest hardships and dangers by a great throng of Christians. And so, at the foot of the mountain [at Varallo], I was met by a priest, a leader of [the Franciscan] order, a man both religious and most experienced with the site where the body of Jesus was actually buried. Leading me across neighboring hills—one moment by climbing, the next moment with an easy descent—he brought me into individual chapels in which images are exhibited, just as the mysteries of the passion of the Lord are narrated in successive order in the gospel and just as it is related that Christ himself was taken to many places among many people and endured diverse humiliations and torments. And he kept assuring me that all these things had been made like the place of the real Sepulchre with the same proportions, the same architecture, and with the same paintings and shapes. Truly, my Lancino, I have never seen anything more religious, more devout. I have never seen anything that could pierce the heart more, which could compel one to neglect everything else and follow Christ alone. Let cease henceforth those so-called Roman stations; let end even the Jerusalem pilgrimage. This new and most pious work repeats [refert] everything, and by the very simplicity of the craft [fabricae] and the artless architecture [structura], the ingenious site surpasses all antiquity. And when three times, now four, now one more time I had surveyed everything and I could not find an end to my visit and admiration, at night I wrote out a description of the site's location and all its mysteries, which I would now like for you to polish; for I will persuade myself that it has been worthwhile if I have been able to invite you and your muses to sing a glorious song. Goodbye! From the Sepulchre of the Lord, 29 September, 1507.[1]

In this letter, Gerolamo Morone, secretary to the Duke of Milan, describes the Sacro Monte of Varallo to Lancino Curtio, another Milanese intellectual. Later, a more famous member of the Milanese elite, Saint Charles Borromeo (1538–84), archbishop of the city, found at the Sacro Monte of Varallo a retreat for reflection after an encounter with the Shroud of Turin: "The contemplation of the relic he had visited left upon the mind of the saint so lively a sympathy for the sufferings of our Lord that he resolved, before returning to Milan, to visit the holy mountain of Varallo to meditate in private on the mysteries of the Passion, commemorated there in little chapels distributed over the mountain."[2] Later, terminally suffering from his labors on behalf of the urban poor during the plague in Milan, Charles Borromeo returned with a few attendants to the site in preparation for his own death. The Franciscan father Francis Adorno directed the regime of his retreat:

Father Adorno gave the points of meditation, and each person chose the chapel he liked best for his own private prayers. . . . St. Charles' two favorite chapels on Mount Varallo were those of the Prayer in the Garden and the Holy Sepulchre. . . . [At the time of his departure, a few days before his death,] he returned to the chapel of the Holy Sepulchre, where he soon became engaged in prayer, as if he could not bear to say a final farewell to it. His attendants had not noticed that he had left them, and were therefore obliged to return to seek him, and make the round of the chapels before they could ascertain where he was.[3]

Varallo is a small town northwest of Milan in the ragged southern foothills of the Alps. The outcrop above the town is its Sacro Monte, or Holy Mountain

1. Morone, *Lettere ed orazioni latine*, 148–49. I want to thank Bart Huelsenbeck for the corrections he made to my translation of this text.

2. Giussano, *The Life of St. Charles Borromeo*, 46.

3. Ibid., 237–40.

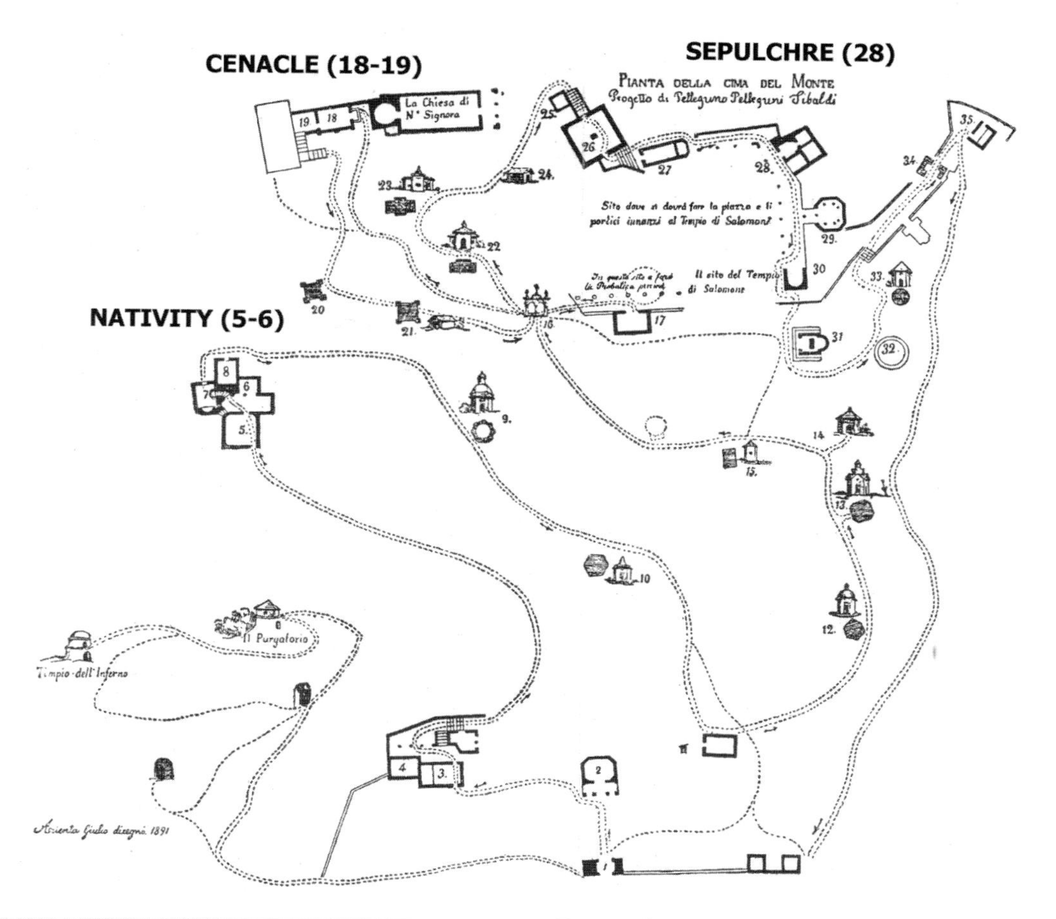

Fig. 29. (*above*) Sacro Monte, Varallo, Italy, plan. Pellegrino Tibaldi's drawing copied by Giulio Arienta and published by Butler, *Ex Voto*.

Fig. 30. Sacro Monte, Varallo, Italy, view from below. Author photo.

Fig. 31. Gaudenzio Ferrari, *Crucifixion,* Sacro Monte, Varallo, Italy. Author photo.

(figs. 29, 30). It was sanctified in the 1490s by the recreation there of Jerusalem. The first piece of this Jerusalem constructed was the Holy Sepulchre. The tomb of the Christ at Varallo is a carefully measured replica of that found in the Rotunda of the Church of the Holy Sepulchre in Jerusalem.[4] Like the tomb

4. For discussion of claims made for the resemblance between the tombs of Varallo and Jerusalem, see Nova, "Popular Art in Renaissance Italy," 119–20. I doubt Nova's suggestion that the contemporaneous emphasis on the sites' identical measurements was a means of alerting visitors to the fact that the tomb was not really Jesus's sepulchre. Quite the opposite: no one making a pilgrimage to Varallo, then as now, believes herself to be in Jerusalem. But, as in Epcot in Disney World, the repeated insistence on the authenticity of representation increases the viewer's sense of the experiential value of the surrogate.

in Jerusalem, the Varallo sepulchre consists of a small apsidal anteroom connected to the tomb chamber by a low door through which the pious visitor must crawl.[5] Golgotha was later constructed on a higher level and to the northeast of the Sepulchre, just as in Jerusalem. In early modern Jerusalem, however, both the tomb and Golgotha were incorporated within the Church of the Holy Sepulchre; at Varallo, they occur in the imagined urban landscape of Herod's Jerusalem.

Varallo's spaces are like those of first-century Jerusalem in another remarkable way. The actions that took place in the ancient Holy City are reproduced along with its structures. At Varallo the holy sites are reanimated with life-size sculptures depicting the events that made them sacred. The Crucifixion and other events of the Passion, each articulated as a distinct episode by its architectural frame, are reenacted.[6] Small chapel-theaters stage these scenes; they are powerfully portrayed by life-size sculptures, naturalistically painted, in some instances draped with brocades and dressed in trousers, provided with real buckets and spears, and often wigged in horsehair. These three-dimensional figures act upon stages of hallucinatory depth. Trompe l'oeil frescoes provide appropriate backdrops occupied by complementary figures, urban elements, and landscape views.[7] The sites associated with Jesus's life and death in fifteenth-century Jerusalem were empty by comparison with those of Varallo.

The scene of the Crucifixion suggests what the tableaux of Varallo desired of their devout observers in the first half of the sixteenth century (fig. 31).[8] Jesus dominates the whole composition by his centrality, elevation, and motionlessness. His static body is framed by hyperactivity—writhing criminals, gawking witnesses, and, most dramatically, a sword-brandishing equestrian figure astride a massive steed that prances out of the composition into real time. Groups of statues play out subnarratives below the cross. Several of these scenes are familiar from the Gospels: the gambling for Jesus's cloak, the swooning Virgin and her supporters. Other figures perform anecdotally: the mother with her squirming infants, the burgher with his pet dog. This voluptuous sculptural narrative is unnaturally flattened along a narrow stage space. The claustrophobic lack of real depth is further exaggerated by the peculiar recession of the narrative behind the Crucifixion. Its picture plane is pitched violently toward the observer. The onlooker shares the viewing field with the sculptured figures but looks down on the scene that extends behind the crosses.

5. For a reconstruction of the pilgrim's experience, see Hood, "*The Sacro Monte of Varallo,*" 300–302.

6. For the Franciscan commitment to the Passion and its representation, see Derbes, *Picturing the Passion in Late Medieval Italy*.

7. For a discussion of the technicalities of controlling the gaze in these chapels, see Langé, "Lo spazio virtuale nell'opera di collaborazione dei fratelli D'Enrico"; Langé and Pensa, *Il Sacro Monte*. These works also provide references to earlier research on Varallo.

8. For the insights into images' desire that have shaped the present study, see Mitchell, *What Do Pictures Want?*

Fig. 32. Duane Hanson, *Museum Guard*. The Nelson-Atkins Museum of Art, Kansas City, Missouri (Gift of the Friends of Art), F76-40. Art © Estate of Duane Hanson/Licensed by VAGA, New York, NY. Photography by Robert Newcombe. By permission of The Nelson-Atkins Museum of Art, Kansas City, Missouri.

The Varallo Crucifixion is a great baroque altarpiece that has exceeded its two-dimensional limitations in its desire to become real.[9] The question remains: is the scene's desire to become real inevitably frustrated? In what ways could it ever succeed? The answers, of course, depend on the observer.[10] The centurion witnessing the Crucifixion at the Sacro Monte is not the Duane Hanson *Museum Guard* at the Nelson-Atkins Museum of Art (fig. 32). The centurion does not fool the viewer into assuming that another living human being shares her space. The illusion of the Duane Hanson polyurethane, molded-from-life *Museum Guard* certainly depends on an advanced technology of visual fraudu-

9. A painting of the Crucifixion in Sta. Maria delle Grazie, Varallo, by Gaudenzio Ferrari, the same artist who executed the scene on the Sacro Monte, already makes an effort to elude its frame. As the insufferable travel writer the Rev. S. W. King comments, "Yet, in some of the accessories, an original quaintness of manner, and caprice of execution, manifest themselves. The trappings of the soldiers' horses, which form conspicuous figures, and also their knightly armor and other details, are embossed in low relief, and gilt; which has a singular effect. . . . But though these materialisms have a quaint and medieval effect when scrutinized, the spirit of the whole composition prevents them obtruding disagreeably." King, *The Italian Valleys of the Pennine Alps*, 505.

10. For an account of the origins in the East of the Western devotional image, see Belting, *The Image and Its Public in the Middle Ages*.

Fig. 33. ACC Tournament, Duke vs. Maryland, Greensboro, North Carolina, 2004. Chris Duhon lays up the ball. Photograph courtesy of Duke University Photography.

lence. But it also works because of the sculpture's limited demands on its audience. The *Museum Guard*'s illusion functions within an unmodified temporal and spatial present. The piece's discretion—a function of its contextual appropriateness and its motionlessness—allows it to be ignored. The shock of realizing the *Museum Guard*'s objecthood might stimulate in the thoughtful observer a new understanding of the human relationship to art. More commonly it is a surprise of the sort elicited by a magician. "I had the experience of walking by this sculpture and confusing it with a museum guard. It had a real effect on me. I couldn't be sure if it was real or not real—I had to go and check. . . . [The sculpture] has an intense reality. I almost felt some kind of fear; I wasn't sure whether he was going to react or not."[11] The *Museum Guard* might startle the viewer; the piece does not, however, move its observer to an alternative plane of consciousness, to a different historical moment, or to an exotic and remote location.

The Crucifixion at Varallo plays different tricks for a larger return. The realism of its scale and form is undone by its stop-action presentation.[12] The exag-

11. The quotation is in response to Duane Hanson's *Policeman*, exhibited in the Whitney and now in a private collection. See "The Art of Judgment," 31.

12. Most commentators simply see an "intense realism" in the works. For example, see Plesch, "A Pilgrim's Progress," 56.

gerated activity of the figures undermines pictorial illusion by its unnatural interruption. Movements that should be completed in nanoseconds remain unchanged. Indeed, the representation presents to the viewer that which could not be seen: the single moment in a violent motion is not perceptible. Now, the ubiquity of photographs like those taken of athletes in action make us forget that they display what we ourselves cannot see (fig. 33). Unless you are a fan, the seductiveness of the photograph of one basketball player dunking over another lies in its aesthetic presentation of the remarkable power of the human body rendered in exquisite detail and in brilliant color. The Crucifixion must have fascinated its early modern audience by revealing what could never otherwise be witnessed—it exposed perceptual mysteries as well as spiritual ones.

Just as photographs of athletes effectively index a particular moment of transient glory, so the aggressive figures of the Crucifixion insist on a particular moment of historical violence. They provide the active frame that accentuates the passive Jesus at its center. The figure of the dead Jesus is so different from the other participants in the scene that it has been perceived by connoisseurs as not fitting. The idiosyncratic nineteenth-century English intellectual Samuel Butler describes others' narratives explaining the distinctiveness of the crucified Jesus:

Fassola says that the figure of Christ on the Cross is not the original one, which was stolen, and somehow or other found its way to the Church of S. Andrea at Vercelli, where according to Colombo, a crucifix, traditionally said to be this one, was preserved until the close of the last century. Bordiga says that there is no reason to believe this story. The present crucifix is of wood, and is probably an old one long venerated, and embodied in his work by Gaudenzio himself, partly out of respect to public feeling, and partly, perhaps, as an unexceptionable excuse for avoiding a great difficulty.[13]

Whether the artist, Gaudenzio Ferrari, produced the crucified figure or chose to include a salvaged image, the effect was the same.[14] Jesus is similarly the passive focus of attention in the other scenes of the Passion at Varallo. By his stillness, he is more real. Isolated in his self-absorption by the theatricality around him, Jesus invites the empathy of the pious beholder.[15]

Empathy is the power of the observer to project herself into an object of contemplation, thereby more fully understanding it.[16] Some images invite an empathetic response from their viewers. The *Museum Guard* is not one of those images; the Jesus of the Varallo Crucifixion is. Saint Bonaventure, the great mystic, theologian, and minister general of the Franciscan order, provides a compelling story of the empathetic potential of an image of the Crucifixion:

13. S. Butler, *Ex Voto*, 205.

14. For a sympathetic consideration of Gaudenzio Ferrari's work at Varallo, see Testori, *Il gran teatro montano*.

15. For the canonical discussion of absorption and theatricality, see Fried, *Absorption and Theatricality*.

16. As defined in the on-line edition of the *Oxford English Dictionary*. In art history, empathy is most familiarly deployed to explain abstract artworks. See, for example, Worringer, *Abstraction and Empathy*.

On a certain morning about the feast of the Exaltation of the Cross, while Francis was praying on the mountainside, he saw a Seraph with six fiery and shining wings descend from the height of heaven. . . . There appeared between the wings the figure of a man crucified. . . . As the vision disappeared, it left in his heart a marvelous ardor and imprinted on his body markings that were no less marvelous. Immediately the marks of nails began to appear in his hands and feet just as he had seen a little before in the figure of the man crucified.[17]

Saint Francis presents a model of extreme empathy with an image of suffering. The Varallo Crucifixion appealed for a similar response. Not all images get what they want. Nevertheless, Morone's letter to Curtio suggests that this one may well have come close to realizing its desire.

CUSTODY

The Sacro Monte of Varallo was, as Morone indicates, a Franciscan production. Bernardino Caimi, a member of the first order of the Franciscans or, officially, the Friars Minor (Ordinis Fratrum Minorum, O.F.M.), initiated the construction of the site in imitation of Jerusalem at the end of the fifteenth century. In the 1470s Caimi, progeny of a distinguished Milanese family, was appointed Custos, the superior and custodian, of the Franciscan community in the Holy Land, where he gained an intimate experience of Jerusalem. The Sacro Monte reproduced his sense of that sacred landscape. The landscape of Caimi's Jerusalem at Varallo was a particular historical mix of the Herodian, Franciscan, and Mamluk; its living occupants were exclusively pious Christians. Caimi's Jerusalem was free of the non-Christians who occupied not only its archetype but also the mercantile cities of Italy.

The spatial hybridity of Caimi's Jerusalem at Varallo proceeded from the real Jerusalem's late medieval history as interpreted by Franciscan piety. The crusaders had conceded Jerusalem to Saladin, the Kurdish founder of the Ayyubid dynasty, in 1187, but they had continued to hold the city of Acre. The first General Chapter of the Franciscan order, held in 1217 outside Assisi, founded the administrative province of the Holy Land and Syria and established the provincial head of the order in Acre. In 1219, Francis himself confronted the Ayyubid sultan al-Malik al-Kamil with the spiritual benefits of Christianity. Saint Bonaventure again tells the tale:

The ardor of his charity urged his spirit on toward martyrdom. . . . He traveled to the regions of Syria, constantly exposing himself to many dangers in order to reach the presence of the Soldan [sultan] of Babylon [Cairo]. . . . The Saracen sentries fell upon [Francis and his companion friar] like wolves swiftly overtaking sheep, savagely seized the servants of God and cruelly and contemptuously dragged them away, insulting them, beating them and putting them in chains. Finally, after they had been maltreated in many ways and were exhausted, by divine providence they were led to the

17. Bonaventure, "Life of St. Francis," 305–6.

Soldan. . . . He preached to the Soldan the Triune God and the one Savior of all, Jesus Christ.[18]

The sultan was apparently impressed, but not converted. Franciscan tradition suggests that al-Kamil arranged for Francis to visit the shrines of Jerusalem before his return to Acre.[19]

The Mamluks, who displaced the Ayyubids in 1250, ended the crusader presence in Palestine with the capture of Acre in 1291. Jerusalem flourished in the early fourteenth century under the Mamluks, though later in the century the city suffered the ravages of the Black Death (1347–51) and then economic and social disorder caused by the late Mongol invasions.[20] The Franciscans became intimately involved with the Mamluks.[21] The Mamluks were interested enough in maintaining economic and political relations with the West to negotiate a reestablishment of a Franciscan presence in the Holy Land. An agreement between James II of Aragon (r. 1291–1327) and Sultan al-Malik an-Nasir (r. 1293–1341) secured the convent and Church of the Nativity in Bethlehem for the Franciscans as early as 1327. As the BBC epigraph of this chapter indicates, the Franciscans are still there; they are also still in Jerusalem.[22] In 1333 the same sultan promulgated a *firman* (decree) awarding the Franciscans the right to live permanently in the Holy Sepulchre and celebrate Latin Christian rites there. They also received titles to the Chapel of the Holy Spirit, the Chapel of Saint Thomas the Apostle, and, most important, the Cenacle on Mount Sion.[23] The United Nations Conciliation Commission for Palestine's Committee on Jerusalem attempts an objective account of the Cenacle:

The Cenacle (Mount Sion). The Cenacle is the place of the Last Supper and of the descent of the Holy Ghost at Pentecost. It was the first meeting place of the Early Christians in Jerusalem. Since 1552 the Cenacle has been under Moslem control and no Christian services may be held therein. The Cenacle was already in use as a church as early as A.D. *135. During the fourth century a basilica was built on the site of the primitive church. The basilica was destroyed by Moslems and Jews in 966; rebuilt by the Crusaders in the twelfth century; and destroyed once again by the Sultan of Damascus in 1219, on which occasion the Cenacle itself escaped destruction. It passed*

18. Ibid., 268–69.

19. It is perhaps worth noting that the same sultan, al-Malik al-Kamil, was later involved in the negotiations with Emperor Frederick II that briefly reestablished Latin control in Jerusalem between 1229 and 1244.

20. Instability continued with the wars against the Ottoman Turks. Only in 1516 did the Ottoman sultan Selim I rout the Mamluk armies and move control of Jerusalem from Cairo to Istanbul.

21. My understanding of the Franciscans in Jerusalem depends heavily on Arce, "The Custody of the Holy Land," 141–55. Also see Ordoardo, "La custodia francescana di Terra Santa."

22. The Franciscans' control of the holy sites in Jerusalem was threatened by the reestablishment of the Latin Patriarchate in 1847. For the papal definition of the Franciscan role, see Collin, *Recueil de documents concernant Jerusalem et les lieux saints,* 3–5.

23. Bulls of Clement VI, *Nuper charissimae* and *Gratias agimus,* Avignon, November 21, 1342, record this history and accord papal approval to the arrangements. For a scholarly review of the establishment of the Franciscan custody of the holy sites, see Lemmens, *Die Franziskanner im Hl. Lande.*

into the care of the Franciscans in the early fourteenth century and remained so until 1552, when the Franciscans were ejected by the Ottoman government. The "Franciscan Chapel of the Cenacle" is listed by the [Franciscan] Custos of the Holy Land as being under the exclusive jurisdiction of the Latin Church.[24]

Though expelled from the Cenacle by the Ottomans, who defeated the Mamluks and extended their empire to include Jerusalem in 1516, the Franciscans blamed the loss of their properties on the Jews.[25] The Franciscan Francesco Suriano, writing in the early sixteenth century, is explicit:

From the foundations of the church of Mount Sion can be gathered its size: the length is 100 braccia [a braccio is the length of a man's arm—a little more than two feet] and the width 50: it has three naves, all covered with slabs of the finest marble with a mosaic floor. Of which building nothing remains save the apse of the high altar, the Cenacle of Christ and the Chapel of the Holy Ghost. [This last was built by Duke Philip of Burgundy who ordered that after his death, his heart be removed and buried in it.] . . . This chapel then so beautiful and so ornate out of envy and hate for the Christian faith was again by the fury of the populace brought to ruins and at the same time were destroyed and broken all the rooms and cells of the cloister within the place. And the reason of such ruin were the dogs of Jews, because they told the Saracens that under the chapel was the tomb of David the prophet. When the Lord Sultan heard this he ordered that the tomb and place be taken from the Friars and dedicated to their cult, and so it was done. And the Saracens considering it a shame that the Friars should celebrate above them, who regarded themselves as superior, destroyed it.[26]

Another Franciscan, Agustín Arce, writing in 1974, uses less abusive language but makes the same accusations:

For more than two hundred years, the Religious lived in this famous Franciscan monastery of Mount Sion (1335–1552). Violently, and unjustly, they were expelled in 1551. . . . So ended a religious drama which began with the so-called Tomb of David, localized in a chamber beneath the Cenacle, an attribution without any basis in ancient tradition, Jewish or Moslem. . . . [Nevertheless,] owing to this popular but highly improbable localization, in which both Jews and Moslems had an interest, the Franciscans were deprived of this part of their residence in 1452. This, followed by similar successive maneuvers, urged them to ask—and they were vouchsafed—a decision from the Jerusalem court forbidding Jews to pass by the monastery of Sion and the Holy Sepulchre.[27]

24. United Nations Conciliation Commission for Palestine, Committee on Jerusalem, "The Holy Places," 22.

25. It has been argued that the first source identifying the tomb of David with the site of the Cenaculum was the Jewish traveler Benjamin of Tudela, who was in Jerusalem in 1169. For a review of the case and a counterargument, see Arce, "El sepulcro de David," 105–15.

26. Suriano, *Treatise on the Holy Land,* 123.

27. Arce, "The Custody of the Holy Land," 144.

The principal sites, as indicated by the nnmbers, are thus explained by the artist:

12-14. The Temple, now the Mosque of Omar.
29. Pilate's House.
30. Herod's House.
31. Supposed place of the Scourging.
32. Arch from which Christ was shown to the people.
33. Church of our Lady's Swoon.
34. Place where Simon of Cyrene came to help our Lord.
35. The Glutton's House.
36. The House of the Pharisee.
37. House of Veronica.
7. Judicial Gate.
38. Church of the Holy Sepulchre.
9. Mount Sion and the Cenacle.

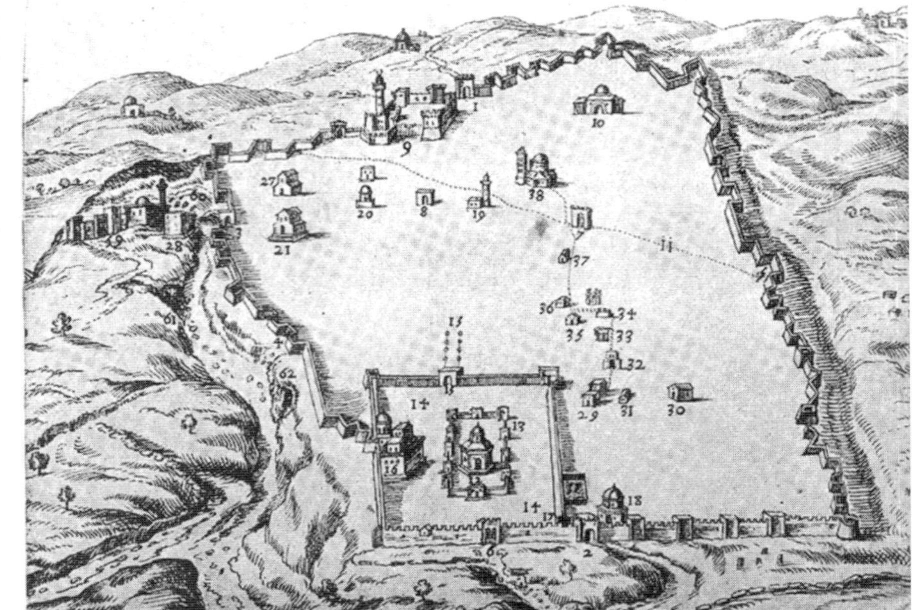

Fig. 34. Jerusalem, plan. Giovanni Cales's illustration for Vincenzo Favi, *Viaggio di Gerusalem*. From Thurston, *The Stations of the Cross,* modified by the author.

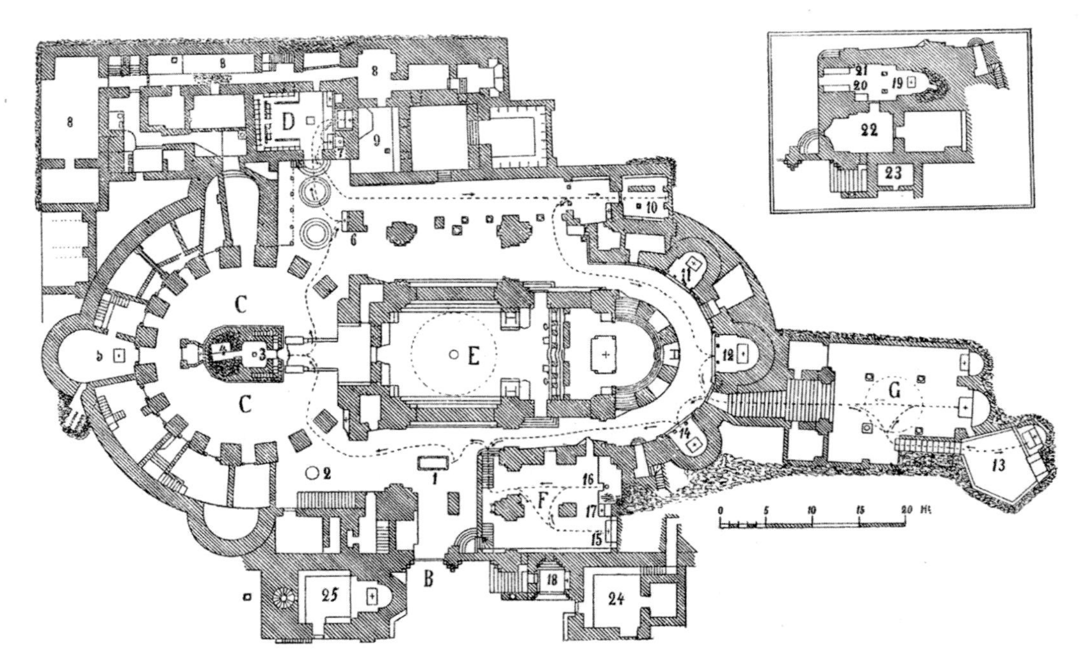

Fig. 35. Holy Sepulchre, Jerusalem, plan. Franciscan sites: *D,* Chapel of the Virgin; 7, scourging column; 8, cloister; 9, Holy Sepulchre; 15–17, section of Calvary; 13, altar in the Chapel of the Finding of the True Cross. Greek sites: *E,* choir; 10, Christ's prison; 12, Chapel of the Division of Jesus's Clothing. Armenian sites: 16, section of Calvary; 13, Chapel of the Finding of the True Cross; 19, Adam's Chapel; 20, 21, tombs of the Frankish kings. Jacobite site: *K,* chapel on the back of the Holy Sepulchre. Abyssinian sites: 14, Chapel of the Crown of Thorns; 23, place where Mary stood by the cross. Surian site: *G,* Chapel of St. Helen. Nestorian site: altar next to 7. Changing possession: 1, Stone of Unction. From Lemmens, *Die Franziskanner im Hl. Lande*.

The international ramifications of the contestation over sacred space in Jerusalem, all too familiar now, were certainly in place in the fifteenth and sixteenth centuries. The Franciscans engineered not only the exclusion of the Jews from the vicinity of the Christian holy places in Jerusalem but also the disruption of their transport from Spain to Palestine after the Spanish pogroms of 1391.[28] Indeed, the interdiction on the Jews sought by the Franciscans in Jerusalem was more radically pursued in early modernity in the cities of northern and central Italy.[29]

PILGRIM

In some remarkable ways, the Franciscans assumed the role previously played by the Knights Templar in the Holy Land.[30] From its origins in the first half of the fourteenth century, the Custody was charged with the guidance, instruction, and care of Latin pilgrims as well as with the guardianship, maintenance, defense, and rituals of the Catholic shrines of the Holy Land.[31] The Franciscans inevitably make their appearance in fifteenth- and sixteenth-century Western pilgrims' journals of their sojourn to the Holy Land. Three accounts suggest how pilgrimage worked: Margery Kempe's description of her journey to Jerusalem in 1413–15; the record made by his chaplain of Sir Richard Guylforde's pilgrimage in 1506; and Francesco Suriano's *Treatise on the Holy Land* of 1524, already quoted. These texts convey something of the political and physical encumbrances of travel. More important, the changing shape of Jerusalem's sacred topography in early modernity emerges from these narratives. By suggesting how the Holy City was understood by the Western traveler, the essays also provide some basis for construing the early functions of the Sacro Monte of Varallo. Of the many available accounts, English texts are privileged here and quoted in length in order to convey with as much immediacy as possible something of the early modern textures of seeing the city. The written accounts have a visual analog. A map of Jerusalem published by Giovanni Cales in 1616 illustrates the pilgrim's reading of the city's topography (fig. 34).[32] An impression of

28. For a brief but useful introduction to Jewish-Franciscan relations, see Schein, "La *Custodia Terrae Sanctae* franciscaine." For the Franciscans' role in the Spanish pogroms and for the emigration of Jews to Palestine, see Baer, *A History of the Jews in Christian Spain,* 1:150–59 and 2:58–62, 292–99.

29. The Franciscan antipathy to the Jews was well established in the thirteenth century. See Cohen, *The Friars and the Jews.*

30. See chapter 2.

31. In Bethlehem: the Grottos of the Nativity, the Milk Grotto, and Shepherds' Field; in Jerusalem: the Holy Sepulchre and Calvary, as well as the sites of the Flagellation, Gethsemane, "Dominus Flevit," and the Ascension; in Bethany: the house of Martha and Mary; in Siyagha (Mount Nebo): the Memorial of Moses; in 'Ain Karem: the House of Zachary, the Birthplace of the Baptist, the site where Mary met Saint Elizabeth, and the Desert of Saint John; in Galilee: the Basilica of the Annunciation in Nazareth and many others, including Mount Tabor, Cana, Tiberius, Capernaum, and the Church of the Primacy.

32. For a discussion of Jerusalem's place in the evolution of Western cartography, see Silver, "Mapped and Marginalized."

how late-medieval pilgrims moved through the space of the Church of the Holy Sepulchre is provided a modern plan made by Leonhard Lemmens O.F.M. for his study of the Franciscans in Jerusalem (fig. 35).[33]

The *Book of Margery Kempe,* which includes her pilgrimage to Jerusalem, is even more problematic as a historical source than most old texts.[34] It is unique in perhaps too many ways. This work, identified as the first autobiography in English, was produced by an illiterate. It provides the only known account of a late medieval/early modern woman's journey to the Holy Land. And the account is peculiarly personal. Despite questions about its authenticity, scholars have embraced the work as a genuine product of fifteenth-century piety. According to the story, Margery buys her contractual freedom from her husband and her fourteen children with an inheritance from her father and leaves for the Holy Land. She travels in the company of other English pilgrims, who vacillate between their dislike of her devout hysteria and their fear that she might actually be divinely inspired, repeatedly evicting her from their company and then soliciting her return. Having traveled overland from England to Venice and by ship from Venice to Jaffa, the pilgrims reach Jerusalem.

So they went forth into the Holy Land till they might see Jerusalem. And, when this creature [Margery], riding on an ass, saw Jerusalem, she thanked God with all her heart, praying him for his mercy that, as he had brought her to see this earthly city Jerusalem, he would grant her grace to see the blissful city Jerusalem above, the city of heaven. Our Lord Jesus Christ, answering to her thought, granted her to have her desire. Then, for the joy she had, and the sweetness that she felt in the dalliance with our Lord, she [swooned].[35]

Margery's collapse at the sight of Jerusalem presages even more dramatic public displays of piety at the holy sites of the city. The Franciscans introduce her first to the most important Christian memorials in Jerusalem: those enshrined in the Church of the Holy Sepulchre.

Then went they to the Temple [Holy Sepulchre] in Jerusalem, and they were let in on the one day at evensong time and abided therein till the next day at evensong time. Then the friars lifted up a cross and led the pilgrims about from one place to another where our Lord had suffered his pains and his passions, every man and woman bearing a wax candle in their hand. And the friars always, as they went about, told

33. Lemmens, *Die Franziskanner im Hl. Lande,* plate 8.

34. For the Middle English text, see Kempe, *The Book of Margery Kempe,* ed. Peck. For the translation into modern English, see Kempe, *The Book of Margery Kempe: A New Translation, Contexts, Criticism,* trans. Staley. References are to chapters in the text, so that either edition may be consulted. A few small modifications have been made in the translation. I want to thank Professor Gail Gibson for sharing with me her insights on Margery Kempe. I recommend Gibson's article, "St. Margery."

35. Kempe, chap. 28.

them what our Lord suffered in every place. And the . . . creature [Margery] wept and sobbed so plenteously as though she had seen our Lord with her bodily eye suffering his Passion at that time. Before her in her soul she saw him verily by contemplation, and that caused her to have compassion. And when they came up onto the Mount of Calvary, she fell down so that she might not stand or kneel but wallowed and twisted with her body, spreading her arms abroad, and cried with a loud voice as though her heart should have burst asunder, for in the city of her soul she saw verily and freshly how our Lord was crucified. Before her face she heard and saw in her ghostly sight the mourning of our Lady, of Saint John and Mary Magdalene. . . . And she had so great compassion and so great pain to see our Lord's pain that she might not keep herself from crying and roaring though she should have died from it. And this was the first cry that ever she cried in any contemplation. And this manner of crying endured many years after this time for aught that any man might do. . . . And she had [spells of hysterical weeping] so often that they made her right weak in her bodily powers, and, namely, if she heard of our Lord's Passion. And sometimes, when she saw the crucifix, or if she saw a man or a beast, where ever it were, had a wound or if a man beat a child before her or smote a horse or another beast with a whip.[36]

The site of the Crucifixion had a transformative affect on Margery. Her vision of the historical event conjured by the present reality of its physical setting was so intense that it affected her behavior for the rest of her life. Tears and wailing were the visible wounds of her empathic response to the crucified Christ. They were a feminized version of Francis's stigmata.

From Calvary, the Franciscans take Margery to the Sepulchre itself, then to the Stone of Unction, where Jesus had been prepared for burial. On another day, the Franciscans show the company the route Jesus traveled to his Crucifixion:

Their [Franciscan] guides told her where our Lord bore the cross on his back, and where his mother met with him, and how she swooned and fell down and he fell down also. And so they went forth all the morning till they came to Mount Sion. And ever this creature [Margery] wept abundantly, all the way that she went, for compassion of our Lord's Passion. In Mount Sion is the place where our Lord washed his disciples' feet and, a little there from, he made his Maundy [Last Supper; the Eucharist] with his disciples. And therefore this creature had great desire to take communion in that holy place where our merciful Lord Christ Jesus first consecrated his precious body in the form of bread, and gave it to his disciples And so she was, with great devotion and plenteous tears and boisterous sobbings, for in this place is plenary [or full] remission [for sins], and so there is in four other places in the Temple [Church of the Holy Sepulchre]. One is on the Mount of Calvary; another at the grave where our Lord was buried; the third is at the marble stone that his precious Body was laid on, when it

36. Ibid.

was taken from the Cross; the fourth is where the Holy Cross was buried; and in many other places in Jerusalem.[37]

Led by the Franciscans, Margery subsequently visits the other sacred sites, including that of the Pentecost and the tomb of the Virgin, where first Jesus and then Mary appear to her to assure her of her personal worthiness. Later she journeys to Bethlehem and other holy places beyond Jerusalem. Because of her incessant weeping and fasting, Margery is shunned by her traveling companions. In compensation, the Franciscans, she relates, embraced her "and gave her many great relics."[38] One of these may have been a measure of the tomb of Jesus, which Margery later exchanged for hospitality en route from Venice to Rome.[39] But Margery's piety was awarded with more than relics. As the passage above indicates, remissions, more commonly identified as indulgences, were earned by pilgrims by the arduousness of their travel and the promise of their penitence.[40] Indulgences, in turn, provided pilgrims the means of discharging the just price of their sins during their lifetimes rather than having to pay those debts after death by undergoing the pains of purgatory. A plenary indulgence remitted the whole of the temporal punishment fairly required by God for sin. Partial indulgences, indulgences for a particular number of days or years, only discharged a fraction of the liability. On leaving Jerusalem after her three-week sojourn, Margery is so anxious about her indulgence account that "then would she have turned again to Jerusalem for the great grace and ghostly comfort that she felt when she was there and in order to purchase herself more pardon." But Jesus himself assures her: "Daughter, as oftentimes as you say or think 'Worshipped be all those holy places in Jerusalem that Christ suffered bitter pain and passion in,' you shall have the same pardon as if you were there with your bodily presence, both for yourself and for all those that you will give it to." Jesus seems here to do the uncanonical: give a laywoman the power to award indulgences to others.[41] Later the pope, who had a legitimate power to offer remissions, awarded the same indulgences to those who witnessed the sites of the Passion on an Italian Holy Mountain as to those who witnessed them in the Holy Land.[42]

Margery Kempe's account of her journey to Jerusalem in the early fifteenth century presents a parody of a pilgrim's spiritual excess. The early sixteenth-century diary of Sir John Guylforde's chaplain, in contrast, offers a prosaic recording of dramatic religious conviction. The anonymous chaplain methodically transcribes, day by day, his and his companions' encounters with the holy. The pilgrims arrived by ship in Jaffa.

37. Ibid., chap. 29.

38. Ibid., chap. 30.

39. Ibid.

40. For the effect of indulgences on pilgrimage, see Miedema, "Following in the Footsteps of Christ."

41. Kempe, chap. 30.

42. For a fuller discussion of indulgences, see below.

We sent to Jerusalem for the [Franciscan] father warden of Mount Sion to come and see us conducted to Jerusalem, as the custom is. Not withstanding all our haste, we lay there in our Galley seven days before he came to us; the cause was for he could no sooner have the lords of Jerusalem and Rama at Layser to come to us, without whose presence and conduct there can no Pilgrim pass; which lords be all Mamluks and under the sultan. . . . At this Jaffa begins the Holy Land; and to every pilgrim at the first foot that he sets on land there is granted plenary remission.[43]

After a difficult trip from Jaffa, the pilgrims finally arrived in the Holy City:

Upon Monday, that was the last day of August, about 2 or 3 o'clock in the afternoon, we came to Jerusalem and were received into the Latin Hospital, called by some the Hospital of Saint John, and there we rested us that night, which hospital is right near the Temple of the Holy Sepulchre, and there the Gray Friars [Franciscans] of Mount Sion ministered wine unto us every day twice, and lent us also carpets to lie upon, for which every pilgrim recompensed the said Friars at their direction and power. . . . And always the warden of the said friars or some of his brethren by his assignment daily accompanied us, informing and showing us the holy places within the Holy Land. (Ibid., 17)

The following morning they begin their tour of the shrines of the city with Mount Sion. On their way there, the Franciscans identify particular locations associated with Jesus, his family, and his followers:

First the place where the Jews would have arrested and taken away the holy body of our blessed Lady when the apostles bore her to the valley of Josaphat to be buried. And thereby we come into a place where saint Peter, after he had denied our Lord thrice, went out of the house of Caiphas into a cave and wept bitterly. And a little from there we come into the church of the Angels, where sometime was the house of Annas the bishop [that is, the high priest], into which our savior Christ was first led from the Mount of Olives, where he suffered many injuries and specially there he took a hit from one of the bishop's servants. . . . From thence we went to a church of saint Savior, where sometime stood the great house of Caiphas, where as our blessed savior was scorned, his face covered and bloodied, and most egregiously beaten, and there suffered many afflictions all the night. There is also a little cave, where they shut him while the Jews had taken their counsel and determined what they would do with him, and it is yet called "Carcer Dni" [Prison of the Lord]. There is also in the same place the most part of the great stone that the Angel, as we read, removed from the door of the Sepulchre. . . . And going out of the same court in the high way on the right hand, in a corner, is a stone where our blessed Lady stood when Peter went out sore weeping, and his weeping was so much that he could give her no answer when she inquired of her sweet son; and there she, desirous to know of her son, most sorrowfully staid until in the morning that she saw them lead him

---

43. The translation into modern English is my own. Chaplain of Sir Richard Guylforde, *Pylgrymage of Sir Richard Guylforde to the Holy Land*, 16.

bound to the house of Pilate the president, wither she most sorrowfully followed him. A little from this church there appears a ruin of an old fallen church, where this most glorious virgin, after the death of our savior her son, dwelt and abode most devoutly for the space of fourteen years until the day of her holy Ascension, and there is a plenary remission [clene remyssyon]. Thereby is the place, and a stone lying, where our blessed Lady died and ascended to Heaven; there is also plenary remission. Nearby also is a part of a stone upon which Saint John the Evangelist often said mass before that blessed Lady, as her chaplain, after the ascension of the Lord. (Ibid., 18)

Also on the way to Mount Sion is the place where the Virgin made her daily devotions both before and after the Ascension. Nearby, the chaplain notes, were two stones: Jesus sat on one when he preached to the disciples, and on the other his mother, who attended his sermons (ibid., 19–20). The pilgrims then reach their destination: the Franciscan church of Sion. The space below the church had been identified as the burial place of David and Solomon and reordered as a mosque; Christians were not admitted. More accessible to them were other places of biblical significance associated with the site: the roasting pit where Jesus's paschal lamb was prepared and water warmed for his washing of the apostles' feet, and the site where David wrote the penitential psalms after his adultery with Bathsheba.

All these foresaid places thus visited, we entered into the place of Mount Sion, where is a right fair church, well vaulted, where at our first entrance the friars sang a solemn mass, and that done, he that sang the mass made a right holy sermon, and showed right devoutly the holiness of all the blessed chosen places of the Holy Land, and exhorted every man to confession and repentance, and so to visit the said holy places in cleanness of life, with such devotion as Almighty God would give unto them of his most special grace; and this sermon done, the Father Warden, with all his brethren, which be in number most commonly about thirty friars, dressed them in ornaments, and went in solemn procession from one holy place to another, whom we followed devoutly . . . and when so ever they come to any holy place, there they made a station, and declared unto us the mysteries of the same, we all bearing lights in our hands. (Ibid., 20–21)

The pilgrims are shown the place of the Last Supper and foot washing; in the loft above, the room of the descent of the Holy Ghost at Pentecost; in the chapel below, the site of the doubting Thomas. As the party returns to its sleeping quarters at the hospital, it also is shown the prison of Saint James and the place of the appearance of Jesus to the Marys after his Resurrection. After this long day of site-seeing, the pilgrims spend the entire night in pious devotion, locked, as Margery had been, in the Church of the Holy Sepulchre.

And you shall understand that the doors of the Temple of the Sepulchre be never opened by the Paynims [pagans or Muslims], but for the coming of pilgrims, at their great suit and cost, or else to change the friars that have the keeping of the holy place within the same temple. (Ibid., 23)

The chaplain identifies the parts of the church held by the Franciscans—namely the Sepulchre itself and the chapel marking the site where Jesus first appeared to the Virgin after his Resurrection—as well as those sections of the church controlled by other Christian communities, including most prominently the Greeks and the Armenians. He then describes the building:

The disposition . . . of the Holy Sepulchre is round at the west end and eastward formed after the making of a church, much like the form and making of the Temple at London, except it is far exceeding in greatness . . . ; and the great round part westward . . . , where stands the Holy Sepulchre of our Lord, which is made all of stone, roof and all, in the form of a little chapel; and first, at the entrance is a little door, where we come into a little round chapel, vaulted, otherwise called a cave [spelunke], of eight feet in breadth and as much in length; and from this we enter into a much less and lower door, and come into a little cave, and upon the right hand of the same, even within the said low door, is the very holy Sepulchre of our Lord, covered with a white marble stone, the length whereof is eight feet, and there is no light into the said little cave of the Sepulchre by no manner whatsoever, but the light is there ministered by many lamps hanging within the said cave over the Sepulchre. (Ibid., 24)

The Franciscans lead the pilgrims in a solemn procession around the sites within the church. "And at every station was showed unto us by one of the friars the mysteries and holiness of the place where they made their stations." At each "station" appropriate hymns are sung and prayers offered. The significant places in the Franciscans' own Chapel of the Virgin include the high altar (the exact location of the first post-Resurrection meeting of Jesus and his mother); a large piece of a pillar (the column to which Jesus was bound in Pilate's house); a window where Saint Helena placed the True Cross after finding it, and which yet retains a fragment of the relic; and finally a round stone in the middle marking the place where the cross established its identity by raising to life a dead woman (ibid., 24–25). The procession next visits a series of hallowed locations: two round white marble stones, ten feet apart, marking where Jesus and the Magdalene stood in their first meeting after the Resurrection; a corner of an aisle where there is a little vault which served as the prison of the Savior while the cross was prepared; an altar where Jesus's clothes were divided in a dice game; a crypt chapel where Helena stood before finding the True Cross and where she later came to say her prayers; an even lower chapel where the cross, spear, nails, and crown of thorns were found; back at the main level of the church, an altar under which there was a piece of stone much like a piece of a pillar, upon which the Savior sat in the court of Pilate, where he was crowned with thorns, scorned, and buffeted; the elevated chapel of Calvary, which "is marvelous holy and venerable above all others," where there is the hole in which the cross was placed and the rift in the rock made at the moment of Jesus's death. Here the chaplain comments:

And it is of truth, as they say there, and as it is assigned by token of a fair stone laid for remembrance, that our blessed Lady and saint John the Evangelist stood not above upon the highest part of the Mount of Calvary at the passion of our Lord, as it is painted and carved in many places, but she stood somewhat beneath, before her dear son, face to face, at the time of his precious death. (Ibid., 26–27)

The list of sites continues: below Calvary is another chapel in which was found the skull of Adam; a white stone marks the location of the lamentation; the Sepulchre; and finally returning to the Chapel of the Virgin. After daybreak, the pilgrims leave the Holy Sepulchre, noting as they go to their hostel the broad stone on which Abraham offered Isaac and the altar on which Melchizedek offered his sacrifice (ibid., 28).

The same day, the friars take the pilgrims to visit the holy sites within Jerusalem: "And so this day aforesaid we visited all the long way by which our savior Christ was led from the house of Pilate to the place of his Crucifixion." This itinerary included the house of Veronica, where her veil, now in Rome, was impressed with the face of Jesus; Dives' house; the place where Jesus warned weeping women of the fate of Jerusalem; the site where Simon Cyrene was forced to bear the cross; the church of Saint Mary of the Spasm, where the Virgin collapsed after seeing Jesus's suffering ("the Saracens have often attempted to build there but their edifices would never stand"); a street with an arch on which stood two white stones—upon which Jesus and Pilate stood opposite each other at the time of judgment; the house of Pilate; the house of Herod; the house of Saint Anne ("and in a vault underneath is the very same place where our blessed Lady was born; and there is a plenary remission. The Saracens will suffer no man to come into this place but privately or for bribes, because it is their mosque. Relics of the stones of the place where our Lady was born is remedy and consolation to women that travail of child"); Probatica Piscina, site of Jesus's healings; and the house where the sins of Mary Magdalene were forgiven. The pilgrims again spend the night in the Holy Sepulchre. The next day the Franciscans take them to shrines in the Jerusalem suburbs.

The pace of pilgrimage was killing. Six days after arriving in Jerusalem, Sir Richard Guylforde died. The Franciscans saw to his burial "with as much a solemn service as might be done for him" (ibid., 40).

The third account of Jerusalem included here was written not by a pilgrim but by a friar. Francesco Suriano, a Venetian merchant, took the Franciscan habit in 1475. His practical knowledge of the East was put to use in his narrative: he served as Custos between 1493 and 1496 and again between 1512 and 1515. Suriano's fiscal responsibility is documented by his attention to functional matters. He suggests, for instance, something of the expense of transport: "Though . . . the Venetians allot two galleys for the service and transport of the pilgrims [once a year leaving after the Ascension], they do not, however, convey them *gratis,* nor for the love of God; but according to the rank and condition of the person, they make them pay 50, 60, 40 and some 30 ducats."[44] The Venetians, the author notes, were obligated to take Franciscans more cheaply. Suriano wrote his trea-

44. Suriano, *Treatise on the Holy Land,* 33.

tise for the benefit of his cloistered sister, a Poor Clare in the Monastery of S. Lucia in Foligno, near Assisi. It takes the rhetorical form of answers to her questions: Why is it called the Holy Land? Because the prophets, saints, and, most important, Jesus, came from there. What was the cause of its sanctity? Just as God makes the heart of the animal first, so he made this land the locus of the spirit (ibid., 21–23). Suriano's explanation of how the somatic touch of Jesus sanctified the land provides an epigraph of this chapter (ibid., 28–29).

Suriano begins his description of the Jerusalem pilgrimage with the Holy Sepulchre and a list of the sacred sites within the complex, along with the indulgences attached to them. He describes the Holy Sepulchre numerically:

And first when you enter by the main door of the church, at a distance of twenty braccia, you find the place where our Lord Jesus Christ was anointed at the time of his burial. Then twenty braccia to the left is the Holy Sepulchre. Upon which is a dome of fifteen cubits high, worked in mosaic and supported by fifteen small columns of fine red porphyry. Upon this there is another smaller one, and in it there is a lamp hanging that is always burning. The Sepulchre is walled all round and forms as it were a small cell, covered inside and outside with very delicate marble slabs. And this room has a small entrance, two cubits high and one in width, where stood the stone that closed the monument. In front of this entrance there is a stone set in the ground upon which sat the angel [who greeted the Marys]. (Ibid., 44)

How the most sacred of Christian sites colonized the territory of the Hebrew Bible is revealed in Suriano's answer to the question, why was Jesus crucified on Calvary? He lists all the testamental events that happened at the site: here was Jacob's ladder and his three pillow-stones; here Jacob wrestled with the angel; here Elias ate unleavened bread; here Melchizedek met Abraham; and here Isaac was offered by his father, Abraham. Indeed, the Holy Sepulchre is the center of the world (ibid., 24, 36).

Suriano also describes the other pilgrimage sites of the city, carefully recording distances and indulgences: the house of Veronica, the house of the rich epicurean, the house of Mary Magdalen, the place of Simon of Cyrene, the place of Jesus's "weep not over me" comment, the church of St. Mary of the Spasm, the two stones from the judgment of Pilate, the house of Pilate, the house of Herod, the church of the Nativity of the Virgin, the pool of Bethesda, the Temple of Solomon, the great church of the Presentation of Our Lady, the Golden Gate "by which Christ entered the Temple on Palm Sunday," the Beautiful Gate, "where St. Peter healed the infirm man," the portico of Solomon, "from which Christ often refuted the Jews," the Church of the Ascension. Woven into the descriptions of the sacred city is the violence involved in its control: "The Saracens dwell in the house of Pilate and that profane place has never been dedicated to things spiritual. Though, where the Tribunal stood and where Christ was scourged there was built a round chapel in circumference fifty braccia which had a marvelous apse of ultramarine blue, but at present it is a horse-stall full of manure" (ibid., 104). The agonistic conditions of the Franciscan presence in

Jerusalem are also written into the narrative. The treatise's emphasis on Franciscan custodial and spiritual privileges as well as its descriptions of Jewish and Muslim transgressions against Christian persons and properties suggests the contentious and provisional nature of Franciscan control (ibid., 80). The shrillness of the text's assertion of the legitimacy of Franciscan claims is evidence of the precariousness of the order's hold on Jerusalem.

The stories told by Margery Kempe, the chaplain of Sir Richard Guylforde, and Francesco Suriano are very different from those reported by earlier pilgrims like Egeria in the early Christian period or the Anonymous Pilgrim whose text is dated to the mid-fourteenth century.[45] Pilgrims no longer traveled independently or in small groups. Rather, they booked package tours, which included round-trip travel with first-class, business-class, and tourist accommodations. Special deals were offered to those with privileged professional affiliations. Within Palestine, the Franciscans had become the organizing agents—the Thomas Cook and Sons—of pilgrimage. Travel within Palestine was measured in days and weeks, not months or years, and restricted to sites under the supervision of the order. By the fifteenth century, pilgrimage had already taken on some of the practical aspects of modern tourism, if not its commercial secularism.

INTENTION

In addition to indicating the changed character of pilgrimage, the narratives of Margery Kempe, the chaplain of Sir Richard Guylforde, and Francesco Suriano provide access to the particular Jerusalem that Varallo was meant to recapitulate. These texts also inform speculation about Bernardino Caimi's intentions in his establishment of the Sacro Monte of Varallo. The distinguished art historian Michael Baxandall established the place of intention in understanding the artwork. Intention, he argues, is "not narrating mental events" but documenting a work's relation to the social circumstances of its production.[46] The discussion here of Caimi's "intentions" has nothing to do with reconstructing individual consciousness but imaging the historical conditions or ground against which his actions appear coherent and intelligible.

Modern assessments of the Sacro Monte commonly assume that the enterprise was a response to the difficulties of travel to Jerusalem.[47] An inscription over the door of the Holy Sepulchre at Varallo is explicit:

On the seventh day of October, 1491, the magnificent Milanus Scarognini, with his own resources, put in place this Sepulchre containing Christ. The most reverend and

45. Anonymous Pilgrim, *Guide Book to Palestine*. For Egeria, see chapter 1 of the present text.

46. Baxandall, *Patterns of Intention*, 72.

47. Riccardo Pacciani has speculated productively on the causes of the *sacri monti*. He argues that they had three specific purposes: to maintain the life of the pilgrimage when access to the Holy Land sites was extremely difficult; to promote a spirituality that internalized pilgrimage; and to formulate experimentally the ideal city, using contemporary humanistic models. Pacciani and Vannini, *La "Gerusalemme" di S. Vivaldo in Valdelsa*, 59.

pious Friar of the Observant Minors Bernardinus Caimi of Milan devised the sacred places on this mountain so that he who could not travel might see this Jerusalem.[48]

Caimi constructed a surrogate Jerusalem at Varallo to compensate for the Holy City's relative unavailability. Certainly, judging from Suriano's account, pilgrimage was very expensive.[49] The costs and charges were high to get to the Holy Land, and exorbitant also after the pilgrim arrived. Pilgrimage was the most important revenue-producing industry in Mamluk Jerusalem; the admission charge at the Church of the Holy Sepulchre was the city's single greatest source of cash revenue.[50] Only the relatively well-to-do could afford to make the journey to the East in early modernity. Reading the Sacro Monte as a surrogate for an inaccessible Jerusalem does not, however, fully satisfy the question of intention. It provides no answers for such questions as why at the end of the fifteenth century? Why at Varallo?

Samuel Butler gives an alternative explanation for the construction of the Varallo Jerusalem: "It was an attempt to stem the torrent of reformed doctrines already surging over many an Alpine pass, and threatening a moral invasion as fatal to the spiritual power of Rome as earlier physical invasions of Northmen had been to her material power."[51] Varallo, Butler posits, was constructed as a Catholic bulwark against northern dissent. He seems here to offer a topographic reason for the *sacri monti.* But the vision of Varallo as a dam blocking the flood of heretical ideas flowing through the crevices in the Alps seems, frankly, ridiculous. The Sacro Monte of Varallo was founded a generation before Luther published his Ninety-five Theses (1517). Clearly, Bernardino Caimi did not build at Varallo in order to frustrate an unknown monk in Wittenberg. Nevertheless, it might be entertainingly argued that although Varallo did not stem the southward tide of Protestantism, it may have contributed to the northward flow of a Franciscan-inspired "theology of the cross"—that is, the religious conviction that the revelation of Christ crucified was the vehicle of salvation—which so engaged Luther.[52] In making Varallo a reaction to Protestantism, Butler privileges the Protestant north. His notion of a "moral invasion" of the north that threatened the "spiritual power of Rome" occurred not in the remote past of the late fifteenth and early sixteenth century but in the author's own late

48. Although the present inscription does not date from the origins of the building, Morone's comments make it clear that the Varallo structure was always presented as an exact replication of the Holy Sepulchre in Jerusalem. For a Latin transcription, see Galloni, *Uomini e fatti celebri in Valle-Sesia,* 84.

49. One Venetian ducat of 1500 was worth about $30 in 2003, so the cheapest fare for a lay traveler would have been $900.

50. Lutfi, *Al-Quds al-Mamlûkiyya,* 136. This, of course, included Jewish and Muslim pilgrims, as well as non-Frankish Christians.

51. S. Butler, *Ex Voto,* 44. Butler's early and isolated interest in Varallo compensates for the limitations of his explanatory device. His position is, however, repeated by Rudolf Wittkower, who has less of an excuse for such an argument. Wittkower, "'Sacri Monti' in the Italian Alps," 175.

52. For an introduction to the ways in which Luther's *theologia cruces* both continues and rejects later medieval meditations on the Passion, see Tomlin, "The Medieval Origins of Luther's Theology of the Cross."

nineteenth-century present. The basic assumption of his entertaining volume is that the Sacro Monte's legitimate function is aesthetic, not religious. For Butler, Varallo is important not for its sanctity but for its art.

Tradition provided the Sacro Monte's local audience with more compelling explanations of Caimi's foundation of the site. According to one story, Caimi sought a landscape that matched the appearance of Jerusalem; according to others the site was revealed to him in a dream or by the sweet singing of a flock of birds.[53] The broader historical and topographic circumstances of the Sacro Monte encourage new foundational stories for a more academic consumption. Whether chosen by God or by Caimi, Varallo perfectly realized the practical requirements of a regional pilgrimage shrine. The setting was extraordinarily beautiful, and remains so. As a pilgrimage destination, the site needed to *feel* remote; immediate proximity to a major city would compromise the Sacro Monte's heterotopic force. As a surrogate for distant travel, however, the site needed to *be* obtainable. Varallo is set at the edge of the heartland of Caimi's own Franciscan order. Saint Francis himself and many of his most renowned followers, from Bonaventure to Bernardino da Feltre, were the products of the mercantile urban culture of northern and central Italy. Many of the great cultural and commercial centers that promoted the financial and intellectual innovations of early modernity were also found there—from Turin and Milan to Florence and Venice, from the Piedmont to the Marches. Though traveling to the Sacro Monte of Varallo seemed a distant journey, it remained part of the Franciscan neighborhood.

INTEREST

It is no coincidence that the Franciscans—the mendicant order that most disdained possessions—emerged at the time and place of Europe's most dramatic progress in monetization. The urban bourgeois legacy of the most prominent Franciscans defined the order. Money was thus as central to Franciscan identity as it was to that of J. P. Morgan, but through its rejection rather than its embrace. Most literally, Franciscans identified themselves by denying their inheritance. Francis established the model for his followers by publicly stripping himself naked and returning even his clothes to his father.

His carnally minded father led this child of grace, now stripped of his money, before the bishop of the town. He wanted to have Francis renounce into his hands his family possessions and return everything he had. A true lover of poverty, Francis showed himself eager to comply; he went before the bishop without delaying or hesitating. He did not wait for any words nor did he speak any, but immediately took off his clothes and gave them back to his father. Then it was discovered that the man of God had a hairshirt next to his skin under his fine clothes. Moreover, drunk with remarkable fervor, he even took off his underwear, stripping himself completely naked before all. . . .

---

53. For Caimi's own account of miracles associated with the Sacro Monte of Varallo, see Motta, *Il Beato Bernardino Caimi*, 17–19.

They brought him a poor, cheap cloak of a farmer who worked for the bishop. Francis accepted it gratefully and with his own hand marked a cross on it with a piece of chalk, thus designating it as the covering of a crucified man.[54]

The identity of the Franciscans depended on their lack of money.[55] Their abhorrence of money is passionately expressed in chapter 8 of the Rule for the Order of Friars Minor (*Regula non bullata*) presented to Pope Innocent III in 1221:

That brothers not receive money. . . . No brother, wherever he is or wherever he goes, should in any manner either receive or demand money or coins, neither for need of clothing, books, or for the price of work, or indeed on any occasion, except out of the manifest necessity of sick brothers, because we must not have more use and regard for money and coins than for stones. And the devil wishes to blind those who seek or esteem them more than stones. Therefore we should be careful that we, who have given up everything, do not lose the kingdom of heaven for such a limited thing. And if anywhere we find coins, of these we should care no more than the dust, which we tread under our feet, which is the vanity of vanities and all vanity. And if it should happen, and may it not come to be, that some brother is found with money or collecting or having coins . . . then all of us brothers must hold him as a false brother and apostate and thief. . . . And by no means may brothers receive or allow receipt nor beg or organize requests for alms nor money for any house or place; and never go with a person to such places of money and coin. . . . Let all brothers beware that they do not travel the world for dirty lucre.[56]

Only an echo of this strong language against money was heard in the rule that was finally accepted by Pope Honorius III in 1223.[57] Nevertheless, Franciscan distinctiveness continued to reside in the order's promotion of poverty.

Though contempt for money was perhaps the Franciscans' most conspicuous characteristic, the order's involvement with money was not limited to its refusal. Franciscans thought very seriously about money.[58] The author of the first surviving published treatise on double-entry bookkeeping, the "father of accounting," was a Franciscan, Luca Pacioli.[59] Friars Minor are to be counted among the greatest economic thinkers of the Middle Ages. Alexander of Hales (1170/85–1245), Peter John Olivi (1248–98), John Duns Scotus (ca. 1270–1308), and San Bernardino da Siena (1380–1444) all contributed to an understanding

54. Bonaventure, "Life of St. Francis," 193–94.

55. For the ironies involved in Saint Francis's rejection of wealth from a modern, liberal perspective, see Wolf, *The Poverty of Riches*.

56. Francis of Assissi, *Regula non bullata* (1221).

57. Francis of Assissi, *Regula bullata* (1223).

58. For a thorough discussion of refinements in thinking about property brought about by the debates between the 1250s and the 1320s concerning Franciscan poverty, see Mäkinen, *Property Rights in the Late Medieval Discussion on Franciscan Poverty*.

59. Pacioli, *Summa de arithmetica*. For distinct perspectives and references to earlier literature, see Fischer, "Luca Pacioli on Business Profits"; Yamey, "Scientific Bookkeeping and the Rise of Capitalism."

of exchange that evolved concurrently with the Western market.[60] Raymond de Roover, the great twentieth-century economic historian of the Middle Ages, wrote a book on Bernardino da Siena, a Franciscan, and Antonino of Florence, a Dominican, subtitled *The Two Great Economic Thinkers of the Middle Ages*. He underlines their importance:

> *Economists may be dismayed at the uncomfortable thought that two toothless, emaciated, and ascetic saints should perhaps be considered as the originators of [modern] utility theory. Incredible as it may sound, such seems to be the case. San Bernardino and Sant'Antonio developed a value theory based on scarcity and utility, both objective and subjective. Today's economic theorists may scoff at this distinction between virtuositas (usefulness) and complacibilitas (desirability), but I am not so sure that [modern economists] are right in pegging their theory entirely on subjective preferences.*[61]

In the end, de Roover concludes that the Franciscan's contribution to economic thought was greater than that of the Dominican "because of [San Bernardino's] ability to write synthesis and to attempt economic analysis."[62] Despite their own poverty, Franciscans were among those of the thirteenth through fifteenth centuries who thought the most deeply and productively about other people's wealth.

The Franciscans' intellectual interest in money is perhaps a little surprising. Even more unexpected was their effective intervention in its actual circulation. Late medieval Christian anxiety over money and its potential to contaminate the soul was expressed in heightened usury-consciousness. At the beginning of the fourteenth century, the identification of interest as usury was still independent of the percentage of return. Whether a borrower was charged 10 percent or 110 percent of the principal was irrelevant. Certainly, exceptions came to be recognized. Interest might be charged if the lender lost expected income by loaning money that she intended to profitably invest, for example in buying seed to plant (*lucrum cessans* [missing gain]) or fixing a house that could be rented (*damnum emergens* [obvious loss]). Two other exceptions to usury were recognized later. The *poena conventionalis* (agreed penalty) was a fine to be paid to the lender for the late return of the borrowed sum, and *periculum sortis* (danger money) was interest taken in compensation for the danger involved in lending, for example for a loan to a merchant for a foreign venture. But these are compensatory monies, not profit.[63] All interest for profit was still usury and a sin.

---

60. For a perfect introduction to the Franciscans and economic thought, see Langholm, *Economics in the Medieval Schools*. I don't know if scholars of the Franciscan movement have compared the order to the supercompanies of the fourteenth century, but there are engaging parallels. For the supercompanies, see Hunt, *The Medieval Super-Companies;* Hunt and Murray, *A History of Business in Medieval Europe*, 1200–1550.

61. De Roover, *San Bernardino of Siena and Sant'Antonino of Florence*, 41.

62. Ibid., 42.

63. Kelly, *Aquinas and Modern Practices of Interest Taking*, 32–33.

A remarkable shift occurs in 1515. In his bull *Inter multiplices nostrae solicitudinis curas,* Pope Leo X allows that a low rate of interest might not, after all, be usury:

Monte di pietà, an institution of Christian piety, may licitly charge money for outlays, losses, and even for a moderate return.[64]

The bull of 1515 predicts the modern understanding of usury as *excessive* interest. The Franciscans were its prophets.[65]

The *monte di pietà,* subject of the papal bull of 1515, emerged in northern and central Italy in the second half of the fifteenth and early sixteenth centuries. The term *mons*—mountain, mass, great rock—was traditionally connected with money as well as with landscapes. In Italy there were, among other monetary mountains, *montes profani,* which acted as banks or insurance agents; *mons mortuorum,* which functioned as funerary societies; and *mons dotis,* a trust fund for children.[66] The *monte di pietà*—money mountain of piety—was a bank for the poor that lent money using goods as collateral. It was, in other words, a publicly run pawnshop. A comparison with modern pawnshops conveys some sense of how these institutions functioned:

Pawnbroking has been characterized as a necessary evil, and while its evils are small compared with the necessities which it supplies, they are conspicuous enough to demand legislative attention and public control. In the course of his business, the average pawnbroker will lend money on the security of any article of value not of a perishable nature that can be delivered into his possession, and without making any inquiry as to the character or responsibility of the applicant or regarding the ownership of the property offered. It may be an article of jewelry worth thousands of dollars, or it may be a household utensil or piece of wearing apparel worth a dollar; it is acceptable collateral to the pawnbroker if, in his judgment, he should be able to sell it for an amount at least equal to his loan, accrued interest and expenses of sale should it not be redeemed. . . . It is a service which may be just as indispensable in one emergency as the services of a doctor or a lawyer in another.[67]

This description of pawning, published in New York in 1924 as a background study for pending legislation on pawning practices, suggests that some things haven't changed. Pawning is a social necessity. Those who lack the credit to conduct business with banks must have access to money from another legitimate source to cope with financial crises which often, like bad health, are beyond

64. In Roman Catholic Church, *Bullarum privilegiorum ac diplomatum Romanorum Pontificum amplissima collectio,* 3:408–9.

65. For an accessible introduction to the relation between the Franciscans and the *monte di pietà,* see Parsons, "Bernadino of Feltre and the Montes Pietatis."

66. Holzapfel, *Die Anfänge der Montes Pietatis (1462–1515),* 18–19. Like everyone else who has considered the *monte di pietà,* I am very dependent on Holzapfel. His remains the classic work in the field.

67. Raby, *The Regulation of Pawnbroking,* 5.

their control. Corresponding concerns are expressed in support of the *monte di pietà* in early modern Italy.[68] The modern definition of acceptable possessions to be held against loans might also be applied to the *monte di pietà*. Any possession of value could be pawned. The 1924 document also emphasizes the need for government control of loans. Here differences between the past and the present emerge. Today, civic oversight of lending is limited. Indeed, the investigations of Citigroup's involvement with "predatory lending practices" suggests that now government supervision is rather too lax.[69] American pawnbrokers are expected to propose an exchange "without making any inquiry as to the character or responsibility of the applicant or regarding the ownership of the property offered." Early modern Roman Catholic Italy required stricter regulation than does the neoconservative America of utility theory and rampant individualism. Officials of the *monte di pietà* interrogated their applicants to establish their character and insure the ethical legitimacy of their need.

Other, more significant differences between the modern American and early modern Italian pawning institutions are not, however, revealed through a discussion of the quoted passage. Piety, not profit, was the object of the *monte di pietà,* as its name suggests. A *monte di pietà* was established by a city for the good of the community, rather than by an entrepreneur for personal profit; it was a civic institution operated by the state, not a private business. Funding for the *monte di pietà* might come in part from the government, but pious donations from individuals were also usually involved. The private benefactors of the *monte di pietà* in many cases received some benefit from their bounty—in the form of a safe depository for funds, a source of limited income, or more commonly in the form of indulgences.[70] But the *monte di pietà* was the product of a social desire that far exceeded the pawnshop's provision of affordable money for the poor and a living for its operator: it was promoted by the Franciscans as the means by which a city might rid itself of its Jews.[71]

---

68. For instance, in the sermons of Bernardino da Feltre, *Sermoni del beato Bernardino Tomitano da Feltre,* vol. 2.

69. Beckett, "Citigroup Is Near a Settlement of 'Predatory Lending' Charges."

70. For an excellent introduction to the workings of the institution, see Holzapfel, *Die Anfänge der Montes Pietatis (1462–1515)*.

71. A commemorative inscription in Savona's meeting hall naming Pope Sixtus IV documents the inextricable relation between Jews and the *monte di pietà;* quoted from Holzapfel, 65n1:

Impia quam coluit proles judaica Sedem,
Hanc jussit Sixtus Papa subesse piam.
Foenus in hac dudum cives sorbebat egenos,
Quos pietatis opus nunc iuvat aere pio.
Octoginta simul centum quater adiice mille
Annos, quo Pietas tempore structa fuit.

[The seat which the impious Jewish race occupied, this [seat] Pope Sixtus made pious under him. Formerly usury was consuming the poor citizens who a work of piety now aids with its pious air. Add a thousand years to four hundred and eighty—this is when piety was built.]

I want to thank Bart Huelsenbeck for his corrections to my translation.

In the twelfth and thirteenth centuries, small and often very expensive loans had been offered in Italian cities by their own citizens. Growing anxiety about the sinfulness of usury precipitated legislation barring Christians from lending money (practicing usury). To meet the needs of those in need, a small number of Jews were, for a fee, given permission to lend at strictly controlled interest rates. The Jews profited the state; they also answered the financial desires of the elites as well as the impoverished. In the later fourteenth and fifteenth centuries, resentment of the Jews escalated into violence, precipitated on occasion by Franciscan preachers. In his Lenten sermons of 1475 in Trent, the Franciscan Bernardino da Feltre (d. 1494), an extraordinarily popular preacher, denounced the Jews, warning that God would soon reveal their iniquity. A few days later the body of Simon, a three-year-old Christian child, was discovered, and the Jews of Trent were accused of his ritual murder. They were imprisoned, tortured, and many were executed. By mid-1476, "blessed Simon of Trent" had reportedly performed 129 miracles; in 1478 Pope Sixtus IV formally endorsed the proceedings against the Jews. The city of Trent profited greatly from the new cult by becoming a popular pilgrimage destination.[72] Bernardino da Feltre's anti-Judaism was enmeshed with his promotion of the *monte di pietà*:

Here is victory. . . . I would speak to you now of the holy mountain of piety [the pawn bank]. Truly here is a victory that conquers the world, one that is pleasing to God, averts sin, saves the soul, nourishes the body, assists the poor, lightens the load of the rich, and drives the Jews into exile.[73]

Scholars debate which came first for him: his hatred of the Jews or his love of the *monte di pietà*.[74] To eliminate the Jews required the establishment of financial institutions that would meet the needs of the poor in the absence of Jewish pawnshops. Correspondingly, the establishment of the *monte di pietà* required the elimination of Jewish competition. The Jews were not disenfranchised without a struggle. They themselves—as well as the civil authorities to whom their tolls were paid—opposed the *monte di pietà*.[75] Moreover, those borrowers who would rather not make public the reasons for their need, preferred to deal with the Jews. Venice never evicted its Jewish bankers.[76]

---

72. According to a popular hagiographic collection, "The synagogue was destroyed, and a chapel was erected on the spot where the child was martyred. God honored this innocent victim with many miracles. The relics lie in a stately tomb in St. Peter's church at Trent: and the name occurs in the Roman Martyrology. See the "authentic" account of Tiberinus, the physician, who inspected the child's body." Butler, "St. Simon, an Infant, Martyr at Trent," 3:243–44.

73. Bernardino da Feltre, *Sermoni del beato Bernardino Tomitano da Feltre,* 1.185.13–15. Symptomatically prominent in the presentation of this publication of Bernardino's sermons are Giordano dell'Amore, president of the Cassa di Risparmio delle Provincie Lombarde (which is located in Milan on the Via Monte di Pietà) and Gino Barbieri, the professor of economic history at the University of Verona.

74. Meneghin, "Bernardino da Feltre"; Segre, "Bernardino da Feltre." For the effect of the Franciscans on the Jews of a single community, see Simonsohn, *History of the Jews in the Duchy of Mantua.*

75. For usury and Jewish law, see Stein, "The Development of the Jewish Law on Interest."

76. Pullan, "Jewish Banks and Monti di Pietà."

Franciscan animosity toward the Jews was not limited to conflicts of interest over banks. The friars—Dominicans even more so than Franciscans—were consistently hostile to the Jews. The mendicant orders contributed to the politics of eviction in the expulsion of Jews from European cities and states throughout the later fifteenth century.[77] The successful Franciscan move to interdict Jews from the vicinity of the Holy Sepulchre and their monastery on Sion inscribed in Jerusalem on a small scale what was occurring in Europe on a large one. A Jew-free Jerusalem was, however, only fully realized in the *sacri monti*.

RESEMBLANCE/DISSEMBLANCE

The *monte di pietà* and the *sacri monti* were both expressions of a Franciscan commitment to redistributing the increased material and spiritual resources of the West to a broader segment of the population.[78] Whether in the form of money or of chits remitting their possessors from time in purgatory, the Franciscans worked to make that excess available to the Christian poor. Their attempt to eliminate the Jews both in Jerusalem and in the West reveals the broader theological project of which charity was a part. Poor relief was integral to the spiritual revival of a homogeneously Christian Europe. Franciscan efforts to establish pawn banks in the later fifteenth and early sixteenth centuries concentrated on northern and central Italy. It was within this same spatial and chronological terrain that the Franciscans also successfully promoted *sacri monti*. Over a dozen *sacri monti* still survive today in northern Italy and Switzerland, most with Franciscan connections.[79] Two of these complexes, the *sacri monti* of San Vivaldo near Florence and that of Varese north of Milan, provide a historical frame for Caimi's Sacro Monte of Varallo.

---

77. Cohen, *The Friars and the Jews*.

78. The *monte di pietà* is tangibly linked to the Jews; it is less tangibly associated with the East. Philippe de Mézières (1327?–1405), who first clearly articulated the institution's anti-Jewish function as well as its administrative form, came from a long experience in the East. The Franciscan promoter of the first successfully established *monte di pietà* in Mantua preached on the *monte* immediately upon his return from the Holy Land. Mézières, *Le Songe du Vieil Pelerin*, 2:38–9.

79. *Sacri monti* may still be visited at Orta, Crea, Santi Trinità di Ghiffa, Belmonte, Domodossola, Montrigone, Graglia, Andorno, Montà d'Alba, Arona, Monte Berico di Vicenza, Torricella Verzate, Cerveno, and Sasso di Locarno. For a clear introduction to these sites in English, see Cannon Brookes, "The Sacri Monti of Lombardy and the Piedmont." Not all of these *sacri monti* are devoted to Jesus's life, and not all were finished. For the incomplete project of Arona devoted to Carlo Borromeo, see Langé, "L'omaggio incompiuto di F. M. Richini a S. Carlo Borromeo per il Sacro Monte di Arona." For an imaginative approach to its completion, see "Per il completamento del sacro monte de San Carlo ad Arona." For the series devoted to the life of Saint Francis, see Schlumberger, "Un théâtre de la foi: le Sacro Monte d'Orta." For the different expressions of piety in France, see Bresc-Bautier, "Les chapelles de la mémoire." There replicas of the Holy Sepulchre were built, but not within the same elaborate narrative context as the Italian *sacri monti*. "Calvaries" were, however, popular in France after the Revolution. There were earlier representations of Jerusalems, but none that I know of with sculptural representations of the events that occurred on the various sites. See Pieper, "The Garden of the Holy Sepulchre in Görlitz."

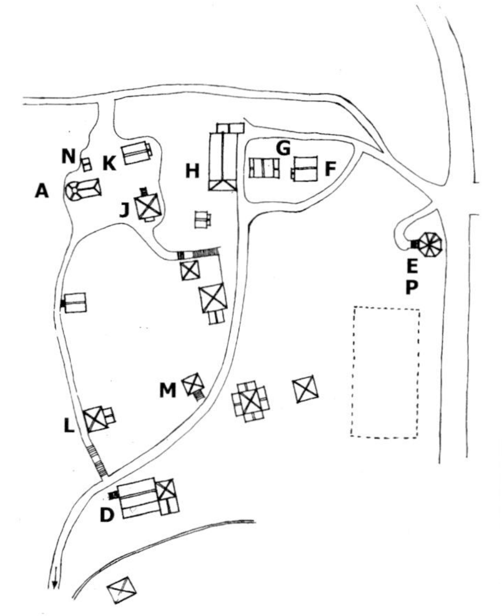

Fig. 36. (*above, left*) San Vivaldo, Tuscany, plan of the complex. San Vivaldo guidebook, modified by the author. *A,* Holy Sepulchre; *D,* Cenacle; *E,* Ascension; *F,* house of Pilate; *G,* house of Herod (now missing); *H,* Our Lady of Sorrows; *J;* road to Golgotha; *K,* prison of Jesus; L, house of Caiaphas; *M,* house of Annas; *N, Noli me tangere; P,* Valley of Jehosaphat.

Fig. 37. (*above*) Holy Sepulchre, San Vivaldo, Tuscany, exterior. Author photo.

Fig. 38. (*left*) Giovanni Della Robbia, Italian, 1469–1529. *Christ and the Samaritan Woman at the Well,* ca. 1500–1530. Sculpture, polychromed terra-cotta, 233.60 x 198.10 cm. © The Cleveland Museum of Art, Gift of Samuel Mather, 1922.210. By permission of The Cleveland Museum.

The Sacro Monte of San Vivaldo was begun a few years after that at Varallo.[80] The promontory chosen for the shrine had an established aura. In the late twelfth and thirteenth centuries, it was occupied by a community identified as the Brothers of the Cross of Normandy; in the fourteenth century, it was associated with the holy hermit Vivaldo.[81] Franciscans were established on the site by 1500. The community's first leader was Cherubino Conzi: "After this brother Cherubino, brother Tommaso of Florence, a holy friar, loved this place and worked hard for it; in that forest he devotedly fabricated chapels and oratories similar to the places of the holy city of Jerusalem, where there are all the mysteries of the Lord's passion."[82] It has been assumed that Cherubino and Tommaso had returned to Tuscany from the Holy Land, though apparently without any documentary substantiation.[83] San Vivaldo appears in the list of convents of the Observant Franciscans compiled about 1509; there it is described as being built near the Holy Sepulchre, "with various chapels and aediculas resembling the holy places on Mount Sion and on the Mount of Olives."[84]

Between 1500 and 1516, about twenty-five chapels were constructed at San Vivaldo that recorded thirty-four sites in and around Jerusalem associated with the life of Jesus. As at Varallo, figures inside the chapels depicted the episodes commemorated, though here the sculptures were not free-standing and life-size but rather smaller, glazed terra-cotta, high-relief panels, with only a few figures in the round (figs. 36, 37, and 38). In 1516, Pope Leo X issued a letter at the behest of the Franciscans, awarding indulgences to those who piously visited the *sacro monte*.[85] Sixteen stations of the itinerary offered indulgences of seven years: Ecclesia Presepii (Church of the Nativity), Templum Domini (Circumcision), Locus Quarantane (place in the desert of Jesus's forty-day fast), church of Mount Sion (Last Supper), cavern in the Valley of Jehosaphat (where Christ preached to the disciples), church where Jesus was captured (Gethsemane), house of Pilate, house of Herod, house of Saint Anne, house of Caiphas, Chapel of Mary of the Swoon, Calvary, Holy Sepulchre, Chapel of the Ascension, Chapel of the Holy Spirit, Church of the Tomb of the Blessed Virgin.[86] The list of sites arranges them in the narrative order of the Gospels, but their form and distribution on the Tuscan hill follows the contemporary topography

80. For an accessible introduction to the history of the site and its chapels, see Comune Montaione, *San Vivaldo*. For a scholarly analysis, see Cardini and Vannini, "San Vivaldo in Valdelsa"; Gensini, *La "Gerusalemme" di San Vivaldo e I Sacri Monti in Europa;* Neri, *Il S. Sepolcro riprodotto in occidente,* 94–139; Pacciani and Vannini, *La "Gerusalemme" di S. Vivaldo in Valdelsa*.

81. Bull issued by Pius X on February 13, 1908. The saint's feast day is May 2.

82. From a manuscript now in the collection of San Francesco in Florence; quoted in Cardini and Vannini, "San Vivaldo in Valdelsa," 36. A full citation for the source is not included in the article.

83. Civilini, *San Vivaldo,* 2.

84. Pacciani and Vannini, *La "Gerusalemme" di S. Vivaldo in Valdelsa,* 22–23.

85. February 19, 1516. For the text of this document, see ibid., 24–25. For the papal concession to Franciscans for granting indulgences in the Holy Land, see Golubovic, *Biblioteca bio-bibliografica della Terra Santa e dell'Oriente Francescano,* 1:180.

86. Indulgences of one year were offered for visits to another eighteen sites in Jerusalem, familiar from pilgrims' itineraries.

of the Holy Land.[87] The landscape to which San Vivaldo refers is that of early modern Jerusalem, overlaying the Jerusalem of Herod the Great in which Jesus lived and died.

At San Vivaldo, as at Varallo, the topographical arrangement of the chapels followed that of the Holy City.[88] A deep ravine to the east of the convent was apparently identified as the Valley of Jehosaphat; the south side of the ravine represented the Mount of Olives; a small plateau to the north realized the Temple Mount; a tertiary hill signified Calvary. As in the Jerusalem of the Gospels, a wall originally surrounded the *sacro monte*. However, the Jerusalems of both San Vivaldo and Varallo included sites on the Franciscan itinerary of the Church of the Holy Sepulchre, whether or not they appeared in the New Testament. For example, the Chapel of the Prison of Christ mentioned by the chaplain of Sir Richard Guylforde as a vaulted chamber in the aisle of the Holy Sepulchre is also represented at San Vivaldo.[89] A *Stabat Mater*—the Virgin supported by her friends—in a separate niche is viewable below the Crucifixion, again in imitation of the late-medieval arrangements at the Church of the Holy Sepulchre.

San Vivaldo and Varallo had, obviously, a great deal in common: the Franciscan religious affiliation of their producers, their chronology, and, most remarkably, their project of fabricating Jerusalem with sculptural groups in an imitative landscape.[90] The two *sacri monti* also had significant differences. From the beginning, San Vivaldo was less ambitious than Varallo—the structures and their terra-cotta tenants were smaller and less elaborately articulated than their equivalents further north. More significantly, their later histories were distinct. San Vivaldo remained a local shrine; Varallo, in contrast, received supraregional attention. As the art historian Peter Cannon Brookes observes, the "Sacro Monte of San Vivaldo was doomed to be ignored outside this corner of Tuscany, whilst the Sacro Monte of Varallo . . . was, through the patronage of Saint Charles Borromeo, to become the model for Northern Italy and subsequently the Roman Catholic world."[91]

San Vivaldo has been progressively marginalized. Although its original plan has been modified by both the addition of new chapels and the decay and destruction of others, it is still imaginable. It has at least in part escaped the

87. For a careful mapping of the Sacro Monte of San Vivaldo against Jerusalem, see Vannini, "S. Vivaldo e la sua documentazione materiale," 250–55.

88. For a more literal mapping of San Vivaldo over Jerusalem, see Pacciani, "L'archittetura delle cappelle di S. Vivaldo," 29.

89. Civilini, *San Vivaldo*, 34–35. The chaplain describes the location: "From thence we descended into a corner of an aisle of the same church where is a little vault, strongly made, wherein our Savior was kept in prison while his cross was in dressing and making ready." Chaplain of Sir Richard Guylforde, *Pylgrymage of Sir Richard Guylforde to the Holy Land*, 25.

90. Interaction between Caimi and Tommaso is undocumented. Consequently, claims have been made that they had no knowledge of the other's project. "The artistic origins of the two Sacri Monti are entirely different and the resemblances between the sculptural complexes created are fortuitous or generic rather than specific. . . . The evidence provided by the surviving chapels of the two Sacri Monti indicates that there was no contact between those teams although they were responding to virtually the same intellectual demands." Cannon Brookes, "The Sculptural Complexes of San Vivaldo," 271. The assumption has also been made that they were intimately linked.

91. Ibid., 272.

later remodelings imposed on Varallo. Consequently, the ways in which pious visitors appropriate the Tuscan site, even now, may reflect something of the *sacri monti*'s earliest functions. A modern visitor's guide reports:

Shrine of the Ecce Homo: The prison of Barabbas, the criminal freed in exchange for Christ, lies under the shrine of the Ecce Homo. Until towards 1900, there was there a mutilated statue of Barabbas. Father Faustino Gilardi explains in his Guide to the Sanctuary of San Vivaldo why the statue was "half ruined by stones being thrown at it. . . . It was a good thing to remove a ridiculous superstition which had grown among the women of the lower order. If they could not find a husband, for some reason or other they believed that commending themselves to Barabbas would help and they brought him a stone, which they threw at the statue. So, though neither rich nor fair, yet they lived in hope. This custom arose with the building of the first chapels."[92]

The interpretation of this "superstition" seems as bizarre as its object. The pamphlet also records the healings and visions of devout visitors. Unmentioned are the rewards that the Sacro Monte of San Vivaldo offered to less-pious travelers. In 1911, Elia Volpi, known for his shady dealings with J. P. Morgan, acquired the terra-cotta sculpture *Christ and the Samaritan Woman at the Well* from San Vivaldo for 8,000 lira, and quickly exported it. This work, now in the Cleveland Museum, is attributed to Giovanni Della Robbia (fig. 38).[93]

In contrast with San Vivaldo, Varallo enjoyed increasing popularity as a pilgrimage destination. It was, consequently, subject to remodeling. Documents of the later sixteenth century prove that a serious effort was made to reorder the site "so that it would be possible for anyone on their own to easily conduct oneself though all the mysteries following the order of the sacred text."[94] The Jerusalem constructed by Varallo's founder nevertheless resisted complete concealment. The Rev. S. W. King, a particularly pompous travel writer, describes his experience of Varallo in a publication of 1858:

The labyrinth of walks leads from one to another, up and down endless steps, through wild gardens and open spaces; and to take the chapels in their right order, as numbered, almost requires the assistance of one of the numerous guides—a set of lazy mendicants and ragged children, who, of course, infest the place.[95]

The Sacro Monte's creator and its remodelers had two very distinct spatial projects. The site originally reproduced Jerusalem. Its metonymic topography

---

92. Civilini, *San Vivaldo*, 21–22. An anthropologist would surely read the actions of these stone-throwers differently.

93. Roberta Ferrazza, *Palazzo Davanzati e le Collezioni di Elia Volpi*, 113, "A Relief by Giovanni della Robbia Given by Samuel Mather."

94. For the documents and plans relevant to the remodeling of Varallo, see Gatti-Perer, "Marino Bassi, il Sacro Monte di Varallo e Sta. Maria presso San Celso a Milano."

95. Rev. S. W. King, *The Italian Valley of the Pennine Alps*, 512.

allowed an envisioning of the Holy City. The Sacro Monte presented an understanding of the landscape that promised to replicate the experience of the pilgrim in a complex space: disordered by geography, marked by incoherence, interrupted by overlap. A city's visitor only understands it partially and pragmatically. Urban space never reveals itself systematically, but rather erratically and through continuous negotiation. Only from a distance is there a glimpse of the city as a whole; within it, it can only be grasped in the fragments of the particular.[96] A city—as distinguished from a utopia—always offers surprises. The space of urban complexity was progressively restructured in the sixteenth and seventeenth centuries. The popes sought to impose order on Rome before Haussmann inflicted it on Paris.[97] In the urban microcosms of the *sacri monti,* space was also progressively systematized. Varallo was reconceptualized. From a replica of the Holy City, it was cleverly reshaped as a fabrication of the life of Jesus.[98] This shift from Varallo as a map of Jerusalem to Varallo as a resumé of Jesus's career involved a programmatic move from experiential to dogmatic space. That change corresponds to the demands of Counter-Reformation piety.[99] The idea to which the remodelers of Varallo hoped to make the site conform was fully realized in the *sacro monte* or *Via dei Misteri* of Varese.

The Sacro Monte of Varese occupies a hilltop popularly associated with a miraculous military victory over heresy (Arianism) ascribed to the intervention of Saint Ambrose, the great fourth-century archbishop of Milan; it was also the home of an image of the Virgin painted from life by Saint Luke.[100] The monastic church on the mountain became a local pilgrimage destination. Its cult of the Virgin was promoted by another great warrior against heresy (Protestantism), the cardinal archbishop of Milan, Saint Charles Borromeo. Charles Borromeo's attachment to Varallo was mentioned at the beginning of this chapter; his patronage contributed significantly to Varallo's reordering in the later sixteenth century. He also promoted Varese, though the construction of the chapels and the realization of their sculptural contents was left largely to his successor and kinsman, Cardinal Federico Borromeo. The initiating plan for the fourteen chapels has been ascribed to another Franciscan (Capuchin) friar, Battista Aguggiari da Monza.[101] The work was virtually complete by 1680.

The Sacro Monte of Varese consists of a series of beautifully designed individual chapels that "come fresh one after the other as a set of variations by

---

96. For a thought-provoking discussion of urban perception, see Koolhaas, *Delirious New York.*

97. Giedion, *Space, Time and Architecture,* 75–106. Also see Burroughs, "Opacity and Transparence."

98. For an excellent reading of the *sacri monti* against the urge for urban order, see Miedema, "Following in the Footsteps of Christ." Also see Pacciani and Vannini, *La "Gerusalemme" di S. Vivaldo in Valdelsa.*

99. Vannini, "S. Vivaldo e la sua documentazione materiale," 242–45.

100. Carlo Alberto Lotti, *Santa Maria del Monte sopra Varese,* 14–26. Of all the *sacri monti,* that of Varese has received the most photographic and scholarly attention, no doubt because of the photogenic character of both its architecture and its sculptures. A lavishly illustrated presentation of the site is offered by Corsini, *Affreschi del Sacro Monte di Varese.* For a serious attempt to put the site into a broader social and political context, see Bianconi et al., *Il Sacro Monte sopra Varese.*

101. Zanzi, "Peak of the Most High," 47.

Fig. 39. Chapel 10 with the Arch of Saint Ambrose (Glory) in the foreground and Santa Maria del Monte in the background. Sacro Monte di Varese. Author photo.

Fig. 40. (*below*) Plan of the Sacro Monte di Varese from 1656, from an undated souvenir reproduction distributed at the site. Author's collection.

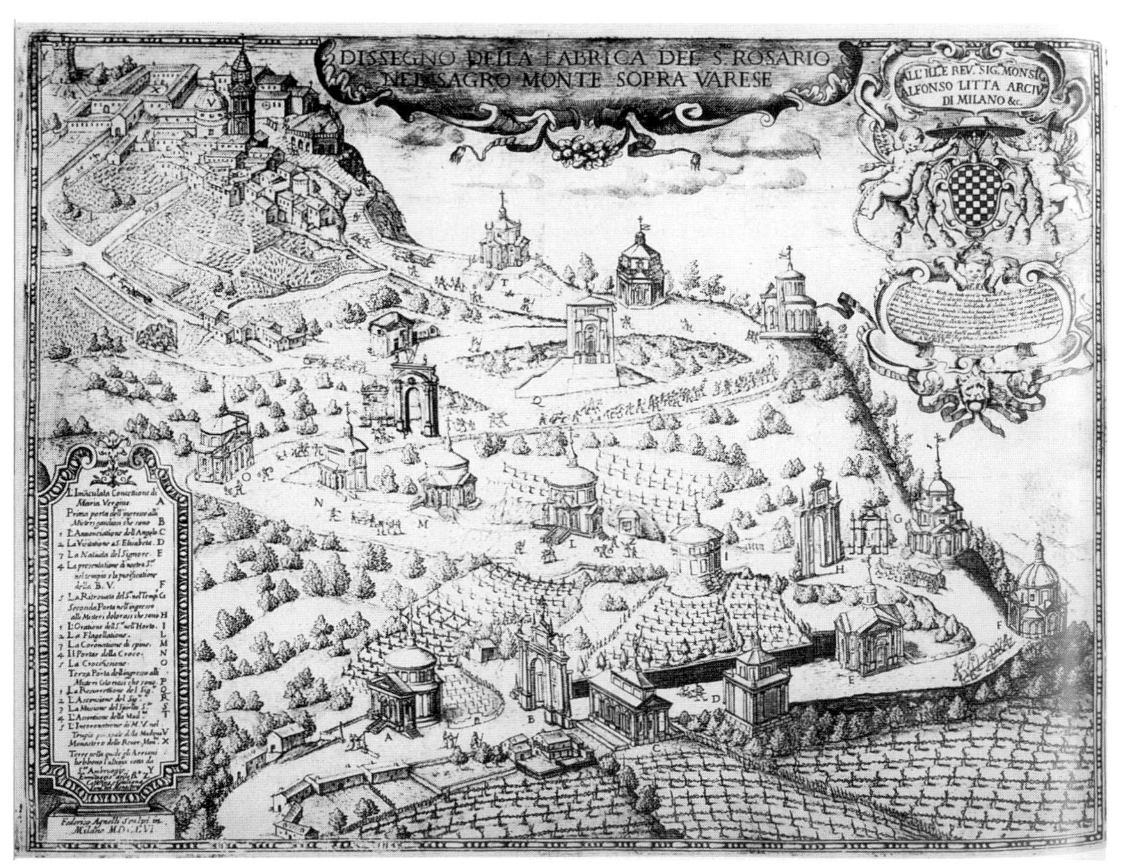

Fig. 41. Chapel 9, interior, Jesus bearing the cross and Veronica with her veil. Sacro Monte di Varese. Author photo.

Handel. Each one of them is a little architectural gem." [102] The buildings appear at regular intervals along the broad pathway that ascends toward the church. They are neatly divided into three groups by triumphal arches, marking the progress of the mystical narratives that they house: joy—the Annunciation, Visitation, Nativity, Presentation, and the Disputation in the Temple; grief—Agony in the Garden, Flagellation, Crown of Thorns, Ascent to Calvary, Crucifixion; glory—Resurrection, Ascension, Descent of the Holy Ghost, Assumption of the Virgin Mary (figs. 39, 40). Samuel Butler offers a lively, if again condescendingly Protestant, view of the interiors of chapels that mark the observer's ascent to the church at the top of the hill:

Then we looked through the grating of the first chapel inside the arch, and found it to contain a representation of the Annunciation. The Virgin had a real washing stand, with a basin and jug, and a piece of real soap. Her slippers were disposed neatly under the bed, so also were her shoes, and, if I remember rightly, there was everything else that Messrs. Heal and Co. [the nineteenth-century British version of Williams-Sonoma] would send for the furnishing of a lady's bedroom. I have already said perhaps too much about the realism of these groups of painted statuary, but will venture a word or two more which may help the reader to understand the matter better as it appears to Catholics themselves. The object is to bring the scene as vividly as possible before people who have not had the opportunity of being able to realize it to themselves through travel or general cultivation of the imaginative faculties. How can an Italian peasant realize to himself the notion of the Annunciation so well as by seeing such a chapel as

102. Butler, *Alps and Sanctuaries of Piedmont and the Canton Ticino*, 252.

that at Varese? . . . We stuff the dead bodies of birds and animals which we think it worth while to put into our museums. We put them in the most life-like attitudes we can, with bits of grass and bush, and painted landscape behind them: by doing this we give people who have never seen the actual animals, a more vivid idea concerning them than we know how to give by any other means. . . . But we are shocked at the notion of giving them a similar aid to the realization of events which, as we say, concern them more nearly than any others in the history of the world. A stuffed rabbit or blackbird is a good thing. A stuffed Charge of Balaclava again is quite legitimate; but a stuffed Nativity is, according to Protestant notions, offensive. . . . They like them as our own people like Madame Tussaud's. Granted that they come to worship the images. . . . But how, pray, can we avoid worshipping images? Or loving images?[103]

The scene of Veronica and Christ Carrying the Cross reproduced here suggests something of the experience of these chapels (fig. 41). To the grille that keeps the pious beholder at a distance is now added the modern supplement of glass. Here glass is not transparent but reflective; the images have become virtually invisible. On a Sunday in May the way of the Sacro Monte provides the perfect venue for a family outing. Young families, older couples, bicyclists—rarely does anyone stop to look at the sacred images.

The Sacro Monte of Varese was never Jerusalem. Just as the images became increasingly detached from their observers, so those images, historically located in the Holy City, were removed from their originating topography. The elimination of Jerusalem modified the work of the sculptural presentations. In late fifteenth/early sixteenth-century Varallo, the images demanded discovery. Glimpses of history from the Gospels were sought amongst the hills of Jerusalem; their finding transformed the witness into a participant. Truth was constructed by the active observer. In later sixteenth-century Varese, truth was presented *systematically* for the pilgrims' examination and, as Butler suggests, delectation. That greatest of all Counter-Reformation texts, the decrees of the Council of Trent (1545–63), sought to discipline images and to control their profligate generation of meaning. It directed the careful ordering of representation:

The holy Synod enjoins on all bishops, and others who sustain the office and charge of teaching, that . . . they especially instruct the faithful diligently concerning the intercession and invocation of saints; the honor (paid) to relics; and the legitimate use of images. . . . The images of Christ, of the Virgin Mother of God, and of the other saints, are to be had and retained particularly in temples, and that due honor and veneration are to be given them . . . because the honor which is shown them is referred to the prototypes which those images represent; in such wise that by the images which we kiss, and before which we uncover the head, and prostrate ourselves, we adore Christ; and we venerate the saints, whose similitude they bear. . . . And the bishops shall carefully teach this: that, by means of the histories of the mysteries of our Redemption,

103. Ibid., 249–51.

portrayed by paintings or other representations, the people is instructed, and confirmed in (the habit of) remembering, and continually revolving in mind the articles of faith; as also that great profit is derived from all sacred images, not only because the people are thereby admonished of the benefits and gifts bestowed upon them by Christ, but also because the miracles which God has performed by means of the saints, and their salutary examples, are set before the eyes of the faithful; that so they may give God thanks for those things; may order their own lives and manners in imitation of the saints; and may be excited to adore and love God, and to cultivate piety. . . . And if any abuses have crept in amongst these holy and salutary observances, the holy Synod ardently desires that they be utterly abolished; in such wise that no images (suggestive) of false doctrine, and furnishing occasion of dangerous error to the uneducated, be set up. . . . In fine, let so great care and diligence be used herein by bishops, as that there be nothing seen that is disorderly, or that is unbecomingly or confusedly arranged, *nothing that is profane, nothing indecorous, seeing that holiness becomes the house of God.*[104]

The mysteries of Varese are dramatized dogma. The chapels focus the mind on the unchanging truth of the events through which Jesus revealed his divinity. The string of chapels of the Sacro Monte of Varese has been described as a built rosary.[105] It might also bring to mind a monumental and cinematic version of the familiar Stations of the Cross.[106] The Stations of the Cross, now found ubiquitously in Roman Catholic churches, offer the faithful a "pious exercise": images of the Lord's Passion, distributed in the church in imitation of "the way in which they are found by pilgrims in holy city of Jerusalem," assist the believer's contemplation of the mysteries of redemption.[107] The Stations of the Cross were promoted by the Franciscans, if not invented by them.[108] In 1686, responding to a petition from the Franciscans, Pope Innocent XI awarded indulgences to the Stations and control over them to the order. As late as the early twentieth century, the Franciscans still claimed some authority over the erection of the Stations of the Cross.[109]

The Franciscan disposition of the Stations in the churches of the West abstracted the drama of the Passion of Jesus from the particularity of Jerusalem. As in the Sacro Monte of Varese, the scenes lost their urban reference. Dogmatic truth superseded didactic drama. This new regularity of the spatial order emerged concurrently with such Counter-Reformation institutions as the Jesuits and a revitalized Inquisition. The new discipline of Roman Catholic orthodoxy

---

104. "On the Invocation, Veneration, and Relics of Saints, and on Sacred Images," in Roman Catholic Church, *The Council of Trent,* 234–36; my emphasis.

105. Zanzi, "Peak of the Most High," 47. The rosary is identified with Dominican piety.

106. For a broad historical survey in English, see Thurston, *The Stations of the Cross.* Also see Halbwachs, *La Topographie légendaire des Évangiles en terre sainte,* 102–12.

107. Benedict XIII, *Const. Inter Plurima, V Nonas Mart. 1726,* quoted by Sleutjes, *Instructio de stationibus S. Viae Crucis deque Crucifixis Viae Crucis,* 9.

108. At least according to the *Catholic Encyclopedia.* See Alston, *Way of the Cross.*

109. Sleutjes, *Instructio de stationibus S. Viae Crucis deque Crucifixis Viae Crucis,* 19–26.

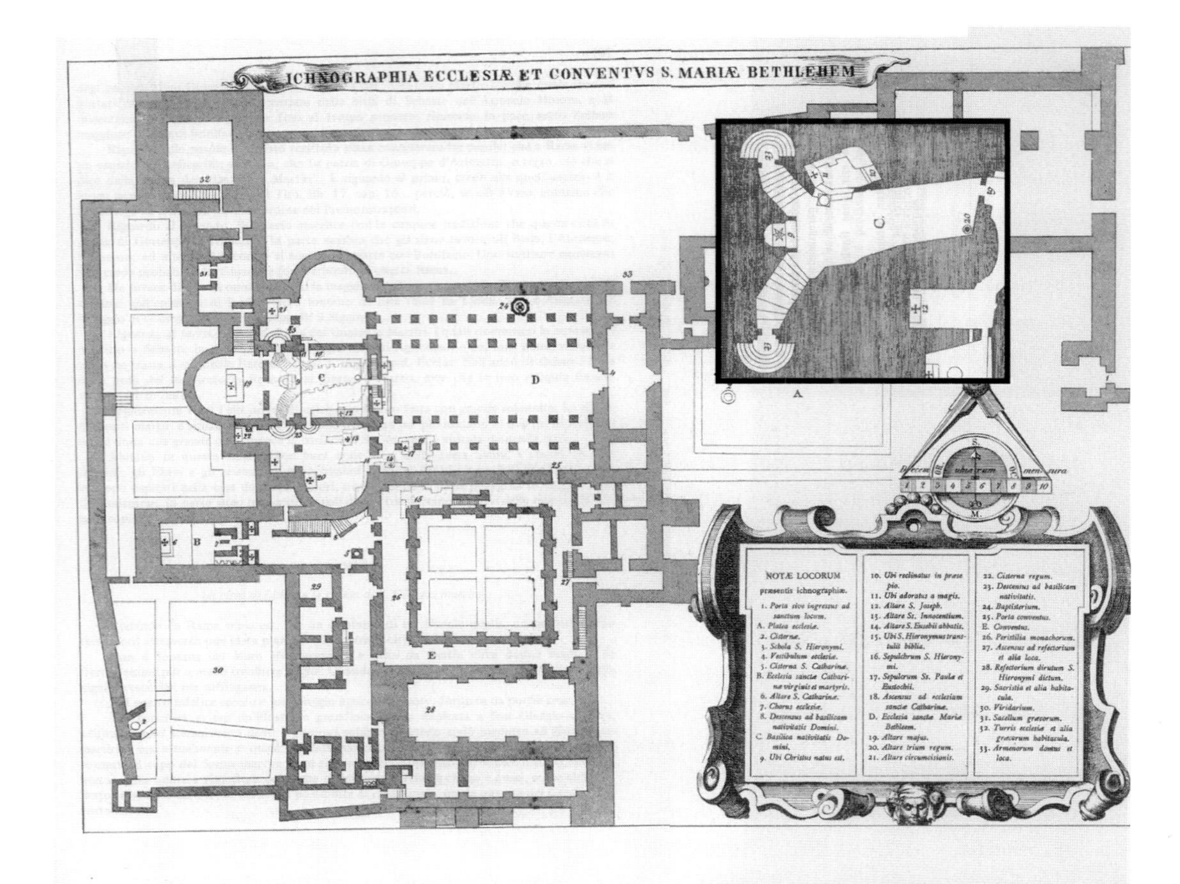

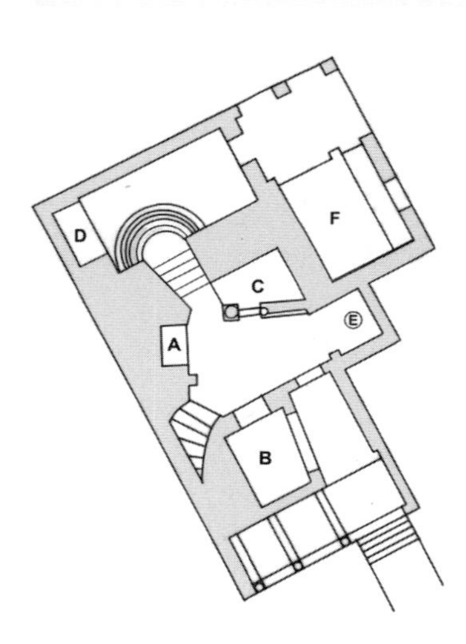

Fig. 42. (*top*) Church of the Nativity, Bethlehem, plan. From Francesco Quaresmio, *Elucidatio Terrae Sanctae*.

Fig. 43. (*bottom, left*) Nativity complex, Sacro Monte, Varallo, sketch plan. *A,* Infant Jesus adored by Mary and Joseph; *B,* arrival of the Magi; *C,* Adoration of the Shepherds; *D,* Circumcision; *E,* pillar; *F,* dream of Joseph. Author drawing.

Fig. 44. (*bottom, right*) Interior of the Nativity complex, Sacro Monte, Varallo. Author photo.

imposed a more transparent sequence of chapels on the old images of Varallo and San Vivaldo. Both sites were remodeled to more closely correspond to the cycle of mysteries found at Varese. At Varallo, some of the original references to specific Holy Land sites survived renovation. The representation of Bethlehem there had been carefully built to the specifications of its archetype—the Church of the Nativity. Like the tomb of Christ, the Church of the Nativity was under the Franciscans' control in the fifteenth century just as it is now. Located down the hill from "Jerusalem," the complex of chapels replicates with remarkable accuracy the Grotto of the Nativity (figs. 42, 43, and 44). At Varallo, of course, the spaces are animated with life-size sculptures depicting the events that occupy them: the three kings approach the stable; inside, the shepherds adore the Child. Marble steps similar to those in the Church of the Nativity lead upward to the representation of the Circumcision. But by the later sixteenth century, the Varallo Bethlehem was no longer an isolated suburb of Jerusalem. Rather, it was ingeniously incorporated into a series of chapels rationally performing Christian history. Bethlehem is preceded by Adam and Eve in Paradise, the Annunciation (in a replica of the Sancta Casa of Loreto), the Visitation, and Dreams of Joseph. It is followed by the Flight into Egypt and the Massacre of the Innocents.

The architectural specificity of Varallo's Nativity Grotto and Holy Sepulchre indicates the sense of the real that was lost in the destruction of another part of the complex. The third important site controlled by the Franciscans in the Holy Land was the Cenacle, site of the Last Supper and Christ's washing the feet of his disciples. This prominent pilgrimage destination on Mount Sion seems to have been reproduced at Varallo with the same care as the Sepulchre and the Grotto. According to Tibaldi's plan of 1570, the Cenacle was attached to the rear of the central church of the complex, not unlike the arrangement of the Franciscan monastery and shrine in the Holy City (fig. 29). Reference to these scenes is made in a description of the Sacro Monte of Varallo written in 1516:

Then ascending to the great compartment built above Mount Sion where Jesus convened the apostles for dinner during which Judas conceived the desire to be ungrateful to his Lord, so at the table Jesus heeded his hatred. All this is revealed in painted forms. It is not possible to tell with how much beauty the construction of this great dining room was decorated and painted. . . . In the middle is found an altar where the Lord with all humility washes the feet of his dear disciples.[110]

In the mid-sixteenth century, the Cenacle in Jerusalem was lost by the Franciscans to the Jews and Moslems. Not long after, the Cenacle of Varallo was lost to the visual protocols of the Counter-Reformation. Now the Last Supper is a feast set in an eighteenth-century structure that bears no relationship to the Cenacle

110. The work is republished in Perrone, *Questi sono li Misteri che sono sopra el Monte de Varalle,* 27–47. See particularly capitulo 33. Also see Brizio, "Configuration del Sacro Monte di Varallo nel 1514," 2.

Fig. 45. Last Supper, Sacro Monte, Varallo. Author photo.

Fig. 46. (*below*) Cenacle, Jerusalem. Author photo.

(figs. 45, 46). Other scenes were modified also, apparently to better conform with contemporary piety. The "Stone of Unction," for example, was the slab of marble on which Jesus was prepared for burial after the Crucifixion; it figures prominently in pilgrims' descriptions of the sites in the Holy Sepulchre. An early chapel at Varallo, located a few steps away from the Holy Sepulchre, was dedicated to this relic and its drama. The image was later replaced by one in which a more currently popular, local relic is displayed—the Shroud of Turin. The dominant shift toward narrative coherence made room for local cults. The complex space of the Holy City receded before the demands of contemporary spiritual practices.

The new visual strategy of the Counter-Reformation reshaped Varallo. Just as fundamentally, the Franciscan understanding of the Via Dolorosa reshaped Jerusalem itself. Though the Franciscans presented a series of Stations of the Cross to pilgrims from at least the fifteenth century, their number and order were irregular and unstable. The old and familiar pilgrimage practice of controlling space by mathematically registering distances seems to have become obsessive by the seventeenth century. For example, in his *Elucidatio Terrae Sanctae* of 1639, the Franciscan Francesco Quaresmio offers a catalog of the Holy Land to travelers, rather than a spiritual guide.[111] By the later seventeenth century, too, the Franciscans, following the model established in western Europe, had imposed the canonical fourteen stations on Jerusalem.[112] The experience of the city was codified and ordered. Urban complexity and contradiction were never eliminated, but the space was regimented for Christian pilgrims. Like the itinerary of a London tour bus, the Franciscan Way of the Cross rescued the Western visitor from the discomfiting complications of the alien urban experience. The encounter with an anticipated sacrality was less disrupted by the spatially unexpected.

The shift in the topography of Varallo from a complexity that replicated the experience of the pilgrim to Jerusalem toward the transparent didacticism of Varese was, in part, a response to the Council of Trent. Nevertheless, both the landscape of the *sacri monti* and the Council of Trent participated in a broad, European-wide social reordering that also involved economic change. In the sixteenth century, currency shifted from gold to silver. The weight of the market moved from the south—Spain and Italy—to the north—the Low Countries, England, and Germany.[113] The century was further marked by "the price revolution," an extended period of serious inflation:[114]

---

111. Quaresmio, *Elucidatio Terrae Sanctae*. The author recorded eight stations on the Way of the Cross.

112. Horn, *Ichnographiae monumentorum Terrae Sanctae*, 8. For a collection of the pilgrimage texts on the Via Crucis, see Baldi, *Enchiridion locorum sanctorum*, 593–616.

113. Charles P. Kindleberger, *Economic and Financial Crises and Transformations in Sixteenth-Century Europe*, 1.

114. The theory of the "price revolution" was well established by the time of Adam Smith. For questions raised about its interpretive validity and for answers to those questions, see Chabert, "More about the Sixteenth-Century Price Revolution"; Cipolla, "The So-Called 'Price Revolution'"; Ramsey, "The European Economy in the Sixteenth Century." For a less radically changing sixteenth-century economy, see Duplessis, *Transitions to Capitalism in Early Modern Europe*.

Throughout Western Europe during the second half of the sixteenth century, peasants, craftsmen and shopkeepers, as well as princes and bishops, all shared one novel experience of some importance for their daily lives. In each decade they found that any standard coin, even if it contained precisely the same quantity of precious metal as in the previous decade, would buy less of almost any commodity bought and sold. . . . For some time historians and economists have been disposed to regard the price revolution as an important cause for the rise of modern capitalism. . . . E. J. Hamilton . . . suggested that the rapid increase in prices stimulated the growth of capitalism mainly by cheapening labor costs, and thus making possible exceptionally large profits during the period of many decades. These profits brought about an unprecedented accumulation of wealth in the hands of enterprising merchants and other rich men, who could afford to invest in large-scale enterprises.[115]

Thus the spiritual anxieties given shape by the Reformation and Counter-Reformation had their economic equivalents: inflation, bank failures, and unemployment.

Contributing to the erosion of material certainty was the progressively powerful abstraction of money. Not only was there more specie in circulation, but the velocity of circulation increased. Capital markets and instruments of credit became progressively more ubiquitous and sophisticated, freeing money from its bullion base and allowing it to move more rapidly.[116] Hoards of gold and silver—savings under the mattress—were replaced by bills of exchange. Both the growing authority of a monetary model and its limits are suggested by an ecclesiastical parallel—indulgences.[117] Thomas Aquinas explained indulgences in terms of double-entry bookkeeping already in the thirteenth century:

Indulgences hold good both in the Church's court and in the judgment of God, for the remission of the punishment which remains after contrition, absolution, and confession, whether this punishment be enjoined or not. The reason why they so avail is the oneness of the mystical body in which many have performed works of satisfaction exceeding the requirements of their debts. . . . And the saints in whom this superabundance of satisfactions is found, did not perform their good works for this or that particular person, who needs the remission of his punishment (else he would have received this remission without any indulgence at all), but they performed them for the whole Church in general. . . . These merits, then, are the common property of the whole Church. Now those things which are the common property of a number are distributed to the various individuals according to the judgment of him who rules them all.

---

115. Nef, "Prices and Industrial Capitalism in France and England, 1540–1640," 155–56. For a clear discussion of the sixteenth- and early seventeenth-century "price revolution" as greater profit dependent on lower wages, also see Keynes, *A Treatise on Money*, 1:152–63.

116. Kindleberger, *Economic and Financial Crises and Transformations in Sixteenth-Century Europe*, 1.

117. For a modern guide to the acquisition of indulgences, see Roman Catholic Church, *The Raccolta; or, A Manual of Indulgences, Prayers and Devotions*. Also see Roman Catholic Church, *Sacraments and Forgiveness*, 321–68.

> *The effective cause of the remission is not the devotion, or toil, or gift of the recipient; nor, again, is it the cause for which the indulgence was granted. We cannot, then, estimate the quantity of the remission by any of the foregoing, but solely by the merits of the Church—and these are always superabundant. Consequently, according as these merits are applied to a person so does he obtain remission. That they should be so applied demands, firstly, authority to dispense this treasure; secondly, union between the recipient and Him Who merited it—and this is brought about by charity; thirdly, there is required a reason for so dispensing this treasury, so that the intention, namely, of those who wrought these meritorious works is safeguarded, since they did them for the honor of God and for the good of the Church in general. Hence whenever the cause assigned tends to the good of the Church and the honor of God, there is sufficient reason for granting an indulgence.*[118]

The sacrifices of Jesus and the saints, as they far exceeded their sins, were deposited in the treasury of the church. These accumulated credits were disbursed by the pope as redemptions from purgatorial punishments in exchange for pious acts.[119] Such deeds included kissing images, visiting shrines, saying prayers, and giving alms for pious causes: building churches, maintaining hospitals, and funding wars against the heathens. Both money and indulgences tended toward inflation.[120]

If a general monetary model usefully informs an understanding of indulgences, the practice of indulgences provides a specific fiscal model for the later Franciscan pawn banks: administrators distribute to the poor the excess wealth contributed by the elite in exchange for redeemable goods. In the sixteenth century, the indulgence and the *monte di pietà* were both under attack because of their suspect relationship to money. Pawn banks were assaulted as usurious; indulgences were assailed for exchanging salvation for money. Martin Luther's 1517 collection of Ninety-five Theses on indulgences is the most famous of such forays. A few of those theses provide a sense of their thrust.

45. *Christians are to be taught that he who sees a man in need, and passes him by, and gives [his money] for pardons, purchases not the indulgences of the pope, but the indignation of God.*
46. *Christians are to be taught that unless they have more than they need, they are bound to keep back what is necessary for their own families, and by no means to squander it on pardons. . . .*
50. *Christians are to be taught that if the pope knew the exactions of the pardon-preachers, he would rather that St. Peter's church should go to ashes, than that it should be built up with the skin, flesh and bones of his sheep. . . .*

---

118. Thomas Aquinas, *Summa Theologica, Supplementum Tertiae Partis,* 27, answer to objection 4.

119. A certain inflationary tendency might well also be ascribed to images; see Belting, *The Image and Its Public in the Middle Ages,* 154–85.

120. For a useful insight into the traditions of Franciscan piety, see the discussion of a late fifteenth-century woodcut, which provided an indulgence of four years to those who kissed it, in Areford, "The Passion Measured." For a more general introduction to the relation between images and indulgences, see Lewis, "Rewarding Devotion."

56. *The "treasures of the Church," out of which the pope grants indulgences, are not sufficiently named or known among the people of Christ.*
57. *That they are not temporal treasures is certainly evident, for many of the vendors do not pour out such treasures so easily, but only gather them. . . .*
82. *To wit:—"Why does not the pope empty purgatory, for the sake of holy love and of the dire need of the souls that are there, if he redeems an infinite number of souls for the sake of miserable money with which to build a Church [St. Peter's]? The former reasons would be most just; the latter is most trivial."*[121]

The Council of Trent answered Protestant critics of indulgences:

Whereas the power of conferring indulgences was granted by Christ to the Church . . . the sacred holy Synod teaches, and enjoins, that the use of Indulgences, for the Christian people most salutary, and approved of by the authority of sacred Councils, is to be retained in the Church. . . . It condemns with anathema those who either assert that they are useless or who deny that there is in the Church the power of granting them. In granting them, however, it desires that, in accordance with the ancient and approved custom in the Church, moderation be observed; lest, by excessive facility, ecclesiastical discipline be enervated. And being desirous that the abuses which have crept therein, and by occasion of which this honorable name of indulgences is blasphemed by heretics, be amended and corrected, it ordains generally by this decree, that all evil gains for the obtaining thereof . . . be wholly abolished.[122]

When the Council of Trent's enactments failed to pass the Protestant test, Pope Pius V, in 1567, canceled all grants of indulgences involving the transfer of money. Indulgences continued to be exchanged for other pious acts. They were still awarded for visits to the *sacri monti*.

CONCLUSION

The Sacro Monte of Varallo manifests shifts in the social space and cultural economy of Italy from the end of the fifteenth through the seventeenth century. At the time of its establishment the site was an explicit expression of its founder's investment in the Franciscan possession of Jerusalem. Varallo was initially imagined as offering its pious Western consumers the experience of exploring the urban complexities of the Holy City; it presented unexpected encounters with the realities of Jesus's life and Passion. The dramatic staging of events from the Gospels within the fabrication of their originating landscape invited the participation of the devout observer. The spectacularity of the images in the *sacro monte* compensated for the absence of the authentic Jerusalem. The Franciscans provided scenes that might be readily imagined at the site of their historical occurrence in the Holy City. By the later sixteenth and seventeenth centuries, depictions of Jesus's suffering and glory superseded the landscape.

121. Luther, *Works of Martin Luther*, 28–38.
122. Roman Catholic Church, *The Council of Trent*, 277–78.

Jerusalem was replaced in the West by a schematic set of images, the Stations of the Cross. A topography often evokes images; it is less clear that images can generate a landscape. Representations without a location frequently suffer a form of homelessness. Though the architecture of the stations at Varese is more elaborate than that at Varallo and the figures more dense and brilliant, there is a certain depthlessness in their experience. They miss Jerusalem. Art was becoming ever more like entertainment, and travel to the Holy City, revised to match the expectations of the Western Stations of the Cross, was becoming ever more like tourism.

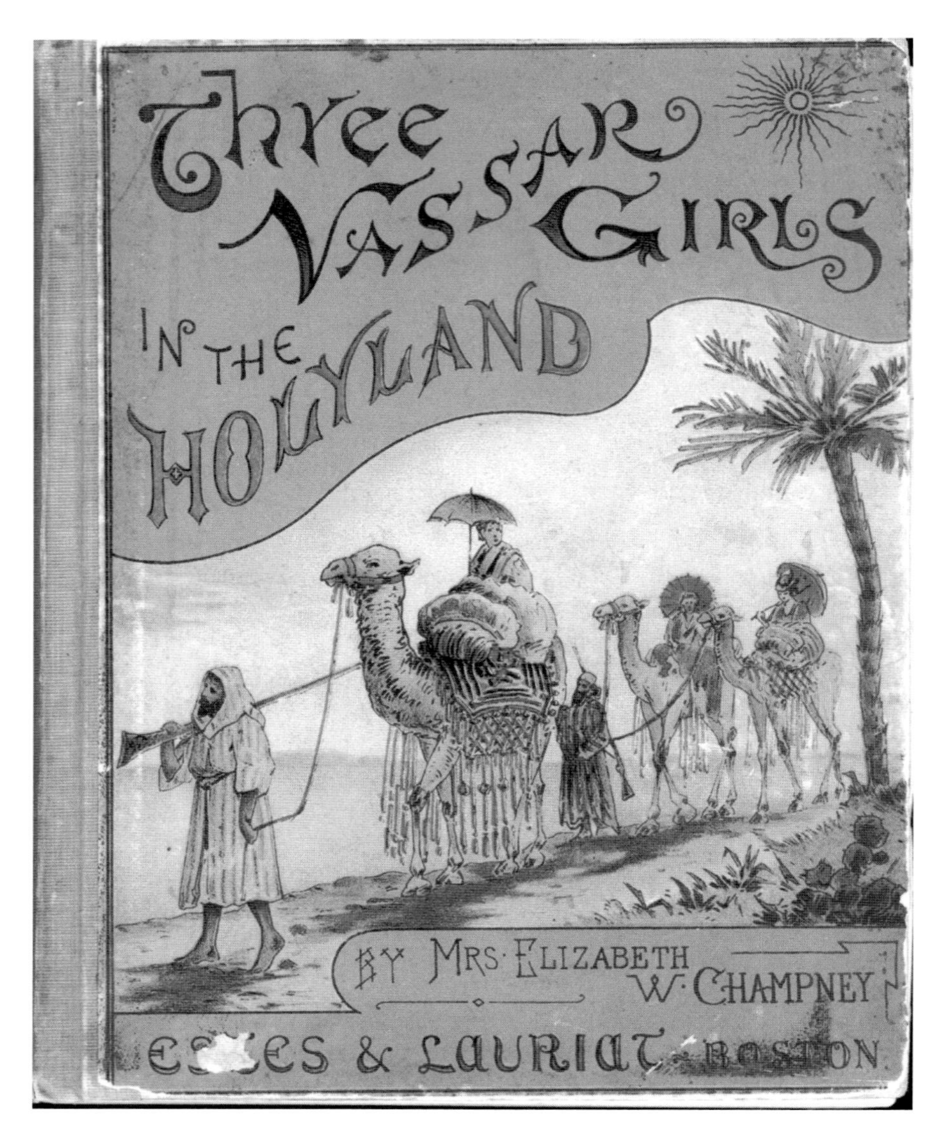

Fig. 47. Elizabeth Champney, illustrated by James Wells Champney, *Three Vassar Girls in the Holy Land*, front cover.

CHAPTER FOUR

Mechanically Reproduced Jerusalem: Entrepreneurs and Tourists

Men moralize among ruins, or, in the throng and tumult of successful cities, recall past visions of urban desolation for prophetic warning. * BENJAMIN DISRAELI, *TANCRED; OR, THE NEW CRUSADE* (1874)

I discovered, at a later period, the secret of my sympathies and antipathies for the memory of certain nations; it lay in the very nature of the institutions and actions of those people. Nations like the Phoenicians, Tyre, Sidon, Carthage—commercial societies, exploring the earth for their profit, and measuring the grandeur of their enterprise only by the material and actual utility of the result. . . . Let us forget them—they were rich and prospered, that is all—they labored only for the present, the future had nothing to do with them—*Receperunt mercedem* ["They have received their reward" (Matt. 6:2)]. But . . . those poetic nations, as the Egyptians, Jews, Hindoos, and Greeks, who have idealized policy, and caused in the lives of their people, the divine principle, the imaginative, to predominate over the human principle, that of mere utility;—it is such I love, such I venerate. * ALPHONSE DE LAMARTINE, *A PILGRIMAGE TO THE HOLY LAND COMPRISING RECOLLECTIONS, SKETCHES AND REFLECTIONS MADE DURING A TOUR IN THE EAST* (1848)

MODERN PILGRIMS

Two popular novels suggest how Jerusalem was consumed in the West in the late nineteenth century. Elizabeth Champney's *Three Vassar Girls in the Holy Land,* published in 1892, is a travelogue in the form of a romance (fig. 47). Zipporah (*bird* in Hebrew) Baumgarten (*orchard* in German), known to her friends as Bird Orchard, is a closet Jewess. Bird and Emma, another Vassar student, are invited by their classmate Violet Remington to accompany her family on an expedition to the East. Bird and Violet's brother, Frank, fall in love on the journey. Bird

I am grateful to Professor Peter McIsaac for his comments on this chapter. I am also deeply indebted to the directors of the surviving Jerusalem panoramas who generously shared their knowledge of panoramas with me and introduced me to the panorama's behind-the-scenes technology—Marc Blouin at Ste.-Anne-de-Beaupré, Canada; Max Fuchs at Einsiedeln, Switzerland; and Gebhard Streicher at Altötting, Germany—and to Sarah Schroth, Nancy Hanks Senior Curator at Duke University's Nasher Museum of Art, for her help in making David Roberts's prints available to me to study.

resists her passion, recognizing the impossibility of a Jewess being accepted into Frank's deeply Protestant, mildly anti-Semitic, American middle-class family.

In the novel, the Holy Land is the site of two conversions. Bird's father, Shear Baumgarten, is transformed. Initially he is represented as "one of those objectionable Jews . . . sordid, worldly, materialistic, his soul had shriveled until his aims and desires were concentrated upon money-getting."[1] At the end, after providing the ransom to save two members of the party from torture and death at the hands of rapacious Bedouins, he is revealed as generous and acceptable.

The second, concurrent conversion is more crucial. Jesus's divinity is progressively revealed to Bird as she experiences the landscape through which he moved. She becomes Christian. At the beginning of the journey, distant from Jerusalem, Bird is a skeptical observer of religion. Outside Cairo, the party stops "to see the Virgin's Tree, an ancient sycamore, which grows near the village of Matariyeh, in whose shade the Holy Family are supposed to have rested during the Flight into Egypt. A fence has been built about it by its owner, to protect it from the ravages of relic-hunters, and beside the fence sat a young Coptic woman holding a beautiful babe upon her shoulder.[2] 'She seems to be posing for us,' Bird said, 'I wonder if she fancies that she will gain our sympathies by enacting this pretty tableau.'"[3] Bird admits her religious skepticism to Frank, though still disguising her ethnicity: "'I do not like to pain you, Frank,' Bird said, 'but I ought to tell you that I am not a Christian, that I do not look upon the character of Jesus as you do.' 'I know it,' he replied; 'but I look forward to the pilgrimages which we shall make together in Palestine to bring us both into a truer knowledge of his life and mission. I am sure that we shall understand him and each other better after talking about him by the way.'"[4] It is not, however, Frank who persuades Bird to become a Christian but the terrain of the New Testament. She is converted only after she decides that marriage with Frank is impossible. The symbolically resonant site of her conversion is Magdala, the home of Mary Magdalene, conventionally identified as the beautiful and repentant prostitute who washed Jesus's feet with her hair. "As Bird read the sacred guide [the New Testament] she felt herself more and more impressed with the character of Jesus. . . . 'I can never say "my Frank,"' she thought, 'but I can say, "my Christ, my Messiah."'"[5]

For modern travelers as for premodern pilgrims, the Bible mapped the Holy Land. Jerusalem was indecipherable without the Hebrew Bible and the New Testament. In *Three Vassar Girls in the Holy Land,* the hero, Frank,

1. Champney, *Three Vassar Girls in the Holy Land,* 54.

2. Scottish artist-traveler David Roberts was one such relic hunter. "Having hired a donkey and a boy, I visited the celebrated sycamore-tree under which the blessed Virgin and infant Savior are said to have taken shelter on their arrival in Egypt. It stands in the middle of an orchard, and close by a small village called Matarieh. After carving my name on the bark and cutting off a twig for Christine, I made a sketch." Ballantine, *The Life of David Roberts, R.A.,* 110.

3. Champney, *Three Vassar Girls in the Holy Land,* 48.

4. Ibid., 123–24.

5. Ibid., 236–37.

TOMB OF THE HOLY SEPULCHRE.

160 *THREE VASSAR GIRLS IN THE HOLY LAND.*

children looked at them curiously, but the men had left their business for the ceremony of the day.

The Jews' Wailing Place is a spot to which, especially on Fridays, Jews of both sexes and every nationality congregate to lament the

THE JEWS' WAILING PLACE.

destruction of the Temple. A portion of the wall of the ancient Temple, supposed to be near to the Holy of Holies, stands here. Some of the stones are bevelled, many are fully twenty-five feet in length. It is the finest and best preserved portion of the wall. The Jews

Fig. 48. (*left*) Elizabeth Champney, illustrated by James Wells Champney, *Three Vassar Girls in the Holy Land*, photograph, *Tomb of the Holy Sepulchre*.

Fig. 49. Elizabeth Champney, illustrated by James Wells Champney, *Three Vassar Girls in the Holy Land*, etching, *The Jews' Wailing Place*.

demonstrates the continued importance of the Bible as the authoritative text for understanding the landscape. In the Garden of Gethsemane on the Mount of Olives, "Frank threw himself upon a seat, and took a book from his pocket. 'Is that a guide-book?' Violet asked. 'It is *the* guide-book,' he replied."[6] A text is required to translate sacred space into a meaningful experience. And that text is the Bible, not a *Baedeker's* guidebook. Even *Baedeker's* acknowledges the preeminence of the Bible as travel guide: "It is scarcely necessary to remark that the traveler is assumed to have his Bible with him."[7]

In the nineteenth century, the landscape without the text remained unreadable for the Christian traveler. More remarkably, in the nineteenth century the text without the landscape also became inadequate. The anonymous reviewer of a public presentation of images from the Holy Land in 1850 puts the case perfectly. The scenes "take hold of the mind and fix themselves there—it is to be felt, not described. The East of the Bible is little better than a dream until this Diorama is studied."[8] This observation suggests that the illusionary landscape of texts, prints, maps, and photographs was more than adequate for its understanding. In *Three Vassar Girls in the Holy Land,* long quotations from recognized biblical and archaeological authorities, a map of the girls' itinerary, and descriptions of sacred sites, photographic and graphic as well as textual, blur the genre boundaries between novel, picture book, and travel guide (figs. 48, 49). The novel's reader experiences the salutary effect of Christian topography vicariously, imagining that its construction of Jerusalem is true.

The conventional heroine of *Three Vassar Girls,* who sets off to Jerusalem as tourist and is transformed by the land into a pilgrim, demonstrates the West's spiritual expectations of travel to the Holy Land. In contrast, the unconventional hero of a second novel, *Tancred; or, The New Crusade,* who begins his journey to Jerusalem as a pilgrim, discovers that the representation of the Holy City is more deeply spiritual than its reality. *Tancred,* first published in 1847, was written by Benjamin Disraeli, novelist, British prime minister, and Jew converted to Christianity. In a literary style more elevated than that of *Three Vassar Girls, Tancred* explicitly describes the spiritual solace that the Holy Land promises to its Western readers. The Duke, Tancred's father, wishes him to take a seat in Parliament. He reminds Tancred of the benefits of industrialization and democracy:

"The general condition of England is superior to that of any other country; it cannot be denied, that on the whole there is more political freedom, more social happiness, more sound religion, and more material prosperity, among us, than in any nation in the world."

[Tancred replies:] "I see nothing in this fresh development of material industry, but fresh causes of moral deterioration. You have announced to the millions that their welfare is to

---

6. Ibid., 172.

7. *Baedeker's Handbook for Travellers*, cxvi.

8. Beverly and Bartlett, *A Pilgrimage through the Holy Land.* Also see J. Davis, "'Each Mouldering Ruin Recalls a History.'"

be tested by the amount of their wages. Money is to be the cupel [test] of their worth, as it is of all other classes. You propose for their conduct the least ennobling of all impulses."[9]

In the novel, the Duke represents the practical politics and economy of empire—through the expansion of markets, both internally and externally, industrialization and domestic social stability were both sustained. The East was needed for raw materials and potential consumers. His son expresses the immaterial supplement to the Duke's pragmatism. For Tancred, the sovereignty of money in the industrialized Aryan West makes the spiritual impossible; spiritual meaning may, however, be recovered in the Semitic East. The East serves the West as a spiritual reservoir as well as a market:

"I wish, indeed, to leave England; I wish to make an expedition; a progress to a particular point; without wandering, without any intervening residence. In a word—it is the Holy Land that occupies my thought, and I propose to make a pilgrimage to the sepulchre of my Savior."

The Duke started, and sank again into his chair. "The Holy Land! The Holy Sepulchre!" he exclaimed, and repeated to himself, staring at his son.

"Yes, sir, the Holy Sepulchre," repeated Lord Montacute [Tancred], and now speaking with his accustomed repose. "When I remember that the Creator, since light sprang out of darkness, has deigned to reveal himself to his creatures only in one land; that in that land he assumed a manly form, and met a human death; I feel persuaded that the country sanctified by such intercourse and such events, must be endowed with marvelous and peculiar qualities, which man may not in all ages be competent to penetrate, but which, nevertheless, at all times exercise an irresistible influence upon his destiny. It is these qualities that many times drew Europe to Asia during the middle centuries. Our castle has before this sent forth a De Montacute [the formidable Norman crusader Tancred] to Palestine. For three days and three nights he knelt at the tomb of his Redeemer. Six centuries and more have elapsed since that great enterprise. It is time to restore and renovate our communications with the Most High. I, too, would kneel at that tomb; I, too, surrounded by the holy hills and sacred groves of Jerusalem, would relieve my spirit from the bale that bows it down."[10]

Tancred, the young Lord Montacute, distracted by the materialism of the West, travels to the East for the particular consolation that the Holy Land offers. Like his ancestral namesake, Tancred seeks solace at the Holy Sepulchre, but in contrast with his forbearer, he fails to find inspiration there.[11] By the nineteenth century the Holy Sepulchre's aura is eroded. Indeed, Disraeli articulates his disdain for the site in his autobiographic novel, *Contarini Fleming*:

The church of the Holy Sepulchre is nearly in the middle of the city, and professedly built upon Mount Calvary, which it is alleged was leveled for the structure. Within

9. Disraeli, *Tancred*, 1.100–102.
10. Ibid., 1.109–11.
11. Ibid., 2.135.

Fig. 50. David Roberts, *Jerusalem from the Mount of Olives*. From Roberts and Croly, *The Holy Land, Syria, Idumea, Arabia, Egypt, and Nubia*.

its walls they have contrived to assemble the scenes of a vast number of incidents in the life of the Savior, with a highly romantic violation of the unity of place. . . . The truth is, the whole is an ingenious imposture of a comparatively recent date, and we are indebted to that favored individual, the Empress Helen, for this exceedingly clever creation, as well as for the discovery of the true cross.[12]

In its inauthenticity the Holy Sepulchre fails to provide the spiritual sustenance that Tancred seeks. At the end of the novel, the West's spiritual interest in the East is revealed for what it is—ideology. In seeking the Holy Sepulchre, the modern Tancred, like the medieval one, discovers the possibilities of a Near Eastern Empire. *Tancred* does not document a spiritual renewal of the West through contact with the East. It acts rather as Disraeli's prophetic fantasy about the English conquest of Syria and Palestine.

Tancred, like *Three Vassar Girls,* demonstrates the place of images in nineteenth-century imaginative constructions of Jerusalem. In *Tancred,* illustrations appear in the narrative, not in the text. Tancred prepares for his pilgrimage to the Holy Land by studying its representations:

12. Disraeli, *Contarini Fleming,* 100.

The enamoured Montacute [Tancred] hung over her [Lady Bertie] with pious rapture, as they examined together Mr. Roberts's Syrian drawings, and she alike charmed and astonished him by her familiarity with every locality and each detail. She looked like a beautiful prophetess as she dilated with solemn enthusiasm on the sacred scene. Tancred called on her every day, because when he called the first time, he had announced his immediate departure, and so had been authorized to promise that he would pay his respects to her every day till he went. It was calculated that by these means, that is to say three or four visits, they might perhaps travel through Mr. Roberts's views together before he left England, which would facilitate their correspondence, for Tancred had engaged to write to the only person in the world worthy of receiving his letters.[13]

Later, to Tancred's horror, Lady Bertie reveals herself as a crass materialist by speculating on how much easier it would be to travel to Jerusalem if there were a train line between Jaffa and the Holy City. Though the affects of Lady Bertie then cease to move Tancred, the effects of David Roberts's lithographs continue. The description of Jerusalem in the novel reads like a collage of images derived from Roberts's prints, populated by a pastiche of figures from the Old and New Testaments (fig. 50):

A lofty wall, with turrets and towers and frequent gates, undulates with the unequal ground which it covers, as it encircles the lost capital of Jehovah. . . . The broad steep of Zion, crowned with the tower of David; nearer still, Mount Moriah, with the gorgeous temple of the God of Abraham, but built, alas! by the child of Hagar, and not by Sarah's chosen one; close to its cedars and its cypresses, its lofty spires and airy arches, the moonlight falls upon Bethesda's pool; further on, entered by the gate of St. Stephen, the eye . . . traces with ease the Street of Grief [Via Dolorosa, the Way of the Cross], a long winding ascent to a vast cupolaed pile that now covers Calvary, called the Street of Grief, because there the most illustrious of the human, as well as of the Hebrew, race, the descendant of King David, and the divine Son of the most favored of women, twice sank under that burden of suffering and shame which is now throughout all Christendom the emblem of triumph and of honor; passing over groups and masses of houses built of stone, with terraced roofs or surmounted with small domes, we reach the hill of Salem, where Melchisedek built his mystic citadel; and still remains the hill of Scopas, where Titus gazed upon Jerusalem on the eve of his final assault. . . . A fortified city, almost surrounded by ravines, and rising in the center of chains of far-spreading hills occasionally offering, through their rocky glens, the gleams of a distant and richer land![14]

In *Tancred,* Roberts's lithographs are not cited as the source for the description of Jerusalem. His prints are, however, recognized as the model for the

13. Disraeli, *Tancred,* 1.309.

14. Ibid., 2.1–3.

A CARAVAN JOURNEY. 81

ARABS OF THE DESERT.

We might manage to let them have a separate dining-tent. At any rate, it is probably wisest to see them and talk the matter over."

The donkey boys of Suez besieged them in very much the same fashion as those of Cairo. Each boy has a different name for his donkey which he thinks will appeal to travellers of different nationalities. In talking with a Frenchman he will assert that M. de Lesseps named

6

Fig. 51. David Roberts, *Arabs of the Desert.* From Roberts and Croly, *The Holy Land, Syria, Idumea, Arabia, Egypt, and Nubia.*

Fig. 52. (*above*) Elizabeth Champney, illustrated by James Wells Champney, *Three Vassar Girls in the Holy Land,* lithograph, *Arabs of the Desert.*

illustrations in *Three Vassar Girls.* Although the images reproduced in *Three Vassar Girls* come from a variety of sources, only one is identified: "David Roberts, R.A., whose sketches are reproduced in the illustration of this volume." [15] A comparison of Roberts's *Arabs of the Desert* with the illustration on page 81 of the novel indicates the appropriateness of the author's acknowledgment (figs. 51, 52).

ENTREPRENEURS

David Roberts's *The Holy Land, Syria, Idumea, Arabia, Egypt, and Nubia, from Drawings Made on the Spot by David Roberts, R. A., with Historical Descriptions by the Reverend George Croly, L.L.D., Lithographed by Louis Haghe* was the most lavish lithographic art-print collection ever produced.[16] His plates were first published between 1840 and 1845 in the form of separate fascicules for subscribers. The collected fascicules comprise a magisterial three-volume set of 257 folio polychrome prints. Further editions of *The Holy Land,* both pirated and legitimate, made Roberts's Holy Land available to a wide range of European

15. Champney, *Three Vassar Girls in the Holy Land,* 268.

16. For Roberts and for bibliographies of earlier studies, see Bendiner, "David Roberts in the Near East"; Bourbon, *The Life, Works and Travels of David Roberts, R.A.;* K. Clark, "Renderings of an Early Master"; Guiterman, "David Roberts, R. A. (1796–1864), part I"; Guiterman, "The Travels of David Roberts"; Mancoff, *David Roberts;* Solon, "Suggestions and Models for Architectural Rendering."

and American consumers.[17] Even more distant progeny of Roberts's renderings of the East proliferated in the West in copies like those that appeared in *Three Vassar Girls*. A toast to Roberts proposed by Lord Cockburn in 1842 offers a contemporary understanding of the broad appeal of his work:

[There was a land] which lay in silence and desolation, and which seemed by the very impressiveness of that silence to demand the eye and the hand and the mind of an artist worthy of conveying its treasures to the latest posterity. That is a region connected with such associations—connected with solemn and interesting events—that so far as we can at present conceive, it is impossible that an equal interest should ever be imparted to any other portion of the globe. . . . [Roberts] explored that patriarchal land; he searched its inmost recesses, and returned to his native country laden with the richest treasures, after having completed the finest pilgrimage of art which ever perhaps has been performed by a single man. The result has been marked by the most distinct and unanimous verdict that the public ever pronounced on a mere triumph of taste. And no wonder it has done so; because, first, the scenes themselves are connected with our earliest, our deepest, our most sacred associations; and in the second place, they were presented to us with all their complement of scenery and figures, not only with the fidelity of portraiture, but adorned with the finest touches of poetry.[18]

The language of this tribute is the language of imperial economics. Roberts appropriates the wealth (treasures) of a defenseless land (silent and desolate) for export to the West. But Roberts is not the CEO of Standard Oil. The object of his exploitation has spiritual as well as commercial value; further, his commerce is not in commodities but in works.[19] What Roberts imports from the East has religion as its content and art as its form. Nevertheless, like Egyptian cotton, before the subject matter procured by Roberts in the East could be marketed, it had to be industrially manufactured. The commercial success of his prints was the consequence of a remarkable set of entrepreneurial, economic, and aesthetic coincidences.

The particular popularity of Roberts's *Holy Land* was the happy result of the simultaneous maturation both of a cheap new mode of graphic reproduction and of a remarkable artist. The lithographic process was invented at the turn of the nineteenth century. The first patents for it date from 1799.[20] Only in the 1830s were techniques refined to the point that images that looked like art could be mass-produced. Lithographers developed the technological capability to cheaply mass-produce simulations of the artist's touch.[21] Some sense of the assembly-line production of the lithographic print is provided by a view of the

17. Pirated editions appeared almost immediately in Europe. In response, the original publisher, Moon, participated in a French edition of sixty plates published in Brussels. Octavo editions appeared in the United States in 1855 and 1860 and in England in 1856. See Mancoff, *David Roberts*, 115.

18. Quoted in Ballantine, *The Life of David Roberts, R.A.*, 150.

19. For the definition of *commodity* used in this text, see the introduction.

20. Twyman, *Lithography, 1800–1850*, 12.

21. Twyman, *Breaking the Mould*, chap. 2.

Fig. 53. Rose-Joseph Lemercier's hall of presses, Paris. Advertisement reproduced from Twyman, *Breaking the Mould.* Reprinted with the author's permission.

factorylike hall of presses of the Parisian publisher Lemercier (fig. 53).[22] David Roberts came of age as an artist at the same time that the new medium reached its prime. He was a brilliant autodidact.[23] Son of a shoemaker, apprentice to a housepainter, understudy of a stage-set designer, then a theater and panorama painter, Roberts observed and sketched nature at every opportunity, refining his skills in watercolor and then oils. But only through travel was Roberts's reputation as an artist established and his fortune assured. A contemporary interest in topographic images complemented his own desire for the foreign. He journeyed to France, visiting "Dieppe, Rouen, and Harvre de Grace, where I made a series of drawings, from which I painted pictures that brought me both profit and fame."[24] Recognizing the appeal of the exotic and novel, Roberts later traveled to more remote regions. "The fact is that nothing is known of Spain; those who could have appreciated the richness of its architecture have generally gone to Italy or Greece. My portfolio is getting rich, the subjects are not only good but of a very novel character."[25] The trip to Spain proved extremely profitable.[26]

---

22. For a description of a labyrinthine setting for the mass production of texts under J.-P. Migne, the master of entrepreneurial publishing, see Bloch, *God's Plagiarist,* 14–16.

23. Still the best access to David Roberts's life is provided by Ballantine, *The Life of David Roberts, R.A.* This work is a compilation of excerpts from Roberts's own journals as transcribed by his daughter and quotations from contemporary sources connected by the narration of the author, one of Roberts's good friends.

24. Ibid., 24.

25. Ibid., 47.

26. Ibid., 76.

Fig. 54. David Roberts, *The Mosque of Omar*. From Roberts and Croly, *The Holy Land, Syria, Idumea, Arabia, Egypt, and Nubia*.

By the late 1830s, Roberts was prepared for the longest and most lucrative excursion of his career. In 1837 and 1838, he traveled through Egypt and then to Palestine and up the Syrian coast, producing hundreds of sketches in the process. He describes to his daughter the pleasures of cross-dressing and image-gathering:

I am so completely transmogrified in appearance that my dear old mother would never know me. Before I could get admission to the mosques, I had to transfer my whiskers to my upper lip, and don the full Arab costume, since which I have been allowed to make sketches, both in oil and water colors, of the principal mosques. I have provided everything requisite for my journey. A tent (a very gay one, I assure you), skins for carrying water, pewter dishes, provisions of all sorts, not forgetting a brace of Turkish pistols, and a warm covering for night. Imagine me mounted on my camel, my black servant on another, and two men with my tent and luggage; the other two gentlemen similarly furnished and accoutred, surrounded by a host of the children of the desert—the wild Arabs; and you will have an idea of what an Eastern monarch I am. From Suez, we intend skirting the Red Sea, visiting Mount Sinai, Petra, Hebron, Jerusalem, Bethlehem, and all the more important places in the Holy Land. All this journey I hope to accomplish in about two months; and if God spares me in life and health, I expect to bring home with me the most interesting collection of sketches that has ever left the East. I told you, I was getting on excellent terms with myself. . . . And thanks to Mahomet Ali, traveling now in Syria is as safe as in England.[27]

Muhammad Ali, the Egyptian despot, reformer, and modernizer, would have overthrown the Ottomans were it not for British intervention.[28] His forces

27. Roberts's letter to his daughter from Cairo, January 31, 1839, quoted in ibid., 112–13.

28. Sayyid-Marsot, *Egypt in the Reign of Muhammad Ali*.

Fig. 55. Luigi Mayers, *Temple of Solomon*. From *Views of Palestine*. Reproduction courtesy of the Houghton Library, Harvard University.

Fig. 56. (*bottom*) William Finden, *Mount Moriah*. Etching, after a drawing by J. M. W. Turner done from a sketch made on the site by Charles Barry. From Finden, Finden, and Horne, *Landscape Illustrations of the Bible*.

occupied Jerusalem in 1831. The position of the religious minorities improved under Egyptian rule, and as Roberts reports, traveling for foreigners became safer and easier. Without Muhammad Ali, his project would have been impossible.

The publication of *The Holy Land* upon his return established Roberts's status as an artist—he became a member of the Royal Academy in 1841—and secured for him a comfortable income for the rest of his life. The success of his endeavor depended on his prints' capacity to represent the Holy Land as it was desired in the West: a material reality which might readily be appropriated by its possessor for her own purposes—religious or antiquarian, as a supplement to travel (Tancred) or as travels' surrogate (Lady Bertie).

The lithographs' literalness was one of the publication's greatest appeals. Critics corroborated the accuracy of the representations. The best-known nineteenth-century authority on art, John Ruskin, comments:

> *It had chanced, in the spring of the year, that David Roberts had brought home and exhibited his sketches in Egypt and the Holy Land. They were the first studies ever made conscientiously by an English painter, not to exhibit his own skill, or make capital out of his subjects, but to give true portraiture of scenes of historical and religious interest. They were faithful and laborious beyond any outlines from nature I had ever seen.*[29]

The veracity of Roberts's images remains compelling. Indeed, the camera lucida (a mirroring device that transfers a view to a sheet of paper for tracing) has been invoked to explain the apparent truthfulness of his sketches.[30] Moreover, the literalism of Roberts's representation of the Holy Land was a novelty. The contrast between his rendering of the Dome of the Rock and examples of earlier depictions of the monument documents Roberts's relative proximity to optical reality (fig. 54). In his depiction of al-Haram al-Sharif, the influential German artist Luigi Mayers imported a stilted baroque onion dome and a well-ordered German town square to Palestine (fig. 55).[31] Just as bizarre is the representation of the Dome of the Rock ascribed to Sir Charles Barry, a well-known British architect, which appeared in 1836 in William Finden's *Landscape Illustrations of the Bible: Consisting of Views of the Most Remarkable Places Mentioned in the Old and New Testaments, from Original Sketches Taken on the Spot* (fig. 56).[32] It sets Jerusalem in the Scottish Highlands and includes a tiny vignette of a Western woman being ravaged by Arab bandits in the foreground.

A comparison of prints by Barry and Roberts also reveals something of the differences between etching and lithography. It suggests that claims for the veracity of *The Holy Land*'s images depended on their medium as well as on their figuration. Etching involves the meticulous paraphrase of an artist's drawing by a master engraver, working with incising tools and acids, on a metal plate. The language of an image radically changes in its translation from drawing to etching: a wash of color may become a lake of stippling; the artist's broad brushstroke, a shadow of delicate parallel lines. The polychrome painting becomes

29. Ruskin, *The Works of John Ruskin*, 35:262.

30. Bourbon, *The Life, Works and Travels of David Roberts, R.A.*, 15. I wrote to the author requesting his source for this information, but received no response. Frederick Catherwood, who worked in Jerusalem at the beginning of the century, certainly used the camera lucida. Ben-Arieh, "Catherwood Map of Jerusalem," 152.

31. For Luigi Mayers as a model for contemporary artists, see Schütz, *Preussen in Jerusalem (1800–1861)*, 28–30.

32. Finden, Finden, and Horne, *Landscape Illustrations of the Bible*, plate 3.

black and white. The plate is inked, then wiped; ink is held in its furrows and scars until transferred to paper by the press.[33]

In the medium of lithography, the language of the print remains that of painting. The lithographer, working with a brush, applies a gluey paint to a polished stone much as a painter applies pigment to a canvas. The stone is moistened, inked, then wiped. The ink, adhering to the sticky paint, is then pressed onto paper.[34] Multiple stones used for a single print added layers of color to the final product. In his reproduction of an artwork, the master lithographer recapitulates the artist's gestures as well as the model's forms. The proximity of lithography to painting is demonstrated by the number of artists who worked directly on the stone. Indeed, in the nineteenth century, master etchers remained craftsmen, while master lithographers were also often painters. William Simpson, the remarkable nineteenth-century lithographer, watercolorist, illustrator, and traveler, comments on this proximity of lithographers and artists:[35]

[There was] a tendency among lithographers . . . to become artists or painters. . . . As a rule engravers, whether on copper, steel, or wood, never became artists, or I should say painters, because the work was mechanical, and merely copying. But in lithography . . . we had to work out rough material into pictures. . . . It was from work like this [lithography] that such artists as Sir John Gilbert, George Thomas, Herkomer, and Gregory, as well as others, have started.[36]

The print of Barry's drawing of the Haram is estranged from its subject by the artist's romantic interpretation of the setting; it is also distanced from the originating hand of the artist by the process of its production. Barry's original drawing was turned into a painting by a second artist, J. M. W. Turner, then translated onto copper by William Finden. The print appears as a stylized fantasy, removed from nature and from art by its obvious craftedness. In contrast, Roberts's print seems to present to the observer the immediacy of an artist's view of Jerusalem. Roberts's prints were executed not by Roberts, of course, but by a team of craftsmen led by Louis Haghe. A master lithographer, Haghe worked first for the publisher Francis Graham Moon, then for Day and Sons before finally leaving lithography to become a professional watercolorist.[37] Nevertheless, the loose, calligraphic rendering of *The Holy Land* image allows it to be read as the direct expression of Roberts's own gaze. Its color, its grand scale, and its touch mark the image as art.

---

33. This is, of course, an oversimplified description of the complex process of making etchings. For an insightful discussion of how the technique was pushed to compete with painting, see Melion, "Hendrick Goltzius's Project of Reproductive Engraving."

34. Again, this is an oversimplified account of lithography. For a full description and history of the technique, see Twyman, *Lithography, 1800–1850.*

35. For a discussion of the attempt to raise the status of etching from a craft to an art, see Chambers, "From Chemical Process to the Aesthetics of Omission."

36. Simpson, *The Autobiography of William Simpson,* 14–15.

37. An excellent discussion of the place of Roberts's project within the technological development of lithography is provided by Twyman, *Lithography, 1800–1850,* 210–20. For William Day, see Simpson, *The Autobiography of William Simpson,* chap. 18.

Roberts was a great draftsman but a weak colorist. John Ruskin describes his artistic limitations as well as his artistic accomplishments:

[Roberts's] drawings were made with a diligence and patience greatly edifying to me, and with a precision of line which I had no pretence to equal though I had been drawing little more than lines for the last seven years. . . . I immediately saw the facilities given by these means for obtaining the essential forms in any subject, and their adoption at once enabled me to use what powers of delineation I had already obtained to the best possible effect. The drawings made on this principle satisfied myself, for the first time, and gave much pleasure to most people interested in the scenes they represented—such of them as I possess remain to this day delightful to me. . . . To the end of his life Roberts remained merely a draughtsman and oil painter in grey and yellow—he never looked for the facts of color in anything but in so far as it was large, varied in picturesque surfaces, and capable of being arranged in a composition of light things against dark ones, and dark against light.[38]

Although Roberts's concern with surface and tone rather than saturation and hue may have kept him from being a great painter, it allowed his work to be more closely replicated in lithography. His limitations as an artist contributed to the aesthetic success of his lithographs.

The ostensible objectivity of *The Holy Land*'s lithographic prints, their obvious artistry, and their relative affordability contributed to the remarkable popularity of the collection. Because Roberts's works functioned both as archaeological documents and as art, they appealed to a variety of consumers. Their factual character gave them a new scientific credibility that was further enhanced by the absence of an exclusively Christian content.[39] The images' independence of the Bible is remarkable. Most earlier representations of the Holy Land, like many later ones, acted as illustrations for the stories of the Old and New Testaments; the landscape of Palestine functioned as a background authenticating the biblical narrative enacted within it. In contrast, the Greco-Roman and Egyptian monuments as well as the Christian ones represented in Roberts's prints demonstrated that his works were "true" depictions of an exotic topography. Moreover, by populating the lithographs with local types in native costume, the artist gave an anthropological gloss to the scenes before anthropology.[40] The scientific posture of Roberts's prints promoted their secular consumption.

At the same time, the denarrativized images allowed a devout viewer to read into them the story of her choice. Indeed, the Arabs represented in the print could

38. Ruskin, *The Works of John Ruskin*, 625.

39. Those who desired a biblical reading had recourse to the unimaginative text by the Reverend George Croly that accompanied the images. Croly's commentary is constructed of excerpts from Roberts's journal laced together with biblical quotations and pious observations. Few positive references to Croly's text are found in either nineteenth-century reviews or in current assessments of Roberts's *Holy Land*. Also, see Bendiner, "David Roberts in the Near East." Bendiner, however, oddly treats Roberts's prints as if they were an "impersonal documentation" of the landscape.

40. Anthropology was not established as a discipline in universities until the end of the nineteenth century. See MacCurdy, "Extent of Instruction in Anthropology in Europe and the United States."

be understood as the same who populated the biblical landscape. Conventional Christians might not have understood Mark Twain's observation as ironic:

> *But maybe you cannot see the wild extravagance of my panorama. . . . The scenery of the Bible is about you—the customs of the patriarchs are around you—the same people, in the same flowing robes and in sandals, cross your path—the same long trains of stately camels go and come—the same impressive religious solemnity and silence rest upon the desert and the mountains that were upon them in the remote ages of antiquity.*[41]

For the pious Protestant beholder, no less than for the antiquarian, the *real* Holy Land, liberated from its Catholic icons, was finally available for purchase.

The absence of religious preference in the prints of *The Holy Land* conforms to the absence of religious motivation in Roberts's enterprise. Pilgrimage was not the object of the artist's journey. Indeed, the purpose of his excursion was explicitly entrepreneurial; the trip was undertaken for profit. Roberts describes with satisfaction the realization of his ambitious project:

> *Previous to my leaving for the East I had promised to give Messrs. Finden [William and Edward Finden, publishers of* Landscape Illustrations of the Bible . . . from Original Sketches Taken on the Spot] *the refusal of the work, and on my return, after having arranged the form in which it was to brought out, these gentlemen promised to let me know what terms they would give me for the copy right and use of the drawings. After having waited four months without having received any offer from them, I applied to Mr. [John] Murray, who at first agreed to my proposal; but after calculating the outlay (£10,000), told me the risk was too great. I had been applied to by Mr. Moon, whom I made acquainted with all these circumstances, and he at once agreed to bring out the work in the manner I had proposed. . . . I was to be paid £3000 for the use of the drawings. This was a great risk on the publisher's part; but by exhibiting the drawings in London and other principal towns, his subscription list in May 1841 was nearly double Murray's estimate of cost. . . . Before the drawings were shown to the public they were submitted to the Queen, to the Archbishops of York and Canterbury, and to the Bishop of London, who all subscribed for the work, the Queen graciously allowing it to be dedicated to her. . . . It was ultimately arranged that [the prints] should all be done by Mr. Haghe, and there can be only one opinion as to the masterly manner in which he executed his work. The notices given by the public journals, wherever those drawings were exhibited, were highly laudatory; the work, when completed, was equally favorably noticed; and the success of the publication was all that could be desired.*[42]

The Holy Land was sold by two clever entrepreneurs, Roberts and his publisher, Francis Graham Moon, before it had been produced. The support of the queen

41. Twain, *The Innocents Abroad; or, the New Pilgrims Progress*, 347.
42. Ballantine, *The Life of David Roberts, R.A.*, 130–31.

ensured the patronage of a broad stratum of the elite. Names on the subscription list, which appeared in the first print volume, include a long list of aristocrats and bishops, as well as such formidable patrons as Miss Burdett-Coutts, Charles Dickens, William Morris, John Ruskin, and Sir David Wilkie, R.A.[43]

That Roberts's *Holy Land* exceeded all earlier lithographic projects in its scale is often noted; that it remained one of the most ambitious collections of lithographically reproduced drawings is less commonly remarked. Almost immediately after the publication of *The Holy Land,* lithography lost its priority as an art form. Simpson remarks that his volume of lithographs from the Crimean War of 1855 "was perhaps the last" of the genre. "The startling thing is that it [the collection of lithographic art prints] was a class of work which came into existence, lasted only about a quarter of a century, and has entirely vanished. Lithography is still carried on, but it is limited to such things as an auctioneer's view of an estate, or a window show-bill, few of which show any pictorial qualities."[44] *The Holy Land*'s claims to veracity exhibited a taste for the real that was, by the late 1850s, more fully satisfied with photography. Indeed, almost immediately after its publication, lithographic drawings were superseded by photographic prints as the favored means of possessing Jerusalem.[45]

By the end of the nineteenth century, Roberts's lithographs had been eclipsed by stereoptic slides and photographic portfolios from Palestine. In 1897, *The Holy Land* was advertised for sale at only $10.50 a volume.[46] By the end of the twentieth century, however, there was a revival of interest in Roberts's works. Photographs have become too painful a vehicle for contemplating the Holy Land; there is now a nostalgia for nostalgic renderings of the sacred landscape. In an op-ed piece on the fate of traditional bookstores in the age of Barnes and Noble and Amazon.com, the *New York Times* quotes the owner of the Argosy: "Some of the books are so rare they are kept in safes, and there is a sophisticated alarm system. Probably the most valuable item is a six-volume set of hand-colored lithographs of the Holy Land by David Roberts, published in 1842–1849, which can be had for 'up to $200,000,' Ms. Cohen said."[47] The complete set of lithographs has also been recently reproduced in

---

43. The subscription list is conveniently accessible in Mezzatesta, *Jerusalem and the Holy Land Rediscovered.*

44. Simpson, *The Autobiography of William Simpson,* 14–15.

45. Twyman, *Lithography, 1800–1850,* 225. For the incursions of photographers in Palestine, see Onne, *Photographic Heritage of the Holy Land 1839–1914.* Onne's appendix B, 93–99, provides a chronological summary.

46. "David Roberts's colored lithographic views of the Holy Land, 3 vols., London, 1842, $10.50 per volume." From "Books Sold This Week at Auction." Even when Roberts's work was less in demand, his facility was acknowledged. In 1926, for example, the well-known art historian Kenneth Clark wrote, "The sense of scale so necessary in the representation of the huge ruins that form the subjects of the series is admirably expressed though perhaps a bit over accented by making the figures a trifle small, but this method adds to the vastness and majesty of the Egyptian architecture. . . . The accuracy of perspective in these drawings is particularly worth study; the most intricate problems are solved perfectly." K. Clark, "Renderings of an Early Master," 58–61.

47. D. Smith, "A Shrine to Books Past Clings to Independence."

its entirety by two different publishers, Duke Press and Rizzoli, and exhibitions of the prints are popular.[48] Roberts's lithographic series has proved to be the most pervasive and enduring of the nineteenth-century renderings of the East circulated in the West.

VIEWING

Lithography was only one of a number of speculative ventures in the nineteenth-century manufacture of vendible images. A few years before patents for lithography were issued, for example, the Panorama was invented. The Panorama, an architectural mechanism for the mass production of illusions, was patented by Robert Barker in 1787.[49] The best description of its machinery is provided by Barker's patent application:

June 19th, 1787. NOW KNOW YE, *that by my invention, called La Nature à Coup d' Oeil [Nature at a Glance, later named Panorama], is intended, by drawing and painting, and a proper disposition of the whole, to perfect an entire view of any country or situation, as it appears to an observer turning quite round; to produce which effect, the painter or drawer must fix his station, and delineate correctly and connectedly every object which presents itself to his view as he turns round, concluding his drawing by a connection with where he began. He must observe the lights and shadows, how they fall, and perfect his piece to the best of his abilities.*

There must be a circular building or framing erected, on which this drawing or painting may be performed; or the same may be done on canvas, or other materials, and fixed or suspended on the same building or framing, to answer the purpose complete. It must be lighted entirely from the top, either by a glazed dome or otherwise, as the artist may think proper. There must be an inclosure within the said circular building or framing, which shall prevent an observer going too near the drawing or painting, so as it may, from all parts it can be viewed, have its proper effect. This inclosure may represent a room, or platform, or any other situation, and may be any form thought most convenient, but the circular form is particularly recommended.

Of whatever extent this inside inclosure may be, there must be over it (supported from the bottom, or suspended from the top,) a shade or roof; which, in all directions, should project so far beyond this inclosure, as to prevent an observer seeing above the drawing or painting, when looking up; and there must be without this inclosure another interception, to represent a wall, paling, or other interception, as the natural objects represented, or fancy, may direct, so as effectually to prevent the observer from seeing below the bottom of the painting or drawing, by means of which interception nothing can be seen on the outer circle, but the drawing or painting intended to

48. Bourbon, *The Life, Works and Travels of David Roberts, R.A;* Mezzatesta, *Jerusalem and the Holy Land Rediscovered.*

49. The most scholarly and thorough history of the panorama is offered by Oettermann, *The Panorama.* Other very useful discussions are provided by Comment, *The Painted Panorama;* Hyde, *Panoramania!;* Lawson, "Time Bandits; Space Vampires"; A. Miller, "The Moving Panorama, the Cinema, and the Emergence of the Spectacular."

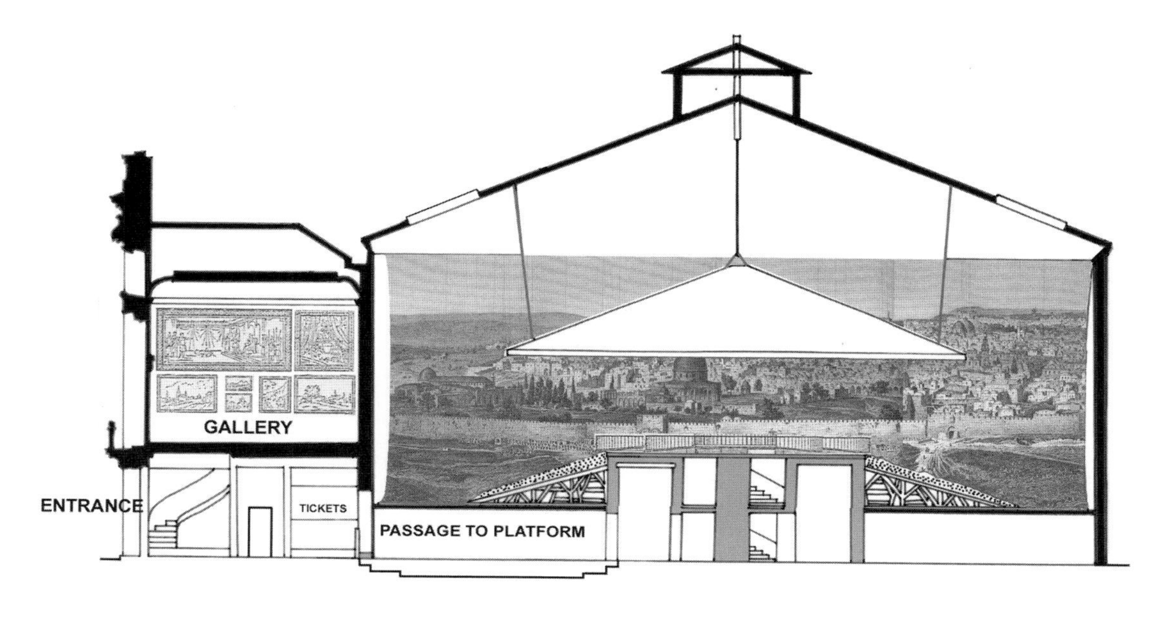

Fig. 57. (*top*) Schematic section of a Panorama. Drawing by the author.

Fig. 58. Stateville Correctional Center, near Joliet, Illinois, view of the interior. Photograph courtesy of the Abraham Lincoln Presidential Library.

represent nature. The entrance to the inner inclosure must be from below a proper building or framing being erected for that purpose, so that no door or other interruption may disturb the circle on which the view is to be represented.

And there should be, below the painting or drawing, proper ventilators fixed, so as to render a current circulation of air through the whole; and the inner inclosure may be elevated, at the will of an artist, so as to make observers, on whatever situation he may wish they should imagine themselves, feel as if really on the very spot. In witness whereof, &c.[50]

No diagram is attached to the patent, but a sketch illustrates this remarkable image-producing machine (fig. 57). The Panorama constructs an optical illusion involving the body as well as the eye. Space is ordered to control the gaze of the observer: she is restricted to a small platform from which the only view is to the periphery; her vision depends on an overhead light source which she can sense but cannot see. The restlessness of her body compensates for the inanimate image that she views: her shifting look enlivens the unmoving clouds and motionless figures of the painting of the circumference.

In the same year that Barker took out his patent for the Panorama, Jeremy Bentham, utilitarian philosopher and economist, published the plans of an uncannily similar architectural machine, the Panopticon.[51] Its author presents a detailed description of the device (fig. 58):

Morals reformed—health preserved—industry invigorated—instruction diffused—public burthens lightened—Economy seated, as it were, upon a rock . . . all by a simple idea in Architecture! . . . A new mode of obtaining power of mind over mind, in a quantity hitherto without example: and that, to a degree equally without example, secured by whoever chooses to have it so, against abuse.—Such is the engine: such the work that may be done with it.[52] . . .

The building is circular. The apartments of the prisoners occupy the circumference. . . . These cells are divided from one another, and the prisoners by that means secluded from all communication with each other, by partitions in the form of radii issuing from the circumference towards the center, and extending as many feet as shall be thought necessary to form the largest dimension of the cell. The apartment of the inspector occupies the center. . . . It will be convenient in most, if not in all cases, to have a vacant space or area all round, between such center and such circumference. . . . Each cell has in the outward circumference, a window, large enough, not only to light the cell, but, through the cell, to afford light enough to the correspondent part of the [inspector's] lodge. The inner circumference of the cell is formed by an iron grating, so light as not to screen any part of the cell from the inspector's view. . . . To the windows of the lodge there are blinds, as high up as the eyes of the prisoners in their cells can, by

50. Barker, "Patent: La Nature à Coup d' Oeil," n.p.

51. For the best-known and still-magisterial treatment of the Panopticon, see Foucault, *Discipline and Punish*, 195–228.

52. Bentham, "Panopticon," 31.

any means they can employ, be made to reach. . . . Small lamps, in the outside of each window of the lodge, backed by a reflector, to throw the light into the corresponding cells, would extend to the night the security of the day.[53]

These two monumental machines for viewing both provide observers at their centers with a new sense of power over the periphery. The Panopticon allows control of the social margins of the state; the Panorama offers surveillance of its actual or potential territorial edges. In both cases, however, power resides in the structure, not the viewer. Both apparatuses coerce the observer as well as the object of observation. Both structures physically constrain the "inspector." The observer's authority, her subjecthood, is illusory—with the Panorama, literally, and with the Panopticon, politically. Only the power of the machine—the building—is absolute. These structures present a metaphor of the evolving capitalist economy: the entrepreneurial classes, like the laboring ones, were both regulated by a new economic system—capitalism—that, once constructed, had its own internal logic.

The Panorama and Panopticon were, of course, actually, as well as metaphorically, linked to the economy: both these devices were expected to produce a profit. Bentham, after all, composed his "Defense of the Usury" at the same time that he wrote his letters describing the Panopticon; Bentham was the man who changed the mind of the great economist Adam Smith about the necessity of usury laws.[54] Bentham's critique of state-imposed limitations on profit from lending was based on his assumption that individuals should be free agents. "No man of ripe years and of sound mind, acting freely, and with his eyes open, ought to be hindered, with a view to his advantage, from making such a bargain, in the way of obtaining money, as he thinks fit; nor (what is a necessary consequence), anybody hindered from supplying him, upon any terms he thinks proper to accede to."[55] But profit, rather than freedom, reveals itself to be the true object of Bentham's social practice in his discussion of the Panopticon. He presents the device as a prison/factory that, because of its exquisite means of visual control, is particularly efficient:

What hold can any other manufacturer have upon his workmen, equal to what my manufacturer would have upon his? What other master is there that can reduce his workmen, if idle, to a situation next to starving, without suffering them to go elsewhere? What other master is there, whose men can never get drunk unless he chooses they should do so? And who, so far from being able to raise their wages by combination, are obliged to take whatever pittance he thinks it most for his interest to allow? . . . What other manufacturers are there who reap their profits at the risk of other people, and who have the purse of the nation to support them, in case of any blameless misfortune? And to crown the whole by the great advantage which is the

53. Ibid., 35–36.
54. Bentham, "Usury Laws," 7–32.
55. Ibid., 7.

peculiar fruit of this new principle, what other master or manufacturer is there, who to appearance constantly, and in reality as much as he thinks proper, has every look and motion of each workman under his eye?[56]

Barker's Panorama, no less than Bentham's Panopticon or Roberts's *Holy Land,* was designed to make a profit. That the description of his invention appears in the form of a patent document proves that its products were meant to be marketable. The development of the patent—a form of government-sanctioned monopoly—paralleled the evolution of manufacturing.[57] The earliest recorded patent, granted by the English crown in 1449 to John of Utynam for a glassmaking process, protected technologies of industrial production; now patent law has been extended to the control of life itself.[58] From defending the inventions of the individual to promoting the monopolies of the globalized corporation, the state has progressively refined its protections for profit-producing processes.[59]

The Panorama proved a lucrative and popular entertainment—the predecessor of the twentieth-century film industry.[60] The subjects depicted in Panoramas were chosen exclusively for their potential appeal to a paying audience. Urban populations were interested in looking at themselves; Panoramas offered views of the cities in which they were constructed. Barker's first Panorama, displayed in Edinburgh, represented Edinburgh. The first panorama painted specifically for display in London represented London. The Mesdag Panorama of Scheveningen, one of the most sophisticated of the surviving Panoramas, presented the neighboring resort beach at the time of the painting.[61] In addition to offering an observer a new visual access to her own surroundings, the panorama performed as the nineteenth century's CNN, providing the viewer with the optic immediacy of the horrors of war. The Panorama of the Battle of Waterloo, on view in the Leicester Square Panorama in London in 1816, was such an economic success that it enabled Henry Aston Barker, the son and heir of Robert Barker, to retire comfortably.[62] *The Battle of Gettysburg* and *The Battle of Atlanta* are among the few nineteenth-century panoramas still in operation in the United States.

---

56. Bentham, "Panopticon," 71–72.

57. For an apology for trusts and monopolies written at a moment of rampant speculation, see J. Jenks, *The Trust Problem*.

58. Most obviously in the corporate struggle to possess the genome. See Resnik, *Owning the Genome*. The author, who introduces his book with a legal disclaimer (he is a philosopher, not a biochemist or a lawyer) and a disclosure statement (that he has no financial interests in the companies that he discusses), suggests that fragments of the human genome are not fully human and therefore subject to limitations, so they may well be exclusively possessed through patents. For a religious perspective, see Nelkin, "God Talk."

59. These observations are more fully argued by Shiva, *Protect or Plunder?,* 11–21.

60. For the importance of the Panorama to Romanticism and the idea of the *Gesamtkunstwerk,* see Eberlein, "Dioramen, Panoramen und Romantik."

61. Halkes, "The Mesdag Panorama"; van Eekelen, *The Magical Panorama*.

62. Comment, *The Painted Panorama,* 23–28.

Panorama speculators also profitably offered surrogate sightseeing.[63] Views of the great European cities fascinated not only their own occupants but also those living elsewhere in Europe and in America. Dramatic landscapes, such as Niagara Falls and the Mississippi River, attracted European as well as American audiences. More exotic locations were also made available to the panorama-going public. The remarkable popularity of the panoramas of Istanbul/Constantinople and Cairo, each of which circulated in several renditions, is indicative of the West's growing interest in the great cities of Middle East. Although the antiquity of these metropolises doubtlessly contributed to their attraction, all versions of which I am aware represented them in the present. Constantinople was depicted the way it would appear to a tourist occupying the same vantage point as the artist. Panoramas functioned as the optical analogue of the emerging travel industry.[64]

Jerusalem was also among the sites produced for panorama audiences. It was, however, always more than an exotic tourist destination. In contrast with Cairo and Constantinople, Jerusalem's past was of greater interest than its present. Amos Lawrence's redemptive reaction to a panorama of Jerusalem is one of the few interesting incidents in the biography of this American philanthropist, commemoratively published with the support of the principal benefactor of his generosity, Williams College:

After a long confinement, with little hope of recovery, he visited, when first able to get out, the Panorama of Jerusalem, then on exhibition in Boston, and remained there till the scene took full possession of his mind. Shortly after, on a fine day, he rode out to Brookline; and, as returning health threw over those hills a mantle of beauty that he had never seen before, they were immediately associated in his mind with the Panorama of Jerusalem, and with the glories of Jerusalem above. This association was indissoluble, and he would take his friends out to see his "Mount Zion."[65]

Early panoramas of Jerusalem were displayed in New York, London, and Edinburgh.[66] In 1819, Pierre Prévost, having returned from travel in the Middle

63. For the economics of panoramas and particularly the remarkable episode of Belgian speculation in the late nineteenth century, see Leroy, "The Maritime Panorama of Scheveningen."

64. As did, of course, orientalist images in all media. For a useful review of the European penetration of the East through drawing, see Conner, "The Mosque through European Eyes."

65. *A. Lawrence, Extracts from the Diary and Correspondence of the Late Amos Lawrence*, 350.

66. The *Panorama of Jerusalem* by Alexander Fink was on display in New York in 1802. See Comment, *The Painted Panorama*, 51–56. New York's Rotunda, which was built to house Vanderlyn's Panorama, is claimed to be the first public art museum in the city. See Avery and Fodera, *John Vanderlyn's Panoramic View of the Palace and Gardens of Versailles*, 19. A panorama of Jerusalem by Frederick Catherwood was displayed first at London's Leicester Square Panorama, then exported to open Catherwood's own panorama building in New York in 1838. That structure, along with several canvases, including that of Jerusalem, burned down in 1842. See "[Catherwood Panorama]." For Catherwood, who should have a larger role in this chapter than I have allotted him, see Bourbon, *The Lost Cities of the Mayas*. A panorama of Jerusalem by Marshall, exhibited in 1843 in Edinburgh, is best known from its representation in a painting by Charles Halkerston. The painting is now in the collection of the City Art Centre in Edinburgh.

East, opened a panorama of Jerusalem in Paris. The remarkable French traveler, the Vicomte François-René Chateaubriand, who had published an account of Jerusalem in his widely read *Itinéraire de Paris à Jérusalem* in 1811, judged the validity of his own description of the Holy City on the basis of its resemblance to the panorama of the same subject on display in Paris:

Had I, in visiting Greece and Palestine, merely had the pleasure of tracing out the route to men of talent who would familiarize us with these lands of great and beautiful memory, I would still be proud of my undertaking. In Paris we saw the Panoramas of Jerusalem and Athens; the illusion was complete; I recognized at first glance the monuments and places that I had mentioned. Never was a traveler put to such a harsh test: I could not have expected that Jerusalem and Athens would be transported to Paris in order to convict me of falsehood or truth. The confrontation with these witnesses was favorable to me: my accuracy was found to be such that citations from the Itinerary were quoted in the program and in the popular explanations of the Panorama's tableaux.[67]

In his short essay, "Paris—the Capital of the Nineteenth Century," Walter Benjamin describes the diorama, the less circular cousin of the panorama, which he uses as a trope for understanding a particular genre of contemporary popular French literature:[68]

Tireless efforts had been made to render the dioramas, by means of technical artifice, the locus of a perfect imitation of nature. People sought to copy the changing time of day in the countryside, the rising of the moon, or the rushing of the waterfall. David counseled his pupils to draw from Nature in their dioramas. While the dioramas strove to produce life-like transformations in Nature portrayed in them, they foreshadowed, via photography, the moving-picture and the talking-picture.[69]

Benjamin's description of this architecture of illusion follows a section on the arcades, those great glass-covered boulevards for the display of commodities. The panorama was an uncannily equivalent space that excited similar desires for consumption.

The early panorama exhibition halls were often at least partially owned and operated by the artists who executed the paintings exhibited in them.[70] At the

---

67. Chateaubriand, "Préface de l'édition de 1827," 13–14. I am grateful to Neil McWilliam for his corrections to my translation.

68. The best introduction to the diorama is that by one of its inventors: Daguerre, *Historique et description des procédés du daguerréotype et du diorama*. For the English patent, taken out in 1824, see Wood, "The Diorama in Great Britain in the 1820s."

69. Benjamin, *Charles Baudelaire*, 161.

70. Roberts was, for example, one of the few artists from outside the Barker family who worked on their panoramas. See Hyde, *Panoramania!*, 60. Roberts himself was not only a painter of panoramas, but also his work provided the model for others: "The Rotonda, a building constructed in Leicester Square especially for exhibitions, displayed a huge panorama of Cairo based on Roberts' drawings." Bourbon, *The Life, Works and Travels of David Roberts, R.A.*, 22.

end of the nineteenth century, when panoramas enjoyed a profitable revival, they tended to be promoted by business consortia. Jerusalem then became the most common single subject displayed. The newly popular Jerusalem was sold primarily as a site of pilgrimage: the viewer was the witness of Christian history as well as of sacred topography. Most of the new spate of Jerusalem panoramas represented the city as it was known by Jesus. A panorama of *Jerusalem at the Time of Herod* by Olivier Pichat was exhibited in Paris in 1887.[71] Most were more specific, representing the city on the day of the Crucifixion.[72] Many of these were the offspring of one grand and highly profitable version of the subject.

In competition with monopolistic Belgian panorama companies, two Germans, Josef Halder from Munich and Franz Josef Hotop from Dresden, established a new panorama enterprise in early 1885.[73] Their first painting represented *Jerusalem on the Day of the Crucifixion*. Bruno Piglhein, a rising academic painter, agreed to design the image and to oversee its execution for 145,000 marks.[74] To ensure the painting's authenticity, Piglhein and his team, including Karl Frosch, who painted the architectural elements of the work, and Joseph Krieger, a landscape artist, journeyed to Palestine in 1885 to see and draw Jerusalem.[75] They traveled with letters of introduction from powerful German churchmen as well as a camera. The painting was exhibited to the public in 1886. The venture proved a great financial success. Piglhein's painting, which was 50 feet high and 390 feet long, delighted critics and the public. It produced a profit not only from admission tickets but also through the sale of experience enhancers and souvenirs: opera glass rentals, guidebooks, and reproductions of assorted quality and expense. The work traveled from Munich to Berlin, then to Vienna, where it was destroyed by fire in 1892.[76]

A foldout print from the 1886 exhibition brochure reproduces the composition of Piglhein's panorama (fig. 59).[77] Half the circumference of the painting is stunningly occupied by the walled city of Jerusalem as viewed from the southeast. The

---

71. Oliver Pichat traveled to the Holy Land in 1886 to prepare for the painting of this panorama, *Jerusalem at the Time of Herod*. He also consulted archaeological texts. The painting was exhibited in the Panorama Marigny Champs-Elysees from May 1888 to December 1890, and then in the Panorama du Sacre Coeur. A Society of the Panorama of Jerusalem was later founded with the purpose of moving the panorama permanently to Lourdes. See Auktionshaus Reinhild Tschöpe Historische Wertpapiere u. Finanzdokumente, 52. *Auktion*.

72. The earliest of the Crucifixion panoramas, dated to 1884, has been attributed to the Belgian Juliaan De Vriendt. See Koller, "Jerusalem in Altötting," 188. This article provides a useful list of the Panoramas of Jerusalem on the day of the Crucifixion.

73. Edward Said pointed out the differences and similarities between the orientalisms of the German and Anglo-French traditions already in the late 1970s. I have, I hope not too misleadingly, ignored the former in this discussion for lack of space. See Said, *Orientalism*, 19.

74. Stephan Oettermann's fundamental study of panoramas offers a genealogy of Bruno Piglhein's panorama of Jerusalem, as well as an insight into the entrepreneurial character of its production. See particularly chapter 4 in Oettermann, *The Panorama*. For a contemporary biographical sketch and commentary on the panorama, see Muther, "Bruno Piglhein."

75. v. B., "Das neue Münchner Panorama."

76. Oettermann, *The Panorama*, 274–77.

77. This foldout is reproduced in ibid., 275–77.

Fig. 59. Souvenir foldout of Bruno Piglhein's panorama, *Jerusalem on the Day of the Crucifixion*. From Oetterman, *The Panorama*. Reprinted with the author's permission.

city's expanse is defined by its major monuments. The towers of Herod's Antonia Fortress, which in antiquity marked the northern corner of the Temple Mount, define its far left. Herod's massive Temple, represented as facing east, away from the observer, rises to the right of the fortress. Herod's great palace, closer to the observer, anchors the south end of the city. In the foreground of the cityscape is a Bedouin tent, with attendant camels and nomads. The other half of the panorama displays a desolate terrain of limestone outcrops, enlivened by a few gnarled trees and a humble building. The Crucifixion and its crowds of witnesses appear on a rise to the left of the city walls. The three crosses are arranged so that those being executed look away from the city, toward the viewer and the empty landscape to the west. The Temple and the crucified turn their backs on one another. The cave in which Jesus is to be buried appears below the rock shelf on which the Crucifixion is staged. The prepared tomb appears here in the desolate landscape, not in a garden as described in the New Testament.

Piglhein's panorama was the mother of end-of-the-century Jerusalems.[78] Its litigious history reveals its function not only as a template but also as a profitable engine for image production. By contract, Piglhein could not reproduce his rendering of the Holy City. His associates, however, were less constrained. Karl Frosch and Joseph Krieger, separately and together, painted at least seven additional Jerusalems. One of these was gainfully installed in London in 1890, where its exhibitors were sued by those who had planned to display the original Piglhein work there. In Europe, if not in the United States, where European copyrights were not enforced, efforts were made to distinguish new Jerusalem panoramas from Piglhein's original.[79] The family resemblance nevertheless

78. For a more detailed discussion of the lawsuit described here, see ibid., 274–85. For the view from Altötting, see Koller, "Zur Planungs- und Enstehungsgeschichte des Panoramas 'Kreuzigung Christi' in Altötting."

79. Frosch and Krieger were apparently successful. A review of their *Jerusalem on the Day of the Crucifixion* for Einsiedeln in the Munich *Allgemeine Zeitung* suggests that the artists sacrificed the authenticity of Jerusalem to protect themselves from legal claims:

Since Piglhein's Crucifixion Panorama, which was a masterpiece capable of evoking tremendous feeling, it has remained an unusually difficult venture to tackle the same subject in a new manner. As previously reported, however, it is just that that has been accomplished for Einsiedeln with noteworthy success by Messrs. Frosch, Krieger and Leigh. Naturally, they mainly avoided the temptation of making references [to the earlier work], for that would have been the best way to have their work remain overshadowed by its precursor. So Frosch composed Jerusalem, which fills half the circumference of the circular picture, in a completely new manner, without depending too much on the contemporary city, it seems, but rather more on all manner of literary sources.

F. Pt., "Münchener kunst"; I want to thank Professor Peter McIsaac for offering improvements to my translation. The newspaper's claims for difference are hard to substantiate. Like so many of the nineteenth-century panoramas, the Frosch-Krieger version of Jerusalem on the day of the Crucifixion in Einsiedeln was destroyed by fire in 1960. A sense of the composition of that image is, nevertheless, preserved in its replacement. This Jerusalem was reconstructed by projecting photographs of the lost work onto a new canvas, then filling in the images with color. It was produced in 1962 by Joseph Fastel and Hans Wulz. The result is thin in its pigmentation but strong in its structure. That structure, despite the declarations of difference made in the *Allgemeine Zeitung*, seems to follow Piglhein in its

Fig. 60. Souvenir foldout of Gerhardt Fugel's *Jerusalem on the Day of the Crucifixion,* Altötting, Bavaria. Author's collection.

general layout—the city occupies half of the canvas. The Crucifixion lies at its left end, with a virtual wasteland filling the gap between the scene of the execution and Herod's palace. The Bedouin tent, the empty tomb and water-carrying attendant, the crowds of onlookers, all occur in only slightly modified forms. The principal parts of the city—the Antonia, the Temple Mount, and Herod's palace—are given greater prominence, and the victims on the three crosses look east toward Jerusalem and the back of the Temple. Much of the information on Einsiedeln was provided by the present president of remains clear, as is demonstrated in the *Jerusalem on the Day of the Crucifixion* that was painted under the direction of Gerhardt Fugel in 1903 for display in Altötting, Bavaria.[80] Fugel's turn-of-the century academic style complemented the realism that was the object of the exercise.[81] The artist worked from life: "The wooden cross [seen in the painting] was planted in the artist's atelier and on it models were fastened."[82] Architecture was taken with the same seriousness. Two of the artists working on Fugel's team, Karl Nadler and the experienced artist of Crucifixion panoramas Josef Krieger, traveled to Jerusalem to prepare for the new work; Krieger also took photographs of the city.[83] The painting follows the Piglhein formula, but its architecture is more monumental than the original, and the sky, which darkens threateningly over Golgotha, is more dramatic than that of the other two surviving Jerusalems (fig. 60).[84] The trompe l'oeil effects in Altötting are also convincing. The space between the canvas and

---

the Panorama Company, Max Fuchs, who I interviewed on May 15, 2001. More tangentially related to the Piglhein *Jerusalem on the Day of the Crucifixion* is the panorama on display at Ste.-Anne de Beaupré, outside Quebec City in Canada. On this image, see Hyde, "Jerusalem for Sale." It was painted under the direction of Paul Philippoteaux, the son of the well-known French panorama entrepreneur, Félix Philippoteaux. The younger Philippoteaux emigrated to the United States and established an atelier in Milwaukee, Wisconsin. There he and his staff produced a number of panoramas, including the *Battle of Gettysburg* that remains on view at the battlefield site. His *Jerusalem on the Day of the Crucifixion,* first displayed in Montreal, was established permanently at Ste.-Anne-de-Beaupré in 1895. The composition repeats the Piglhein formula: the expansive city, with soldiers and the Bedouins' tents; the desolate landscape with a few structures and large groups of spectators; the Crucifixion. Features of this version that diverge from the archetype generate topographic incoherence. The Temple, oddly oriented to the west toward the site of the Crucifixion, is no longer raised on Herod's great platform. It rather looks like a preview of Montmartre. The importation of Absalom's tomb from the east side of the city to the west contributes to the visitor's dislocation. Cutout figures on the constructed surface between the observation deck and the painting decrease rather than increase the illusion. Most disconcerting, the Canadian panorama shifts the position of the observer. In the other three panoramas, the modern audience occupies a fantasy outcrop at the level of Calvary; like the crowds of ancient viewers, they look up at the victims. In Philippoteaux's painting, the viewer stands on a level with Jesus, looking down on the painted onlookers.

80. My assessment is the inverse of that of the preeminent scholar of panoramas, Stephan Oettermann, who writes: "Of all the subjects treated in the panoramas, the Crucifixion was no doubt the most sensitive and the most questionable. The Crucifixion itself was always depicted in the traditional manner familiar from thousands of easel paintings, creating an awkward contrast to the rest of the panorama surrounding it. It is difficult not to feel that the striking realism of the depiction and the alleged historical accuracy were meant to present an article of religious belief to visitors as reality. There is a false note in the whole that cannot be ignored. This is particularly true of the Altötting picture; perhaps it is caused by the general tenor of the shrine itself. Certainly of all the surviving panoramas this is the stalest and most dated." Oettermann, *The Panorama,* 285.

81. Koenigs, "Die Architektur des alten Jerusalem auf dem Panorama von Altötting."

82. Staudhamer, "Vom Panorama in Altötting," 60; my translation.

83. Three of these—details of the city—are reproduced in Koller, "Zur Planungs- und Enstehungsgeschichte des Panoramas 'Kreuzigung Christi' in Altötting." These photographs are apparently now lost. Gebhard Streicher, interview, May 18, 2001.

84. See Koenigs, "Das Werk Gebhard Fugels (1863–1939)"; Koenigs, "Die Architektur des alten Jerusalem auf dem Panorama von Altötting"; Koller, "Jerusalem in Altötting"; Koller, "Zur Planungs- und Enstehungsgeschichte des Panoramas 'Kreuzigung Christi' in Altötting."

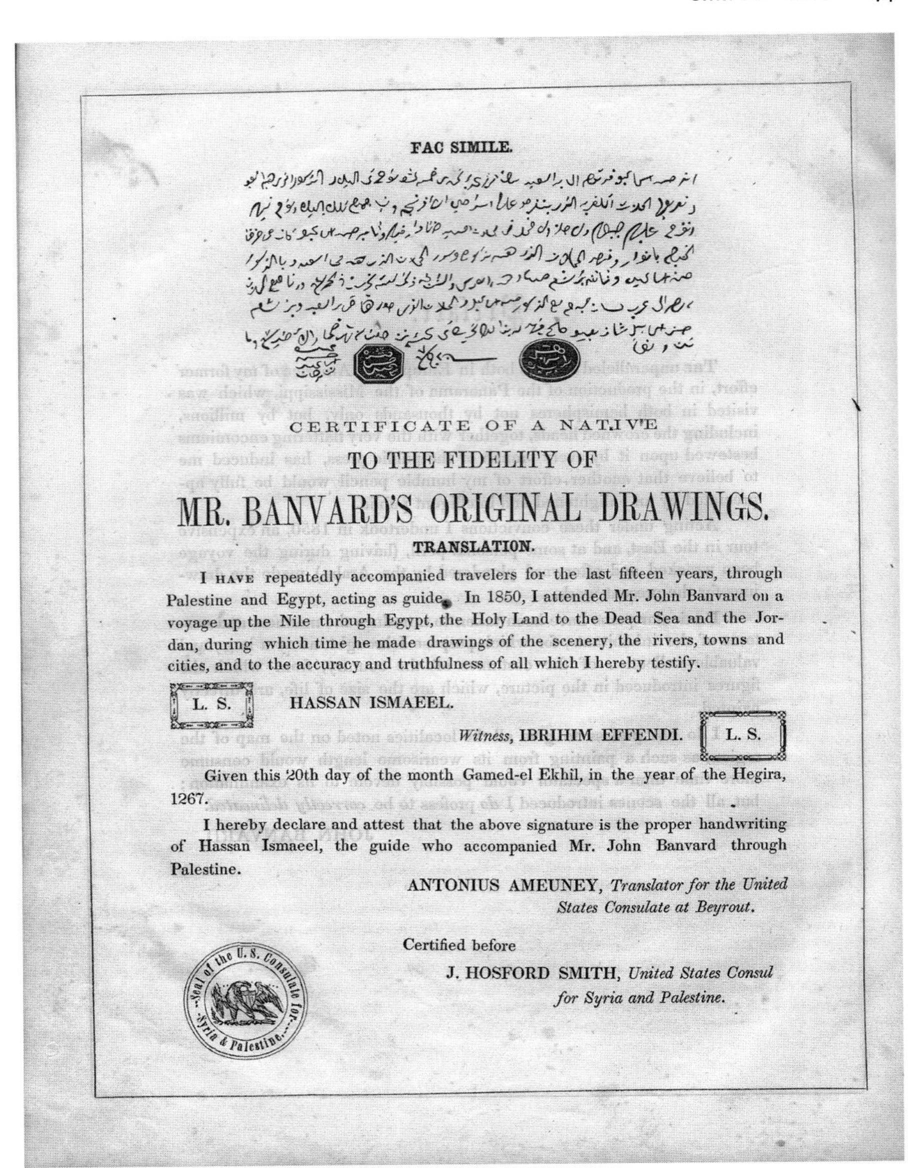

FAC SIMILE.

CERTIFICATE OF A NATIVE

TO THE FIDELITY OF

MR. BANVARD'S ORIGINAL DRAWINGS.

TRANSLATION.

I HAVE repeatedly accompanied travelers for the last fifteen years, through Palestine and Egypt, acting as guide. In 1850, I attended Mr. John Banvard on a voyage up the Nile through Egypt, the Holy Land to the Dead Sea and the Jordan, during which time he made drawings of the scenery, the rivers, towns and cities, and to the accuracy and truthfulness of all which I hereby testify.

L. S. HASSAN ISMAEEL.

Witness, IBRIHIM EFFENDI. L. S.

Given this 20th day of the month Gamed-el Ekhil, in the year of the Hegira, 1267.

I hereby declare and attest that the above signature is the proper handwriting of Hassan Ismaeel, the guide who accompanied Mr. John Banvard through Palestine.

ANTONIUS AMEUNEY, *Translator for the United States Consulate at Beyrout.*

Certified before

J. HOSFORD SMITH, *United States Consul for Syria and Palestine.*

Seal of the U. S. Consulate for Syria & Palestine.

Fig. 61. Statement of the authenticity of John Banvard's panoramas of the Holy Land, reproduced from the pamphlet that accompanied his performance: Banvard, *Description of Banvard's Pilgrimage to Jerusalem and the Holy Land.* Author's collection.

the viewing deck is filled with a persuasive papier-mâché landscape and architectural features that provide a compelling visual transition from a material three-dimensional world to an immaterial two-dimensional one.

Like the claims of authenticity made for other versions of Jerusalem on the market, the publicists of the panoramas of the Holy City asserted the truthfulness of their renderings (fig. 61). Those declarations were embraced by their patrons.[85] An anonymous review in the *Buffalo Morning Express* of the 1888

85. The effects of the panorama's "reality" are discussed by Wilcox, "Introduction: Unlimiting the Bounds of Painting."

opening of another, now lost, *Jerusalem on the Day of the Crucifixion* Panorama provides a typical Protestant reaction to the work:

> *Before us is spread out the Jerusalem of song; the Jerusalem of the Holy Bible! Lovely, treacherous, perfidious Jerusalem! Beautiful? Ah, yes—but its beauty marred by the enactment of the most woeful of all tragedies—The Divine Sacrifice. . . . Here before us, like a page of legible type, large enough for even the skeptic to read—is an object lesson, which lends to the pulpit a potent factor in the education of the masses in the truths upon which are based Christian belief—Christian civilization. There is no memoriter [rote memorization] process here. All understand it. Look. Observe well, and the lesson of Christ's precept and suffering is learned. The realism is overpowering—proselytizing almost. Genius seeks expression not alone through the medium of literature or pulpit oratory. It depends primarily for its effects upon the force of its appeal to an outward sense—the eye. It is demonstrated by the pre-eminent and invariable popularity of skillful imitation of nature in art. . . . In the creation of this great work, "Jerusalem on the Day of the Crucifixion," a realism is attained that does not hurt the reverential element of the theme. . . . Skilled and intelligent artists have studied Josephus, and the profane writers, for the purpose of truthfully portraying these noted structures. Historically accurate in location and carefully drawn, they are sure to satisfy even the most argumentative. The investigations of the distinguished artists, savants and theologians, conscientiously compiled, have been admirably reproduced in this masterpiece of panoramas.*[86]

The panorama is legitimated by its function as text and as virtually unmediated nature. Its archaeological correctness allows the work's divine message to be understood intuitively. It competes successfully in its religious effectiveness with literature and sermons. The painting's professed didactic religious value veils its origins as profit-producing entertainment, much like Mel Gibson's more recent cinematic version of the Crucifixion, *The Passion of the Christ*.

The panorama's archaeological landscape also rendered its brand of Christianity perfectly ambivalent. For Protestants, the representation was opportunely empty of the accretions of post-apostolic (heretical) Catholicism. This Crucifixion had the status not of a devotional icon but of a history painting. The panorama was fully free of the idolatry Protestants ascribed to Catholic practice.

86. "A Great Work of Art." The educational value of the panorama was explicitly claimed by John Vanderlyn in promoting his own work in New York: "Panoramic exhibitions possess so much of the magic deception of the art, as irresistably [*sic*] to captivate all classes of Spectators, and to give them a decided advantage over every other description of pictures; for no study nor a cultivated taste is required fully to appreciate the merits of such representations. They have further the power of conveying much practical and topographical information, such as can in no other manner be supplied, and if instruction and mental gratification be the aim and object of painting no class of pictures have a fairer claim to the public estimation than panoramas." Quoted in Avery and Fodera, *John Vanderlyn's Panoramic View of the Palace and Gardens of Versailles*, 30–31.

Simultaneously, for Catholics, the panorama presented one of the focal images of their piety. The iconography of the work conformed to Catholic tradition; the executors of the Council of Trent would have been proud. Perhaps for the assimilated Catholics of North America, the vagueness of the painting's religiosity was something of a relief. The ambiguous attitude of American Catholics toward the church's traditional use of images is revealed in the *Catholic Union and Times* review of the same Crucifixion panorama that went on display in Buffalo in 1888:

When some years ago the announcement was made that the famous [Catholic] passion plays of Ober-Ammergau in Tyrol were to be reproduced in this country, and that the closing scenes in the life of the founder of the Christian religion were to be brought upon the dramatic stage, a general protest went up from all quarters against this endeavor as sacrilegious. . . . The reason for the protest and the failure it produced is not hard to find. The scenes of Golgotha have for our people the grandest result and fulfillment of all the promises contained in what is called the Christian era, in the history of humanity, far too great and solemn a meaning than to permit their reproduction or perpetuation to be entrusted to blundering supes [supernumeraries], moving about in the limited space of the stage, even if forming only the back-ground for the greatest of dramatic artists, simply because the spirit which founded a new era is too gigantic to submit to personification. We feel, intuitively, that a dramatization of great events is a desecration, a sacrilege, which grows in proportion to the grandeur and importance, for all humanity, of the event. A drama with the signing of the Declaration of Independence as one of its scenes, would arouse nothing but ridicule and indignation; that moment has outgrown the possibility of adequate reproduction by the means of living human forms. Yet we gladly admire pictorial representations of such grand events and consider them the painter's and sculptor's true field, the pictorial representation rising in acceptability in the same degree as an attempt at dramatization would meet with disapproval and indignation. . . .

[The Cyclorama of Jerusalem] . . . may be called a faithful reproduction of all that is absolutely known, by authentic record and tradition, as well as from ruins and other preserved evidence, of the scenes surrounding the death upon the cross of Jesus of Nazareth. The most remarkable preparations were made for this work. The backbone of the cyclorama was the work of Professor Carl Frosch, who has made himself familiar with every ruin in and about Jerusalem. The splendid composition of the work was due to F. W. Heine, and the wonderful atmosphere and perspective to A. Lohr.

Buffalo's Cyclorama of Jerusalem on the day of the crucifixion will be recognized not only as a superior work of art, but as the most faithful representation from sacred and secular sources of the scene on Golgotha and that which surrounded it. It revives the scene in all its solemn reality.[87]

87. "The Cyclorama of Jerusalem."

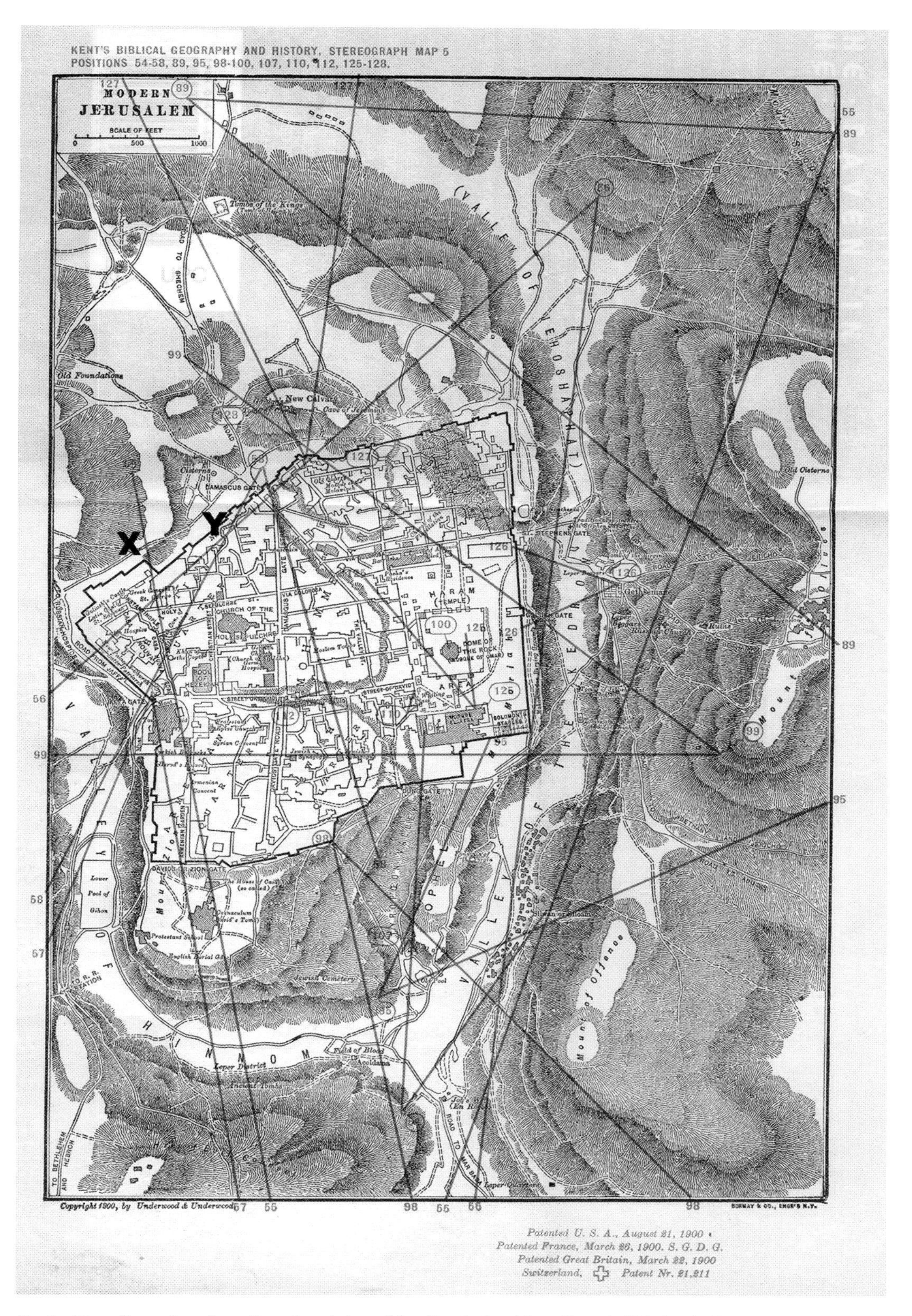

Fig. 62. Plan of Jerusalem. From Kent, *Descriptions of One Hundred and Forty Places in Bible Lands*. *X* marks the approximate location of the Panorama viewer; *Y* indicates the site of the Crucifixion.

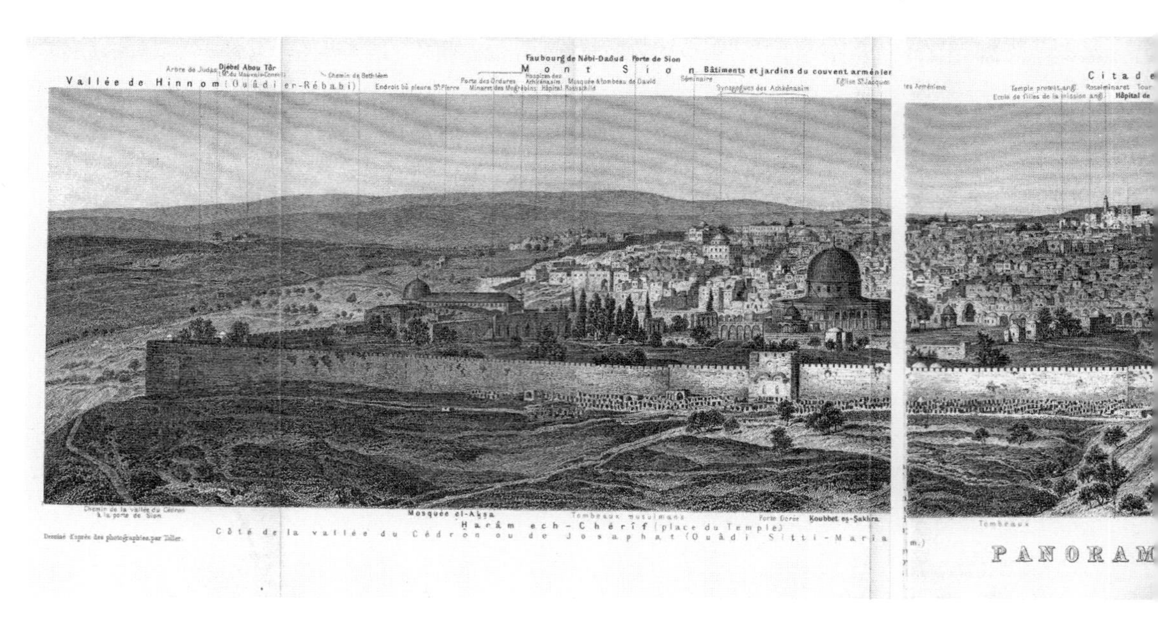

The compelling religiosity of the painting is contrasted to the blasphemy of traditional Catholic live performances of the Crucifixion. For American Catholics, the painted panorama, with its claims for archaeological accuracy and its realization in an elite medium, was a legitimate means of rendering biblical truth; real bodies in a theatrical setting were not.

Audiences—Protestant or Catholic—tended not to question the panorama's authenticity. Viewers became witnesses. Even those critical of the contemporary desire for illusion might embrace the panorama's "reality." The distinguished nineteenth-century art historian Cornelius Gurlitt, like Sir Joshua Reynolds, believed that the pursuit of the "real" was unworthy of true art.[88] Indeed, Gurlitt prefaced his discussion of Piglhein's Panorama with a critique of the current fashion for archaeological veracity. He chides Holman Hunt, who went to Palestine in order to provide authentic backgrounds for his religious paintings, and Adolf Menzel, who similarly sought Jewish models for his images of the Virgin: "One can say in both cases, that when art became the slave of science, it sought reality [*Wirklichkeit*] rather than truth [*Wahrheit*]."[89] But, he suggests, there is an exception to his condemnation:

The painter Bruno Piglhein, one of the most talented among the artists stimulated by Leibl in Munich, took up the notion of the Rationalists. He too went to Jerusalem to study the land and the people before undertaking the painting of the Crucifixion panorama. A panorama, however, is absolutely associated with realism. It should deceive; it should eliminate the border between reality—the three-dimensionally modeled foreground—and effigy. . . . I went to the panorama in Munich and saw there

88. For example, Sir Joshua's third Discourse. Reynolds, *Discourses on Art*, 41–53.
89. Gurlitt, *Die deutsche Kunst des Neunzehnten Jahrhunderts*, 545.

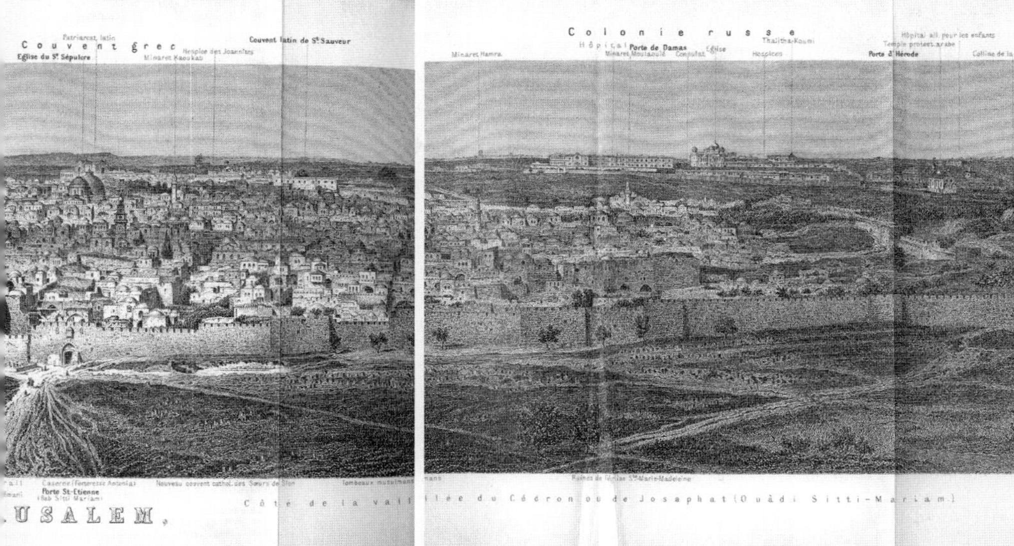

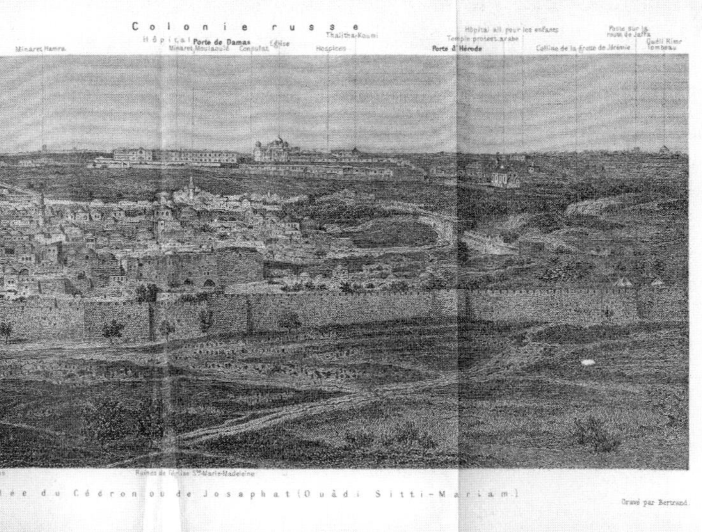

Fig. 63. Foldout panorama of Jerusalem from *Baedeker's Handbook for Travellers*. Author's collection.

clergy and—I would almost like to say—pilgrims in dumb wonder and devotion. The strongest objective of realism, of true deception, indeed of that which has always been the most contemptible and lamentable in art, has indeed had a disturbing effect only on those who were conscious of such aesthetic principles.[90]

Professor Gurlitt, like the less sophisticated members of the panorama's audience, assumed that Piglhein represented the optic reality of Jerusalem.

Actually, the appearance of reality required considerable deceit. The authenticity of the image resides only in its illusion. Piglhein's representation, like those of his imitators, inflates the space of the city. Its extent is exaggerated. More specifically, the paintings greatly expand the distance of Golgotha/Calvary from city. I have marked the approximate location of the viewer (X) and the panorama's site of the Crucifixion (Y) on Charles Foster Kent's map of Jerusalem; the plan indicates the discrepancy between the view presented by the panoramas and the location of the Holy Sepulchre (fig. 62). Calvary is represented outside the west wall of the city, at its northern end. The painted Calvary thus stands in the same general relation to Jerusalem as does the Church of the Holy Sepulchre. The producers of the panoramas accepted as historical the traditional site of the Crucifixion marked by the ancient church. A poster for the panorama at Einsiedeln notes that the "view is taken of the place where the church of the Holy Sepulchre now stands."[91] Nevertheless, Calvary is rendered remote from the city walls, not immediately outside its gate as convention dictates.

Most remarkably, the general view of Jerusalem, as displayed in the panoramas, could never have been seen by those who produced them. The approach

90. Ibid., 547. I want to thank Professor Peter McIsaac for offering improvements to my translation.

91. Kunz, *Panorama Einsiedeln Kruezigung Christi;* my translation.

from the west did not present such a view. The city spread itself before the beholder as a unified urban landscape only from the east—most famously from the Mount of Olives. The *Baedeker's* panorama of the city presents this familiar aspect of Jerusalem (fig. 63). David Roberts offered two views of Jerusalem from the east: one from the north, and one from the south; he published no sketch of the city from the west. Photographers, too, did not represent the city from the northwest. This absence is most clearly demonstrated in the map that accompanied Charles Foster Kent's *Descriptions of One Hundred and Forty Places in Bible Lands to Be Seen through the Stereoscope or by Means of Stereopticon Slides,* an exhaustive collection of views of Palestine (fig. 62).[92] On the map, the numbers (in red in the original) correspond to the stereoscopic slides and to text descriptions of the view. The point from which the photograph was taken is marked by the circled numbers; the terminations of each of the two red lines which define the angle of vision bear the same number, uncircled. There are no general views of the city from the west marked on the map.

Despite the makers' assertions of the truth of their representation, the panoramas thus deviate from an optic reality of Jerusalem. The demands of illusion and spectacle required an unreal representation.[93] The deception was convincing; panoramas were remarkably successful in passing off illusion as reality.[94]

At the time of their greatest popularity, panoramas were generally an urban phenomenon. They depended on changing exhibitions to maintain the large audiences essential to their profitability. The paintings themselves tended to renew their audiences by shifting locations; they were migrants dependent on local spectators. At the end of the nineteenth century, new technologies for the mass production of illusion displaced the panorama as urban spectacle. To remain economically viable, panoramas sought sites that attracted everchanging audiences; they became permanent residents dependent on transient spectators. The most viable surviving panoramas complement popular tourist destinations. The *Battle of Atlanta,* the *Battle of Gettysburg,* and the *Battle of Waterloo* are all subordinate historical markers of that sort. Less successful in their quest for a profitable permanent residence are the three surviving Panoramas of *Jerusalem on the Day of the Crucifixion.* All three are located in the aura of venerable Catholic pilgrimage shrines—Ste.-Anne-de-Beaupré near Quebec, Einsiedlung in Switzerland, and Altötting in Bavaria. With the decline of pilgrimage to traditional shrines, the panoramas struggle to maintain themselves.

---

92. The maps are attached at the end of his text.

93. The modification of the actual for the impression of truth in art was an acknowledged necessity. It was nevertheless recognized that in the nineteenth century there was an increased concern for correctness. For example, Charles Eastlake, the important Victorian artist and art historian, commented, "The extent of modern antiquarian researches, in increasing information in archaeology, has increased the number of critics; and to be true even to the imagination, now, a painter requires to be more attentive to the details in question than the earlier artists were." Eastlake, *Contributions to the Literature of the Fine Arts,* 58.

94. For scholarly arguments on the credibility of the Altötting panorama, see Koenigs, "Die Architektur des alten Jerusalem auf dem Panorama von Altötting."

TRAVEL

With the displacement of bullion by paper bills, the institution of national banks, the erosion of usury laws, and the development of sophisticated credit conveyances, the velocity of exchange increased dramatically in the nineteenth century. So did the traffic of people. Inventions of the industrial age made foreign travel cheap. Railroads and steamships, Thomas Cook and Son, *Baedeker's*, and hotels like the Pera Palas in Istanbul and Shepheard's in Cairo all obviously contributed to the popularization of travel among the middle classes. The working classes also traveled, as Charles Dickens describes:

In person Mr. Booley is below the middle size, and corpulent. His countenance is florid, he is perfectly bald, and soon hot; and there is a composure in his gait and manner, calculated to impress a stranger with the idea of his being, on the whole, an unwieldy man. It is only in his eye that the adventurous character of Mr. Booley is seen to shine. It is a moist, bright eye, of a cheerful expression, and indicative of keen and eager curiosity.

It was not until late in life that Mr. Booley conceived the idea of entering on the extraordinary amount of travel he has since accomplished. He had attained the age of sixty-five before he left England for the first time. In all the immense journeys he has since performed, he has never laid aside the English dress, nor departed in the slightest degree from English customs. Neither does he speak a word of any language but his own.

Mr. Booley's powers of endurance are wonderful. All climates are alike to him. Nothing exhausts him; no alternations of heat and cold appear to have the least effect upon his hardy frame. . . . An intelligent Englishman may have occasionally pointed out to him objects and scenes of interest; but otherwise he has traveled alone and unattended. . . .

His first departure from the sedentary and monotonous life he had hitherto led, strikingly exemplifies, we think, the energetic character, long suppressed by that unchanging routine. Without any communication with any member of his family—Mr. Booley has never been married, but has many relations—without announcing his intention to his solicitor, or banker, or any person entrusted with the management of his affairs, he closed the door of his house behind him at one o'clock in the afternoon of a certain day, and immediately proceeded to New Orleans, in the United States of America. . . .

It might have been expected that at his advanced age, retired from the active duties of life, blessed with a competency, and happy in the affections of his numerous relations, Mr. Booley would now have settled himself down, to muse, for the remainder of his days, over the new stock of experience thus acquired. But travel had whetted, not satisfied, his appetite. . . . [At the] "opening the Nile," at Cairo, Mr. Booley was present.

Along that wonderful river, associated with such stupendous fables, and with a history more prodigious than any fancy of man, in its vast and gorgeous facts; among temples, palaces, pyramids, colossal statues, crocodiles, tombs, obelisks, mummies, sand and ruin; he proceeded, like an opium-eater in a mighty dream. . . . Upon the walls of temples, in colors fresh and bright as those of yesterday, he read the conquests of great Egyptian monarchs: upon the tombs of humbler people in the same blooming symbols, he saw their ancient way of working at their trades, of riding, driving, feasting, playing games; of marrying and burying, and performing on instruments, and singing songs, and healing by the power of animal magnetism, and performing all the occupations of life. . . .

[Mr. Booley travels to the Arctic where] the desolate sublimity of this astounding spectacle was broken in a pleasant and surprising manner. In the remote solitude to which he had penetrated, Mr. Booley . . . had the happiness of encountering two Scotch gardeners; several English compositors, accompanied by their wives; three brass-founders from the neighborhood of Long Acre, London; two coach-painters, a gold-beater and his only daughter, by trade a staymaker; and several other working-people from sundry parts of Great Britain who had conceived the extraordinary idea of "holiday-making" in the frozen wilderness. . . .

It was only at the close of Easter week that, sitting in an armchair, at a private club called the Social Oysters, assembling at Highbury Barn, where he is much respected, this indefatigable traveler expressed himself in the following terms: "It is very gratifying to me," said he, "to have seen so much at my time of life, and to have acquired a knowledge of the countries I have visited, which I could not have derived from books alone. When I was a boy, such traveling would have been impossible, as the gigantic-moving-panorama or diorama mode of conveyance, which I have principally adopted (all my modes of conveyance have been pictorial), had then not been attempted. It is a delightful characteristic of these times, that new and cheap means are continually being devised for conveying the results of actual experience to those who are unable to obtain such experiences for themselves: and to bring them within the reach of the people—emphatically of the people; for it is they at large who are addressed in these endeavors, and not exclusive audiences. Hence," said Mr. Booley, "even if I see a run on an idea, like the panorama one, it awakens no ill-humor within me, but gives me pleasant thoughts. Some of the best results of actual travel are suggested by such means to those whose lot it is to stay at home. New worlds open out to them, beyond their little worlds, and widen their range of reflection, information, sympathy, and interest. The more man knows of man, the better for the common brotherhood among us all. . . ." The Social Oysters having drunk [to his proposed] toast with acclamation, Mr. Booley proceeded to entertain them with anecdotes of his travels.[95]

Mr. Booley, a retired grocer, encounters the world through its panoramic reproductions. For him, as for many who left accounts of the panorama, only the aggravations of travel are missing from their experience of the exotic land that they see. Dickens's amusing sketch of 1850 of Mr. Booley's voyages is complemented by the author's own travelogues from the 1840s, *American Notes* and *Pictures from Italy*.[96] These also are characterized by a brilliantly described

95. Dickens, "Some Account of an Extraordinary Traveller," 511–20.

96. Dickens, *American Notes;* Dickens, *Pictures from Italy*. For the resemblance between travelogues and panoramas, see Flint, *The Victorians and the Visual Imagination.*

landscape with urban interludes variegated by anecdotal incidents that reveal the peculiar characteristics of the native population. Dicken's travelogues are themselves panoramas.

The mass-produced textual and pictorial panoramas of the nineteenth century allowed the working and middle classes in the West to participate in the colonization of the East. Panoramas and picture albums were performative inventions that both simulated and promoted tourism. Nineteenth-century travelogues, like those of Champney and Dickens, as well as illustrated lectures and exhibitions of indigenous peoples and architectures, all contributed to the Western sense of entitlement. Images of the Holy Land—prints, panoramas, photographs—were a provocation for its possession.[97]

Lamartine, the French poet and traveler cited in the epigraph, ascribes to prints his desire to experience the Holy Land:

My mother had received from her's, on the bed of death, a beautiful copy of the Bible of Royaumont, in which she taught me to read when I was a little child. This Bible had engravings on sacred subjects in every page; they depicted Sarah, Tobit and his angel, Joseph and Samuel; and, above all, those beautiful patriarchal scenes, in which the solemn and primitive nature of the East was blended with all the arts of the simple and wonderful lives of the fathers of mankind. When I had repeated my lesson well, and read with only a fault or two the half page of historical matter, my mother uncovered the engraving, and holding the book open on her lap, showed and explained it to me as my recompense. She was endowed, by nature, with a mind as pious as it was tender, and with the most sensitive and vivid imagination; all her thoughts were sentiments, and every sentiment was an image.[98]

Pictures incited Lamartine's longing for the sacred landscape of the Holy Land. In turn, his own very popular *A Pilgrimage to the Holy Land Comprising Recollections, Sketches and Reflections Made During a Tour in the East* stimulated in others a desire for the East.

Tourism and its less costly optical analogues invidiously whetted the appetites of the industrializing states of Europe and America. The narratives that accompanied some of those pictures document Western desire—descriptions present the Ottoman East not only as a site to visit but also as a place to possess. Further, the imperialist assumptions of the West are articulated explicitly in travel texts and, later, implicitly in guidebooks.[99] European and American travelers of the nineteenth and early twentieth centuries, experiencing the East under the control of the Turks, willed Western domination of the old Ottoman Empire. The apparent

97. For the similar effect of images in the American absorption of the West, see A. Miller, *The Empire of the Eye*.

98. Lamartine, *A Pilgrimage to the Holy Land*, 1:9.

99. For an insightful description of the relationship between travelogues and guidebooks, see Behdad, "Orientalist Tourism." For a discussion of the penetration of capitalism into the Ottoman Empire in the nineteenth century, see Pamuk, "The Ottoman Empire in Comparative Perspective."

vulnerability of the Ottoman state aggravated jealousies among the Western industrialized states; "The Eastern Problem" names their anxieties about the others' potential intervention. The accounts of travelers to the Ottoman Empire almost all comment on the inevitability of its Western occupation. The American diplomat and travel writer Edwin de Leon gives characteristic expression to this sentiment: "The Turcoman came as a scourge from his far wilds, to chastise the vices of an effete and decaying civilization [Byzantium]. Those vices he has aggravated and perpetuated. . . . The Turk cannot stay much longer, nor will he make more than a feeble resistance against his expulsion."[100]

Similar assumptions are expressed by John L. Stoddard, a traveler and popular lecturer on the circuit of American cities in the late nineteenth century. Stoddard presented illustrated talks on the East, including a series on Constantinople/Istanbul and Jerusalem. The *New York Times* in 1888 reports on one of his presentations:[101]

In the future Mr. Stoddard dreams of Constantinople in the hands of a Christian Government, which will make of it the powerful and influential city which its position geographically entitles it to be. . . . The pictures are the finest which Mr. Stoddard has ever exhibited during his present course of lectures, and elicited many expressions of delight on the part of the spectators.[102]

Stoddard's veneration of the great city and his detestation of its government is better expressed in his own high rhetorical style:

The Turk, by nature and religion, belongs not to Europe, but to Asia; and when sufficient unanimity is found among the jealous European nations to insure united action, to Asia will the Sultan and his evil government depart. Such thoughts recurred to me with special force, as, on a recent visit to the Bosphorus, I saw again the form of fair Stamboul, stretched out in indolent repose. . . . For, whether it be Russia, Austria, Germany, England or a joint protectorate of nations, some Christian power must ere long occupy this site, and lift it to the rank designed for it by destiny,—that of the immortal Queen of the East, throned on the Eden of the world, and holding as a scepter in her hand the Golden Horn.[103]

For Stoddard, as for many other European observers, Istanbul is a beautiful European princess held hostage in the sultan's harem.

Stoddard uses a similar analogy in a later lecture, observing that the Holy Land "has lain for ages like a beautiful slave in the marketplace, contended

100. Leon, *Thirty Years of My Life on Three Continents,* 2:141–42.

101. "John Lawson Stoddard, noted American author, who had lived in Italy for several years, died today at his villa near Merano, at the age of 81. He was born in Brookline, Mass., and attended Williams College and Yale Divinity School. For nearly twenty years he promoted the Stoddard Lectures in the larger American cities, retiring from the platform in 1897." "J. L. Stoddard Dies; Author, Lecturer."

102. "The City of the Sultans."

103. Stoddard, *Lectures,* 108–9.

for by wrangling rivals."[104] Jerusalem is thus presented to the American audience as a body for sale.[105] Possession is available as experience through travel; tourism is latent occupation. The *New York Times* reports on Stoddard's performance in 1892:

An excursion to "Jerusalem and the Holy Land" was made from the stage of Daly's Theatre yesterday morning under the guidance of John L. Stoddard, this being the subject of the fourth of his illustrated lectures. The audience, which filled the theatre to overflowing, was afforded a rare treat in the large collection of photographic views of Jerusalem, Hebron, Joppa, the Church of the Holy Sepulchre, the Mosque of Omar, the Garden of Gethsemane, the Mount of Olives, and other points of interest in the Holy Land. Mr. Stoddard's lecture was the most interesting of his entire course thus far delivered. He described the peculiarities of the people who now inhabit Palestine, the features of the country, and the alleged relics of the Savior which are exhibited to tourists, some of which may be genuine, but the majority of which are probably frauds.[106]

As in descriptions of other exotic cities, Stoddard's published account answers the reader's questions about travel to Jerusalem. He comments, for example, on accommodation: "If there be any part of the world where management like that of this experienced cicerone [Thomas Cook] is needed, Palestine is the place. Here, where practically no traveling conveniences existed twenty-five years ago, arrangements have been so perfected, that one can now journey through Judaea in comparative luxury as well as safety."[107] The Holy Land is ever more accessible.

In his *Pilgrimage to the Holy Land,* Lamartine reveals how modern pilgrimage might be converted to colonial occupation. He provides a resolution to "The Eastern Problem": a clandestine European congress should establish by force free European cities within the Ottoman Empire; in the rush of neighboring communities to associate themselves with the social and economic advantages of these metropolises, the old empire would collapse. Moreover, for Lamartine, imperialism solves not only the problems of the East but also those of the West, convulsed as it is in revolutionary struggles:

The exuberance of her unemployed population, industry, and intellectual forces, ought to lead her to bless that Providence which so opportunely opens to her so boundless a career of thought, activity, noble ambition, civilizing proselytism, manufacturing and agricultural industry; offices and emoluments in every shape; fleets and armies to direct; ports to construct; cities to erect; colonies to found; fertile solitudes to

---

104. Ibid., 114.

105. The city as a reclining, vulnerable body is a familiar topos for Jerusalem, as it is for Istanbul. "Go with me then. Let us mount yon winding path up Olivet's sacred height, hallowed by the footsteps of the Son of God. Now from its *cülm* follow my pencil while I rapidly sketch the scene spread out beneath, where rests the unhappy city, like an invalid lingering out a sickly existence, under the atmosphere of a false religion." Banvard, *Description of Banvard's Pilgrimage to Jerusalem and the Holy Land,* n.p.

106. "A Trip to Jerusalem: Lecture by John L. Stoddard."

107. Stoddard, Lectures, 124.

cultivate; new manufactures to establish; new discoveries to turn to account; new regions to explore; alliances to attempt; young and sound populations to educate; systems of legislation to study and to prove; religions to investigate and rationalize; fashions of people and of customs to consummate; Europe, Asia, and Africa to draw nearer to each other, and to unite by new communications.[108]

Colonization productively redirects the frustrations of the underemployed and undercompensated working classes of the industrialized West. Western civilization will be advantageously exchanged for new colonial commodities. Labor, as well as overaccumulated capital, will be profitably recycled in the East to make the East act more like the West.

CONCLUSION

Novels are a diagnostic product of the industrializing nineteenth century. The novel, like the print and photograph, was a mass-produced form of popular entertainment. Two novels framed and documented this chapter's argument; a third provides its conclusion. Émile Zola's *L'Argent* (Money), published first in a serialized form in 1890, stages the peculiar mixture of venality and religiosity with which the West coveted the East.[109] More dramatically than the travelogues of Stoddard or Edwin de Leon, Zola's text presents the West's religious and economic desire for the East as inextricably intertwined. The principal character of the narrative is Aristide Saccard, an obsessive, anti-Semitic financier whose identity is formed by speculation. His activities perfectly describe the manipulation of money in the underregulated arena of high finance in the late nineteenth century, as well as the scandals and tragedies that resulted from the extortions of speculators. Drawn with astutely observed detail are the complex mechanisms of speculation as well as its physical settings, from Paris's public Bourse and street cafés to the city's private parlors and tenements. Zola reveals the profoundly demoralizing effects of modern speculation by contrasting two brothers. The eldest, Busch, represents the lowest form of entrepreneurial life, feeding parasitically on the catastrophic failures of speculation. He collects bankruptcies and forgotten debts, then finds and persecutes already destitute debtors. Busch's brother, Sigismond, is also a product of capitalism, killing himself in an attempt to remedy its excesses. Sigismond is "utterly ignorant of all that frightful traffic in depreciated stock, and of the purchase of bad debts; he lived in a loftier region, in a sovereign dream of justice. . . . He admitted naught but justice, the rights of each individual man regained and adopted as the unchangeable principles of a new social organization. And thus, following the example of Karl Marx, with whom he was in constant correspondence, he

108. Lamartine, *A Pilgrimage to the Holy Land*, 308–9.

109. Cousins, "The Serialization and Publication of *L'Argent*." The English version of the novel, translated by Ernest A. Vizetelly, appeared in 1894. For fear of prosecution for pornography, the explicitly sexual episodes of the narrative were expurgated. It is the Vizetelly translation that has been reprinted as a Pocket Classic by Sutton. The scandal described in the novel is based on that of *L'Union Générale* of 1878–85. See Richardson, *Zola*, 141–42.

spent his days in studying this organization, incessantly modifying and improving upon paper the society of tomorrow."[110] Sigismond learns of his brother's heartless scavenging among the poor and dies of consumptive despair.

Representing the survival of middle-class honesty are Saccard's innocent friends, the brother and sister Caroline and George Hamelin. Caroline is an intelligent woman who, as Saccard's opposite, feels compassion and disdains wealth. Also a foil to Saccard, George is a true entrepreneur. He is a piously Catholic engineer who, with his sister, has spent a great deal of time in the Middle East and dreams of the European development of the region—steam lines, mines, and railroads. Hamelin's vision provides the pretext for Saccard's swindle.

Then, one morning, Hamelin quietly broached the secret program to which he sometimes alluded, and which he smilingly called the crowning of his edifice. "When we have become the masters [of Syria by means of railway and other monopolies]," said he, "we will restore the kingdom of Palestine, and put the Pope there. At first we might content ourselves with Jerusalem, with Jaffa as a seaport. Then Syria will be declared independent, and can be annexed. . . ."

Saccard listened open-mouthed whilst Hamelin said these things in a thoroughly unaffected way. . . . "It's madness!" he cried. "The Porte won't give up Jerusalem."

"Oh! Why not?" quietly rejoined Hamelin. "It is always in such desperate need of money! Jerusalem is a burden to it; it would be a good riddance. The Porte, you know, often can't tell what course to take between the various sects which dispute for possession of the sanctuaries. Moreover, the Pope would have true supporters among the Syrian Maronites. . . . In fact, I have thought the matter over carefully, have calculated everything, and this will be a new era, the triumphant era of Catholicism. It may be said that we should be sending the Pope too far away, that he would find himself isolated, thrust out of European affairs. But with what brilliancy and authority would he not radiate when once he was enthroned in the holy places, and spoke in the name of Christ from the very land where Christ Himself spoke! And, rest easy, we will build this kingdom up, firm and powerful; we will put it beyond the reach of political disturbances, by basing its budget—guaranteed by the resources of the country—on a vast bank for the shares of which the Catholics of the entire world will scramble."

Saccard, who had begun to smile, already attracted by the magnitude of the project, although not convinced, could not help christening this bank with a joyous "Eureka! The Treasure of the Holy Sepulchre, eh? Superb!"[111]

Saccard uses Hamelin's plans as the basis for his own scheme of a Universal Bank, whose politically conservative Catholic mission is linked with that of producing wealth. Initially, Saccard's speculative fraud is a remarkable success, attracting monies from pensioners and widows as well as from great bankers. The collapse of the Universal Bank brings bankruptcy and impoverishment,

110. Zola, *Money*, 36.
111. Ibid., 77–78.

but not the end of the dream of colonizing Jerusalem. The Western occupation of the Holy City, if not the installation there of the pope, dreamt of through the nineteenth century, became a reality in the twentieth. In 1917, British and Allied troops under General Edmund Allenby entered Jerusalem.

Those who wish to understand Enron and other twenty-first-century financial scandals would do well to read Zola's *Money*. The novelist offers a forensic examination of capitalism's vicious extremity; his analysis of the speculative bubble puts our own economic textbooks to shame. Speculation as "the faculty or power of seeing; sight, vision, especially intelligent or comprehending vision," or as "the contemplation, consideration, or profound study of some subject" is, as the *Oxford English Dictionary* observes, archaic and obsolete; rather, by the late nineteenth century speculation was "a conjectural consideration or meditation; an attempt to ascertain or anticipate something by probable reasoning" and "the action or practice of buying and selling goods, land, stocks and shares, etc., in order to profit by the rise or fall in the market value, as distinct from regular trading or investment; engagement in any business enterprise or transaction of a venturesome or risky nature, but offering the chance of great or unusual gain."[112]

Speculators are only in the market for the money. The shift in the meaning of *speculation* from a profound study to a venturesome transaction is symptomatic of the changed economy of the nineteenth century. From the cautious introduction into general circulation of paper bills at the beginning of the century to the wild circulation of unbacked notes at its end, illusory forms of wealth, like illusory Jerusalems, became the new reality of the West.

112. *Oxford English Dictionary*, on-line edition.

CHAPTER FIVE

Spectacularized Jerusalem: Imperialism, Globalization, and the Holy Land as Theme Park

Whereas the name of Walt Disney is synonymous with love of children, the joy and freedom of youth, and the strength of the family bond; and

Whereas twenty-five years ago, Walt Disney made tangible these most basic and cherished values in a magic land where age relives fond memories of the past and youth may savor the challenge and promises of the future; and

Whereas Walt Disney's dream embodies the ideals, the hopes, and the hard work that have created America; and

Whereas this embodiment contributes to the international understanding of American life and purpose; and

Whereas official recognition of Walt Disney and his dream-come-true will enhance the United States, nationally and internationally, as a land where wholesome family past times are both encouraged and enjoyed; and

Whereas the silver anniversary of Walt Disney's creation makes appropriate a salute to its creator: Now, therefore, be it

Resolved by the Senate and House of Representatives of the United States of America in Congress assembled, That the President is authorized and requested to issue a proclamation honoring the memory of Walt Disney on the twenty-fifth anniversary of his contribution to the American dream. * *CONGRESSIONAL RECORD*, VOL. 126 (1980)

Whereas, Southern Baptists and their children have for many decades enjoyed and trusted the Disney Co.'s television programming, feature-length films and theme parks which have reinforced basic American virtues and values; and

Whereas, The virtues promoted by Disney have contributed to the development of a generation of Americans who have come to expect and demand high levels of moral and virtuous leadership from the Disney Co.; and

Whereas, In recent years, the Disney Co. has given the appearance that the promotion of homosexuality is more important than its historic commitment to traditional family values and has taken a direction which is contrary to its previous commitment. . . . Now, therefore,

Be it resolved, We as Southern Baptist messengers meeting in annual session on June 11–13, 1996, go on record expressing our deep disappointments for these corporate actions by the Disney Co.; and. . . .

This chapter depends on conversations with Daniel Monk, Yoram Tsafrir, and Rev. Marvin Rosenthal.

Fig. 64. Visitor's souvenir map, The Holy Land Experience, Orlando, Florida. Author's collection.

Be it further resolved, That we encourage Southern Baptists to give serious and prayerful reconsideration to their purchase and support of Disney products and to boycott the Disney theme parks and stores if they continue this anti-Christian and anti-family trend. * ETHICS AND LIBERTY COMMISSION OF THE SOUTHERN BAPTIST CONVENTION (PROPOSED AND PASSED BY THE CONVENTION, 1996)

THEME PARK

In the globalized economy of the turn of the millennium, Jerusalem is experienced in the West as spectacle.[1] Spectacle is a performance that demands attention, but refuses reciprocity; it is a display that avoids local content, but produces a local effect. Spectacle is politics or ideology that pretends to be entertainment; it is the theatrical figuration of capital and an expression of its excesses. When spectacle seems safe, it is probably dangerous; when spectacle seems dangerous, it certainly is. Present Jerusalem is represented as the violent spectacle of suicide bombers on CNN. Past Jerusalem is rendered as the violent spectacle of

1. My understanding of *spectacle* depends on Marx and Debord, who respectively reveal money as a fetish and its display as spectacle. Marx, *Capital;* in particular, see "Commodities," vol. 1, pt. 1, 35–83; Debord, *Society of the Spectacle,* 34. For an exemplary application of spectacle in art-historical writing, see the introduction in T. J. Clark, *The Painting of Modern Life.*

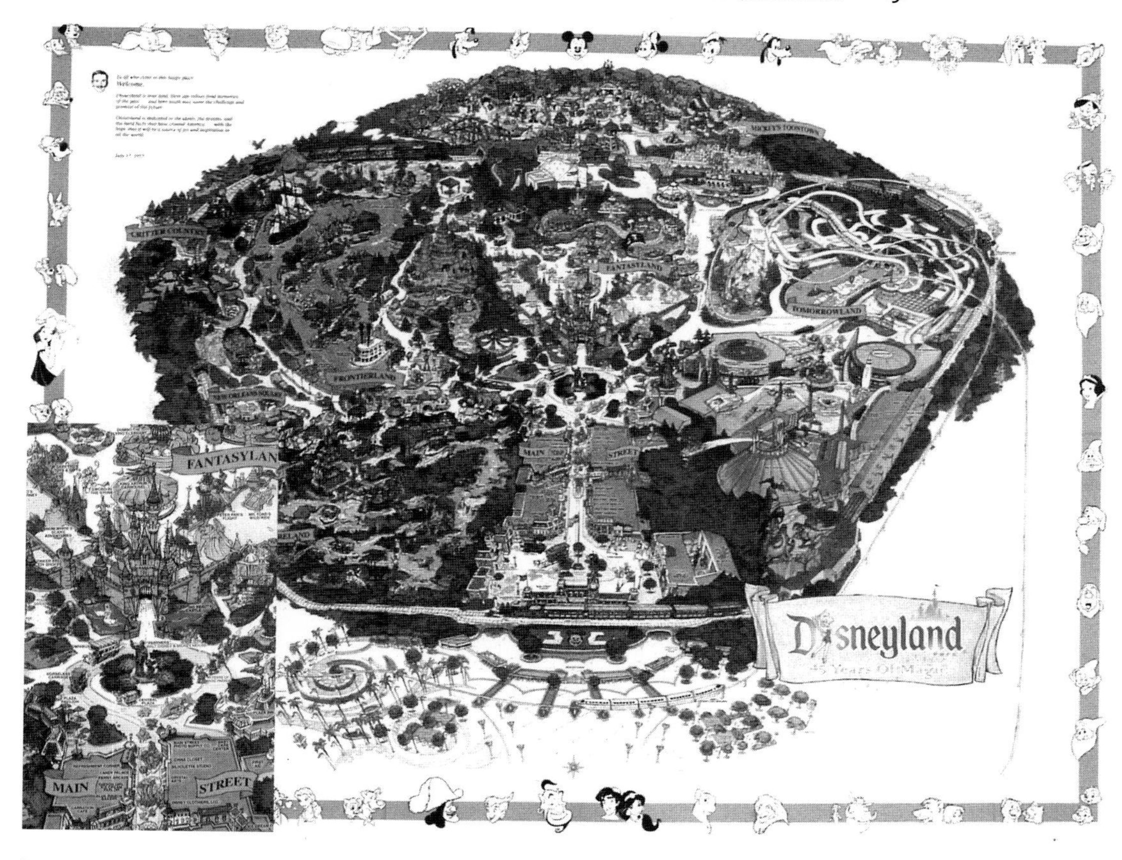

Fig. 65. Tourist plan of Disneyland, Anaheim, California. Inset of the core of the park added by the author. Author's collection.

torture by Mel Gibson in *The Passion of the Christ.*[2] In February 2001, Jerusalem opened as an apparently safe spectacle in Orlando, Florida. There, in The Holy Land Experience, Jerusalem appears in the guise of a theme park (fig. 64).

Theme park can be usefully defined by contrasting an archetypal theme park, Disneyland in California, with an archetypal religious shrine, the Holy Sepulchre (figs. 65, 35).[3] The principal subject of Disneyland is the tourist; that of the Holy Sepulchre is the pilgrim. Possession of Disneyland is corporate, and admission is pricey—it is maintained for profit; control of the Holy Sepulchre is communal, and access is free—it is supported by gifts. Time is experienced by a visitor to Disneyland as a synchronic present. Everything happens just once for her pleasure—the ride, the parade, the fireworks. And once may well be enough. Every effort is made by the corporation to erase the marks of the others who have been there before. Disneyland is famously clean. In contrast, the Holy Sepulchre is messy. The building bears the marks of its history—its

---

2. Gibson, *The Passion of the Christ,* screenplay by Fitzgerald.

3. *Theme park* is defined as "chiefly *U.S.,* an amusement park organized round a unifying idea or group of ideas" in the on-line edition of the *Oxford English Dictionary.* For an attempt to read Walt Disney World as a pilgrimage site rather than its antithesis, see G. Moore, "Walt Disney World."

Fig. 66. The Holy Land Experience, Orlando, Florida, view from the parking lot. Author photo.

Fig. 67. (*bottom*) Jerusalem Street Market at The Holy Land Experience, Orlando, Florida. Author photo.

fabric demonstrates how it has been worn, blackened, reconstructed. The pilgrim sees, touches, and even smells the antiquity of the shrine's veneration. Time for the pilgrim in the church is isochronic, repeated—the power of the place for the pilgrim comes from her confrontation with a ritually recurring deep past.

The material forms of the theme park and the shrine are obviously distinct. Disneyland, which opened to the public on July 17, 1955, is homogeneous despite its various themes; it was unitary in its conception. Walt Disney conceived and refined the idea of Disneyland. All its vital parts were in place in the presentation drawing produced by Walt Disney and Herb Ryman over a weekend in 1953, in preparation for a sponsor meeting with the television network ABC.[4] Disneyland's attractions are coherently arranged around a "wienie"—Disney's term for a dominant vertical landmark, like Cinderella's castle—within a sphere isolated from the real world by a berm, a transport system, and parking lots. Accessibility is strictly controlled; the tourist pays a high price for her admission.[5] The Holy Sepulchre is a heterogeneous site; its hybrid collection of shrines is irregularly ordered. The space of the Holy Sepulchre is porous; entrance may be watched and ritualized, but it is not exclusive. Entry is not by ticket; donations are voluntary. Behavior is invisibly policed in the theme park; decorum is witnessed in the shrine. The tourist pursues pleasure and transient oblivion in Disneyland; the pilgrim seeks solace and redemption in the Holy Sepulchre.

The Holy Land Experience may well attract both the pilgrim and the tourist. Nevertheless, it looks and acts more like a theme park than a shrine. It more closely resembles a truncated version of Disneyland than an expanded type of Holy Sepulchre. The Holy Land Experience is physically separated from the rest of Orlando by a wall and a parking lot. Its formidable faux-stone city gate—claimed to be a pastiche of the Old City's Damascus Gate, Jaffa Gate, and Golden Gate—provides the park's only public access (fig. 66).[6] Through it, the guest enters the Jerusalem Street Market (fig. 67). Most of the commodities presented in this mock Middle Eastern bazaar are similar to those offered on Main Street, Disneyland's equivalent admission-mall: souvenirs, tee shirts, and fast food. There is no falafel stand. Beyond the Market are the attractions, clustered around a "wienie." Herod's Temple stands in for Cinderella's castle. In Disneyland the principal attractions are themed rides, many of which serve also as advertisements for their corporate sponsors. In The Holy Land Experience the attractions are replicated biblical sites, each of which acts as a stage for periodically performed entertainments.

These biblical sites in The Holy Land Experience were designed and constructed by ITEC Entertainment Corporation, whose corporate headquarters are located, appropriately enough, on Commodity Circle in Orlando. ITEC's press release describes its product as "meticulous re-creations of some of the Bible's greatest landmarks—from Jerusalem's revered Herodian Temple to the Wilderness Tabernacle."[7] Each of these sites is more fully described in *The Holy Land Experience Fact Sheet*. An excerpt indicates something of ITEC's intentions:

The Wilderness Tabernacle: Exiting the street market, guests are transported back in time to circa 1450 B.C. A colorful, authentic-looking Bedouin tent beckons them

4. Marling, "Imagineering the Disney Theme Parks," 75–76.
5. In May 2004, an adult day-pass to Disneyland cost $50.
6. See ITEC Entertainment Corporation, *ITEC Projects*.
7. Ibid.

inside and provides pertinent pre-show information for the dramatic Wilderness Tabernacle. The interior creates the illusion of being outdoors at dusk, and guests find themselves among the 12 tribes of Israel making camp during their long journey to the Promised Land. Suddenly, the entrance to the adjoining Wilderness Tabernacle building materializes from the darkness and guests are directed inside for a 20-minute, sit-down, fully automated multi-media presentation, a dramatic and biblically accurate look at Israel's ancient priesthood and their sacrificial system. The tabernacle—which is recreated in three-quarter scale within the show building—was a mobile temple that provided a place for God to dwell among the Israelites during their 40 years of wandering through the desert. The Wilderness Tabernacle presentation is shown two times each hour, and is the most technologically advanced production in The Holy Land Experience. . . .

Calvary's Garden Tomb: As guests move from one area to another throughout the complex, the music and the atmosphere change. Soon guests find a beautifully landscaped and tranquil garden, but it is the tomb carved into the garden bedrock—a replication of the actual tomb of Jesus near Jerusalem—that attracts their attention. The stone that once sealed the tomb has been rolled to the side, exposing the empty tomb. Inside the tomb guests can pray, read the Scriptures, and reflect on the stirring events surrounding them. Throughout the day dramatists and/or musicians depict the death, burial, and resurrection of Jesus.

Plaza of the Nations/The Temple of the Great King/Theater of Life: Leaving the Garden Tomb, guests pass under a regal archway and find themselves in the spectacular Plaza of the Nations, surrounded by 30 columns crowned with golden Corinthian capitals and facing the majestic and splendorous six-story-high Temple of the Great King, a one-half-scale representation of Herod's Temple which stood upon hallowed Mount Moriah in first-century Jerusalem. It was in that Temple that Jesus reasoned with the Pharisees and scribes as a boy. Sixteen spectacular oil lamps are suspended over guests in the Plaza, and in the afternoon the sun reflects off the simulated white Jerusalem limestone and golden filigree of the Temple. In the evening, floodlights bathe the Temple's exterior, creating an ambience that is both reverential and peaceful. The 13 rounded steps that are the Temple's main entrance provide a dramatic venue for on-going sacred concerts and biblical drama reenactments.

From the Plaza of the Nations, guests enter The Temple of the Great King's "Theater of Life" through a side queuing entrance, to be seated for a 20-minute emotionally immersing film presentation, "The Seed of Promise," shot on location in Jerusalem exclusively for The Holy Land Experience and enhanced with a variety of special effects. The large-screen presentation, which can accommodate 170 guests per seating, opens with Roman soldiers battering down the massive door of the Temple, while fire rages across the screen. The film also includes scenes from creation and the Garden of Eden, Abraham's unquestioning response to God, the crucifixion, resurrection, and second coming of Christ and much more.

The Byzantine Cardo/Jerusalem Model A.D. 66: Guests exit the Theater of Life onto the Byzantine Cardo (the main Byzantine Road) and are directed to the nearby structure that houses the world's largest indoor model of first-century Jerusalem. The 45-foot-long by 25-foot-wide model is a historically authentic reproduction of the city of Jerusalem, circa A.D. *66, including the ancient Temple of Jerusalem as it had been rebuilt by King Herod the Great while the city was under Roman rule. Live 30-minute presentations detailing the history of the city and the movements of Jesus during the last week of his life, leading up to Calvary, are presented daily around the model.*[8]

Authentic or *authenticity* appears seven times in the unabridged Holy Land Experience Fact Sheet. Throughout the text, the strong claim for truth is weakened by a vocabulary of deception: "sandstone-like structure," "authentic-looking," "historically authentic reproduction," "simulated . . . limestone," and the like. The will to authenticity revealed in the fact sheet articulates the intentions of Rev. Marvin Rosenthal, founder of The Holy Land Experience.[9] Rev. Rosenthal brought to the project his personal experience of landscape as essential to an understanding of the Gospels. "After eighty teaching tours to the Holy Land, I had seen the advantage for teaching the Bible of seeing, touching, feeling the landscape in which biblical events happened. I thought that it would give our teaching a great advantage if we replicated some of those things."[10] He took the lead designer from ITEC with him to Palestine so that he might "get a sense of the color and touch of the place."[11]

For Rev. Rosenthal, The Holy Land Experience is more like a shrine than a theme park. Its landscape functions as an essential element in an evangelical education, behaving like a postmodern version of earlier evangelical geographies. Just as in the second half of the nineteenth century Rev. J. H. Vincent, in his itinerant ministry, used Palestine to persuade his pupils of the material reality of biblical truth, so Rev. Rosenthal deploys Israel to embody that part of the physical past essential to his message.[12] Like the promoters of David Roberts's lithographic folios, the advertisers for the panoramas of Jerusalem, and the sponsors of Kent's stereopticon, The Holy Land Experience promises its consumers what Disneyland does not: the "real" experience of a space that is somewhere else.[13] If The Holy Land Experience doesn't, in the end, deliver what it promises, Disney is to blame.

The modes of popular entertainment developed by Disney for Disneyland synthesized the great public diversions of the late nineteenth and twentieth centuries. Disney transfigured the visual excitements and haptic pleasures offered by the grand international expositions and pleasure parks of the industrial age through a new narrative derived from film and television, the brilliant entertainment technologies of modernity. Disneyland works effectively by deploying the consumer's nostalgia for an idealized childhood that was itself informed by Disney. The visitor reassuringly encounters those Disney cartoon figures—

8. Zion's Hope Inc., *The Holy Land Experience™ Fact Sheet.*

9. J. Jackson, "Holy Land Founder Resigns."

10. Rev. Marvin Rosenthal, interview, Orlando, Fla., October 21, 2001.

11. Ibid.

12. See chapter 2. Vincent, introduction to Hurlebut, *Manual of Biblical Geography*, vii.

13. In Walt Disney World in Orlando, of course, the Epcot Center presents different countries for the tourist's consumption. For further discussion of Epcot and its EPCOT predecessor, see below.

Mickey Mouse, Donald Duck, Goofy—and characters from Disney's brilliant animated full-length feature films—Snow White, Dumbo, Bambi—who populate the collective American consciousness. Moreover, these encounters take place in an appropriately narrativized setting. Disneyland is about visual and aural excitation; it produces pleasurable experience through sight and sound rather than touch or feel. Even its rides, like Splash Mountain, are less about the physical, bodily thrill of the drop than about singing along with B'rer Rabbit and his automata-buddies playing "Zippity-Doo-Da." Disney is a memory masseur.

The enormous success of Disneyland generated multiple copies, perhaps the most profitable being the one produced by the Disney Company itself: Walt Disney World. Governor Hayden Burns claimed November 15, 1965, the day he announced the plans for a new "Disneyland East," to be "the most significant day in the history of Florida."[14] Busch Gardens and Universal Studios have produced full-scale variations on Disney's theme park. The Holy Land Experience may be identified among its numerous small-scale derivatives. Certainly Rev. Rosenthal consciously appropriated Disney's entertainment technologies. "We recognize that the media changes—from scrolls, to the Gutenberg press and printing, to television. We have a message from the Bible that is fixed. The truth doesn't change. But we recognize that the medium changes. We are attempting to realize the medium that most effectively conveys the truth now."[15]

But is the medium not the message?[16] Technologies of pleasure developed by Disney offer magic, not miracle. Indeed, the absence of any religious content in Disneyland, a setting so ubiquitously identified with the quintessential American Way, has gone oddly unremarked.[17] There is no church on Main Street. Walt Disney was an anticommunist, a patriot, and a Freemason; he was not a conventional Christian.[18] He seems to have reacted against his dictatorial father's two fanaticisms: socialism and evangelical Christianity.[19] Socialism and Christianity may, however, have both contributed to the particular variety of authoritarian utopianism that informed Disneyland and, more patently, EPCOT, Walt Disney's unrealized utopian Experimental Prototype Community of Tomorrow.[20] The only Creator represented in Disneyland is Walt himself.

---

14. Quoted by Landsbury, *"Chronology,"* 221. For a thorough, well-documented denunciation of Walt Disney World, see Fjellman, *Vinyl Leaves*. For a less scholarly, but very punchy condemnation, see Hiassen, *Team Rodent*.

15. Rev. Marvin Rosenthal, interview, Orlando, Fla., October 21, 2001.

16. McLuhan, *Understanding Media*. McLuhan's observations remain remarkably relevant forty years after their publication.

17. For a useful analysis of the relation between Disney and fundamentalism, see Juschka, "Disney and Fundamentalism." The author's argument that pre-Eisner Disney productions embodied "family values" is, I think, problematic. No mention is made of the lack of Christian reference in Walt Disney's own works.

18. Walt Disney's religious views are suggested in his contribution to a peculiar collection of famous Americans' opinions on prayer. Disney, "Deeds Rather Than Words."

19. The biographies of Walt Disney, both the encomiastic ones (authorized) and the critical ones (unauthorized), seem formulaic after reading the first few. Eliot, *Walt Disney;* Green and Green, *Inside the Dream;* Hollister, "Genius at Work"; Jackson, *Walt Disney;* Mosley, *The Real Walt Disney*.

20. For a fuller discussion of EPCOT and Epcot, see below.

Fig. 68. Plaza of Nations performance at The Holy Land Experience, Orlando, Florida. Author photo.

A medium that promotes pleasure is adopted in The Holy Land Experience for spiritual instruction. If God is absent in Disneyland, he is always available at The Holy Land Experience. He takes different forms—a voice-over in the Tabernacle, a brilliant red cross unfurled over the altar of Herod's Temple, a filmic Jesus in the Theater of Life (fig. 68). Where God does not make an appearance—at the Empty Tomb and the Model of Jerusalem—his absence is carefully explained. The Empty Tomb and the Model of Jerusalem each has its own distinct history leading to its inclusion in The Holy Land Experience. Both histories reveal the attractions' attachment to Western imperialism in the nineteenth and early twentieth centuries.

EMPTY TOMB

The modern turn to nature is familiarly read as spiritual compensation for the rampant materialism of industrial society.[21] The industrialized urban West desired its Jerusalem to be as natural as possible. Western Protestants in the nineteenth century worked hard to imagine the sacred landscape free from its later accumulations.[22] In their panoramas and prints, they sought a view of the topography not as it was but as it might have been in the first century of the Common Era. The landscape itself was dramatized and the architectural accretions of the Middle

21. For a brilliant introduction to this subject, see Schama, *Landscape and Memory*.

22. There were, of course, exceptions, notably among Roman Catholic travelers. See Géramb, *Pilgrimage to Jerusalem and Mount Sinai;* Vetromile, *Travels in Europe, Egypt, Arabia Petræa, Palestine and Syria*. For an assessment of Catholic pilgrimage to Jerusalem in the late nineteenth and early twentieth centuries, see Klatzker, "American Catholic Travelers to the Holy Land 1861–1929."

Ages and early modernity erased. The distant view, the view of the great panoramas of Jerusalem on the day of the Crucifixion, was sought. It eliminated historical detritus. The evangelical preacher and long-time sojourner in the East, Rev. William M. Thomson, expresses the sentiment perfectly:

Our position on this mount [Olivet] is indeed delightful, and whichever way one turns he sees objects of the highest and most sacred interest. From a dozen points I have been gazing down into the Holy City, and my utmost anticipations are more than realized. Jerusalem, as I see it this morning, is all I could desire, and, if a nearer acquaintance is going to disappoint and disgust, let me not enter, but depart from this "Mount of Ascension" carrying away the picture already imprinted on my heart.[23]

Perhaps the most significant monument to be displaced was the Church of the Holy Sepulchre. For Protestants, the Holy Sepulchre of all Christian sites in the Holy Land obscured the aura of the landscape.[24] William Mason Turner, a popular American travel essayist, expresses this Protestant disdain:

On account of this ubiquity of holy objects and curiosities, the whole church and its wonders necessarily appear as a sham, and the high religious awe with which we should view these wonders, subsides into a stoical, indifferent credulity, which plainly expresses our opinion of everything shown us, as humbug.[25]

John Stoddard, in his popular travel accounts, also describes the fetishization of the Holy Land by those who just can't get religion right:

For fifteen hundred years the majority of pilgrims to the Holy Land, coming from the steppes of Russia, from the mountains of Syria, from Egypt, and even from Abyssinia, expected and demanded to see all the localities mentioned in the Bible. This demand inevitably created the supply, in order to satisfy those who probably needed some such tangible souvenirs to help them to appreciate and understand the life of Him whom they were taught to reverence. Inspired by intense religious zeal, the early pilgrims and Crusaders must have gone about Jerusalem intoxicated with their own enthusiasm and utterly undirected by a critical spirit of investigation. Hence, as years rolled by, the influence of tradition and antiquity gave to these places a sanctity which it is now almost impossible to disturb.[26]

Stoddard dismisses the credibility of the Holy Sepulchre and reiterates the familiar features of the site that inevitably offended Protestants—the miraculous claims made for it and the sectarian factionalism of its non-Protestant occupants:

---

23. Thomson, *The Land and the Book*, 2 : 467.

24. These points have been compellingly argued elsewhere. For an excellent study of the consumption of the Holy Land in the United States, see J. Davis, *The Landscape of Belief.* Also see Bowman, "Christian Ideology and the Image of a Holy Land," 98–121.

25. Turner, *El-Khuds, the Holy*, 231.

26. Stoddard, *Lectures*, 158–59.

The Church of the Holy Sepulchre is not so much a church, as a sacred exposition building. Its enormous roof covers a multitude of altars, chapels, stairways, caves and natural elevations; under this one canopy, as if miraculously concentrated into a small area, are gathered almost all the places mentioned in the Bible, which could by any possibility be located in Jerusalem. The "Holy Sites" are owned by various Christian sects, who hate each other cordially; so much so, indeed, that officers, appointed by the Turkish Government, are always present to protect the property, and to prevent the owners from flying at one another's throats. This is, alas! no exaggeration. . . . Not long ago, during Holy Week, a priest of the Greek Church hurled a bottle of ink at the head of the Franciscan Superior who was conducting a procession round the Holy Sepulchre. [Though the mark was missed], it created a disturbance which Turkish soldiers were obliged to quell.[27]

In 1854, Fisher Howe published a popular travelogue of his journeys, *Oriental and Sacred Scenes: From Notes of Travel Greece, Turkey, and Palestine.* For Howe, as for Turner and Stoddard, these scenes had been unfortunately defaced by non-Protestants:

The impressions of sacredness, which would seem almost instinctively to attach to many localities, are measurably effaced by Mohammedan appropriation, or the gross superstitions engrafted by the ignorant and corrupt Christian sects. These remarks are specially applicable to the Church of the Holy Sepulchre.[28]

Howe's language, recycled from his own earlier text, becomes more violent in his *True Site of Calvary, and Suggestions Relating to the Resurrection* of 1871:

The impressions of sacredness, which would seem almost instinctively to attach to many localities are effaced by the absurd superstitions and baptized paganism engrafted by the ignorant and corrupt sects [Catholics, Greek Orthodox, Armenians, Copts], who claim concurrent rights within the enclosure. The veritable spot which indicates the exact centre of the earth, and from which dust was taken for the creation of Adam, is shown with the same confident assertion as is the so-called tomb of Joseph, from which our Lord is said to have arisen. As we witnessed the mummery of the blessing of trinkets for a "bakhshish" within the tomb, we were relieved by the conviction that our Savior's body neither rested in, nor rose from, this place.[29]

27. Ibid., 2 : 154–55.

28. Howe, *Oriental and Sacred Scenes*, 352–53.

29. Howe, *The True Site of Calvary*, 13–14. Howe's views were broadly absorbed. In Elizabeth Champney's novel, *Three Vassar Girls*, his work is quoted:

[Mr. Remington took the girls to the] Grotto of Jeremiah, near the Damascus Gate, which Dr. Robinson and many other eminent archaeologists regard as the true site of Calvary. Mr. Remington had been much interested in the discussion, and before visiting the spot he went over the views of different authorities with the young people. Mr. Fisher Howe, an able student and Oriental traveler, published a book on this subject in 1871. . . . [His six points of biblical requirements for the site are summarized.] It is impossible to meet these

The relief felt by the Protestant traveler at not having to take the Holy Sepulchre seriously is vividly recorded by Samuel Wheelock Fiske, a traveler of the mid-nineteenth century:

> *The town itself . . . is a filthy, muddy, Oriental town, full of dogs and vermin, and intolerable smells, habitable by decent people only on Mt. Zion and near the Jaffa gate. The so-called sacred places have been described a thousand times, and even if they had not been, are not worth the trouble, as no one now believes in their genuineness. . . . You are thankful to know that Calvary and the Holy Sepulchre could not possibly have been where the Greeks and Catholics locate them, and quarrel so fiercely about their possession that the Turk is obliged to interfere as a peacemaker in these* Christian *brawls.*[30]

The ancient Christian communities with traditional property rights in the holy sites certainly quarreled with one another. But the disdain that Protestants expressed for such infighting may have masked their own sense of disenfranchisement. Protestants, after all, fought among themselves, sometimes violently, over what they might possess—including the Protestant bishopric and the few Jews who converted.[31] The Protestant turn from the monument to the landscape was only partially sour grapes. In most Protestant comments on the traditional tomb of Jesus, the scientific evidence against the Holy Sepulchre is presented first, then confirmed by reports of the church's distressing materiality. Protestant Christians found the ancient church, with its architectural irregularities and multiple miracle-chapels, its candles, icons, ex-votos, incense, and complex religious politics, too crudely corporeal and human for their more cerebral and Romantic piety (fig. 48). Despite the order of the argument, it seems likely that revulsion preceded its rationalization.

For pious medieval travelers, every landscape through which they passed on their way to Jerusalem had its own sacredness—provided by the prophets who predicted there, the apostles who preached there, the martyrs who died there, the

---

> *requirements by the traditional site, now occupied by the Church of the Holy Sepulchre; and the so-called Grotto of Jeremiah is the only locality which perfectly meets them all. The young people took up this view with enthusiasm, on examination of the ground. . . . So convinced were they all that they had visited the true site of Calvary, that Emma acknowledged she had no desire to visit the so-called Church of the Holy Sepulchre, with its collection of legendary holy places; but Violet felt that there would be an interest in standing in a place which had been held sacred for ages, and was consecrated by the faith and strong emotion of many loving and trusting souls.*

Champney, *Three Vassar Girls in the Holy Land*, 154–57.

30. Fiske, *Mr. Dunn Browne's Experiences in Foreign Parts*, 157–58. The italics are Fiske's.

31. A sense of the bitterness and pettiness of Protestant squabbling is provided by Finn, *A View from Jerusalem, 1849–1858*. The case of the converted Jew, Mendel John Diness, suggests something of the ordeal of being fought over by Anglicans and American evangelists: Diness et al., *Capturing the Holy Land*. A particularly powerful description of the violence of Protestant infighting in Jerusalem is provided by Lagerlöf, *The Holy City*.

anchorites who lived there, the relics which were displayed there.[32] They embraced the accretions of devotion—candles, icons, ex votos, monks—that marked a sacred site. Pilgrims added to those tokens of belief, if it were within in their means, as well as carrying them home as relics. Protestants, in contrast, sought a landscape free from pious accretions. In the published version of his travel lectures, John Stoddard describes three kinds of travelers to the Holy Land: "first, those who are wisely content to see the natural localities connected with the life of Christ, and therefore gain from Palestine the solemn inspiration of its priceless memories; secondly, those who lose themselves within the slough of superstition there; and thirdly, those who, thoroughly offended by the false, forget the value of the true, and ridicule it all."[33] Only the first sort of traveler gets it right.

In the sixth century, the Piacenza Pilgrim, pausing at Cana, venerated those clay vessels that had held the water that Jesus miraculously changed to wine on the occasion of a marriage feast.[34] In the nineteenth century, shards became souvenirs. In Elizabeth Champney's *Three Vassar Girls in the Holy Land,* one of the protagonists insists on the sacrality of the fountain of Cana. "I am going to bottle some of this water to be served at my wedding,—if I ever have one; and to me it will be the best wine at the feast." Her brother then "picked up some broken fragments of water jars near the fountain, suggesting that they would make pleasant souvenirs to give as wedding presents to friends."[35] By the early twentieth century, the vessels were commodities. In 1930, Evelyn Waugh, the English novelist and travel writer, reported, "We went to Cana of Galilee, where a little girl was offering wine jars for sale. They were the authentic ones used in the miracle. If they were too big she had a smaller size indoors; yes, the small ones were authentic too."[36] Souvenirs displaced relics; the commodity superseded the blessing *(eulogia)*.[37]

Protestant aversion to the tactility of the Church of the Holy Sepulchre required a more idyllic, contemplative site for Jesus's burial. General George

---

32. For a study of the early Christian pilgrim's sense of the holy itinerary, see Frank, *The Memory of the Eyes.*

33. Stoddard, *Lectures,* 177. Despite the author's insistent lack of gullibility, he, of course, reproduces all the stories associated with the holy monuments.

34. Antoninus of Piacenza, "Antonini Placentini Itinerarium," 161.7–11.

35. Champney, *Three Vassar Girls in the Holy Land,* 245–47. See also note 37 in this chapter.

36. Waugh, *Labels,* 53.

37. For the relation between souvenirs and relics, see the discussion at the beginning of chapter 2. In *Three Vassar Girls in the Holy Land,* Stoddard's three travelers are encountered at Cana. There Jesus performed his first miracle: the transformation of water into wine at a wedding party. Voicing her desire to be married in Cana, Violet expresses a too literal attachment to the place: "It would be more to me all my life to know that my wedding had taken place where Christ once blessed a marriage . . . than to have had the most magnificent ceremonies in the greatest of cathedrals." Violet's mother asserts a too crassly functionalist detachment by objecting that a proper wedding dinner could not be obtained on the site. Only Frank represents the proper Protestant response to the site:

"I understand you, Violet," Frank replied; "but after all, the place does not matter,—only the spirit."
"It matters to me," Violet replied with enthusiasm; "and I am going to bottle some of this water to be served at my wedding,—if I ever have one; and to me it will be the best wine at the feast."
Frank picked up some broken fragments of water jars near the fountain, suggesting that they would make pleasant souvenirs to give as wedding presents to friends.

Gordon, with help from the Palestine Exploration Fund, discovered an appropriately Protestant Holy Sepulchre. Established in London in 1865, the Palestine Exploration Fund promoted the study of the Holy Land by financing research expeditions and publishing their findings. Like all scholarship, the work of the Fund had a politics. Though the articulated objective of the Fund was the scientific understanding of the region, the mapping of Jerusalem and its vicinity by the British also had military, economic, and religious motives.[38] The British military was intimately involved in the Palestine Exploration Fund from its origins; the earliest Fund-sponsored scholarly investigations were undertaken by officers of the Royal Engineers and assisted by the British War Office. Napoleon's deployment of archaeologists and cartographers during the French occupation of Egypt at the beginning of the nineteenth century provided the model as well as the prod for British military engagement in similar activities.[39] Among the Royal Engineers working for the Fund in the mid-1860s were Charles Wilson, Charles Warren, and Horatio Herbert Kitchener, all of whom contributed so greatly to empire-building that they were later titled. Kitchener was distinguished for his military service in Egypt and South Africa and during World War I. Warren also served in South Africa and Egypt; he was police commissioner in London at the time of Jack the Ripper's murderous spree. Wilson, in addition to his work in Palestine, surveyed the forty-ninth parallel as the border between the United States and Canada and laid the institutional foundations for British intelligence.[40] The British government's interest in charting the Middle East was part of the project of colonization. The Fund seems to have acted as a "cover for military mapping."[41] Its maps were used to their great advantage by the British in World War I.

The publications that resulted from the Fund's research program significantly contributed to the circulation of Jerusalem in the West and, consequently, to the promotion of tourism. In 1880, Warren published his influential *The Temple or the Tomb*. Between 1881 and 1884, Wilson edited the enormously popular *Picturesque Palestine, Sinai, and Egypt*. Earlier, in 1871, Wilson and Warren had together produced *The Recovery of Jerusalem: A Narrative of Exploration and Discovery in the City and the Holy Land*. This was followed by the nine-volume *Survey of Western Palestine*, to which they both contributed. These texts were essential to further scholarly research on the city. Travel guides indicate that

---

"And I will write something appropriate on each one," Violet replied. "John 2.1–2, and Milton's 'The conscious water saw its Lord, and blushed.'"

Champney, *Three Vassar Girls in the Holy Land*, 246–47.

38. "For its first twenty-five years of existence the PEF doubled up as a research body and learned society, a tool for extending British imperial influence and as a cover for obtaining strategic information to support British military interests." Moscrop, *Measuring Jerusalem*, 3.

39. Reid, *Whose Pharaohs?*, 21–63.

40. Watson, *The Life of Major-General Sir Charles William Wilson, Royal Engineers*.

41. Moscrop, *Measuring Jerusalem*, 221. Also, see Benvenisti, *Sacred Landscape*, 15–17, Biger, *An Empire in the Holy Land*, 21–31.

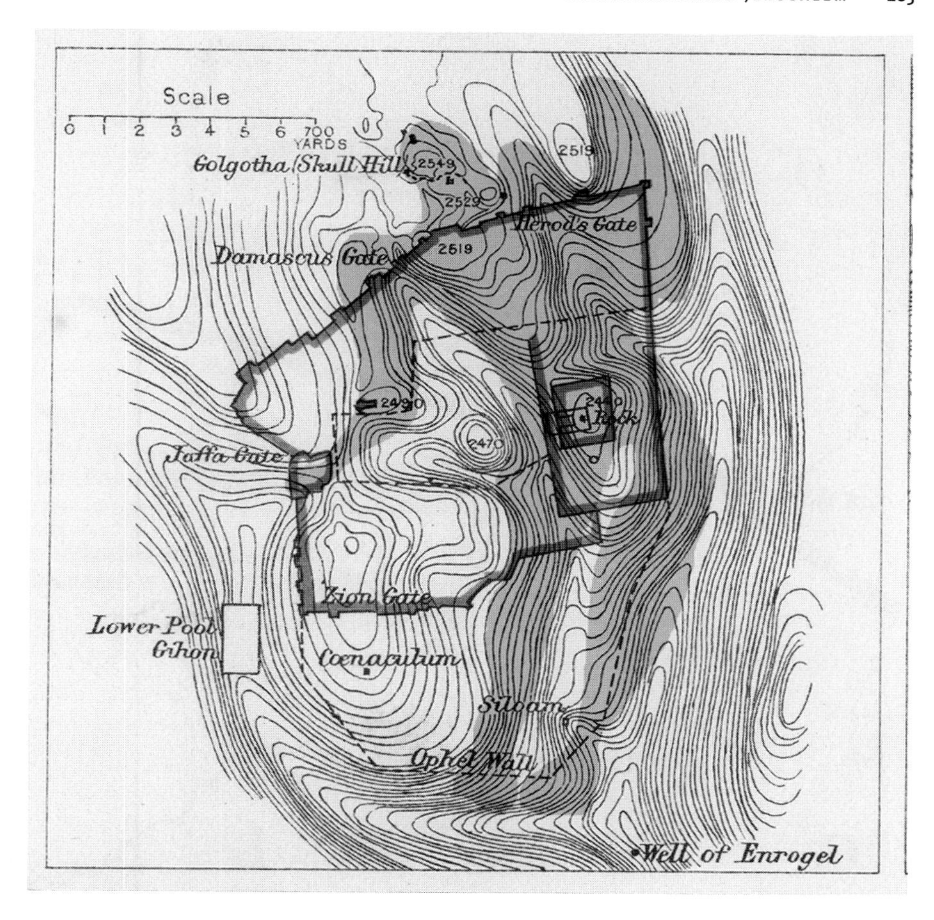

Fig. 69. Colonel Charles Warren's topographical map of Jerusalem. From Gordon, *Reflections in Palestine*. Plan modified with the addition of shading by the author.

they also contributed to the touristic consumption of Jerusalem. In *Baedeker's Handbook for Travelers: Syria and Palestine* of 1898, the bibliography of books for the tourist to consult begins with the *Survey of Western Palestine*. It is the only citation accompanied by a note: "These works, published for the Palestine Exploration Fund, are the foundation of all modern exploration in Palestine, and practically supersede all books of travel of earlier date."[42]

The pious impetus of the Palestine Exploration Fund was evident from its foundation. Many of the its first members and benefactors were devout Christians, including Lord Shaftesbury, a leading evangelical reformer, the bishop of Ely, and the archbishop of York.[43] A remarkable and pious philanthropist, Baroness Burdett-Coutts, supported the survey of Palestine.[44] The Fund's publications were also put to religious work. General George Gordon offers a most remarkable example of the Fund's contribution to Protestant piety.[45]

42. *Baedeker's Handbook for Travellers*, cxvi.

43. The first meeting of the Fund in 1865 was appropriately held in the Jerusalem Chamber at Westminster Abbey. See Moscrop, *Measuring Jerusalem*, 67.

44. C. W. Wilson, *The Recovery of Jerusalem*, 3.

45. For a remarkable biographical sketch of Gordon, see Strachey, *Eminent Victorians*, 189–267.

Fig. 70. Garden Tomb, Jerusalem. Author photo.

Gordon, who was not only a famous British military figure but also a fervent Christian, demonstrated how the topographies of the Holy Land produced by his fellow officers might be used in Palestine's Protestantization. While in Jerusalem on holiday after his campaigns in India and before his heroic death at Khartoum, Gordon sought to identify the "true" Calvary.[46] He found what he was looking for in Warren's topographical map of Jerusalem. For Gordon, the orthogonal lines of the survey figured the body of the crucified Jesus in the landscape itself—the Temple Mount located the groin, and the head was the new Golgotha (fig. 69).

I refer to Colonel Sir Charles Warren, R.E., Brompton Barracks, Chatham, for the explanation of the plan of Jerusalem without débris, *which is in his book,* The Temple

46. For Gordon's identification of the new site, see Gordon, *Reflections in Palestine*. For another assessment, see Silberman, *Digging for God and Country*, 152–53. For the theoretically sophisticated reading of this material that inspired my use of it, see Monk, *An Aesthetic Occupation*, 17–44. Monk's study offers a powerful assessment of the political implications of the architecture of Jerusalem.

Fig. 71. Garden Tomb, The Holy Land Experience, Orlando, Florida. Author photo.

and the Tomb. *His plan shows very clearly the human figure, and only wants the skull hill to be considered with it to complete it.*[47]

Warren thus explains his map:

This plan as now exhibited has been made from observations gained during the excavations, and also from rock-levels obtained during the building of houses, and it will be at once apparent from inspection of it, that the rocky site about the Jebus of the ancients, with its precipitous hills and deep valleys, presents a very different aspect at the present day, when the valleys are filled up, in some cases to heights of a hundred feet or more, with millions of cubic yards of débris *or rubbish. From this contoured plan it will be seen that this ancient site then consisted of three principal hills, to east, north-west, and south-west, separated by deep valleys.*[48]

"Without *débris*" refers to Jerusalem without the effects of history: the city freed from its Catholic and Islamic garbage. Jesus was immanent in the land itself, not in its architectural trappings. The topography produced by Warren's map is the dramatically mountainous one of nineteenth-century renderings and Mel Gibson's *Passion of the Christ*. Warren's reconstruction of Jerusalem's contours

47. Gordon, *Reflections in Palestine*, vii–viii.
48. C. Warren, *The Temple or the Tomb*, 32–33.

was imaginative as well as scientific: it matched the Holy City more closely to the West's expectations.

Gordon's refiguring of the Jerusalem landscape placed Golgotha in a charming garden outside the Damascus Gate, complete with a nearby tomb of an appropriate date and emptiness. A group of English Protestants, the Garden Tomb (Jerusalem) Association, U.K., bought the site, which they continue to maintain as unbuilt (fig. 70).[49] Gordon's Calvary and the Garden Tomb are a clear expression of a Protestant piety that required an immediacy in its experience of God that only nature seemed to offer.

The land where the Word-made-flesh dwelt with men is, and must ever be, an integral part of the Divine Revelation. Her testimony is essential to the chain of evidences, her aid invaluable in exposition. Mournful deserts and mouldering ruins rebuke the pride of man and vindicate the truth of God. . . . The very hills and mountains, rocks, rivers, and fountains, are symbols and pledges of things far better than themselves. In a word, Palestine is one vast tablet whereupon God's messages to men have been drawn, and graven deep in living characters by the Great Publisher of glad tidings, to be seen and read of all to the end of time. The Land and the Book—with reverence be it said—constitute the ENTIRE and ALL-PERFECT TEXT, and should be studied together.[50]

So wrote Rev. William Thomson. Only the land, not the monuments that polluted it, satisfied the Protestant desire to encounter religious truth.

Like the representation of Jerusalem in the great end-of-the-century panoramas, Gordon's Calvary was an illusion of imaginative reconstruction masquerading as truth. Archaeologists now unanimously doubt the authenticity of the Garden Tomb. Evangelical Protestants, who generally have little regard for those who misconstrue revelation on the basis of empirical evidence, still embrace the New Calvary. In The Holy Land Experience in Orlando, it is a replica of the Garden Tomb that tourists visit (fig. 71).

JERUSALEM REMODELED

When the opportunity arose, the West reconstructed Jerusalem to look like the city represented in the images that had been produced and circulated for consumption in Europe and the United States. Warren refigured the landscape of the Holy City to make it look more like David Roberts's prints. Another British officer, Ronald Storrs, governor of Jerusalem from 1917 to 1927, materially reconstructed the city to the same end.[51] Born in Bury Saint Edmunds in

---

49. For this group's historical perspective, see Izzett, White, and Hardcastle, *The Garden Tomb Jerusalem*.

50. Thomson, *The Land and the Book*, 1:xv.

51. For a general sense of the British relationship to Palestine, see Tuchman, *Bible and Sword*. For a balanced history of the British governance of Palestine between 1917 and 1928, see Wasserstein, *The British in Palestine*.

1881, Storrs was the eldest son of the Reverend John Storrs, a vicar who became dean of Rochester. Storrs was educated at Charterhouse and Pembroke College, Cambridge. At Cambridge he received a first-class degree in the Classical Tripos of 1903.[52] There he also was elected to the elite Decemviri, whose ten at his time included Charles Tennyson, John Maynard Keynes, and Lytton Strachey.[53] Storrs moved directly from Cambridge into the Egyptian Civil Service in 1904.[54] In Cairo he served as Oriental Secretary under Sir Eldon Gorst, Lord Kitchener, and Sir Henry McMahon. During the early years of World War I, Storrs was involved with such figures as Sharif Hussein, later King Hussein of Jordan, and T. E. Lawrence, better known as Lawrence of Arabia. Lawrence describes Storrs in his *Seven Pillars of Wisdom*:

The first of us was Ronald Storrs, Oriental Secretary of the Residency, the most brilliant Englishman in the Near East, and subtly efficient, despite his diversion of energy in love of music and letters, of sculpture, painting, of whatever was beautiful in the world's fruit. None the less, Storrs sowed what we reaped, and was always first, and the great man among us. His shadow would have covered our work and British policy in the East like a cloak, had he been able to deny himself the world, and to prepare his mind and body with the sternness of an athlete for a great fight.[55]

As Lawrence suggests, Storrs was never willing to abstain from the arts, whatever his military and administrative obligations. Another of Lawrence's anecdotes, describing their shipboard passage to Jidda to meet with Sharif Hussein's representative, Abdullah, to help plan the Arab Legion's war against the Turks, suggests something of Storrs's sophistication:

Storrs' intolerant brain seldom stooped to company. But today he was more abrupt than usual. He turned twice around the decks, sniffed, "No one worth talking to," and sat down in one of the two comfortable armchairs, to begin a discussion of Debussy with Aziz el-Masri. Aziz, the Arab-Circassian ex-colonel in the Turkish Army, now general of the Sharifian Army, was on his way to discuss with the Emir of Mecca the equipment and standing of the Arab regulars he was forming at Rabegh. A few minutes later they had left Debussy, and were depreciating Wagner: Aziz in fluent

---

52. The honorary archivist of Pembroke College made a valiant effort to explain to me the mysteries of Cambridge degrees: "According to his entry in the University Archives, Storrs matriculated as a member of the University on 22 October 1900. He was placed in Class I division 3 in the first part of the Classical Tripos of 1903 and graduated BA on 23 June of that year. (The obtaining of honours in Part one of the Classical Tripos was then sufficient to qualify for an honours BA.) The First class was divided into three sections according to merit. Storrs subsequently took the MA degree by proxy on 12 October 1928. This was of course awarded upon completion of a certain number of terms after the BA, and not by examination. Storrs would have qualified to take the MA as early as 1907 but for unrecorded reasons chose not to do so." Jayne Ringrose, email, July 17, 2003.

53. Storrs, *Orientations*, 15.

54. Ibid., chaps. 2–12. For a summary of Storrs's Egyptian service, see "Colonel R. Storrs, C. M. G."

55. T. E. Lawrence, *Seven Pillars of Wisdom*, 30.

German, and Storrs in German, French and Arabic. The ship's officers found the whole conversation unnecessary.[56]

Emblematic of Storrs's close connections with those in the arts was his intimate friendship with the well-known American art connoisseur Bernard Berenson and his wife, Mary.[57] His administrative posts were always extended to include the fine arts. In Cairo he was a member of the Comité pour la Conservation des Monuments Arabes; he was also central to the establishment of the Coptic Museum in Cairo. But Storrs's most notable contribution to the arts and to preservation was made in Jerusalem during his tenure as governor of the city.

On December 11, 1917, British and Allied troops under General Edmund Allenby entered Jerusalem. Storrs was appointed governor of the city on December 28, in the immediate aftermath of the Turkish evacuation of the city and its occupation by the British army. He was confronted with a population that had been on starvation rations for three years; the Turkish withdrawal left the city entirely without provisions.[58] Foodstuffs and movables had been confiscated by the retreating army. Water supplies were contaminated. Roads were impassable and the rails of the Jaffa–Jerusalem train line had been dismantled. Despite the enormous fiscal pressures on the civil order of the city, Storrs's commitment to archaeology and the preservation of Jerusalem was a focus of his administration from the beginning.

In a speech reported by the *Times* of London, Storrs identified Jerusalem as "a city unparalleled in the world, with an appeal to the imagination that not Rome, nor even Athens, could rival. Even in its appearance . . . there was an impression of something strange and moving. The austere gray walls and battlements, stone-built on hills of stone, commanded and dominated the gaunt Judean plateau. Travelers . . . would pass the ancient walls, whose stones were hewn from the quarries of Solomon, and climb the Mount of Olives, from whose summit they could look over the city, of which, though its towers, pinnacles, and minarets wore the work of more recent ages, the general appearance was, and he hoped would be allowed to remain, very much what it was 2,000 years ago."[59]

Storrs worked to construct a historic Jerusalem. He deployed two strategies to accomplish the task: rebuild the old and resist the new. The administrative vehicle for Storrs's reconstruction effort was the Pro-Jerusalem Society. Storrs established the Pro-Jerusalem Society as an independent, nongovernmental association of distinguished representatives of the city's various ethnic communities. Members included the Grand Mufti, the most powerful religious

56. Ibid., 39.

57. The Berensons acted as liaisons in Storrs's unsuccessful courtship of the wealthy American Margaret Strong, the only daughter of Bessie and Charles A. Strong and granddaughter of J. D. Rockefeller. Storrs, "The Papers of Sir Ronald Storrs (1881–1956) from Pembroke College, Cambridge."

58. For an overview of the economic history of Jerusalem, see Lieber, "An Economic History of Jerusalem."

59. "The New Era in Jerusalem."

representative of the Muslim community; the Palestinian mayor of Jerusalem; the Orthodox patriarch; the Latin patriarch; the head of the Armenian Convent in Jerusalem; the Franciscan Custodian of the Holy Land; and the head of the Jewish community. Storrs served on the committee for the eight years of its existence. As secretary to this society as well as the Civic Advisor, he appointed C. R. Ashbee, a friend and follower of William Morris and committed Arts and Crafts advocate.[60] In a city tense with ethnic and religious hostility, project decisions made within this group might escape charges of preference or prejudice. Indeed, the Pro-Jerusalem Society, comprised of individuals whose only shared commitment was to the physical well-being of the city, seems to have been the one setting in which representatives of the different factions regularly worked productively together.

The funds available to Storrs for his planned improvements were extremely limited. The British were well practiced in imperialism by the time Palestine was associated with its empire. The historian Gideon Biger explains the "Cromer System," the model deployed by the British to regulate its domains: it "emphasized the importance of low taxation, efficient fiscal administration, careful expenditure on remunerative public work, and a minimal interference in the internal and external traffic of goods. This system was most effective in countries with a clear-cut native ruling class. . . . Development programs and services in the colonies were funded by local tax revenues, British government loans, and public or private investment. . . . Since tax revenues were much lower than in Britain, the services provided in the colonies were obviously more limited."[61] Moreover, not all local income was devoted to local needs. The British imposed heavy external loads on public income in Palestine. Notably, the British treasury insisted that Palestine contribute to the repayment of the Ottoman debt, which, of course, included British creditors. Further, concessions granted by the Ottomans before the war were deemed still valid after it was over. Standard Oil had a concession for oil development; a French company, for the operation of various railroads and cargo and passenger ships; there were also foreign monopolies on water, power, and tobacco farming. In addition, costs of construction undertaken by the British army for its use during the war were charged to the local civilian administration when the buildings were no longer needed by the military. Finally, the British government refused to guarantee a loan that was repeatedly requested by Herbert Samuel, the first high commissioner of Palestine, because Palestine was never intended to be part of the empire. The British were willing to pay only for military expenditures—and when that proved too costly, in 1948, they withdrew.[62]

---

60. Ashbee, *A Palestine Notebook, 1918–1923;* Gitler, "C. R. Ashbee's Jerusalem Years"; Crawford, *C. R. Ashbee.*

61. Biger, *An Empire in the Holy Land,* 20–21.

62. Ibid., 94–95.

Storrs finally extracted an annual subsidy of between £500 and £2000 from Samuel, through the threat of a tourist tax.[63] All other monies had to be raised privately. His 1923 trip to the United States—exploiting his connections to the very wealthy—represents his most notable effort in fund-raising on behalf of the Pro-Jerusalem Society. The organization's yearbooks, which provide the most useful documentation of its activities, were actually published by Ashbee and privately circulated as part of Storrs's fund-raising efforts. Storrs describes the funding of the society in his autobiography:

Many of the leading merchants, realizing how greatly the future prosperity of Jerusalem depended upon its preservation as Jerusalem (and not an inferior Kiev, Manchester or Baltimore), subscribed liberally to our funds; and in Egypt, England and America, Moslems, Christians and Jews, suspicious of any creed, culture or policy other than their own, gave gladly to a Jerusalem which represented all three. I realized then the power of the name of Jerusalem; I realized it even more afterwards when appealing for other countries or causes; I became, I am happy to believe, a convincing and successful Schnorrer (Yiddish for professional beggar). My subscription list, of cheques ranging from £3 to £600, included from Cairo the names of Smouha and Btesh, the Syrian Community, and the editor of the Mokattam; *in Jerusalem the Anglo-Egyptian Bank, Sir Abbas Effendi Abd al-Bahá, the Mufti, several Jewish firms, the Imperial Ottoman Bank, the Crédit Lyonnais, the Anglo-Palestine Bank, the Banco di Roma, the 51st Sikh Regiment, the Zionist Commission, the Municipality, and the Administration; in Europe and America, Lord Milner, Sir Basil Zaharoff, Lord Northcliffe, Sir Alred Mond, Mrs. Holman Hunt, Mrs. Carnegie, Messrs Pierpont Morgan, and Messrs Keun Loeb. I found institutions more generous than individuals, and (especially in America) men than women.*[64]

Storrs also requested financial support from King George V, but was sharply rebuffed for his impertinence.[65]

Despite limited funds, during the first years of British occupation a number of important repairs were made to the fabric of Jerusalem under the aegis of the Pro-Jerusalem Society.[66] The Dome of the Rock received desperately needed attention.

The supervision of this important work has been since the outset in the hands of Mr. Ernest Richmond, the advisor architect of the Wakf, from whose report of

63. Storrs, "The Papers of Sir Ronald Storrs (1881–1956) from Pembroke College, Cambridge."

64. Storrs, *Orientations*, 364–65.

65. A letter from J. A. C. Dilley to Sir Herbert Samuel, August 30, 1920, indicates that Storrs's request to the king for the patronage of the Pro-Jerusalem Society was an "irregularity." "His Majesty does not as a rule give his patronage to new undertakings until they have become firmly established, both financially and otherwise, and he very rightly points out that such a communication should have reached him through you and through this Department." In Storrs, "The Papers of Sir Ronald Storrs (1881–1956) from Pembroke College, Cambridge," 7.2.

66. An idea of the complexity involved in disbursing monies is conveyed by a letter from Ashbee to Storrs, December 4, 1920. Ibid.

The Jaffa Gate reconstruction as at present, looking towards the city. *No. 44.*

The same, as suggested when the unsightly obstructions that hide the wall line are cleared away. *No. 45.*

Fig. 72. Jaffa Gate, Jerusalem. Photograph and reconstruction from Ashbee, *Jerusalem, 1918–1920.*

March 1919 the following extract is given: "To ensure complete immunity from decay, especially in the case of the more modern tiles, is impossible. The surface of this kind of tile . . . is bound to disappear much sooner than that of the earlier tiles, thereby seriously increasing the denuded areas. . . . 'Is the method adopted in the sixteenth century of decorating the outer walls of this building with glazed tiles to be continued . . . or abandoned?' . . . All skin decays, but so long as there is life in the body which it covers its tissues are continually renewed. So long as the Dome of the Rock remains a live building—a building that is to say which is an integral part in the life that surrounds it—so long as it fulfils the functions it has fulfilled for 1,200 years, so long must its skin be continually renewed."[67]

The medieval kilns were restored and tile makers brought from Turkey to provide the high-quality tiles essential to a credible restoration of the structure.

67. Ashbee, *Jerusalem, 1918–1920,* 9.

Fig. 73. Jaffa Gate, Jerusalem. Photographs before and after the removal of the Turkish clock tower. From the *Graphic* (April 19, 1924).

Greater effort, however, was required to remodel the city as *old*—its walls, moat or fosse, and markets had to be remade. The Citadel was purged of the remains of a late Turkish fortress, guardrooms, and offices. The fosse was cleared. The Turks had used its southern and eastern parts as a dump; they had planned to fill in its western section to serve as a roadbed and building site. It was suggested that the Turks had also intended to sell the ancient ramparts. Supposedly, the walls were to be dismantled to the level of the fosse as a means of providing new construction space. This proposal was later repeated by David Ben-Gurion, who "called for 'the demolition of the walls of Jerusalem because they are not Jewish.'"[68] In contrast, Storrs rebuilt the walls, removed unsightly additions, and constructed a sentry walk at their summit, which was subsequently opened to tourists. The great gates into the city—Damascus Gate, St. Stephen's Gate, Herod's Gate, and Jaffa Gate—were also restored. Guardhouses at the gates, functioning in their decrepit state as hovels for the dispossessed or, in one case, a latrine, were demolished or redeemed. Illustrations in Ashbee's published *Records of the Pro-Jerusalem Committee* of 1921 exemplify Storrs's resolve: a contemporary photograph of Jerusalem from south of Jaffa Gate is offered in contrast with Ashbee's pencil sketch of the same space as it was meant to become, after "the unsightly obstructions that hide the wall line are cleared away" (fig. 72).

68. Benvenisti, *City of Stone,* 136.

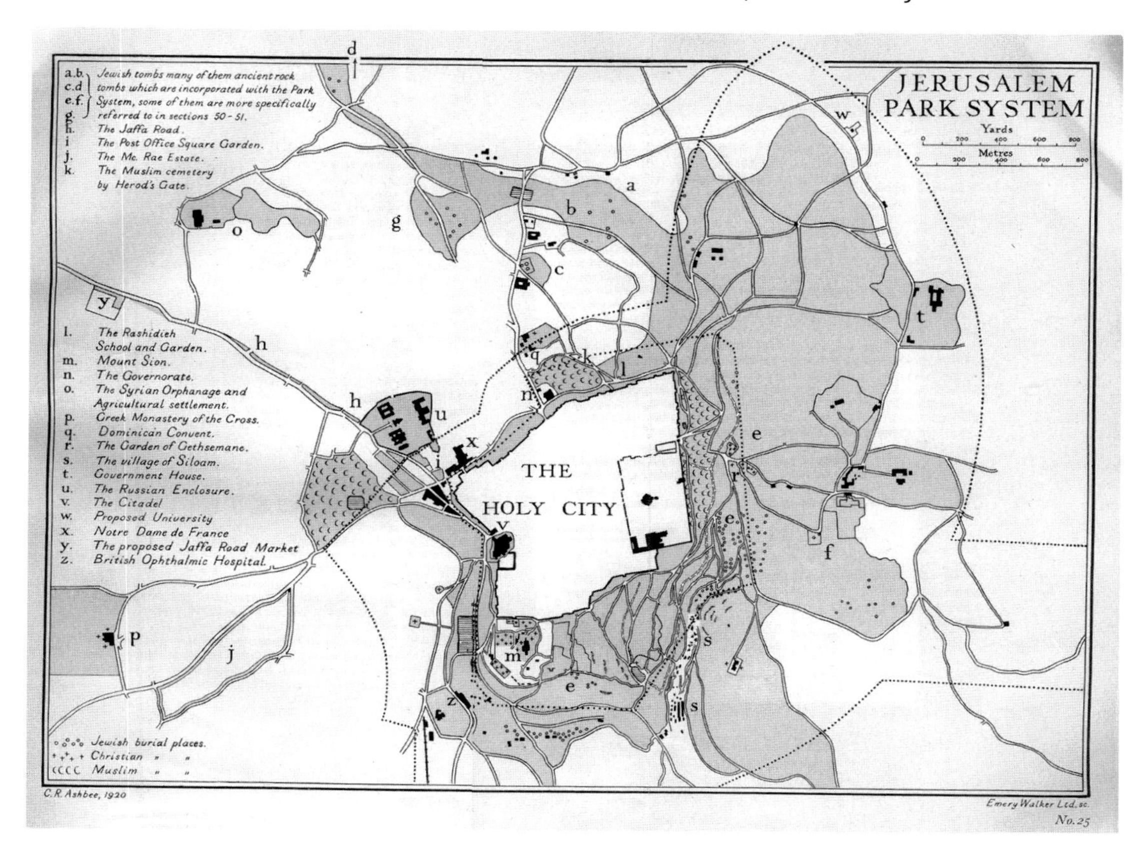

Fig. 74. Jerusalem park system. From Ashbee, *Jerusalem, 1918–1920.*

Storrs sought to produce ancient Jerusalem, not only by reconstructing what it once might have been, but also by eliminating that which it might become. His opposition to the modern was vehement: "Replying to a request for a tram line [from Jerusalem] to Bethlehem, I said that the first rail laid would be laid over the dead body of the Military Governor. The cars did seem so wholly out of keeping with the surroundings that I forbade them throughout the province of Judea."[69] Storrs also supervised the elimination of the more modern reminders of Jerusalem's connection to Britain's enemies. "The clock tower erected by the loyal burgesses of Jerusalem, in a style midway between that of the Eddystone lighthouse and a jubilee memorial to commemorate the thirty-third year of the auspicious reign of the late Sultan Abdul Hamid, has been bodily removed from the north side of the Jaffa Gate, which it too long disfigured" (fig. 73).[70] As described in the popular press,

The famous Clock Tower at the Jaffa Gate, in Jerusalem, has been taken down on the grounds that it was ugly and not in keeping with the ancient wall. It was put up in

69. Reported by the *Evening Standard,* December 21, 1920; included in Storrs, "The Papers of Sir Ronald Storrs (1881–1956) from Pembroke College, Cambridge," 10.3.

70. Storrs's preface in Ashbee, *Jerusalem, 1920–1922,* vi.

1907, and boasted of a fine timepiece, giving both European and Arabic times. . . . The tower was removed at the instigation of the Pro-Jerusalem Society, which was founded by Sir Ronald Storrs, the Present Governor of the Holy City, some eighteen months ago, and whose object is "to preserve the ancient monuments, encourage technical education, plant trees, and in general beautify the ancient and historic city of Jerusalem."[71]

The breach in the wall at Jaffa Gate opened for Kaiser Wilhelm II's triumphal entry into Jerusalem in 1898 was also repaired. Storrs not only reconstructed the old walls of the city, but also sought to establish parkland around it so that Jerusalem might be seen as the distinct and ancient artifact it was meant to be (fig. 74).[72]

The objective of producing Jerusalem as a living museum required the refusal of many forms of Western modernity. Storrs closed bars serving alcoholic beverages. Advertising, except minimally on shop fronts, was proscribed.

Stricter measures are being enforced for the preservation of the traditional building style of Jerusalem, offensive and unsuitable materials are being prohibited or removed, and an effective control of new buildings and town planning sections has been instituted. The size of shop signs, which had become of recent years a serious disfigurement to the city, has been regulated by Municipal By-laws, under which also the posting of bills, placards, and advertisements is restricted to moderate-sized notice boards displayed in specially chosen localities.[73]

But at the core of Storrs's opposition to allowing Jerusalem to show the effects of the modern was his ban on local construction in any nonlocal form.[74] Within four months of the British seizure of the city, Storrs had published in English, French, Arabic, and Hebrew—all languages in which he was reasonably adept—a proclamation concerning construction:

No person shall demolish, erect, alter, or repair the structure of any building in the city of Jerusalem or its environs within a radius of 2,500 meters from the Damascus Gate (Bab al Amud) until he has obtained a written permit from the Military Governor. Any person contravening the orders contained in this proclamation, or any term or terms contained in a license issued to him under this proclamation, will be liable upon conviction to a fine not exceeding £E.200. R. Storrs, Colonel, Military Governor, Jerusalem, April 8th, 1918.[75]

---

71. Shepstone, "Restoring the Walls of Jerusalem."

72. The city-in-a-garden concept that was proposed in 1918 by William McLean and subsequently adopted by Patrick Geddes, a distinguished urban theoretician, is described by Ashbee: "It isolates the Holy City; sets it, so to speak, in the center of a park, thus recognizing the appeal it makes to the world—the city of an idea—that needs as such to be protected." Ashbee, *Jerusalem, 1918–1920*, 12. For an overview of town planning in Jerusalem during this period, see Kark and Oren-Nordheim, *Jerusalem and Its Environs*, 142–88.

73. Storrs, preface in Ashbee, *Jerusalem, 1920–1922*, vi.

74. Ashbee, *Jerusalem, 1918–1920*, 37–38.

75. Storrs, preface in ibid., iv.

Another decree of about the same time prohibited the use of stucco and corrugated iron within the city walls. Red tiles were also forbidden.

Stucco and iron were suspect as imported technologies; red roof tiles were mistrusted on ideological grounds. Red roof tiles were then and still remain politically loaded indices of an alien European occupation of Palestine. As Arthur Ruppin, a Zionist administrator of the Jewish National Fund, reported to the Jewish Colonization Society of Vienna in 1908, "In contrast with the pitiful Arab villages, with their huts of baked clay, the Jewish colonies, with their wide streets, their strong stone houses and their red-tiled roofs, look like veritable oases of culture."[76] The continued ideological power of "red roofs" is indicated by the use of that epithet in the political struggles over Jewish settlements in the occupied territories.[77] For Storrs, Jerusalem was no place for red roofs. He mandated the use of Jerusalem stone. The tradition of stone vaulting was maintained, thus salvaging "the heritage in Jerusalem of an immemorial and a hallowed past."[78]

Storrs recovered the old Jerusalem and opposed the external modernization of a new Jerusalem for a purpose. He worked to realize an image of the Holy City that had circulated in the West throughout the nineteenth century. The New York *Globe* quoted Storrs: "We must preserve the character of the Holy City. The repose of its sacred sites, the colorful beauty of its vaulted streets, must not be disturbed. The sentiment that brings thousands of pilgrims here is our trust, the force by which Jerusalem attracts the homage of the whole world. We can have a sound and yet an ancient city."[79] Ashbee further articulated the undertaking set by Storrs for the Pro-Jerusalem Society:

The disaster of the Great War has forced upon all men and women the necessity of preserving all that is possible of the beauty and purpose, in actual form, of the civilizations that have passed before. We have come to see, moreover, that this is not a mere matter of archaeology or the protection of ancient buildings. In the blind mechanical order with which we are threatened everything that we associate with our sense of beauty is alike in danger. Landscape, the unities of streets and sites, the embodied vision of the men that set the great whole together, the sense of color which in any oriental city is still a living sense—all these things have to be considered practically; they must, to put it plainly, be protected against the incursions of the grasping trader, the ignorant workman, the self-interested property owner, the well-intentioned Government Department. In Jerusalem, perhaps more than in any other city, these facts are brought home to us.[80]

---

76. From Arthur Ruppin's address, delivered on February 27, 1908. Published as "The Picture in 1907," in Ruppin, *Three Decades of Palestine*, 9.

77. For an ideological assessment of "red roofs," see Monk, review of Herbert and Sosnovsky, *Bauhaus on the Carmel and the Crossroads of Empire*, 94–99. This article begins with Labor Party leader Shim'on Peres's 1991 attack on Itzhak Shamir's Likud government and Jewish settlements on the West Bank through reference to their "red roofs."

78. Storrs, preface in Ashbee, *Jerusalem, 1918–1920*, iv.

79. "Jerusalem Now Basks in Rule That Is Tactful," *Globe*, March 12, 1919; included in Storrs, "The Papers of Sir Ronald Storrs (1881–1956) from Pembroke College, Cambridge," 6.1.

80. Ashbee, *Jerusalem, 1920–1922*, 4.

The popular press certainly embraced Storrs's mission: the means of renewing Jerusalem lay not only in revealing its antiquity but also in eliminating its modernity. The *Aberdeen Free Press* reported:

The only "new Jerusalem" is the old one. The gray, austere, ancient, rock-built Palestinian capital, which has for ages appealed to the imagination of the world as no other city has done . . . is experiencing the greatest transformation it has undergone since its destruction by Titus. . . . It is gratifying to find that the British Administration is setting its face against forms of modernization which would interfere with the traditional appearance of the city, and, if it had its way, would macadamize Gethsemane and rebuild Solomon's Temple with corrugated iron.[81]

In July 1918, Storrs wrote to his mother: "I only regret that I was not here 50 years ago when Jerusalem would have been in practice, as it is in effect, an absolutely unique City in the world surrounded by its medieval walls (which are quite perfect) and without houses or monasteries concealing any part of them."[82] He did his best to return the city to its premodern state.

Storrs's historicizing of Jerusalem seems an uncanny prefiguration of later twentieth-century reinventions of history. In the 1960s, decaying, premodern city centers of numerous Italian towns were restored; the up-market *centro storico* (historical center) has now become another term in Italian for "shopping mall."[83] Storrs's Jerusalem might equally be construed as a prototype of Colonial Williamsburg, America's most successful construction of history for the tourism market. It might even be regarded as a distant antecedent of Celebration, the pseudo–New England 1950s town constructed by the Disney Company in Orlando as a theme park for daily living.[84] But Storrs did not plan the city as a means of cashing in on authenticity. Historical Jerusalem was not packaged for sale to tourists. His strategy for the city was less venal, but in the end more dangerous: Jerusalem would serve as an appropriate vessel of aesthetic or religious experience.

Ronald Storrs's commitment to the aestheticization of Jerusalem is apparent from his diary entry of December 25, 1917:

So far as I can recall them, my impressions, though aesthetically and architecturally better founded, resume what we felt seven years ago: firstly, that the faking of the sites and the indignity with which even when authentic they are now mispresented, is an

81. "Jerusalem Transformed," *Aberdeen Free Press*, December 24, 1920; included in Storrs, "The Papers of Sir Ronald Storrs (1881–1956) from Pembroke College, Cambridge," 10.5.

82. From Storrs, "The Papers of Sir Ronald Storrs (1881–1956) from Pembroke College, Cambridge," 6.1.

83. Dainotto, "The Gubbio Papers."

84. For familiar introductions to these two sites, see Handler and Gable, *The New History in an Old Museum*; A. Ross, *The Celebration Chronicles*.

irritation, an imposition, and an affront to the intelligence; secondly, that the pathos, grandeur and nobility of the ancient City of the Heart easily countervails these very real annoyances:

'How beautiful, if sorrow had not made
Sorrow more beautiful than beauty's self.'

Aesthetic death is swallowed up in spiritual victory.[85]

For Storrs, Jerusalem transcended time and existed outside history:[86] "Not the hopeless beauty of Venice, the embalmed majesty of Thebes, the abandon of Ferrara, or the melancholy of Ravenna; but some past yet unalloyed and throbbing, that seems to confound ancient and modern, and to undate recorded history."[87] Patrick Geddes, the well-known Scottish town planner, embraces Storrs's project in his report on the beautification of Jerusalem, naming the city "the most extensive Sacred Park in the world."[88]

The apparent fixity of the city to which Storrs fundamentally contributed provided no resistance to the observer's desire to see in it the material proof of a particular religious past. Most of the vernacular buildings dated from the period of Ottoman rule (1517–1917 CE), but the streets, the buildings, and the gardens are still treated by pilgrims from the West as surviving witnesses to the holiness of the city's remote past. Storrs was not a Christian pilgrim. Although his conception of Jerusalem was deeply informed by his own spiritual idealization of the city and its romanticized Western images, he did not attempt to impose on the city a particularly Christian form. Rather, Storrs confirmed Jerusalem's transcendental character by consolidating its antiquity and denying its present. He treated it as the embodiment of a Western, Hegelian notion of religion and art as elevated above life. Jerusalem thus preserved as an aesthetic experience authorized ominously tendentious religious anxieties and historical claims, as Daniel Monk has demonstrated in his book *An Aesthetic Occupation*.

Storrs assumed that his own obsession with Jerusalem as the physical embodiment of a transcendent history was shared by the contentious population he governed. He supposed that a common concern with the preservation of their city would establish a communal ground for the belligerent ethnic groups of Jerusalem—Arabs, Christians, and Jews. His expectations were frustrated. All parties involved cared passionately for Jerusalem, but their Jerusalems were not the same. Most particularly, the historical Jerusalem that Storrs imagined and struggled with some success to realize had been shaped by images of the city circulated in the Protestant West in the nineteenth century. It was not the city as it had become by the late nineteenth century.

---

85. Storrs, *Orientations*, 333.

86. Storrs had great disdain for those who were not able to experience the city's transcendental qualities: "Many were 'disappointed with Jerusalem' because 'it was so different to what they had expected'. The roads were even worse than the hotels and in place of the Holy City they found—a smell." Ibid., 361.

87. Ibid., 327.

88. Geddes, "Jerusalem Actual and Possible."

A speech by Lord Northcliffe suggests the confidence with which the British embraced the redemptive task of restoring the city to its spiritual inheritance:

Jerusalem is a small city among the cities of the earth; in its great period it was never more than chief town, almost the only town, of a small and pastoral people: yet there is no city in the world's history that has made a longer or a stronger appeal to the spiritual and romantic sense of the human soul. . . . Jerusalem has remained the City of Cities to millions who have never entered her gates, the capital of the ideal State, the goal of the unending pilgrimage. . . . Throughout England, as throughout Europe, generation after generation sent its sons in thousands across unknown lands and seas, through dangers undreamed of, on the mystical quest of the Crusaders, eternal and unsatisfied for the Holy City of Jerusalem. . . . Jerusalem has dominated the minds and spirits of men throughout the centuries, until that great day . . . when it was peacefully conquered by a British Army, and it became our privilege to restore Jerusalem and Palestine to their place among the nations.[89]

John H. Finley, head of the American Red Cross in Palestine at the onset of the British occupation of the territory, more ecstatically expressed the spiritual fervor of the West's delirious optimism that the British would finally put Jerusalem in order:

But even as I looked toward the place of the ancient and holy city, the gray curtain of mist or fog parted as if drawn aside by invisible hands. A golden rift immediately over the city—over the Church of the Holy Sepulchre itself—slowly widened, till in a few minutes there stood as in an Apocalypse before me, a city shut away from the outer city, and from all about, as if rebuilded in the golden and jeweled image of itself. . . . This sight of Jerusalem given to me in such a dramatic way will always remain as an intimation of that which Americans, in common with all who are fighting for justice in the earth, must help to bring into this Holy City. Many that make abominations and lies in the world have entered in the past, but under the British Government it is being cleansed, and prepared for the genius of the nations, and especially of those whose religions found a cradle here—Moslem, Jewish, and Christian—to adorn it, make it the most beautiful city on the planet and give it most fit setting amid the mountains round about it—"as the stars of a crown glistening upon his land."[90]

For Ronald Storrs, getting Jerusalem right meant imposing modernity invisibly through government bureaucracy and, at the same time, erasing modernity from the visible city. His governorship of Jerusalem and the work of the Pro-Jerusalem Society collapsed under the pressure of rising ethnic and religious antagonisms in 1927. The optimism with which many in the West had

89. Northcliffe, greeting to the governor of Jerusalem at a joint meeting in London of the Overseas Club and Patriotic League. Northcliffe was ill on the occasion; his speech was read in his absence. Reported in "The New Era in Jerusalem."

90. Finley, *A Pilgrim in Palestine after Its Deliverance*, 60–62.

viewed the British control of Palestine at the beginning of the occupation was unfounded; the interests of the various factions engaged in Palestine proved irreconcilable. Storrs's understanding of Jerusalem, which misrepresented the city and its buildings as beyond ideology, allowed them to remain underexamined at the lethal core of the city's politics.

MODEL

Storrs never realized his desire for a historically intact Jerusalem. His dream of witnessing the Old City as a whole did, however, come true for others. The complete city came in the form of a model. Models work in many ways. *Model,* like *copy,* implies a strong but unbalanced relationship between an object and its archetype.[91] *Copy* inevitably identifies a thing as derivative and, therefore, secondary. In contrast, *model* is ambivalent in respect to its source; the power of origination is unattributed.[92] *Model* can be the dominant subject that determines its weak object. It may be an archetypal image or configuration (Alan Greenspan's economic model is golden). It may also be an exemplar of moral or aesthetic form (George Bush is a model world citizen) and of physical type (Cindy Crawford is a supermodel). But *model* can also be the weak object of a dominant subject. *Model* is commonly used to describe a thing that bears a resemblance to another thing. Further, *model* often implies a copy on a reduced scale—a diminutive replica of the original (Tonka sells model trucks). Thus, the definition of *model* is characterized by an ambiguity of causality. Curiously, an entity identified as a model may manifest the same ambivalence of authority as the term itself. This certainly is the case with city models. Most obviously, the model of a city is a small-scale imitation of a full-scale urban order. It reduces the size of the city and gives it the appearance of comprehensibility. The dependence of the model on its archetype is self-evident. Less apparent, but always potential, is the function of the model as a paradigm for the city of which it is a copy.

The promise of a city model to function paradigmatically explains the construction of the best-known examples. Gismondi's Plastico di Roma in the Museo della Civiltà Roma presents Rome as it was at the time of Constantine. It was created for the Augustan Exhibition of the Roman World in 1937–38. In it, the Fascists produced the city as a promise to themselves that it would perform again as the Christian capital of a world empire.[93] Athens has the plaster model of the fifth-century Acropolis constructed by Gorham Phillips Stephens, the director of the American School of Classical Studies there, during the Nazi

---

91. *The Oxford English Dictionary,* on-line edition, reviews the various definitions of the terms *model* and *copy*. That summary of meanings allowed me to formulate my own.

92. For an approach which cites earlier thinking about models and for an introduction to philosophical and scientific models, see Handelman, *Models and Mirrors,* 22–62. On the metaphors of miniaturization, see Stewart, *On Longing.*

93. Satorio, "The Reconstruction of Rome in Bigot and Gismondi's Models"; Scriba, "Die Mostra Augustea della Romanità in Rom 1937/38."

occupation of the city.[94] In the maw of fascist barbarism, the model perpetuated the dream of freedom in the disguise of an idealized past. New York has the Panorama of the City of New York in the Queens Museum.[95] This model claims to describe all of the approximately eight hundred thousand buildings constructed in the five boroughs that constitute the 320 square miles of the city. Robert Moses, autocrat of urban development in New York City in the 1940s and '50s, had the model constructed at enormous cost, purportedly for two purposes: to display the magnitude and modernity of the city to visitors to the 1964–65 World's Fair and to aid in the city's future planning. It ultimately served as a surrogate city for its producer. Moses had lost his official hold on New York in 1962; thereafter he controlled only its model.[96] The politics of such replicas is apparent; their effectiveness, of course, depended on who and how they were observed.

Models of Jerusalem work in the same way. The most impressive model of the city is that of the Holy Land Hotel in the western suburbs of Jerusalem itself (fig. 4).[97] There a model of Jerusalem, representing the city as it appeared before its destruction by the Romans in AD 70, was begun in 1964 with the sponsorship of the hotel's proprietor, Hans Kroch. Like the earliest panoramas of the nineteenth century, this model allows its observer to index her collection of partial glimpses and fragmented perceptions of the city in which she finds herself.[98] The fantasy of coherence sustains other predilections to which the model appeals: the Holy Land Hotel replica of Jerusalem responds to the distinct expectations of its various viewers both by what is present and by what is absent.

The first audience of any model is its producer. The Holy Land Hotel model of Jerusalem was built and is renewed and augmented by craftsmen working under the direction of distinguished Israeli archaeologists. Between 1964 and 1974, Michael Avi Yonah managed the construction of the model. After that Yoram Tsafrir superintended the model's periodic elaboration and refinement. For its scholarly makers, the model describes archaeological—that is, scientific—objectivity. It is constructed as fully as possible with authentic materials—Jerusalem stone and marble for the buildings, miniature ceramic tiles for the roofs, and true gold leaf for adornments of the Temple and palaces. Ceramic trees are now being added to the landscape. The replica is built to a scale of

94. Stevens, "Plaster Model of the Acropolis of Athens."

95. M. H. Miller, *The Panorama of New York City.*

96. Bussel, "The City That Moses Built." For Moses's life and his role in the World's Fair, see Caro, *The Power Broker.*

97. I am grateful to Yoram Tsafrir for giving me a personal tour of the model and providing me with much of the information presented here. The Holy Land Hotel has been displaced by land speculators since this text went to press.

98. In his essay, "Walking in the City," Michel de Certeau contrasts the power of seeing the whole city from above with the powerlessness of experiencing it within its textures. He suggests that the view from above offers the "exultation of the scopic and gnostic drive: the fiction of knowledge is related to this lust to be a viewpoint and nothing more." Certeau, *The Practice of Everyday Life,* 92. This is a very productive oversimplification.

1:50. Most critically, the archaeologists in charge of its planning and development strive for historical correctness in its topographical order and in the reconstruction of individual buildings.

A booklet written by Avi Yonah and revised by Tsafrir provides a description of the model; it is beautifully illustrated with comparisons between the model and its contemporary archetype.[99] The text of this pamphlet indicates that decisions about the form and location of the model's various structures are based on the close reading of primary sources, including Flavius Josephus (37/38–100 CE), the city's most significant ancient historian; the Mishna; the Tosephta; the Talmuds; and the New Testament. Past and present archaeological and art-historical findings are carefully sifted and appropriated for use. Texts and artifacts are the means by which fully or partially lost buildings are reconstituted. The archaeologists' desire for accuracy perhaps contributed to the choice of first-century CE Jerusalem as the subject of their work. The relative abundance of evidence for the shape of the first-century CE city is much greater than that for, say, Solomon's tenth-century BCE Jerusalem.

In addition to staking the scholarly claims of the replica, the pamphlet for the Holy Land Hotel model concedes the limitations of science. A final source for the reconstruction is cited: "Local traditions about the location of holy sites in Jerusalem were also taken into account" in the design of the model.[100] "Local traditions" is the frank acknowledgment that some marks on the model are there principally because the model's broader audience expects them. Nevertheless, to its producers the model is a historically conditioned replica of an ancient city; like an excavation report, it functions as an archive.

Though a model's makers are its most familiar viewers, the Holy Land Hotel Jerusalem was produced for the visual consumption of a variety of other audiences. For each of its audiences, the model served a different function. For Jewish visitors before the 1967 war, the model was prosthetic. Like pre-1989 Berlin, Jerusalem was divided by a wall. A barrier separated east Jerusalem and the Old City from its western extensions; Jews and Arabs were unable to cross the divide. The Holy Land Hotel model of Jerusalem served as a surrogate Old City for Jewish sightseers. Even after the Old City came under Israeli control, the model supplemented the Jewish experience of Jerusalem. The model evokes for such viewers a more authentic Jerusalem than the present provides. It offers them not the contemporary Jerusalem or the Jerusalem of the British Mandate. It presents, rather, Herod the Great's Jerusalem, the city before the last great diaspora—capital of a unified domain and center of a coherent community.[101] Herod's magnificent Temple, a site of unparalleled sacredness, the center of religious life and sign of the Jewish state, dominates the replica; the model displays the city as the lavish frame for its sacred Jewish center. The destruction

99. Avi-Yonah and Tsafrir, *Pictorial Guide to the Model of Ancient Jerusalem at the Time of the Second Temple in the Grounds of the Holy Land Hotel Jerusalem, Israel.*

100. Ibid.

101. See the complementary descriptions of Jerusalem in chapters 1 and 2 of the present text.

of Herod's Temple less than a decade after its completion as well as the site's later evolution is described in earlier chapters of this book. But the chronology of Jewish Jerusalem's obliteration and the city's rebuilding as Roman, Christian, and Islamic is relevant here because the model undoes that history. For Jewish tourists, the model manifests the memory of what the city once was. It gives material form to a nostalgia for the pre-traumatic time of unfractured community. For such observers, the model is a dream from which they awake with longing.

The choice of Herod's Jerusalem as the subject of replication is solicitous of Christian as well as Jewish attention. Herod's Jerusalem was not only the city of the latest and largest Jewish temple; it was also the Jerusalem that Jesus knew, the one that he experienced during his ministry and Passion. This particular Jerusalem was the Christian city in its purest apostolic form, untainted by the decadence of the Eastern Christian Empire or the excesses of the Catholic crusaders. Moreover, the model is marked for its Christian viewers as always already Christian. Included in the replica in deference to Christian desire is the site west of the "Second Wall" traditionally identified with Jesus's Crucifixion. This place is mentioned in the visitor's pamphlet and represented in the replica as a quarry with a dramatic skull-shaped outcrop in its center. For the archaeologists who constructed the model, it offers the experience of historical truth insofar as it can be recovered, like an archaeological excavation. Sites without viable historical credentials are left out. Unmarked on the model and unmentioned in the pamphlet, for example, is the second, competing locus of Jesus's Crucifixion and burial, the Protestant's Garden Tomb.

Christian pilgrims go to Jerusalem to experience the presence of God embodied in a material absence. For most of them, the city's most sacred site is an empty tomb, proof of Jesus's Resurrection.[102] Jerusalem is thus the object of pilgrimage for the marks left behind by a once-manifest divinity. What is marked, but absent—the site of the Resurrection—and what is present, but which will soon be merely marked—the Temple—are both legible signs of Christian triumph. If for Jews the model is a prosthesis for the memory and a longing, for Christians the replica is the proof of prophecy. Another audience, a conjectural Muslim audience, might also understand the model in terms of absence. For that audience, however, the model would not be full of signs—documentary, memorial, and promissory—but dangerously empty.

Since the 1967 war, the Islamic monuments of Jerusalem have been under constant threat.[103] Jewish and Christian extremists seek to return al-Haram al-Sharif to its guise as the Temple Mount. The purge began at the base of the Temple Mount on June 10, 1967, immediately after the Old City was taken by Israelis. The medieval Maghariba or Moors' Quarter, site of a mosque and Muslim shrine of Shaikh 'A'id, the Afdaliyya Madrassa of the twelfth century,

102. See Bowman, "Christian Ideology and the Image of a Holy Land," 98–121; Wharton, *Refiguring the Post Classical City*, 64–104.

103. I use some of this same material in Wharton, *Building the Cold War*, 121–24.

was bulldozed.[104] The area had been designated an Islamic holy place by the League of Nations in 1930. The destruction of these monuments was symptomatic of the religious right's aggressive appropriation of sacred space.[105] At least two dozen attacks have been launched against the Dome of the Rock by anti-Muslim fanatics since the Israeli occupation of Jerusalem in 1967.[106] "Clear Away the Abomination!," a chapter in a book by a member of the West Bank Jewish Underground, describes a particularly elaborate plot to blow up the Dome of the Rock.[107] For the hypothetical Muslim viewer, then, the city depicted in the Holy Land Hotel model is not a historical representation. It is, rather, a future Jerusalem, cleared of the archives, longings, and promises of a millennium of Islamic presence. The hypothetical Muslim audience looks at the model and sees not what the city once was but what it will be. For Jewish and Christian fundamentalists also, the copy of the past city has become the model of its future. The Holy Land Hotel model of Jerusalem may thus function as a site of speculation as well as a repository of memory.

The Holy Land Hotel model of Jerusalem is the archetype of a future Jerusalem not only for Jewish religious extremists but also for many American evangelicals. Both hold the millenarian assumption that the Messiah's advent depends on the return of the Jews to Israel and the rebuilding of the Temple. Despite profound differences between Christian and Jewish believers as to who and what this Messiah intends to salvage, they both promote Jewish immigration and collude in preparing the new Temple. Indeed, the evangelical Christian right has become one of the great political and financial contributors to the Jewish State of Israel, deeply affecting the present administration's Middle Eastern policies.[108] Clyde Lott, a cattle rancher and ordained minister of the National Pentecostal Assemblies of Jesus Christ, represents the collaboration between millenarian evangelicals and Israeli extremists.

If Clyde Lott has his way, several hundred cows will fly to Israel this December. . . . The cows, the first of what Lott hopes will be 50,000 sent to the Jewish state, are part of his plan to fulfill a biblical prophecy that a red heifer be born in Israel to bring about the "Second Coming" of Jesus. The return of Jesus is part of a Christian apocalyptic

104. Moshe Safdie, Israel's best-known architect, describes the moment: "Within an hour [of first breaching the defenses of Jerusalem], the soldiers had reached the [Wailing] Wall. The words of the announcer moved a nation: 'I cannot believe it. Here it is, I am seeing the Wall. The great stones. Everyone around me is touching the Wall. They are crying. I'm crying myself.' Within forty-eight hours, Jerusalem had become a unified city. Bulldozers moved in and razed the concrete walls that had divided it. They also razed the Maghariba Quarter that had surrounded the Western Wall, creating a large open space in front of it. To this day it is not clear who ordered the bulldozers in." Safdie, *Jerusalem*, 104.

105. See Dumper, *The Politics of Sacred Space*.

106. For the contemporary political history of the Temple Mount/al-Haram al-Sharif, see Friedland and Hecht, "The Politics of Sacred Space." For a not unbiased account of legal conflicts over the site, see Adler, "Israeli Court Finds Muslim Council Destroyed Ancient Remains on Temple Mount."

107. H. Segal, *Dear Brothers*, 50–60.

108. Broadway, "The Evangelical-Israeli Connection."

Fig. 75. Model of Jerusalem, The Holy Land Experience, Orlando, Florida. Author photo.

vision of the end of time, which includes the slaughter of those who don't accept the Christian messiah as their savior. . . . The modern state of Israel, of course, was established in 1948, and since 1967, the Jewish state has controlled all of Jerusalem. That leaves the rebuilding of the Temple, and since a red heifer was part of the sacrificial ritual in the Temple—mentioned several times in the Bible, including in the Book of Numbers, chapters 19–22—many believe the birth of a red heifer in Israel will signal the Temple's return. . . .

Lott's project is not the only one in which Israelis and Christians are working together to birth red heifers in the Jewish state. At least two other American Christians are breeding similar cows in the United States in hopes of bringing them to Israel, according to Gershon Solomon, the leader of the Temple Mount Faithful, another group dedicated to rebuilding the Temple.[109]

Evangelical Christian commitment to the construction of a new Temple provides a certain political spin to the reconstructions of Jerusalem found

109. Ephross, "Approaching the Millennium."

Fig. 76. Jesus and Veronica. Still from Mel Gibson's *The Passion of the Christ*.

in the United States, like that at Eureka, Arkansas, and Holy Land U.S.A., in Bedford, Virginia. The Holy Land Experience—which reproduces a Holy Land dominated by the Jewish Temple—seems indicative of the place of the Temple in evangelical eschatology. For emphasis, The Holy Land Experience represents a Jerusalem dominated by the Temple twice: once in the park itself and again in a model that serves as one of its major attractions. On display in the building next to the Temple is a somewhat smaller version of the Holy Land Hotel model of Jerusalem (fig. 75). The Orlando version modifies its prototype: it privileges theology rather than history. Golgotha appears not as a proxy for the Holy Sepulchre but at the site of the Protestant Garden Tomb. The location of the Church of the Holy Sepulchre goes unmarked in the copy. The Orlando model makes another significant change: the area on the Temple Mount/al-Haram al-Sharif now occupied by al-Aksa Mosque is excavated for a lecture platform. Not only is the Dome of the Rock displaced by the Temple, but an evangelical lecturer literally stands in for al-Aksa Mosque. The comment of a skeptical observer of the model suggests something of the lecturer's role:

A guy in an Indiana Jones hat pointed out the alleys and buildings where Jesus probably would have been, explained that "The Herodian Temple was the Wal-Mart of sacrifice," and barked at an old man with a video camera. "Sir, we don't allow videotaping. This material is copyrighted. If you want the lecture, we have our own videotape for sale."[110]

110. Kirby, Smith, and Wilkins, *The Holy Land Experience*.

Fig. 77. Jesus and Veronica, Sacro Monte, Varallo. Author photo.

The model is not allowed to speak for itself. It is no longer an archaeological archive but rather an evangelical homily.

The evangelical embrace of Jerusalem is based on revelation, not historical understanding. Evangelicals' enthusiasm for Mel Gibson's *The Passion of the Christ* demonstrates their distance from history.[111] Claims are made for the "truth" of the film. Reportedly, the aging Pope John Paul II pronounced the film as showing the Passion "as it was."[112] Indeed, the film replaces the

111. Teaching has its obligations. As a professor of early Christian art, seeing Mel Gibson's *The Passion of the Christ* was one of mine. After all, most of my future students will be more familiar with Mel Gibson's account of the Passion than with Matthew's version of the story.

112. "Pope Said to Find 'Passion' Accurate."

archaeology of Jerusalem with a Catholic landscape. Certainly *The Passion of the Christ* offers a good bit of visual history, but the history it references is that of late medieval and early modern Europe, not that of Roman first-century Jerusalem. The film is set in Matera, in southern Italy; it describes the landscape of Italo-Byzantine monasticism, not, as presumed by its viewers, Herodian Jerusalem. The extreme bodily affliction described in the film is not Roman turn-of-the-millennia but late fifteenth-century Franciscan. It attempts to produce a hyper-real experience of the Passion for a broad audience through the most persuasive visual technologies available, just as the Franciscans did with their life-size terra-cotta figures in their trompe-l'oeil fresco settings in the *sacri monti* (figs. 76, 77). In both the film and the sculpture, exaggeration in gesture and expression puts a privilege on pain: suffering is the way to salvation.

The spirituality of *The Passion of the Christ* is certainly not early Christian; the film is, rather, controlled by late medieval, pre–Vatican II sacramental theology. The film works to make credible the astonishing relics that gained widespread popularity in medieval Europe. Pilate's wife provides the fine linen cloth by which Jesus's blood might be preserved by his mother and the Magdalene for the proliferation of blood relics in the thirteenth century. Veronica's veil looks suspiciously like the Shroud of Turin. The Stations of the Cross, which weren't invented by the Franciscans until the early modern period, are neatly inscribed on first-century Jerusalem. Mel Gibson also punctuates his film with loving vignettes of popular Catholic icons, such as Michelangelo's *Pietá,* and venerated relics, such as the nails and crown of thorns. Even the politics of *The Passion of the Christ* conform to those of the late medieval West. The film re-presents the violent hatred of the Jews that marked the Franciscan and Dominican orders in the fifteenth and sixteenth centuries. Gibson's Ash-Wednesday release of the film uncannily evokes the Lenten sermons of the friars, which so often incited pogroms.[113]

The question remains: Why does the anti-Jewish archaeology of the late medieval Catholicism in Mel Gibson's *The Passion of the Christ* appeal to modern evangelical Christians? The answer is obvious. Modern evangelical Christians don't see it. In contrast with Luther, Calvin, and other leaders of the Reformation, modern lay Protestants know virtually nothing about Roman Catholicism. For these viewers, the many references to Catholicism and its history in *The Passion of the Christ* are invisible. There are two reasons why such blindness should worry evangelical Christians. First, their founding fathers railed against those same Catholic sacramental practices that the film professes. Second, the evangelical embrace, conscious or unconscious, of the film's anti-Semitism erodes the fragile foundation of the awkward alliance between the Israeli and evangelical Christian right.[114] *The Passion of the Christ* may be set in "Jerusalem," but it is not legally screened in Jerusalem.[115]

---

113. See chapter 3.

114. Cooperman, "Ideas about Christ's Death Surveyed."

115. Pirated versions are apparently readily available. Harris, "Israelis Battling Intellectual Piracy."

If the evangelical understanding of Jerusalem were a simple problem of ignorance, the solution would be a simple matter of education. But it is a complex, historical problem that is not limited to evangelical Christians. The most popular images of Jerusalem now circulating in the United States (*The Passion of the Christ,* UCLA's computer-generated reconstructions of Jerusalem, the myriad of Jerusalems, such as The Holy Land Experience in Orlando, produced as spectacle) present the city as oddly emptied of history. The "archaeological" model of Herod's Jerusalem on display at The Holy Land Experience is symptomatic. It empties the city of the debris of those religions that, for both Jewish and Christian extremists, got it wrong—Byzantine Orthodoxy, Roman Catholicism, and, most obviously, Islam. For devout Jews and Christians, such a model represents respectively the moment of a unitary Judaism and apostolic purity. For extremists, Christian and Jewish, the model functions also as a site of radical speculation about a city without a Muslim presence. The most familiar images of the past city collude in producing the archetype of its future.

CONCLUSION

Money is the medium of the turn-of-the-millennium spectacle. Mel Gibson's *The Passion of the Christ* is the most profitable religious film ever made.[116] The *Wall Street Journal* reports: "Mel Gibson is on track to reap at least $350 million in personal profits from his controversial 'The Passion of the Christ'—one of the biggest individual windfalls in Hollywood's long history of oversized payouts."[117] No less than David Roberts's journey to Jerusalem in the nineteenth century, *The Passion of the Christ* was undertaken for profit. The capital outlay for the film, however, was exponentially greater than that required by the artist, as is the size of the audience and the scale of the performance. Money lies at the core of both projects, but Roberts sold a landscape and Gibson sells a religion. Like Islamic fundamentalism and ultra-Orthodox Judaism, the Christianity retailed by *The Passion of the Christ* claims an exclusive grasp on the truth.

In early Christianity, a false prophet was one who asked for money.[118] In the age of TV evangelicals and megachurches, such a directive is utterly alien. Money drives religion no less than it controls the rest of Western culture. Admission to biblical "truths," simulated as entertainment, at The Holy Land Expe-

116. "Passion Film Beats *Rings* Record"; Waxman, "Hollywood Rethinking Films of Faith after 'Passion.'" The *New York Times* comments on the pope's endorsement of the film: "In what is surely the most bizarre commercial endorsement since Eleanor Roosevelt did an ad for Good Luck Margarine in 1959, the ailing pontiff has been recruited, however unwittingly, to help hawk *The Passion of the Christ,* as Mel Gibson's film about Jesus's final 12 hours is now titled. While Eleanor Roosevelt endorsed a margarine for charity, John Paul's free plug is being exploited by the Gibson camp to aid the movie star's effort to recoup the $25 million he personally sank into a biblical drama filmed in those crowd-pleasing tongues of Latin and Aramaic." Rich, "The Pope's Thumbs Up for Gibson's 'Passion.'"

117. "Hollywood Report."

118. According to the *Didache*: "Now, in respect to those sent by God to preach and [to] prophets, act strictly according to the precept of the Gospel. . . . If he asks for money, he is a false prophet." *The Didache,* 1 : 11.3–6.

rience is available to an individual adult for $30.[119] At least in 2002, some of that ticket price went to the government. The Holy Land Experience, Inc., was then in litigation with the State of Florida over the organization's tax status. The state claimed The Holy Land Experience was a for-profit organization. The Holy Land Experience, a.k.a. Zion's Hope Evangelical Mission, claimed the status of a tax-free religious institution. Both claims are warranted.[120] For an evangelical Christian, The Holy Land Experience looks and acts like the practice of religion. For the Orlando County Council, The Holy Land Experience looks and acts like a corporate, profit-producing theme park. What explains this particular ?[121]

Walt Disney World's EPCOT offers an instructive analog. EPCOT—the acronym for Experimental Prototype Community of Tomorrow—began as Walt Disney's last obsession. He envisioned a "utopian" company town:[122]

EPCOT will be an experimental city that would incorporate the best ideas of industry, government, and academia worldwide, a city that caters to the people as a service function. It will be a planned, controlled community, a showcase for American industry and research, schools, cultural and educational opportunities. In EPCOT there will be no slum areas because we will not let them develop. There will be no landowners and therefore no voting control. People will rent houses instead of buying them, and at modest rentals. There will be no retirees; everyone must be employed. One of the requirements is that people who live in EPCOT must help keep it alive.[123]

EPCOT died with Disney in 1966. A vendible version of EPCOT was constructed as Celebration, an Orlando suburb posing as a circa-1950 New England village.[124] I visited Celebration during the town's Fall Festival; to compensate for Florida's lack of seasons, colored paper leaves were blown into the streets from the top of lampposts.[125]

EPCOT itself became Epcot. In the World Showcase, Epcot is transformed from an ideal model for human daily life at the core of Walt Disney World to a profit-producing spectacle of imitation cities without inhabitants.[126] Distributed

---

119. In spring 2004.

120. The Holy Land Experience won its appeal. Schlueb, "Holy Land Experience Exempt from Property Tax."

121. For a discussion of the duck/rabbit, see chapter 1.

122. For an assessment of the models and plans for EPCOT, as well as for a bibliography, see Mannheim, *Walt Disney and the Quest for Community*.

123. Quoted by Alexander Wilson from a 1966 Disney documentary. A. Wilson, "The Betrayal of the Future," 118.

124. For more on Celebration, see Frantz, *Celebration, U.S.A.*; A. Ross, *The Celebration Chronicles*.

125. Walt Disney's suspicion of religion clung to Celebration. Only one lot was designated for a religious structure. It was leased to the highest bidding denomination—the Presbyterians. Winner, "Praise at Celebration."

126. Epcot's simulation of exotic places of course has precedents in the great exhibitions of the nineteenth and early twentieth centuries. The 1893 World's Columbian Exposition in Chicago, for example, included displays of exotic places:

And, in addition to the assignment of space for regular exhibits and buildings, concessions were granted for the purpose of conducting theatres, shops, restaurants, or of furnishing representations of native life, to the

Fig. 78. "England," Epcot Center, Walt Disney World, Orlando, Florida. Author photo.

picturesquely around a small lake, these urban forms represent eleven nations (the USA is in the center, flanked by Italy, Germany, China, Norway, and Mexico on one side, and Japan, Morocco, France, the United Kingdom, and Canada on the other).[127] Imaginatively produced by the Imagineers (Disney's oddly anonymous in-house architectural firm), Epcot offers a high-cholesterol visual experience. A visitor needs to fondle the facade of the Georgian structure in "England" to realize that it is constructed of Drivit (stucco on Styrofoam), Werzalite (glued sawdust), or fiberglass, not brick and stone (fig. 78). The Disney Company's move from Walt Disney to Michael Eisner and from Fantasy Land and EPCOT to Epcot and Celebration coincides with the move from modernity to globalization. Or, as Stephen Fjellman notes, the shift from the Magic Kingdom to Epcot parallels the political shift from colonial to corporate.[128]

Epcot provided the model for the most recent version of Las Vegas. Modern Las Vegas had gambling sheds marked by elaborate signs to attract the pass-

---

following governments; Algeria, Australia, China, India, Dahomey, Egypt, Hungary, Pacific Islands, Italy, Japan, Morocco, Persia, Sandwich Islands and [xxv] Tunis. All this may be said to be enough to give the display at Jackson Park and the Midway Plaisance something of an international character.

Walton, *Art and Architecture [of the World's Columbian Exposition]*. These "representations of native life" were produced and occupied by the "natives" themselves. Moreover, they were transient. Epcot offers, in contrast, a permanent collection of sites with corporate sponsors.

127. For discussions of EPCOT, see Flower, *Prince of the Magic Kingdom*, chap. 5; Marling, "Imagineering the Disney Theme Parks," 148–63. For the function of museums in Epcot, see Kratz and Karp, "Wonder and Worth."

128. Fjellman, *Vinyl Leaves*, 237.

ing motorist.[129] In the city's postmodern present, the casinos themselves have become advertisements. Disneyfied versions of New York, Venice, and ancient Egypt present images of escape, not to tourists already in Las Vegas, but to potential consumers in Chicago, Milan, and Riyadh. Epcot also provided the archetype for The Holy Land Experience. The identification of The Holy Land Experience with Epcot has been made before. A tourist posted the same observation on the Web:

Anyone expecting [at The Holy Land Experience] some sort of Disney World of the soul is likely to be disappointed. There are no rides here, and the park itself is small; its public areas are about the size of a single World Showcase pavilion at Epcot. It feels a bit like World Showcase, too—rather than giving the sense of actually being in the Holy Land, with the compression of landmarks and the somewhat synthetic feel of the place, it's more like being transported to the set of some Biblical epic.[130]

As the epigraph at the beginning of this chapter suggests, members of the Southern Baptist Convention are suspicious of Disney. Their clearly articulated sense of betrayal responds to a very real transformation in Disney practices.[131] Disney still identifies itself as a company, but everyone knows that it is a corporation. Of course, the change to which the convention leadership really objects comes from another side of globalization—the economically driven embrace of diversity. The quotation demonstrates that the convention is most deeply offended not by Disney's films but by its legitimating acknowledgment of homosexuality. The Southern Baptist Convention's boycott of Disney has failed.

Like Las Vegas, The Holy Land Experience is a colony of Disney. Despite the intentions of their producers, evangelical Jerusalems bear with them the implications of the entertainment commodity. The Jerusalem of The Holy Land Experience is not a relic; it lacks the material connection to an originating power that distinguishes a fragment of the True Cross. Nor is it a replica; it doesn't allow the recreation of ritual as did the Temple Church. The Holy Land Experience certainly does not reproduce Jerusalem; Jesus's footsteps cannot be followed there in the same way that they can at Varallo. And it certainly isn't an industrially fabricated encounter with Jerusalem of the sort presented by Roberts's lithographs or Piglhein's panorama. Evangelical truths are performed at The Holy Land Experience; it is the space of spectacle.

As bills replaced bullion in the nineteenth century, so electronic transfers supplanted paper in the twentieth. As money dematerializes it becomes increasingly ubiquitous. Shedding the last residue of its moral ambiguity, money has moved from being the measure of all things to their equivalent. An eye is no longer worth an eye but only a certain dollar amount, depending on whose eye

---

129. This is the Las Vegas we were taught by Venturi, Brown, and Izenour, *Learning from Las Vegas*.
130. R. Brown, *The Holy Land Experience Guide to Theme Parks, 2002*.
131. Gushee, "The Speck in Mickey's Eye"; H. Warren, "Southern Baptists as Audience and Public."

it is. Images provide a parallel case. Through the early modern period, produced images retained evidence of the labor expended in their making. The work involved in the creation of an image provided explicit or implicit evidence of its relation to the world and the objects within it. It bore the marks of its associations—whether it was an archetype or a copy, a multiple or a unicum, an authentic thing or a fraudulent one. Now the popular image is generally free from the signs of its construction. Academics and other holdouts in archaic institutions might raise questions about the history of particular images—like those in *The Passion of the Christ*—but their observations have no resonance for the images' broader audience. Like money, images no longer seem to bear any moral responsibility for their actions.

Conclusion: Illusion and Immateriality

In contrast to Marx, who relied on the notion of the fetish as a solid object whose stable presence obfuscates its social mediation, we should assert that fetishism reaches its acme precisely when the fetish itself is "dematerialized," turned into a fluid "immaterial" virtual entity; money fetishism will culminate with the passage to its electronic form, when the last traces of its materiality have disappeared—it is only at this stage that it will assume the form of an indestructible spectral presence. * SLAVOJ ŽIŽEK, *WELCOME TO THE DESERT OF THE REAL!* (2002)

Jerusalem has always been available in the West in some guise or another, although the dominant form by which the city was appropriated changed over time. In the early Middle Ages, Jerusalem was most commonly acquired as a relic—a bone, fragment of the True Cross, rock, or other material bit of the city. In the later Middle Ages and in early modernity, the city was requisitioned in the form of a replica or fabrication—the Holy Sepulchre, a *sacro monte,* the Way of the Cross. In modernity, Jerusalem was even more widely dispersed. The city was popularly possessed as a reproduction or an exhibition—a lithograph, photograph, or a panorama. In the era of globalization, Jerusalem—experienced in theme parks, film, Web sites, and television—is consumed as spectacle.

Certainly all the past forms of possessing the Holy Land continue to remain active. For example, Jerusalem can still be found in the form of its fragments. At Holy Land U.S.A. in Bedford, Virginia, the guide begins the walking tour of the 250-acre park with an orientation lecture that makes good use of the large relief map of Israel on the wall behind him.[1] The map is a little unconventional. Not only is it oriented east/west rather than north/south, but it is constituted of materials from the regions it depicts—sand from the Negev, soil from Jerusalem, earth from the Dead Sea basin. Reproductions of a nail from

1. This was the arrangement at least in October 2002, when I took my class on pilgrimage there.

the filmic Crucifixion are offered on *The Passion of the Christ* Web site. Indeed, the remarkable popularity of the film occasioned a traveling exhibition of relics from Rome.[2] The possession of Jerusalem in its material manifestations still operates, but relics now have neither the reach nor the power that they exercised in the earlier centuries of Christianity.[3]

This text argues that the forms by which Jerusalem has been appropriated in the West have shifted sequentially. They have progressively dematerialized even as they became ever more visually persuasive. Indeed, the change in the West's figurations of Jerusalem suggestively corresponds to the developing illusionism of Western images: from the powerful planarity and intimate immediacy of the Fieschi-Morgan reliquary through the faux *tableaux vivants* of the early modern *sacri monti* and the trompe-l'oeil canvases of the great nineteenth-century panoramas, to the compelling cinematic representations of Jerusalem now.

Distinguished art historians have honored the compulsive desire for illusionism as the essence of Western art. For Ernst Gombrich, the character of the Western visual tradition was its relentless effort to realize the truth of nature. "In the Western tradition, painting has indeed been pursued as a science. All the works of tradition that we see displayed in our great collections apply discoveries that are the result of ceaseless experimentation."[4] Even Clement Greenberg, who contributed so significantly to the triumph of abstract expressionism, identifies Western illusionism as that unique product of Western culture necessary for the invention of abstraction. "Realism, naturalism, illusion have attained extremes in Western art that were reached nowhere else. But nowhere else, either, has art ever become as opaque and self-contained, as wholly and exclusively art, as it has in the very recent Western past."[5]

If illusionism has been recently privileged by some art historians as quintessentially Western, it has also long been denounced by philosophers and theologians as unethical or unholy deception. Plato famously banned artists from the Republic because of the false illusions that they produced. For Plato, "imitative art is far removed from the truth."[6] A good artist can mislead the innocent viewer into thinking that the falsehood she depicts is reality. Learned bishops have also denounced as deceitful the painting of the holy figure because "it draws

2. "'The Passion' Unleashed."

3. Similarly, miracle-working images, such as the Black Madonnas of Einsiedlung and Altötting, are still venerated, but they attract and cure fewer pilgrims than they did in the past. Apparitions of the Virgin were witnessed in the Middle Ages, but they were the dominant form of manifestation of the holy in the nineteenth century. For earlier and later apparitions, see Christian, *Apparitions in Late Medieval and Renaissance Spain*. Our Lady of Lourdes is perhaps the most familiar of these appearances. For a remarkable evocation of Lourdes, see Zola, *Lourdes*. For a political reading of Lourdes, see Perry and Echeverría, *Under the Heel of Mary*. Images of Mary still mysteriously appear. In 2004, a ten-year-old grilled-cheese sandwich with the Virgin figured on its face was sold for $28,000. See Aucoin, "Iconic Grilled Cheese Feeds Internet Frenzy." Such curious Virgins, however, attract attention more for the price paid for them than for their aura. Now the Holy Land is more credibly presented in graphic or filmic productions.

4. Gombrich, *Art and Illusion*, 34.

5. Greenberg, "Byzantine Parallels," 167–68.

6. Plato, *Republic*, 10.598b.

down the spirit of man from the lofty adoration of God to the low and material adoration of the creature."[7] By the late eighteenth century, the critique of illusionism seems to have shrunk to a debate in aesthetics. Sir Joshua Reynolds, in his third Discourse, writes, for example, that "nature herself is not to be too closely copied. . . . A mere copier of nature can never produce any thing great; can never raise and enlarge the conceptions, or warm the heart of the spectator."[8] The critical and commercial success of the photo realists and Duane Hanson in the later twentieth century suggests that illusionism is no longer the least bit suspicious.[9] It is possible to trace the increasing dependence of Western culture on the visual as a source of truth. Nevertheless, as I hope that I made clear in chapters 4 and 5, the most realistic images of Jerusalem that have circulated in the West are the least truthful ones.

My treatment of illusion as a peculiarly Western mode of deception in the present work, then, is hardly novel and requires no elaborate argument. Less familiar are the claims offered here of the intimate relationship between the economy and modes of representation in the West. The progressive dematerialization of Western expressions of Jerusalem curiously corresponds to the progressive dematerialization of expressions of exchange. I have argued that the ascendancy of each of the distinct invocations of Jerusalem—fragment, replica, fabrication, reproduction, spectacle—was conditioned by its peculiar embodiment of contemporary economic practice. The economy in the West evolved from gift and barter in the early Middle Ages through monetization and primitive accumulation in the later Middle Ages to capitalism and globalization in modernity. The market, like the Jerusalems that circulated within it, becomes progressively immaterial or virtual. The increasing abstraction of the economy is perhaps most clearly expressed in the shifting vehicles of exchange: from physical treasure, bullion, and coin through bills of exchange to paper money and finally, and most abstractly, to digital credit. By reading the changing representations of Jerusalem against shifts in the Western economy, it is possible to chart the ways in which markets mediate the relationship between the human subject and the spiritual landscape. The progressive abstraction or commodification of sacred space—from a physical presence to a dangerously deceptive illusion—can be understood as the cultural counterpart to the evolving market.

In the past, iconophobic philosophers and iconoclastic theologians feared the representation of the divine. An image's capacity to challenge an assumed distinction between the real and the imaginary threatened the social stability of truth. Now, either because the image has lost its power to confound us or because the truth no longer matters, illusion in popular visual culture is taken for granted. Indeed, illusion is often truth itself. Similarly, philosophers and

---

7. "Epitome of the Definition of the Iconoclastic Conciliabulum, Held in Constantinople, a.d. 754," 543–44.

8. Reynolds, *Discourses on Art*, 41.

9. See, for example, Tom Wolfe's characteristically hysterical denunciation of critical thinking about illusion in the introduction to his *The Painted Word*.

theologians distrusted the power of money: money's tendency to self-generate was suspected of corrupting the communal fabric by promoting inequities. Aristotle revealed his anxiety on the issue in the *Politics* in a passage discussed more fully in chapter 2: "The most hated sort [of wealth-getting], and with the greatest reason, is usury [all interest on money], which makes a gain out of money itself, and not from the natural object of it. . . . And this term interest, which means the birth of money from money, is applied to the breeding of money because the offspring resembles the parent. Wherefore of all modes of getting wealth this is the most unnatural."[10] By the eighteenth century, money's fertility was so thoroughly embedded in social interaction that it could be celebrated. Benjamin Franklin reverses Aristotle; money's generative capacity is eulogized:

Remember that Money is of a prolific generating Nature. Money can beget Money, and its Offspring can beget more, and so on. Five Shillings turn'd, is Six: Turn'd again, 'tis Seven and Three Pence; and so on 'til it becomes an Hundred Pound. The more there is of it, the more it produces every Turning, so that the Profits rise quicker and quicker. He that kills a breeding Sow, destroys all her Offspring to the thousandth Generation. He that murders a Crown, destroys all it might have produc'd, even Scores of Pounds.[11]

Money's generation, like human reproduction, might even be explained to children as a kind of conjuring trick: "Here's where the magic begins. If you take the money you've saved to the bank, it will grow while it sits in the bank, whether you add more money or not!"[12] Money is family.

If society has lent to money and to money's operations a naturalness that it once lacked, how has money repaid its debt? Has it reciprocated by making us less natural, less human? Max Weber observed that interaction in the modern market is highly abstract and coldly impersonal:

Within the market community every act of exchange, especially monetary exchange, is not directed, in isolation, by the action of the individual partner to the particular transaction, but the more rationally it is considered, the more it is directed by the actions of all parties potentially interested in the exchange. The market community as such is the most impersonal relationship in practical life into which humans can enter with one another. . . . The reason for the impersonality of the market is . . . its orientation to the commodity and only to that. . . . Such absolute depersonalization is contrary to all the elementary forms of human relationship.[13]

Weber assumes that humans are humanized by human contact (whether that interaction takes the form of art or politics). Money and commodities—abstract

10. Aristotle, *Politics*, 1141. Also see Aristotle, *Nicomachean Ethics*, bk. 5.

11. Franklin, "Advice to a Young Tradesman, Written by an Old One," 321–22.

12. Harman, *Barron's Money Sense for Children*, 42.

13. Weber, *Economy and Society*, 1:636–7.

Table 2. From early medieval to postmodern; from materiality to illusion

PERIOD	MATERIAL (PHYSICAL REALITY)	→			(ILLUSION) IMMATERIAL
EARLY MEDIEVAL	Relics Fragments of the True Cross *Gifts, bullion* *Profit is usury; it is illegal and immoral*				
MEDIEVAL		Replicas of the Holy Sepulchre *Money* *Usury is hidden*			
EARLY MODERN			Reproductions of urban spaces *Bills of exchange* *Delimited profit*		
MODERN				Images of mass consumption: Prints and panoramas *Paper currency* *Profit legitimated*	
POSTMODERN					Spectacle: Theme parks and digitalization *Electronic credit* *Profit escapes all ethical restraints*

forms that reveal few signs of human touch and which diminish the interaction of individuals—dehumanize their users. The evolving market economy has become more abstract and more impersonal since Weber made his observations at the beginning of the twentieth century. Whether the exchange involves cornflakes or derivatives, the human cost of the exchange is now virtually invisible.[14]

By tracing my own discovery of the remarkably intimate relationship between money and the representations of Jerusalem, I have attempted to show that the increasing abstraction of Western financial exchange collaborates with its visual equivalent (table 2). Economic abstraction and visual illusion don't just appear together: the Templars, the Franciscans, and the entrepreneurs of Holy Land spectacles demonstrate the intimate relation between Jerusalem image-makers and developments in the Western economy. From the somatic encounter with the spaces of the Passion and Resurrection in the *sacri monti* of early modern Italy to the mass consumption of images of Jerusalem in the modern Protestant north, there is a shift from a participatory space that encouraged a haptic engagement with the sacred to a distant view of a historic space available

14. As described in the epigraph. Žižek, *Welcome to the Desert of the Real!*, 36.

for an admission fee. This shift marks both the changed location of the holy and the increased value of visual goods in the industrializing West.

The forms of Jerusalem that circulate in the West thus provide a sense of the city they represent and describe the economy of which they are a part. I hope that my book has persuaded you to entertain the notion that the evolution of illusionism can be mapped against developments in the economy. Just as critically, I hope it has convinced you that both the escalating abstraction of the economy and the progressive illusionism in visual culture involve an increasing suspension of disbelief bordering on the gullible. If *Selling Jerusalem* manages to convince its readers to think about two propositions, it will have accomplished its main task. The first is a historical observation: as the illusionism of both images and the market has accelerated in the West, anxiety about money and representation has, in inverse proportion, diminished. The second is a mental exercise: perhaps the abandonment of all those old anxieties about money and representation is not such a good thing.

BIBLIOGRAPHY: CITED WORKS

PRIMARY SOURCES

Abel, F. M. "Lettre d'un templier." *Revue biblique* 35 (1926): 288–95.

Adamnan and Arculfus. In *De locis sanctis*, edited by Denis Molaise Meehan. Scriptores latini hiberniae, vol. 3. Dublin: Dublin Institute for Advanced Studies, 1958.

Ambrose. "De obitu Theodosii." In *Sancti Ambrosii opera, pars VII*, edited by Otto Faller, 370–401. Vol. 73 of *Corpus scriptorum ecclesiasticorum Latinorum*. Vienna: F. Tempsky, 1955.

Anonymous Pilgrim. *Guide Book to Palestine*. Translated by J. H. Bernard. Vol. 4 of *Palestine Pilgrims' Text Society*. London: Palestine Pilgrims' Text Society, 1894.

Anonymous Pilgrim V. Translated by Aubrey Stewart. Vol. 6 of *Palestine Pilgrims' Text Society*, 27–36. London: Palestine Pilgrims' Text Society, 1896.

Antoninus Placentinus. *Itinerarium*. In Geyer, *Itinera Hierosolymitana saeculi IIII-VIII*, 157–91. Vienna: F. Tempsky, 1898.

Aquinas, Thomas. *Commerce: Being Extracts from the "Summa Theologica" of S. Thomas Aquinas*. Translated by Fathers of the English Dominican Province. Ditchling, Sussex: St. Dominic's Press, 1919.

———. *Summa Theologica*. Translated by Fathers of the English Dominican Province. New York: McGraw-Hill, 1964.

Aristotle. *Nicomachean Ethics*. In *The Basic Works of Aristotle*, edited by Richard McKeon, 935–1126. New York: Random House, 1941.

———. *Politics*. In *The Basic Works of Aristotle*, edited by Richard McKeon, 1127–316. New York: Random House, 1941.

Ashbee, Charles Robert. *A Palestine Notebook, 1918–1923*. Garden City, NY: Doubleday, 1923.

———, ed. *Jerusalem, 1918–1920, Being the Records of the Pro-Jerusalem Council during the Period of the British Military Administration*. London: John Murray for the Council of the Pro-Jerusalem Society, 1921.

———, ed. *Jerusalem, 1920–1922, Being the Records of the Pro-Jerusalem Council during the First Two Years of the Civil Administration*. London: John Murray for the Council of the Pro-Jerusalem Society, 1924.

Aucoin, Don. "Iconic Grilled Cheese Feeds Internet Frenzy." *Boston Globe*, November 24, 2004.

Augustine. "De opere monachorum." *Patrologia Latina* 40 : 547–82.

Auktionshaus Reinhild Tschöpe. 52. *Auktion: Historischer Wertpapiere und Finanzdokumente* 2003. http://www.tschoepe.de/auktion51/katalog/Los304bis315.pdf (accessed December 2003).

Avitus Viennensis. Epistolae 18 and 23. *Patrologia Latina* 59 : 236, 239–40.

Baedeker's Handbook for Travellers: Syria and Palestine. 3rd ed. Leipzig: Karl Baedeker, 1898.

Baldi, Donatus. *Enchiridion locorum sanctorum: Documenta S. Evangelii loca respicientia*. Jerusalem: Typis PP. Franciscanorum, 1955.

Banvard, John. *Description of Banvard's Pilgrimage to Jerusalem and the Holy Land; painted from authentic drawings made upon the spot during an extensive journey, undertaken expressly for the work . . . presenting in minute detail, the sacred localities; the cities, mountains, plains and rivers; celebrated in spiritual history*. New York, 1853.

Barker, Robert. "Patent: La Nature à Coup d' Oeil" [1787]. In *The Repertory of Arts and Manufactures: Consisting of Original Communications, Specifications of Patent Inventions, and Selections of Useful Practical Papers from the Transactions of the Philosophical Societies of All Nations, &C. &c.*, no. 20. London: G. and T. Wilkie, and G. G. and J. Robinson, 1796.

Baudonivia. "Life of Radegund." Translated by McNamara and Halborg in *Sainted Women of the Dark Ages*, 60–105.

———. *Vita Radegundis*. Edited by Bruno Krusch. Vol. 2 of *Monumenta Germaniae historica, Scriptores rerum merovingicarum*, 358–95. Hannover: Bibliopolii Hahniani, 1885.

Beckett, Paul. "Citigroup Is Near a Settlement of 'Predatory Lending' Charges." *Wall Street Journal*, September 6, 2002.

Bentham, Jeremy. "Panopticon; or, the Inspection-House, Containing the Idea of a New Principle of Construction Applicable to Any Sort of Establishment, in which Persons of Any Description Are to be Kept Under Inspection; and in Particular to Penitentiary-Houses, Prisons, Houses of Industry, Work-Houses, Lazarettos, Manufactories, Hospitals, Mad-Houses, and Schools: with a Plan of Management Adapted to the Principle: in a Series of Letters, Written in the Year 1787, from Crecheff in White Russia to a Friend in England by Jeremy Bentham, of Lincoln's Inn." In *The Panopticon Writings*, edited by Miran Božovič. London: Verso, 1995.

———. "Usury Laws; or, An Exposition of the Impolicy of Legal Restraints on the Terms of Pecuniary Bargains; in the Form of a Series of Letters Addressed to a Friend" [1787]. In *Usury Laws: Their Nature, Expediency, and Influence*, edited by Executive Committee of the Society for Political Education, 7–32. New York: Society for Political Education, 1881.

Berger, Eric. "Enron Gets $250 Million Credit Line." *Houston Chronicle*, July 3, 2002.

Bernardino Tomitano da Feltre. *Sermoni del beato Bernardino Tomitano da Feltre: Seque il Quaresimale di Pavia del 1493 e altri sermoni tenuti in diversi luoghi dal 1493 al 1494*. Edited by Carlo Varischi da Milano. 2 vols. Vol. 2. Milan: Stedar, 1963.

Bernard of Clairvaux. "In Praise of the New Knighthood." Translated by Conrad Greenia in *Treatises III*, 113–67. Vol. 19 of *Cistercian Fathers Series*. Kalamazoo, MI: Cistercian Publications, 1977.

———. *La Règle du Temple*. Edited by H. de Curzon. Société de l'histoire de France, vol. 228. Paris: Librairie Renouard, 1886.

———. *The Rule of the Templars: The French Text of the Rule of the Order of the Knights Templar*. Edited and translated by J. M. Upton-Ward. Woodbridge, Suffolk, UK: Boydell Press, 1992.

Beverly, W., and William Henry Bartlett. *A Pilgrimage through the Holy Land: Explanatory of the Diorama of Jerusalem and the Holy Land Painted under the Direction of W. Beverly from Original Sketches, Made on the Spot, During Repeated Journeys in the East*. London, [1850?].

Bonaventure. "Life of St. Francis." Translated by Ewart Cousins in *Bonaventure: The Soul's Journey into God, The Tree of Life, The Life of St. Francis*, 177–327. Mahwah, NJ: Paulist Press, 1978.

"Breviarius de Hierosolyma." In Geyer, *Itinera Hierosolymitana saeculi IIII-VIII*, 107–12.

Broadway, Bill. "The Evangelical-Israeli Connection: Scripture Inspires Many Christians to Support Zionism Politically, Financially." *Washington Post*, March 27, 2004.

Brown, Dan. *The Da Vinci Code*. New York: Doubleday, 2003.

Butler, Alban. *The Lives of the Fathers, Martyrs, and Other Principal Saints*. 4 vols. Dublin: James Duffy, 1866–1906.

Butler, Samuel. *Alps and Sanctuaries of Piedmont and the Canton Ticino* [1881]. London: Jonathan Cape, 1924.

———. *Ex Voto* [1888]. London: Jonathan Cape, 1928.

B., V. "Das neue Münchner Panorama." *Kunstchronik* 21, no. 37 (1885–86): 617–20.

[Catherwood Panorama]. *New York Times,* July 31, 1842.

Champney, Elizabeth. *Three Vassar Girls in the Holy Land.* Boston: Estes and Lauriat, 1892.

Chaplain of Sir Richard Guylforde. *Pylgrymage of Sir Richard Guylforde to the Holy Land, A.D. 1506.* Edited by Sir Henry Ellis. London: J. B. Nichols and Son, 1851.

Chateaubriand, François-René. "Préface de l'édition de 1827: Itinéraire de Paris à Jérusalem." In *Oeuvres complètes de Chateaubriand,* edited by Charles Augustin Sainte-Beuve, 13–16. Paris: Garnier, 1859.

"The City of the Sultans." *New York Times,* March 16, 1888.

Codex Theodosianus. Edited and translated by Clyde Pharr. Princeton, NJ: Princeton University Press, 1952.

"Colonel R. Storrs, C. M. G." *The Sphinx,* February 23, 1918, 164.

Concilium universale Chalcedonense. Vol. 2, tome 1 of *Acta conciliorum oecumenicorum,* edited by Eduard Schwartz. Berlin: W. de Gruyter, 1933.

Cooperman, Alan. "Ideas about Christ's Death Surveyed. Growing Minority: Jews Responsible." *Washington Post,* April 3, 2004.

"The Cyclorama of Jerusalem." *Catholic Union and Times,* September 6, 1888.

Cyril of Jerusalem. "Catechetical Lectures." *Patrologia Greca* 33:331–1128.

———. "Catechetical Lectures." Translated by Edward Hamilton Gifford. Ser. 2, vol. 7 of *A Select Library of the Nicene and Post-Nicene Fathers,* edited by Philip Schaft and Henry Wace. New York: Christian Literature Company, 1894.

Daguerre, Louis Jacques Mandé. *Historique et description des procédés du daguerréotype et du diorama.* With an introduction by Beaumont Newhall. New York: Winter House, 1971.

Dickens, Charles. *American Notes.* New York: Modern Library, 1996.

———. *Barnaby Rudge.* London: Oxford University Press, 1954.

———. *Pictures from Italy.* London: Penguin, 1998.

———. "Some Account of an Extraordinary Traveller." *Household Words,* April 20, 1850. Reprinted in *Selected Journalism 1850–1870,* edited by David Pascoe, 511–20. New York: Penguin, 1997.

The Didache. Translated by Kirsopp Lake. Vol. 1 of *The Apostolic Fathers.* Loeb Classical Library. London: William Heinemann, 1924.

Disney, Walter Elias. "Deeds Rather Than Words." In *Faith Is a Star,* edited by Roland Gammon, 7–9. New York: Dutton, 1963.

Disraeli, Benjamin. *Contarini Fleming: An Autobiography.* New York: D. Appleton and Co., 1870.

———. *Tancred; or, The New Crusade* [1847]. London: Henry Colburn, 1871.

Dubois, Pierre. *De recuperatione Terre Sancte.* Edited by Charles Victor Langlois. Paris: A. Picard, 1891.

Eastlake, Charles. *Contributions to the Literature of the Fine Arts with a Memoir compiled by Lady Eastlake.* London: John Murray, 1848.

eBay. "Auction: Relic True Cross & Crown of Thorns." http://cgi.ebay.com/aw-cgi/eBayISAPI.dll?ViewItem&item=1080381927#DESC (accessed March 5, 2002).

Egeria. *Egeria: Diary of a Pilgrimage.* Translated by George E. Gingras. Vol. 38 of *Ancient Christian Writers.* New York: Newman Press, 1970.

———. *Itinerarium Egeriae.* Edited by A. Franceschini and Robert Weber, 27–103. Vol. 175 of *Corpus Christianorum.* Turnhout, Belgium: Brepols, 1965.

Elliott, Stuart. "Advertising: Mom, Apple Pie and Motor Oil." *New York Times,* May 10, 1995.

Ephross, Peter. "Approaching the Millennium: Mississippi Preacher Devotes Life to Birthing Red Heifer in Israel." *Jewish Telegraphic Agency,* September 3, 1999, 3.

"Epitome of the Definition of the Iconoclastic Conciliabulum, Held in Constantinople, A.D. 754." In *The Seven Ecumenical Councils of the Undivided Church,* edited and translated by H. R. Percival, 543–44. Ser. 2, vol. 14 of *A Select Library of Nicene and Post-Nicene Fathers,* edited by Philip Schaft and Henry Wace. Grand Rapids, MI: Eerdmans, 1955.

Eusebius. *Life of Constantine.* Translated by Averil Cameron. Oxford: Clarendon Press, 1999.

———. *Vita Constantini*. In *Eusebius Werke*, edited by Friedhelm Winkelmann, 481–540. Berlin: Akademie Verlag, 1975.

Finden, William, Edward Francis Finden, and Thomas Hartwell Horne. *Landscape Illustrations of the Bible: Consisting of Views of the Most Remarkable Places Mentioned in the Old and New Testaments, from Original Sketches Taken on the Spot*. London: John Murray, 1836.

Finley, John H. *A Pilgrim in Palestine after Its Deliverance: Being an Account of Journeys on Foot by the First American Pilgrim after General Allenby's Recovery of the Holy Land*. New York: Scribner, 1919.

Finn, James. *A View from Jerusalem, 1849–1858: The Consular Diary of James and Elizabeth Anne Finn*. Edited by Arnold Blumberg. Ruthford, NJ: Associated University Presses, 1980.

Fiske, Samuel Wheelock. *Mr. Dunn Browne's Experiences in Foreign Parts*. Cleveland: H. P. B. Jewett, 1857.

Fleury, Charles Rohault de. *Mémoire sur les instruments de la Passion de N.-S. J.-C.* Paris: L. Lesort, 1870.

Flusfeder, David. *The Gift*. London: Fourth Estate, 2003.

Fortunatus, Venantius Honorius Clementianus. *Fortunatus: Poésies mêlées/Opera poetica*. Edited by Charles Nisard and Eugène Rittier. Paris: Firmin-Didot, 1887.

———. *Opera poetica*. Edited by Fridericus Leo and Bruno Krusch. Vol. 4 of *Monumenta Germaniae historica, Auctorum antiquissimorum*. Berlin: Weidmann, 1881.

———. *Personal and Political Poems*. Edited by Judith W. George. Vol. 23 of *Translated Texts for Historians*. Liverpool: Liverpool University Press, 1995.

———. "Vexilla Regis." In *The Seven Great Hymns of the Mediaeval Church*, edited by Charles C. Nott, 140–45. New York: Edwin S. Gorham, 1911.

———. "Vita sanctae Radegundis." In *Venanti Honori Clementiani Fortunati presbyteri italici opera pedestria*, edited by Bruno Krusch. Berlin: Weidmannos, 1885.

Francis of Assissi. *Regula bullata* 1223. http://www.san-francesco.org/regola_eng.html. For the Latin: http://www.franciscanos.org/esfa/regb-a.html. Accessed January 1, 2003.

———. *Regula non bullata*, Franciscan Friars of Mary Immaculate, 1221. http://www.franciscanos.org/esfa/regnb-b.html (Latin); http://www.ofmi-ofmi.org/ofmihome/rule1221/rule1221.htm (problematic English translation). Accessed January 1, 2003.

Franklin, Benjamin. "Advice to a Young Tradesman, Written by an Old One" [1748]. In *Benjamin Franklin: Writings*, edited by J. A. Leo Lemay, 320–23. New York: Literary Classics of the United States, 1987.

Fry, Roger. *Letters of Roger Fry*. Edited by Denys Sutton. 2 vols. New York: Random House, 1972.

Fulcher of Chartres. *The Chronicle of Fulcher of Chartres*. 2nd ed. Sources of Medieval History, edited by Edward Peters. Philadelphia: University of Pennsylvania Press, 1998.

Garcia Canon of Toledo. *Tractatus Garsiae or The Translation of the Relics of SS. Gold and Silver*. Translated by Rodney M. Thompson. Vol. 46 of *Textus Minores*. Leiden: E. J. Brill, 1973.

Geddes, Patrick. "Jerusalem Actual and Possible: A Preliminary Report to the Chief Administrator of Palestine and the Military Governor of Jerusalem on Town Planning and Improvements." In *Central Zionist Archives Jerusalem, File Z4/10.202*, 1919.

Géramb, Marie Joseph de. *Pilgrimage to Jerusalem and Mount Sinai* [1835]. Philadelphia: Carey and Hart, 1840.

Geyer, Paul, ed. *Itinera Hierosolymitana saeculi IIII-VIII*. Vol. 39 of *Corpus scriptorum ecclesiasticorum Latinorum*. Vienna: F. Tempsky, 1898.

Gibson, Mel. *The Passion of the Christ*. Screenplay by Benedict Fitzgerald. Icon Productions, 2004.

Giussano, John Peter. *The Life of St. Charles Borromeo, Cardinal Archbishop of Milan* [1610]. London: Burns and Oates, 1884.

Golubovic, Girolamo. *Biblioteca bio-bibliografica della Terra Santa e dell'Oriente Francescano*. Vol. 1 (1215–1300). Florence: Tipografia del Collegio di S. Bonaventura, 1906.

Gordon, General Charles George. *Reflections in Palestine*. London: Macmillan, 1884.

Gospel of Nicodemus or Acts of Pilate. In *The Apocryphal New Testament Being the Apocryphal Gospels, Acts, Epistles, and Apocalypses*, edited by Montague Rhodes James, 117–46. Oxford: Clarendon Press, 1975.

"A Great Work of Art." *Buffalo Morning Express*, September 9, 1888.

Gregory of Nyssa. *The Life of Saint Macrina*. Translated by Kevin Corrigan. Vol. 12 of Peregrina Translation Series. Toronto: Peregrina, 1996.

———. "Vita Macrinae Junioris." *Patrologia Greca* 46:960–1000.

Gregory of Tours. *Glory of the Martyrs*. Translated and edited by Raymond van Dam. Vol. 3 of *Translated Texts for Historians, Latin Series*. Liverpool: Liverpool University Press, 1988.

———. *Miracula et opera minora*. Vol. 1, pt. 2 of *Monumenta Germaniae historica, Scriptores rerum merovingicarum*, edited by Bruno Krusch. Hannover: Bibliopolii Hahniani, 1885.

Harris, Aaron Keith. "Israelis Battling Intellectual Piracy." *Washington Post*, June 6, 2004.

"Hollywood Report." *Wall Street Journal*, March 12, 2004.

Horn, Elzear. *Ichnographiae monumentorum Terrae Sanctae* [1724–44]. Publications of the Studium Biblicum Franciscanum, vol. 15. Jerusalem: Franciscan Press, 1962.

Howe, Fisher. *Oriental and Sacred Scenes: From Notes of Travel in Greece, Turkey, and Palestine*. New York: M. W. Dodd, 1854.

———. *The True Site of Calvary, and Suggestions Relating to the Resurrection*. New York: A. D. F. Randolph, 1871.

Howell, James, and John Stow. *Londinopolis, an historicall discourse or perlustration of the city of London, the imperial chamber, and chief emporium of Great Britain*. London: J. Streater, 1657.

Hugo, Victor. *The Hunchback of Notre-Dame*. Translated by Walter J. Cobb. New York: Penguin, 1965.

Hurlebut, Jesse Lyman. *Manual of Biblical Geography: A Text-Book on the Bible History especially prepared for the use of Students and Teachers of the Bible, and for Sunday School Instruction*. Chicago: Rand, McNally, 1884.

ITEC Entertainment Corporation. *ITEC Projects: Fact Sheet*. ITEC Entertainment Corporation, 2001. http://www.itec.com/productions.htm (accessed March 5, 2002).

Jackson, Jerry W. "Holy Land Founder Resigns: The Rev. Marvin Rosenthal Cites 'A Difference of Opinion' with the Board." *Orlando Sentinel*, July 21, 2005.

Jacques de Vitry. *The Exempla; or, Illustrative Stories from the* Sermones vulgares *of Jacques de Vitry*. Edited by Thomas Frederick Crane. Nendeln, Liechtenstein: Kraus Reprint, 1967.

James, Henry. *The Outcry*. New York: C. Scribner's Sons, 1911.

Jerome. Letter 108 to Eustochium, in *Epistulae*. Vol. 55 of *Corpus scriptorum ecclesiasticorum Latinorum*, 306–51, edited by Isidorus Hilberg and Margit Kamptner. Vienna: Verlag der österreichischen Akademie der Wissenschaften, 1996.

"J. L. Stoddard Dies; Author, Lecturer." *New York Times*, June 6, 1931.

John Chrysostom. "Homilia adversus Judaeos et Gentiles demonstratio, quod Christus sit Deus." *Patrologia Greca* 48:813–38.

John the Deacon. "Liber de ecclesia lateranensi." *Patrologia Latina* 194:1543–60.

Joinville, Jean, sire de. *The History of St. Louis*. Translated by Natalis de Wailly. London: Oxford University Press, 1938.

Kempe, Margery. *The Book of Margery Kempe*. Edited by Russell A. Peck. Middle English Texts. Kalamazoo: Medieval Institute Publication, Western Michigan University, 1996.

———. *The Book of Margery Kempe: A New Translation, Contexts, Criticism*. Translated by Lynn Staley. New York: Norton, 2001.

Kent, Charles Foster. *Descriptions of One Hundred and Forty Places in Bible Lands to be Seen through the Stereoscope or by Means of Stereopticon Slides*. New York: Underwood and Underwood, 1911.

King, Rev. S. W. *The Italian Valleys of the Pennine Alps: A Tour through all the Romantic and Less*

Frequented "Vals" of Northern Piedmont, from the Tarentaise to the Gries, with Illustrations from the Author's Sketches. London: John Murray, 1858.

Kunz, Fritz. "Panorama Einsiedeln Kruezigung Christi." Einsiedeln: Panorama-Gesellschaft Einsiedeln, 1893.

Lagerlöf, Selma. *The Holy City: Jerusalem II.* Garden City, NY: Doubleday, 1918.

Lamartine, Alphonse de. *A Pilgrimage to the Holy Land Comprising Recollections, Sketches and Reflections Made During a Tour in the East.* 2 vols. New York: D. Appleton and Company, 1848.

Lawrence, Amos. *Extracts from the Diary and Correspondence of the Late Amos Lawrence with a Brief Account of Some Incidents in his Life.* Boston: Gould and Lincoln, 1856.

Lawrence, Thomas Edward. *Seven Pillars of Wisdom: A Triumph.* Garden City, NY: Doubleday, 1966.

Leo I. "Epistola 139: Ad Juvenalum Jerosolymitanum episcopum." *Patrologia Latina,* cols. 1103–7.

Leon, Edwin de. *Thirty Years of My Life on Three Continents.* 2 vols. London: Ward and Downey, 1890.

Lewis, Roy. *The Cross Bearer.* New York: St. Martin's Press, 1994.

Lizerand, Georges, ed. and trans. *Le dossier de l'affaire des Templiers.* Vol. 2 of *Les classiques de l'histoire de France au moyen âge.* Paris: H. Champion, 1923.

Luther, Martin. *Works of Martin Luther,* edited by Henry Eyster Jacobs. Philadelphia: A. J. Holman, 1915.

Makiya, Kanan. *The Rock: A Tale of Seventh Century Jerusalem.* New York: Pantheon Books, 2001.

Mézières, Philippe de. *Le Songe du Vieil Pelerin.* Edited by G. W. Coopland. 2 vols. Cambridge: Cambridge University Press, 1969.

Michael the Syrian. *Chronique de Michel le Syrien.* Edited and translated by J.-B. Chabot. 5 vols. Paris: Ernest Leroux, 1905.

Morone, Girolamo. *Lettere ed orazioni latine di Girolamo Morone.* Edited by Giuseppe Müller. In *Miscellanea di storia italiana,* vol. 2. Turin: Stamperia Reale, 1863.

Motta, Emilio. *Il Beato Bernardino Caimi: Fondatore del santuario di Varallo; Documenti e lettere inedite.* Milan: Tipografia Bartolotti dei Fratelli Rivara, 1891.

Mukaddasi, Muhammad ibn Amad al-. *Descriptio imperii Moslemici.* Edited by M. J. de Goeje. Lyon: E. J. Brill, 1906.

———. *Description of Syria Including Palestine.* Edited by Guy Le Strange. Vol. 3 of *Palestine Pilgrims' Text Society.* London: Palestine Pilgrims' Text Society, 1886.

"The New Era in Jerusalem." *London Times,* December 22, 1920.

O'Faolain, Julia. *Women in the Wall.* New York: Viking Press, 1975.

Oliver, Rev. George. *History of the Holy Trinity Guild at Sleaford, with an Account of Its Miracle Plays, Religious Mysteries, and Shows as Practiced in the Fifteenth Century.* Lincoln, UK: Edward Bell Drury, 1837.

Pacioli, Luca. *Summa de arithmetica, geometria, proportione & proportionalita.* Venice: Paganino de Paganini, 1494.

Palmieri-Billig, Lisa. "Shetreet: Pope Likely to Visit Next Year." *Jerusalem Post,* January 18, 1996.

Paris, Matthew (Matthew of Westminster). *The Flowers of History, Especially Such as Relate to the Affairs of Britain from the Beginning of the World to the Year 1307.* Translated by C. D. Yonge. 2 vols. London: Henry G. Bohn, 1853.

"Passion Film Beats *Rings* Record: Mel Gibson's *The Passion of the Christ* Has Broken the US Five-Day Box Office Record Held by *The Lord of the Rings: The Return of the King.*" BBC News, March 3, 2004. http://www.wnd.com/news/article.asp?ARTICLE_ID=37645 (accessed April 4, 2004).

"'The Passion' Unleashed: Relics of Crucifixion Coming to U.S. Cities; Washington, St. Louis to See Pieces of Cross and Other Artifacts." *World Daily Net,* 2004. http://www.wnd.com/news/article.asp?ARTICLE_ID=37645 (accessed March 21, 2005).

Patrologia Greca. Edited by J.-P. Migne. Paris: Migne, 1857ff.

Patrologia Latina. Edited by J.-P. Migne. Paris: Migne, 1844ff.

Paulinus of Nola. *Epistulae: Letters of St. Paulinus of Nola.* Edited by P. G. Walsh. Vols. 35, 36 of *Ancient Christian Writers.* New York: Newman Press, 1966, 1967.

———. *Sancti Pontii Meropii Paulini Nolani epistulae.* Edited by Wilhelm August Hartel and Margit Keamptner. Vol. 29 of *Corpus scriptorum ecclesiasticorum Latinorum.* Vienna: Österreichische Akademie der Wissenschaften, 1999.

Plato. *Republic.* Translated by G. M. A. Grube. Indianapolis: Hackett Publishing Company, 1974.

Pliny. *Natural History.* Translated by H. Rackham. 10 vols. Loeb Classical Library. Cambridge, MA: Harvard University Press, 1938–63.

"Pope Said to Find 'Passion' Accurate." *New York Times,* December 20, 2003.

Pt., F. "Münchener kunst." *Allgemeine Zeitung,* April 12, 1893.

Quaresmio, Francesco. *Elucidatio Terrae Sanctae* [1639]. Translated by Sabino De Sandoli. Vol. 32 of *Studium Biblicum Franciscanum, collectio maior.* Jerusalem: Franciscan Printing Press, 1989.

"Religious Reliques; or, The Sale at the Savoy, upon the Jesuits Breaking up their School and Chappel." 1688. Houghton EBB65, Harvard University Library, Cambridge, MA.

Reynolds, Sir Joshua. *Discourses on Art* [1797]. Edited by Robert R. Wark. New Haven, CT: Yale University Press, 1997.

Rich, Frank. "The Pope's Thumbs Up for Gibson's 'Passion.'" *New York Times,* January 18, 2004.

Roberts, David, and Rev. George Croly. *The Holy Land, Syria, Idumea, Arabia, Egypt, and Nubia, from Drawings Made on the Spot by David Roberts, R. A., with Historical Descriptions by the Reverend George Croly, L.L.D., Lithographed by Louis Haghe.* London: F. G. Moon, 1842–45.

Roman Catholic Church. *Bullarum privilegiorum ac diplomatum Romanorum Pontificum amplissima collectio.* Edited by Charles Cocquelines. 18 vols. Rome: Hieronymus Mainardus, 1733–62.

———. *Cartulaire général de l'Ordre du Temple, 1119?–1150.* Edited by Marquis d'Albon. Paris: Librairie ancienne, 1913.

———. *The Council of Trent: The Canons and Decrees of the Sacred and Oecumenical Council of Trent.* Translated by J. Waterworth. London: Dolman, 1848.

———. *The 1917 or Pio-Benedictine Code of Canon Law.* Translated by Edward N. Peters. San Francisco: Ignatius Press, 2001.

———. *The Raccolta; or, A Manual of Indulgences, Prayers and Devotions (Enchiridion indulgentiarum: preces et pia opera).* Translated by John F. Rowan. New York: Benziger Brothers, 1957.

———. *Sacraments and Forgiveness: History and Doctrinal Development of Penance, Extreme Unction and Indulgences.* Edited by Paul F. Palmer. Vol. 2 of *Sources of Christian Theology.* Westminster, MD: Newman Press, 1959.

Ruppin, Arthur. *Three Decades of Palestine: Speeches and Papers on the Upbuilding of the Jewish National Home.* Jerusalem: Schocken, 1936.

Ruskin, John. *Praeterita and Dilecta.* Vol. 35 of *The Works of John Ruskin,* edited by E. T. Cook and A. Wedderburn. London: George Allen, 1908.

Schlueb, Mark. "Holy Land Experience Exempt from Property Tax." *Orlando Sentinel,* July 12, 2005.

Scott, Sir Walter. *Ivanhoe* [1819]. New York: Random House, 2001.

———. *Talisman* [1825]. Edited by Frederick Treudley. New York: Macmillan, 1907.

Simpson, William. *The Autobiography of William Simpson.* Edited by George Eyre-Todd. London: T. F. Unwin, 1903.

Sleutjes, Michaëlus. *Instructio de stationibus S. Viae Crucis deque Crucifixis Viae Crucis.* 4th ed. Rome: Typographia Collegii S. Bonaventurae, 1909.

Smith, Adam. *Wealth of Nations; or, An Inquiry into the Nature and Causes of the Wealth of Nations* [1776]. Amherst, NY: Prometheus Books, 1991.

Smith, Dinita. "A Shrine to Books Past Clings to Independence." *New York Times,* October 13, 1997.

Socrates. *Ecclesiastical Church History.* Translated by Phillip Schaff. Ser. 2, vol. 2 of *A Select Library of Nicene and Post-Nicene Fathers.* New York: Christian Literature Company, 1890.

Solin, Heikki, and Marja Itkonen-Kaila. *Graffiti del Palatino. I: Paedagogium.* Acta Instituti Romani Finlandiae, edited by Veikko Väänänen, vol. 3. Helsinki: Akateeminen Kirjakauppa, 1966.

Sozomen. *Ecclesiastical History.* Translated by Phillip Schaff. Ser. 2, vol. 2 of *A Select Library of Nicene and Post-Nicene Fathers.* New York: Christian Literature Company, 1890.

Spenser, Edmund. *Prothalamion* (2RP.1.124, ed. N. J. Endicott) [1596]. University of Toronto, 2000. http://www.library.utoronto.ca/utel/rp/poems/spenser10b.html (accessed 2002).

Stephanus de Borbone. *Anecdotes historiques, legends et apologues.* Société de l'histoire de France, publications, vol. 185. Paris: Librairie Renouard, 1877.

Stoddard, John L. *Lectures: Constantinople, Jerusalem, Egypt.* Vol. 2 of *John L. Stoddard's Lectures.* 10 vols. Boston: Balch Brothers, 1897.

Storrs, Ronald. *Orientations.* London: Nicholson & Watson, 1937.

———. "The Papers of Sir Ronald Storrs (1881–1956) from Pembroke College, Cambridge." In *Middle East Politics and Diplomacy, 1904–1950.* Marlborough, Wiltshire: Adam Matthew Publications, 1999.

———. Preface to Ashbee, *Jerusalem, 1918–1920.*

———. Preface to Ashbee, *Jerusalem, 1920–1922.*

Suriano, Francesco. *Treatise on the Holy Land* [1524]. Edited by Eugene Hoade. Jerusalem: Franciscan Press, 1949.

Tabari, Abu Ja'far Muhammad b. Jarir al-. *The History of al-Tabari. The Battle of al-Qadisiyyah and the Conquest of Syria and Palestine (A.D. 635–637/A.H. 14–15).* Translated by Yohanan Friedmann. SUNY Series of Near Eastern Studies, vol. 12. Albany: State University of New York Press, 1992.

Templar of Tyre. *The Templar of Tyre: Part III of the "Deeds of the Cypriots."* Translated by Paul Crawford. Vol. 6 of *Crusader Texts in Translation.* Aldershot, UK: Ashgate Publishing Limited, 2003.

Theophanes. *The Chronicle of Theophanes Confessor: Byzantine and Near Eastern History, AD 284–813.* Translated by Cyril Mango, Roger Scott, and Geoffrey Greatrex. Oxford: Clarendon Press, 1997.

———. *Chronographia.* Edited by Carl de Boor. Hildesheim: G. Olms, 1963.

Thomson, William M. *The Land and the Book; or, Biblical Illustrations Drawn from the Manners and Customs, the Scenes and Scenery of the Holy Land.* 2 vols. New York: Harper and Brothers, 1859.

"A Trip to Jerusalem: Lecture by John L. Stoddard." *New York Times,* April 8, 1892.

Turner, William Mason. *El-Khuds, the Holy; or, Glimpses in the Orient.* Philadelphia: James Challen and Son, 1861.

Twain, Mark. *The Innocents Abroad; or, the New Pilgrims Progress* [1869]. New York: Penguin, 2002.

United Nations Conciliation Commission for Palestine, Committee on Jerusalem. "The Holy Places: Working Paper Prepared by the Secretariat." Report A/AC.25/Com.Jer/W.14. New York: United Nations, 1949.

Usama ibn Munqidh. "Autobiography." In *Arab Historians of the Crusades,* edited by Francesco Gabrieli, 73–84. Berkeley and Los Angeles: University of California Press, 1969.

Vetromile, Eugene. *Travels in Europe, Egypt, Arabia Petræa, Palestine and Syria.* New York: D. and J. Sadlier and Company, 1871.

Vincent, John Heyl. Introduction to Hurlebut, *Manual of Biblical Geography.*

Viollet-le-Duc, Eugène. *Dictionnaire raisonné de l'architecture française.* Paris, 1854–68.

Walton, William. *Art and Architecture [of the World's Columbian Exposition]: The Official Illustrated Publication, Printed Only for Subscribers.* Philadelphia: G. Barrie, 1893.

Warren, Sir Charles. *The Temple or the Tomb: Giving further Evidence in Favour of the Authenticity of the Present Site of the Holy Sepulchre, and Pointing Out Some of the Principal Misconceptions Contained in Fergusson's "Holy Sepulchre" and "The Temples of the Jews."* London: Richard Bentley, 1880.

Waugh, Evelyn. *Helena, a Novel.* Boston: Little, Brown and Company, 1950.

———. *Labels: A Mediterranean Journal* [1930]. London: Methuen, 1991.

Waxman, Sharon. "Hollywood Rethinking Films of Faith After 'Passion.'" *New York Times,* March 15, 2004.

Weiss, Rick. "Techy to Trendy: Products Hum DNA's Tune." *New York Times*, September 8, 1992.
William of Tyre. *A History of Deeds Done beyond the Sea*. Translated by Emily Atwater Babcock and A. C. Krey. 2 vols. New York: Columbia University Press, 1943.
———. "Incipit historia rerum in partibus transmarinis." *Patrologia Latina* 201:209–892.
Wilson, Sir Charles William. *Picturesque Palestine, Sinai, and Egypt*. 4 vols. New York: D. Appleton and Co., 1881–84.
———. *The Recovery of Jerusalem: A Narrative of Exploration and Discovery in the City and the Holy Land*. Edited by Walter Morrison. London: Palestine Exploration Fund, 1871.
Zion's Hope Inc. *The Holy Land Experience™ Fact Sheet* 2002. http://www.theholylandexperience.com/press/index.html (accessed February 19, 2004).
Zola, Émile. *Lourdes* [1894]. Pocket Classics edition, Dover, NH: Alan Sutton, 1993.
———. *Money* [1891]. Translated by Ernest A. Vizetelly. Stroud, Gloucestershire: Sutton Publishing, 1991.

SECONDARY SOURCES

Addison, Charles Greenstreet. *The Temple Church*. London: Longman, Brown, Green and Longmans, 1843.
Adler, Stephen J. "Israeli Court Finds Muslim Council Destroyed Ancient Remains on Temple Mount." *Biblical Archaeology Review* 20 (July–August 1994): 39.
Alcalay, Ammiel. *After Jews and Arabs: Remaking Levantine Culture*. Minneapolis: University of Minnesota Press, 1993.
Algeri, Giuliana. *Il Museo diocesano di Chiavari*. Vol. 22 of *Guide turistiche e d'arte*. Genoa: Sagep, 1986.
Allen, Frederick Lewis. *The Great Pierpont Morgan*. New York: Harper Brothers, 1949.
Alston, G. Cyprian. *Way of the Cross*. New York: Robert Appleton Company, [1912] 2003. http://www.newadvent.org/cathen/15569a.htm (accessed January 28, 2005).
Anderson, Gary M., Robert B. Ekelund Jr., Robert F. Hebert, and Robert D. Tollison. "An Economic Interpretation of the Medieval Crusades." *Journal of European Economic History* 21 (1992): 339–63.
Andrault-Schmitt, Claude. "Les églises des templiers de la Creuse et l'architecture religieuse au XIIIe siècle en Limousin." *Bulletin de la Société des antiquaires de l'Ouest et des musées de Poitiers* 10 (1996): 73–141.
Andreade, Rena, Panagiotes L. Bokotopoulos, Cyril Mango, Jean-Pierre Sodini, and Manoles Hatzedakes, eds. *Thumíama ste mneme tes Laskarínas Mpoúra*. Athens: Mouseío Mpenáke, 1994.
Appadurai, Arjun, ed. *The Social Life of Things: Commodities in Cultural Perspective*. Cambridge: Cambridge University Press, 1986.
Arce, Agustín. "The Custody of the Holy Land." In *Miscelánea de Tierra Santa*, vol. 3, edited by Agustín Arce, 141–55. Jerusalem: Franciscan Printing Press, 1974.
———. "El sepulcro de David en un texto de Benjamin de Tudela (1169)." *Sefarad* 23 (1963): 105–15.
Areford, David S. "The Passion Measured: A Late-Medieval Diagram of the Body of Christ." In MacDonald, Ridderbos, and Schlusemann, *The Broken Body*, 211–38.
"The Art of Judgment: *Policeman* Sculpture by Duane Hanson." *Sculpture Review* 48, no. 1 (1999): 29–31.
Asia News. "'The Passion of the Christ' Resounding Success as Moviegoers Search for Traces of Anti-Semitism." *Glacom* (Global Advertising Communication), April 2, 2004. http://www.asianews.it/view.php?l=en&art=571 (accessed April 6, 2004).
Avery, Kevin J., and Peter L. Fodera. *John Vanderlyn's Panoramic View of the Palace and Gardens of Versailles*. New York: Metropolitan Museum of Art, 1988.
Avigad, Nahman. *Discovering Jerusalem*. Oxford: Blackwell, 1983.

Avi-Yonah, Michael, and Yoram Tsafrir. *Pictorial Guide to the Model of Ancient Jerusalem at the Time of the Second Temple in the Grounds of the Holy Land Hotel Jerusalem, Israel.* Herzlia, Israel: Palphot, [1987?].

Baer, Yitzhak. *A History of the Jews in Christian Spain.* Translated by Louis Schoffman. 2 vols. Philadelphia: Jewish Publication Society of America, 1961.

Baldwin, John W. *The Medieval Theories of Just Price: Romanists, Canonists, and Theologians in the Twelfth and Thirteenth Centuries. Transactions of the American Philosophical Society,* n.s., vol. 49, pt. 4. Philadelphia, 1959.

Ballantine, James. *The Life of David Roberts, R.A.* Edinburgh: Adam and Charles Blace, 1866.

Bann, Stephen. *The True Vine: On Visual Representation and the Western Tradition.* Cambridge: Cambridge University Press, 1989.

Barag, Dan. "Glass Pilgrim Vessels from Jerusalem." *Journal of Glass Studies* 12, 13 (1970, 1971): 35–63, 45–63.

Barber, Malcolm. "The Templars and the Turin Shroud." *Catholic Historical Review* 68, no. 2 (1982): 206–25.

———. *The Trial of the Templars.* Cambridge: Cambridge University Press, 1978.

Barnes, Timothy D. *Constantine and Eusebius.* Cambridge, MA: Harvard University Press, 1981.

Baudrillard, Jean. *For a Critique of the Political Economy of the Sign.* Translated by Charles Levin. New York: Telos Press, 1981.

———. *Simulations.* Translated by Paul Foss. New York: Semiotext[e], 1983.

Baxandall, Michael. *Patterns of Intention: On the Historical Explanation of Pictures.* New Haven, CT: Yale University Press, 1985.

Baylis, Thomas Henry. *The Temple Church and Chapel of St. Ann: An Historical Record and Guide.* London: G. Philip and Son, 1900.

Behdad, Ali. "Orientalist Tourism." *Peuples Méditerranéens* 50 (January–March 1990): 59–73.

Belayche, Nicole. *Iudaea-Palaestina: The Pagan Cults in Roman Palestine (Second to Fourth Century).* Edited by Hubert Cancik and Jörg Rüpke. Religion der Römischen Provinzen, vol. 1. Tübingen: Mohr Siebeck, 2001.

Belting, Hans. *The Image and Its Public in the Middle Ages: Form and Function of Early Paintings of the Passion.* Translated by Mark Brtusis and Raymond Meyer. New Rochelle, NY: Aristide D. Caratzas, 1990.

Ben-Arieh. "Catherwood Map of Jerusalem." *Quarterly Journal of the Library of Congress* (July 1974): 150–60.

Ben-Asher Gitler, Inbal. "C. R. Ashbee's Jerusalem Years: Arts and Crafts, Orientalism and British Regionalism." *Assaph: Studies in Art History* 5 (2000): 29–52.

Bendiner, Kenneth Paul. "David Roberts in the Near East: Social and Religious Themes." *Art History* 6, no. 1 (1983): 67–81.

Benjamin, Walter. *The Arcades Project.* Translated by Howard Eiland and Kevin McLaughlin. Edited by Rolf Tiedemann. Cambridge, MA: Harvard University Press, 1999.

———. *Charles Baudelaire: A Lyric Poet in the Era of High Capitalism.* Translated by Harry Zohn. London: Verso, 1983.

———. "The Work of Art in the Age of Mechanical Reproduction." Translated by Harry Zohn in *Illuminations,* edited by Hannah Arendt, 217–51. New York: Schocken Books, 1969.

Benvenisti, Meron. *City of Stone: The Hidden History of Jerusalem.* Berkeley and Los Angeles: University of California Press, 1966.

———. *Sacred Landscape: The Buried History of the Holy Land since 1948.* Translated by Maxine Kaufman-Lacusta. Berkeley and Los Angeles: University of California Press, 2000.

Bianconi, Piero, Silvano Colombo, Aldo Lozito, and Luigi Zanzi. *Il Sacro Monte sopra Varese.* Milan: Electa, 1981.

Biddle, Martin. *The Tomb of Christ.* Stroud, Gloucestershire: Sutton, 1999.

Biger, Gideon. *An Empire in the Holy Land: Historical Geography of the British Administration in Palestine, 1917–1929*. New York: St. Martin's Press, 1994.

Billings, Robert William, and Edward Clarkson. *Architectural Illustrations and Account of the Temple Church, London*. London: T. & W. Boone, 1838.

Blaauw, Sible de. "Jerusalem in Rome and the Cult of the Cross." In *Pratum Romanum: Richard Krautheimer zum 100. Geburtstag*, edited by Renate L. Colella, 55–73. Wiesbaden: Reichert, 1997.

Black, John. *Oxford Dictionary of Economics*. Oxford: Oxford University Press, 1997.

Bloch, R. Howard. *God's Plagiarist: Being an Account of the Fabulous Industry and Irregular Commerce of the Abbé Migne*. Chicago: University of Chicago Press, 1994.

Bode, Wilhelm. *Kunst und Künstler* 1 (1902–3): 5–12.

Bony, Jean. *The English Decorated Style: Gothic Architecture Transformed, 1250–1350*. Ithaca, NY: Cornell University Press, 1979.

———. *French Gothic Architecture of the 12th and 13th Centuries*. Berkeley and Los Angeles: University of California Press, 1983.

"Books Sold This Week at Auction." *New York Times*, February 27, 1897.

Bourbon, Fabio. *The Life, Works and Travels of David Roberts, R.A.* New York: Rizzoli, 2000.

———. *The Lost Cities of the Mayas: The Life, Art, and Discoveries of Frederick Catherwood*. New York: Abbeyville Press, 2000.

Bourdieu, Pierre. *Algeria, 1960*. Cambridge: Cambridge University Press, 1979.

Bowman, Glenn. "Christian Ideology and the Image of a Holy Land: The Place of Jerusalem Pilgrimage in the Various Christianities." In *Contesting the Sacred: The Anthropology of Christian Pilgrimage*, edited by John Eade and Michael J. Sallnow, 98–121. London: Routledge, 1991.

Brand, Paul. "Legal Education in England before the Inns of Court." In *Learning the Law: Teaching and the Transmission of Law in England, 1150–1900*, edited by Jonathan A. Bush and Alain Wijffels, 51–84. London: Hambledon Press, 1999.

Branner, Robert. *Gothic Architecture*. New York: G. Braziller, 1961.

Braudel, Fernand. "Prices in Europe from 1450 to 1750." In *The Economy of Expanding Europe in the Sixteenth and Seventeenth Centuries*, edited by E. E. Rich and C. H. Wilson, 378–485. Cambridge: Cambridge University Press, 1967.

Bredero, Adriaan H. "Jérusalem dans l'Occident médiéval." In *Mélanges offerts à René Crozet*, edited by Pierre Gallais and Yves-Jean Riou, 259–71. Poitiers: Société d'Études Médiévales, 1966.

Bresc-Bautier, Geneviève. "Les chapelles de la mémoire: Souvenir de la terre saint et vie du Christ en France (XVe–XIXe siècles)." In Gensini, *La "Gerusalemme" di San Vivaldo e i Sacri Monti in Europa*, 215–31.

Brizio, Anna Maria. "Configuration del Sacro Monte di Varallo nel 1514." In Perrone, *Questi sono li Misteri che sono sopra el Monte de Varalle*, 1–6.

Brown, Katharine Reynolds. "The Morgan Collection and Related Migration Period Material." In *From Attila to Charlemagne: Arts of the Early Medieval Period in the Metropolitan Museum of Art*, edited by Katharine Reynolds Brown, Dafydd Kid, and Charles T. Little, 8–11. New York: Metropolitan Museum of Art, 2000.

Brown, Peter. "Relics and Social Status in the Age of Gregory of Tours." In *Society and the Holy in Late Antiquity*, 222–50. Berkeley and Los Angeles: University of California Press, 1982.

Brown, Robert. "The Holy Land Experience." In *Guide to Theme Parks, 2002*. http://themeparks.about.com/library/weekly/aa031201a.htm (accessed March 5, 2002).

Buckton, David. "Bogus Byzantine Enamels in Baltimore and Washington, D.C." *Journal of the Walters Art Gallery* 46 (1988): 11–24.

———. "Byzantine Enamel and the West." In *Byzantium and the West c. 850–c. 1200: Proceedings of the XVIII Spring Symposium of Byzantine Studies, Oxford 30 March–1 April 1984*, edited by J. D. Howard-Johnstone, 235–44. Amsterdam: Verlag Adolf M. Hakkert, 1988.

Buettner, Brigitte. "Past Presents: New Year's Gifts at the Valois Courts, ca. 1400." *Art Bulletin* 83, no. 4 (2001): 598–625.

Burke, Peter, ed. *Economy and Society in Early Modern Europe.* New York: Harper & Row, 1972.

Burroughs, Charles. "Opacity and Transparence: Networks and Enclaves in the Rome of Sixtus V." *Res* 41 (Spring 2002): 56–71.

Burrows, Toby. "The Templars' Case for Their Defence in 1310." *Journal of Religious History* 13 (1985): 248–59.

Bussel, Abby. "The City That Moses Built." *Progressive Architecture* 70, no. 7 (June 1989): 21.

Butler, Alan, and Stephen Dafoe. *The Warriors and the Bankers: A History of the Knights Templar from 1307 to the Present.* Belleville, Ontario: Templar Books, 1998.

Bynum, Caroline Walker. *Metamorphosis and Identity.* New York: Zone Books, 2001.

Cadei, Antonio. "Gli Ordini di Terrasancta e il culto per la Vera Croce e il Sepolcro di Cristo in Europa nel XII secolo." *Arte medievale,* n.s., 1 (2002): 51–70.

Cameron, Averil. "The Artistic Patronage of Justin II." *Byzantion* 50 (1980): 62–84.

———. "The Early Religious Policies of Justin II." *Studies in Church History* 13 (1976): 51–68.

Cannon Brookes, Peter. "The Sacri Monti of Lombardy and the Piedmont." *Connoisseur* 186 (August 1974): 286–95.

———. "The Sculptural Complexes of San Vivaldo." In Gensini, *La "Gerusalemme" di San Vivaldo e i Sacri Monti in Europa,* 271–79.

Caputo, John D. "The Time of Giving, the Time of Forgiving." In *The Enigma of Gift and Sacrifice,* edited by Edith Wyschogrod, Jean-Joseph Goux, and Eric Boynton, 117–47. New York: Fordham University Press, 2002.

Cardini, Franco, and Guido Vannini. "S. Vivaldo in Valdelsa: Problemi topografici ed interpretazioni simbologiche di una 'Gerusalemme' cinquecentesca in Toscana." In *Due casi paralleli: La Kalwaria Zebrzydowska in Polonia e la 'Gerusalemme' di San Vivaldo in Toscana,* 21–71. Florence: Società storica della Valdelsa, 1983.

Caro, Robert A. *The Power Broker: Robert Moses and the Fall of New York.* New York: Knopf, 1974.

Certeau, Michel de. *The Practice of Everyday Life.* Translated by Steven F. Rendall. Berkeley and Los Angeles: University of California Press, 1984.

Chabert, Alexandre R. E. "More about the Sixteenth-Century Price Revolution." In Burke, *Economy and Society in Early Modern Europe,* 47–54.

Chambers, Emma. "From Chemical Process to the Aesthetics of Omission: Etching and the Languages of Art Criticism in Nineteenth-Century Britain." *Art History* 20, no. 4 (1997): 556–74.

Chazan, Robert. *Medieval Stereotypes and Modern Antisemitism.* Berkeley and Los Angeles: University of California Press, 1997.

Cheal, David. *The Gift Economy.* London: Routledge, 1988.

Chernow, Ron. *The House of Morgan: An American Banking Dynasty and the Rise of Modern Finance.* New York: Atlantic Monthly Press, 1990.

Christian, William A. *Apparitions in Late Medieval and Renaissance Spain.* Princeton, NJ: Princeton University Press, 1981.

Cipolla, Carlo M. *Before the Industrial Revolution: European Society and Economy 1000–1700.* Translated by Christopher Woodall. 3rd ed. New York: W. W. Norton, 1993.

———. "The So-Called 'Price Revolution': Reflections on 'the Italian Situation.'" In Burke, *Economy and Society in Early Modern Europe,* 43–46.

Civilini, Luigi. *San Vivaldo: Jerusalem in Tuscany.* Bologna: Italcards, n.d.

Clark, Kenneth. "Renderings of an Early Master—David Roberts, Parts I and II." *Pencil Points* 7 (1926): 2–18, 171–76.

Clark, T. J. *The Painting of Modern Life.* Princeton, NJ: Princeton University Press, 1986.

Cohen, Jeremy. *The Friars and the Jews: The Evolution of Medieval Anti-Judaism.* Ithaca, NY: Cornell University Press, 1982.

Cohn, Norman. *Europe's Inner Demons: An Enquiry Inspired by the Great Witch-Hunt*. New York: Meridian, 1977.

Coleman, Simon, and John Elsner. *Pilgrimage: Past and Present in the World Religions*. Cambridge, MA: Harvard University Press, 1995.

Collin, Bernardin, ed. *Recueil de documents concernant Jerusalem et les lieux saints*. Jerusalem: Franciscan Printing Press, 1982.

Comment, Bernard. *The Painted Panorama*. New York: Harry N. Abrams, 1999.

Comune Montaione. *San Vivaldo 1999*. http://www.comune.montaione.fi.it/doc/vivaint.html (accessed January 15, 2003).

Conner, Patrick. "The Mosque through European Eyes." *Apollo* 120 (1984): 44–49.

Conway, Sir W. Martin. *The Sport of Collecting*. London: T. F. Unwin, 1914.

———. "St. Radegund's Reliquary at Poitiers." *Antiquaries' Journal* 3, no. 1 (1932): 1–12.

Corbo, Virgilio C. *Il Santo Sepolcro di Gerusalemme: Aspetti archeologici dalle origini al periodo crociato*. Vol. 29 of *Collectio maior. Studium Biblicum Franciscanum*. Jerusalem: Franciscan Printing Press, 1981.

Cormack, Robin. "Reflections on Early Byzantine Cloisonné Enamels: Endangered or Extinct." In Andreade et al., *Thumíama ste mneme tes Laskarínas Mpoúra*, 67–72.

Corsini, Roberta. *Affreschi del Sacro Monte di Varese*. Gavirate: Nicolini, 2000.

Cousins, Russel. "The Serialization and Publication of *L'Argent:* The Genesis of a Literary Event in France and in England." *Bulletin of the Emile Zola Society* 14 (1996): 9–14.

Crary, Jonathan. *Techniques of the Observer: On Vision and Modernity in the Nineteenth Century*. Cambridge, MA: MIT Press, 1990.

Crawford, Alan. *C. R. Ashbee: Architect, Designer and Romantic Socialist*. New Haven, CT: Yale University Press, 1985.

Crook, J. Mordaunt. "The Restoration of the Temple Church: Ecclesiology and Recrimination." *Architectural History, Journal of the Society of Architectural Historians of Great Britain* 8 (1965): 39–51.

Curzon, Henri de. *La maison du temple de Paris, histoire et description*. Paris: Librairie Hachette, 1888.

Cutler, Anthony. "Gifts and Gift Exchange as Aspects of the Byzantine, Arab, and Related Economies." *Dumbarton Oaks Papers* 25 (2001): 247–78.

———. "Les échanges de dons entre Byzance et l'Islam (IXe-XIe siècles)." *Journal des Savants* (Jan.–June, 1996): 51–66.

Dainotto, Roberto Maria. "The Gubbio Papers: Historic Centers in the Age of the Economic Miracle." *Journal of Modern Italian Studies* 8, no. 1 (2003): 67–83.

D'Amico, Rob. "South Austin's Neon Transformers Light Up Life South of the River." *Austin Chronicle*, January 19, 2001.

Davis, John. "'Each Mouldering Ruin Recalls a History': Nineteenth-Century Images of Jerusalem and the American Public." In *America and Zion: Essays and Papers in Memory of Moshe Davis*, edited by Eli Lederhendler and Jonathan D. Sarna, 49–74. Detroit, MI: Wayne State University Press, 2002.

———. *The Landscape of Belief: Encountering the Holy Land in Nineteenth-Century American Art and Culture*. Princeton, NJ: Princeton University Press, 1995.

Davis, Natalie Zemon. *The Gift in Sixteenth Century France*. Madison: University of Wisconsin Press, 2000.

Davis, W. D. *The Gospel and the Land: Early Christianity and Jewish Territorial Doctrine*. Berkeley and Los Angeles: University of California Press, 1974.

Debord, Guy. *Society of the Spectacle*. Detroit: Black and Red, 1983.

Delisle, Léopold. *Mémoire sur les opérations financières des Templiers*. Mémoires de l'Académie des Inscriptions et Belles-Lettres, vol. 33, pt. 2. Paris: Académie des Inscriptions et Belles-Lettres, 1889. Reprint, Geneva: Slatkine-Megariotis Reprints, 1975.

Derbes, Anne. *Picturing the Passion in Late Medieval Italy: Narrative Painting, Franciscan Ideologies, and the Levant.* New York: Cambridge University Press, 1996.

Derrida, Jacques. *The Gift of Death.* Translated by David Willis. Chicago: University of Chicago Press, 1995.

Dierkens, Alain. "Du bon (et du mauvais) usage des reliquaires au Moyen Âge." In *Les reliques: Objets, cultes, symboles; Actes du colloque international de l'Université du Littoral-Côte d'Opale (Boulogne-sur-Mer), 4–6 septembre 1997,* edited by Edina Bozóky and Anne-Marie Helvétius, 239–52. Turnhout, Belgium: Brepols, 1999.

Diness, Mendel John, Dror Wahrman, Carney E. S. Gavin, and Nitza Rosovsky. *Capturing the Holy Land: M. J. Diness and the Beginnings of Photography in Jerusalem.* Cambridge, MA: Harvard Semitic Museum, 1993.

Douglas, Mary. "Primitive Rationing: A Study in Controlled Exchange." In *Themes in Economic Anthropology,* edited by Raymond William Firth, 119–47. London: Travistock, 1967.

Dove, W. "The Temple Church and Its Restoration." *Transactions of the London and Middlesex Archeological Society* (1967): 164–72.

Doyle, Paul A. "Waugh, Evelyn." In *Dictionary of Literary Biography,* edited by Bernard Oldsey, 570–86. Detroit: Gale Research Co., 1983.

Drijvers, Jan Willem. *Cyril of Jerusalem: Bishop and City.* Supplements to *Vigiliae Christianae,* vol. 72. Leiden: E. J. Brill, 2004.

———. *Helena Augusta: The Mother of Constantine the Great and the Legend of Her Finding of the True Cross.* Brill's Studies in Intellectual History, vol. 27. Leiden: E. J. Brill, 1992.

———. "Marutha of Maipherqat on Helena Augusta, Jerusalem and the Council of Nicaea." *Studia Patristica* 34 (2001): 51–64.

Duby, Georges. *The Early Growth of the European Economy.* Translated by Howard B. Clarke. Ithaca, NY: Cornell University Press, 1974.

Dumper, Michael. *The Politics of Sacred Space: The Old City of Jerusalem in the Middle East Conflict.* Denver: L. Rienner, 2002.

Duplessis, Robert S. *Transitions to Capitalism in Early Modern Europe.* New Approaches to European History, edited by William Beik, T. C. W. Blanning, and R. W. Schribner, vol. 10. Cambridge: Cambridge University Press, 1997.

Durkheim, Émile. *The Elementary Forms of Religious Life.* Translated by Carol Cosman. Oxford: Oxford University Press, 2001.

Eberlein, Kurt Karl. "Dioramen, Panoramen und Romantik." *Das Nationaltheater* 1 (1928/29): 35–43.

Eekelen, Yvonne van, ed. *The Magical Panorama: The Mesdag Panorama, an Experience in Space and Time.* Translated by Arnold Pomerans and Erica Pomerans. The Hague: Zwolle, 1996.

Eichengreen, Barry, and Marc Flandreau. *The Gold Standard in Theory and History.* London: Routledge, 1997.

Eliot, Marc. *Walt Disney: Hollywood's Dark Prince; a Biography.* Secaucus, NJ: Carol Publishing Group, 1993.

Elsner, John. "Replicating Palestine and Reversing the Reformation: Pilgrimage and Collecting at Bobbio, Monza and Walsingham." *Journal of the History of Collections* 9, no. 1 (1997): 117–30.

Engemann, Josef. "Der 'corna'-Gestus: Ein antiker und frühchristlicher Abwehr- und Spottgestus." In *Pietas: Festschrift für Bernhard Kötting,* edited by E. Dassmann and K. Suso Frank, 483–89. Münster: Aschendorff, 1980.

———. "Palästinensische Pilgerampullen im F. J. Dölger-Insitutut in Bonn." *Jahrbuch für Antike und Christentum* 16 (1973): 5–25.

Étienne, Geneviève. "Étude topographique sur les possessions de la maison du Temple à Paris (12–14 siècles)." *Positions de thèses: École nationale des chartes* (1974): 83–90.

Evans, Helen C., Melanie Holcomb, and Robert Hallman. *The Arts of Byzantium.* New York: Metropolitan Museum of Art, 2001.

Ferrazza, Roberta. *Palazzo Davanzati e le Collezioni di Elia Volpi.* Florence: Cassa di Risparmio di Firenze, 1993.

Fichtenau, Heinrich. "Zum Reliquienwesen im früheren Mittelalter." *Mitteilungen des Instituts für österreichische Geschictsforschung* 60 (1952): 66–78.

Fischer, Michael J. "Luca Pacioli on Business Profits." *Journal of Business Ethics* 25, no. 4 (2000): 299–313.

Fjellman, Stephen M. *Vinyl Leaves: Walt Disney World and America.* Boulder, CO: Westview Press, 1992.

Flint, Kate. *The Victorians and the Visual Imagination.* New York: Cambridge University Press, 2000.

Flower, Joe. *Prince of the Magic Kingdom: Michael Eisner and the Re-Making of Disney.* New York: J. Wiley, 1991.

Folda, Jaroslav. *The Art of the Crusaders in the Holy Land, 1098–1187.* Cambridge: Cambridge University Press, 1995.

———. *The Nazareth Capitals and the Crusader Shrine of the Annunciation.* University Park: Pennsylvania State University Press for the College Art Association of America, 1986.

Forey, Alan. *The Military Orders: From the Twelfth to the Early Fourteenth Centuries.* Toronto: University of Toronto Press, 1992.

Foucault, Michel. *Discipline and Punish: The Birth of the Prison.* Translated by A. Sheridan. New York: Random House, 1979.

Frank, Georgia. *The Memory of the Eyes.* Berkeley and Los Angeles: University of California Press, 2000.

Frankl, Paul, and Paul Crossley. *Gothic Architecture.* New Haven, CT: Yale University Press, 2000.

Frantz, Douglas. *Celebration, U.S.A.: Living in Disney's Brave New Town.* New York: Henry Holt, 1999.

Freiberg, Jack. *The Lateran in 1600: Christian Concord in Counter-Reformation Rome.* New York: Cambridge University Press, 1995.

Fried, Michael. *Absorption and Theatricality: Painting and Beholder in the Age of Diderot.* Berkeley and Los Angeles: University of California Press, 1980.

Friedland, Roger, and Richard D. Hecht. "The Politics of Sacred Space: Jerusalem's Temple Mount/al-haram al sharif." In *Sacred and Profane Spaces: Essays in the Geographics of Judaism, Christianity and Islam,* edited by Jamie S. Scott and Paul Simpson-Housley, 21–61. New York: Greenwood Press, 1991.

Frolow, Anatole. *La relique de la Vraie Croix: Recherches sur le développement d'un cult.* Archives de l'orient chrétien, vol. 7. Paris: Institut français d'études byzantines, 1961.

———. *Les reliquaires de la Vraie Croix.* Archives de l'orient chrétien, vol. 8. Paris: Institut français d'études byzantines, 1965.

———. "The Veneration of the Relic of the True Cross at the End of the Sixth and the Beginning of the Seventh Centuries." *St. Vladimirs Seminary Quarterly* 2, no. 1 (1958): 13–30.

Gadamer, Hans Georg. *Truth and Method.* Translated by Garrett Barden and John Cumming. New York: Seabury Press, 1975.

Galloni, Pietro. *Uomini e fatti celebri in Valle-Sesia.* Varallo, Italy, 1873.

Gatti-Perer, Maria Luisa. "Marino Bassi, il Sacro Monte di Varallo e Sta. Maria presso San Celso a Milano." *Arte Lombarda* 9, no. 2 (1964): 21–57.

Geary, Patrick. *Furta Sacra: Thefts of Relics in the Central Middle Ages.* 2nd ed. Princeton, NJ: Princeton University Press, 1990.

———. "The Ninth Century Relic Trade: A Response to Popular Piety?" In *Religion and the People, 800–1700,* edited by James Obelkevich, 8–19. Chapel Hill: University of North Carolina Press, 1979.

———. "Sacred Commodities: The Circulation of Medieval Relics." In Appadurai, *The Social Life of Things,* 169–91.

Gensini, Sergio, ed. *La "Gerusalemme" di San Vivaldo e i Sacri Monti in Europa (Firenze-San Vivaldo, 11–13 September, 1986)*. Centro Internazionale di studi "la 'Jerusalemme' di San Vivaldo" Montaione, 1. Montaione, Italy: Pacini editore, 1989.

Gibson, Gail. "St. Margery: The Book of Margery Kempe." In *Equally in God's Image: Women in the Middle Ages*, edited by Julia Bolton, Constance S. Wright, and Joan Bechtold, 144–63. New York: Peter Lang, 1990.

Giedion, Sigfried. *Space, Time and Architecture: The Growth of a New Tradition*. 5th ed. Cambridge, MA: Harvard University Press, 1967.

Gilmour-Bryson, Anne. *The Trial of the Templars in Cyprus*. Boston: E. J. Brill, 1998.

Godelier, Maurice. *The Enigma of the Gift*. Translated by Nora Scott. Chicago: University of Chicago Press, 1999.

Godfrey, Walter Hinds. "Recent Discoveries at the Temple, London, and Notes on the Topography of the Site." *Archaeologia: Miscellaneous Tracts Relating to Antiquity* 95 (1953): 123–40.

Gombrich, Ernst H. *Art and Illusion: A Study in the Psychology of Pictorial Representation*. 2nd ed. Vol. 35/5, The A. W. Mellon Lectures in the Fine Arts 1956, National Gallery of Art, Washington. Bollingen Series. New York: Random House, 1961.

Goussen, Heinrich. *Über georgische Drucke und Handschriften: Die Festordnung und der Heiligenkalender des altchristlichen Jerusalems*. München-Gladbach, 1923.

Grabar, André. *Ampoules de Terre Sainte (Monza, Bobbio)*. Paris: Klincksieck, 1958.

———. *Martyrium: Recherches sur le culte des reliques et l'art chrétien antique*. 2 vols. Paris: Collège de France, 1943–46. Reprint, London: Variorum, 1972.

Grabar, Oleg. *The Shape of the Holy: Early Islamic Jerusalem*. Princeton, NJ: Princeton University Press, 1996.

———. "The Shared Culture of Objects." In *Byzantine Court Culture from 829 to 1204*, edited by Henry Maguire, 115–30. Washington, DC: Dumbarton Oaks, 1997.

Green, Katherine, and Richard Green. *Inside the Dream: The Personal Story of Walt Disney*. New York: Disney Editions, 2001.

Greenberg, Clement. "Byzantine Parallels." In *Art and Culture: Critical Essays*, 167–70. Boston: Beacon Press, 1961.

Gregory, C. A. *Gifts and Commodities*. London: Academic Press, 1982.

Grierson, Philip. "Commerce in the Dark Ages: A Critique of the Evidence." *Transactions of the Royal Historical Society*, ser. 6, vol. 9 (1959): 123–40.

Griffith-Jones, Robin. "'Hearty and unanimous sentiment': The Monarchy and the Temple Church." *Inner Temple Yearbook* (2002/2003): 46–50.

Grisar, Hartmann. *Die römische Kapelle Sancta Sanctorum und ihr Schatz: Meine Entdeckungen und Studien in der Palastkapelle der mittelalterlichen Päpste*. Freiburg: Herder, 1908.

Grodecki, Louis, Anne Prache, and Roland Recht. *Gothic Architecture*. New York: Rizzoli, 1985.

Guiterman, Helen. "David Roberts, R. A. (1796–1864), part I." *Old Water-Colour Society's Club* 59 (1984): 53–75.

———. "The Travels of David Roberts." *Archaeology* 40, no. 6 (1987): 46–51.

Gurlitt, Cornelius. *Die deutsche Kunst des Neunzehnten Jahrhunderts: Ihre Ziele und Thaten*. Berlin: G. Bondi, 1899.

Gushee, David P. "The Speck in Mickey's Eye." *Christianity Today*, August 11, 1997, 13.

Habermas, Jürgen. *The Structural Transformation of the Public Sphere*. Translated by Thomas Burger and Frederick Lawrence. Cambridge, MA: MIT Press, 1989.

Hahn, Cynthia. "Collector and Saint: Queen Radegund and the Relic of the True Cross." Typescript.

Halbwachs, Maurice. *La topographie légendaire des Évangiles en terre sainte: Étude de mémoire collective*. Bibliothèque de sociologie contemporaine. Paris: Presses Universitaires de France, 1971.

Halkes, Petra. "The Mesdag Panorama: Sheltering the All-Embracing View." *Art History* 22, no. 1 (1999): 83–98.

Halpern, Richard. *The Poetics of Primitive Accumulation: English Renaissance Culture and the Genealogy of Capital.* Ithaca, NY: Cornell University Press, 1991.

Handelman, Don. *Models and Mirrors: Towards an Anthropology of Public Events.* Cambridge: Cambridge University Press, 1990.

Handler, Richard, and Eric Gable. *The New History in an Old Museum: Creating the Past at Colonial Williamsburg.* Durham, NC: Duke University Press, 1997.

Harman, Hollis Page. *Barron's Money Sense for Children.* Hauppauge, NY: Barron's Educational Series, 1999.

Harvey, David. *The New Imperialism.* Oxford: Oxford University Press, 2003.

Hiassen, Carl. *Team Rodent: How Disney Devours the World.* New York: Library of Contemporary Thought, 1998.

Hollister, Paul. "Genius at Work: Walt Disney." *Atlantic Monthly* 166, no. 6 (June 1940): 689–701.

Holum, Kenneth G. "Pulcheria's Crusade A.D. 421–22 and the Ideology of Imperial Victory." *Greek, Roman and Byzantine Studies* 18 (1977): 153–72.

Holzapfel, Heribert. *Die Anfänge der Montes Pietatis (1462–1515).* Munich: J. J. Lentner'schen Buchhandlung, 1903.

Honeybourne, Marjorie B. "The Temple Precinct in the Days of the Knights Templar." *Transactions of the Ancient Monuments Society* 16 (1969): 33–36.

Honigmann, Ernest. "Juvenal of Jerusalem." *Dumbarton Oaks Papers* 5 (1950): 209–79.

Hood, William. "The *Sacro Monte* of Varallo: Renaissance Art and Popular Religion." In *Monasticism and the Arts,* edited by Timothy Gregory Verdon, 291–312. Syracuse, NY: Syracuse University Press, 1984.

Horwitz, Howard. *By the Law of Nature: Form and Value in Nineteenth-Century America.* New York: Oxford University Press, 1991.

Hunt, Edwin S. *The Medieval Super-Companies: A Study of the Peruzzi Company in Florence.* Cambridge: Cambridge University Press, 1994.

Hunt, Edwin S., and James M. Murray. *A History of Business in Medieval Europe, 1200–1550.* Cambridge: Cambridge University Press, 1999.

Hyde, Ralph. "Jerusalem for Sale." *Art Newspaper* 103 (2000): 66.

———, ed. *Panoramania! The Art and Entertainment of the "All-Embracing" View.* London: Trefoil for the Barbican Art Gallery, 1988.

Izzett, David S. T., W. L. White, and W. S. Hardcastle. *The Garden Tomb Jerusalem.* London: Committee of the Garden Tomb Association, 1967.

Jackson, Kathy Merlock. *Walt Disney: A Bio-Bibliography.* Westport, CT: Greenwood Press, 1993.

Jacoby, David. "Pèlerinage médiéval et sanctuaires de terre sainte: La perspective vénitienne." *Ateneo Veneto,* n.s., 24 (1986): 27–58.

Jameson, Fredric, and Masao Miyoshi, eds. *The Cultures of Globalization.* Durham, NC: Duke University Press, 1998.

Jaspert, Nikolas. "Vergegenwärtigungen Jerusalem in Architektur und Reliquienkult." In *Jerusalem im Hoch- und Spätmittelalter: Konflikte und Konfliktbewältigung, Vorstellungen und Vergegenwärtungen,* edited by Dieter Bauer, Klaus Herbers, and Nikolas Jaspert, 219–70. Frankfurt: Campus Verlag, 2001.

Jastrow, Joseph. *Fact and Fable in Psychology.* Boston: Houghton, Mifflin and Company, 1900.

Jenks, Jeremiah Whipple. *The Trust Problem.* Edited by Walter Ernest Clark and John Joseph Quigley. 5th ed. New York: Doubleday, 1929.

Jenks, Martha Gail. "From Queen to Bishop: A Political Biography of Radegund of Poitiers." Ph.D. diss., University of California, Berkeley, 1999.

Jevons, W. Stanley. *The Theory of Political Economy.* London: Macmillan, 1888.

Juschka, Darlene. "Disney and Fundamentalism: The Fetishisation of the Family and the Production of American Family Values." *Culture and Religion* 2, no. 1 (2001): 21–39.

Kark, Ruth, and Michal Oren-Nordheim. *Jerusalem and Its Environs: Quarter, Neighborhoods, Villages, 1800–1948.* Detroit: Wayne State University Press, 2001.

Kartsonis, Anna D. *Anastasis: The Making of an Image.* Princeton, NJ: Princeton University Press, 1986.

Kaye, Joel. *Economy and Nature in the Fourteenth Century: Money, Market Exchange, and the Emergence of Scientific Thought.* Cambridge: Cambridge University Press, 1998.

Kelly, John P. *Aquinas and Modern Practices of Interest Taking.* Brisbane: Aquinas Press, 1945.

Keynes, John Maynard. *A Treatise on Money.* 2 vols. London: MacMillan, 1960.

Kindleberger, Charles P. *Economic and Financial Crises and Transformations in Sixteenth-Century Europe.* Essays in International Finance, vol. 208. Princeton, NJ: Department of Economics at Princeton University, 1998.

Kiraz, George, ed. "Special Issue: Michael the Syrian." *Hugoye: Journal of Syriac Studies* 3, no. 2 (2000).

Kirby, Doug, Ken Smith, and Mike Wilkins. "The Holy Land Experience." Roadside America, 2004. http://www.roadsideamerica.com/attract/FLORLholyland.html (accessed April 1, 2004).

Klatzker, David. "American Catholic Travelers to the Holy Land 1861–1929." *Catholic Historical Review* 74, no. 1 (1988): 55–74.

Kluncker, Karlhans. "Die Templer: Geschichte und Geheimnis." *Zeitschrift für Religions- und Geistesgeschichte* 41 (1989): 215–47.

Koenigs, Wolf. "Die Architektur des alten Jerusalem auf dem Panorama von Altötting." In Petzet, *Das Panorama in Altötting,* 36–43.

———. "Das Werk Gebhard Fugels (1863–1939): Zur Situation der christlichen Kunst um 1900." In Petzet, *Das Panorama in Altötting,* 45–53.

Koller, Gabriele. "Jerusalem in Altötting: Das Panorama religiöser Thematik im 19. Jahrhundert." *Das Münster* 46, no. 3 (1993): 185–96.

———. "Zur Planungs- und Enstehungsgeschichte [*sic*] des Panoramas 'Kreuzigung Christi' in Altötting." In Petzet, *Das Panorama in Altötting,* 23–33.

Koolhaas, Rem. *Delirious New York.* New York: Monacelli Press, 1994.

Kötsche-Breitenbruch, L. "Pilgerandenken aus dem Heiligen Land." In *Vivarium: Festschrift Theodor Klauser zum 90 Geburtstag,* edited by E. Dassmann and K. Traede, 229–46. Münster: Aschendorff, 1984.

Kratz, Coninne A., and Ivan Karp. "Wonder and Worth: Disney Museums in World Showcase." *Museum Anthropology* 17, no. 3 (1993): 32–42.

Krautheimer, Richard. "Introduction to an 'Iconography of Medieval Architecture.'" *Journal of the Warburg and Courtauld Institutes* 5 (1942): 1–33.

Lambert, C., and P. P. Demeglio. "Ampolle devozionali ed itinerari di pellegrinaggio tra IV e VII secolo." *Antiquité Tardive* 2 (1994): 205–31.

Lambert, Élie. *L'architecture des templiers.* Paris: A. and J. Picard, 1955.

Landsbury, Andrew. "Chronology." In Marling, *Designing Disney's Theme Parks,* 219–22.

Langé, Santino. "Lo spazio virtuale nell'opera di collaborazione dei fratelli D'Enrico: L'iconografia della Passione al Monte Varallo." *Arte Lombarda* 105–7 (1993): 142–48.

———. "L'omaggio incompiuto di F. M. Richini a S. Carlo Borromeo per il Sacro Monte di Arona." *Arte cristiana* 75, no. 706 (1985): 17–24.

Langé, Santino, and Alberto Pensa. *Il Sacro Monte: esperienza del reale e spazio virtuale nell'iconografia della passione a Varallo.* Milan: Jaca Book, 1991.

Langholm, Odd Inge. *Economics in the Medieval Schools: Wealth, Exchange, Value, Money, and Usury according to the Paris Theological Tradition, 1200–1350.* Leiden: E. J. Brill, 1992.

———. *The Legacy of Scholasticism in Economic Thought: Antecedents of Choice and Power; Historical Perspectives on Modern Economics.* Cambridge: Cambridge University Press, 1998.

Lauer, Philippe. *Le Trésor du Sancta Sanctorum.* Monuments et mémoires publiés par l'Académie des Inscriptions et Belles-Lettres, Fondation Eugène Piot, vol. 15.1–2. Paris: E. Leroux, 1906.

Lawson, Thomas. "Time Bandits; Space Vampires." *Art Forum International* 26 (1988): 88–95.

Leclercq, Jean. "Un document sur les débuts des Templiers." *Revue d'histoire ecclesiastique* 52 (1957): 81–91.

———. "Reliques et reliquaires." In *Dictionnaire d'archéologie chrétienne et de liturgie*, edited by Fernand Cabrol and Henri Leclerq, vol. 14, part 2, 2294–359. Paris: Librairie Letouzey et Ané, 1948.

Lees, Beatrice A., ed. *Records of the Templars in England in the Twelfth Century*. Records of the Social and Economic History of England and Wales, vol. 9. London: British Academy, 1935. Reprint, Munich: Kraus Reprint, 1981.

LeGoff, Jacques. *Your Money or Your Life: Economy and Religion in the Middle Ages*. Translated by Patricia Ranum. Cambridge, MA: Zone Books, 1988.

Lemmens, Leonhard. *Die Franziskanner im Hl. Lande: Die Franziskanner auf dem Sion (1335–1552)*. Münster: Aschendorff, 1925.

Leroy, Isabelle. "The Maritime Panorama of Scheveningen: A Brussels Initiative." In van Eekelen, *The Magical Panorama*, 37–43.

Lesley, Parker. "An Echo of Early Christianity." *Art Quarterly* 2 (1939): 214–32.

Levine, Lee I. *Jerusalem: Its Sanctity and Centrality to Judaism, Christianity, and Islam*. New York: Continuum, 1999.

Lewer, David. "The Anniversary Address: Restorations in the Temple Church, London, with Notes on Middle Temple Hall." *Transactions of the Ancient Monuments Society* 16 (1969): 23–31.

Lewer, David, and Robert Dark. *The Temple Church in London*. London: Historical Publications, 1997.

Lewis, Flora. "Rewarding Devotion: Indulgences and the Promotion of Images." In *The Church and the Arts: Papers Read at the 1990 Summer Meeting and 1991 Winter Meeting of the Ecclesiastical History Society*, edited by Diana Wood, 179–94. Oxford: Blackwell, 1992.

Lieber, Alfred E. "An Economic History of Jerusalem." In *Jerusalem: City of the Ages*, edited by Alice L. Eckhardt, 161–83. New York: University Press of America, 1987.

Ligato, Giuseppe. "The Political Meanings of the Relic of the Holy Cross among the Crusades and in the Latin Kingdom of Jerusalem: An Example of 1185." In *Autour de la première croisade: Actes du Colloque de la Society for the Study of the Crusades and the Latin East (Clermont-Ferrand, 22–25 June 1995)*, edited by Michel Balard, 315–30. Paris: Publications de la Sorbonne, 1996.

Little, Lester K. *Religious Poverty and the Profit Economy in Medieval Europe*. Ithaca, NY: Cornell University Press, 1978.

Loftie, W. J. *The Inns of Court and Chancery* [1893]. Curdridge, Southampton: Ashford Press, 1985.

Long, Burke O. *Imagining the Holy Land: Maps, Models and Fantasy Travels*. Bloomington: Indiana University Press, 2003.

Lopez, Robert S. *The Commercial Revolution of the Middle Ages 950–1350*. Cambridge: Cambridge University Press, 1976.

———. "The Trade of Medieval Europe: The South." In *The Cambridge Economic History of Europe*, vol. 2, *Trade and Industry in the Middle Ages*, edited by Michael Postan and E. E. Rich, 257–354. Cambridge: Cambridge University Press, 1952.

Lord, Evelyn. *The Knights Templar in Britain*. Harlow, UK: Longman, 2001.

Lotti, Carlo Alberto. *Santa Maria del Monte sopra Varese: Il monte sacro Olona e il Sacro Monte del Rosario; Guida per il pellegrino del terzo millenio*. Genoa: Silvana Editoriale, 2000.

Lucchesi Palli, Elisabetta. "Der syrisch-palästinensische Darstellungstypus der Höllenfahrt Christi." *Römische Quartalschrift* 57 (1962): 250–67.

Lutfi, Huda. *Al-Quds al-Mamlûkiyya: A History of Mamlûk Jerusalem Based on the Haram Documents*. Islamkundliche Untersuchungen, vol. 113. Berlin: Klaus Schwarz Verlag, 1985.

Luxemburg, Rosa. *The Accumulation of Capital*. Translated by Agnes Schwarzschild. London: Routledge, 1951.

MacCurdy, George Grant. "Extent of Instruction in Anthropology in Europe and the United States." *Science* 10, no. 260 (1899): 910–17.

MacDonald, A. A., H. N. B. Ridderbos, and R. M. Schlusemann, eds. *The Broken Body: Passion Devotion in Late-Medieval Culture.* Groningen, Netherlands: Egbert Forsten, 1998.

MacLeod, Christine. *Inventing the Industrial Revolution: The English Patent System, 1660–1800.* Cambridge: Cambridge University Press, 1988.

Mäkinen, Virpi. *Property Rights in the Late Medieval Discussion on Franciscan Poverty.* Vol. 3 of *Recherches de théologie et philosophie médiévales.* Leuven, Belgium: Peeters, 2001.

Mancoff, Debra N. *David Roberts: Travels in Egypt and the Holy Land.* San Francisco: Pomegranate, 1999.

Mannheim, Steve. *Walt Disney and the Quest for Community.* Aldershot, UK: Ashgate, 2002.

Marling, Karal Ann. "Imagineering the Disney Theme Parks." In *Designing Disney's Theme Parks: The Architecture of Reassurance,* edited by Karal Ann Marling, 29–189. Paris: Flammarion, 1997.

Marx, Karl. *Capital.* Edited by Frederick Engels. New York: International Press, 1967.

Mauss, Marcel. *The Gift: The Form and Reason for Exchange in Archaic Societies.* Translated by W. D. Halls. New York: Norton, 1990.

McIsaac, Peter M. "Wilhelm (von) Bode, the Public Museum, and the Case for Public Support of the Arts in Second Empire Germany." Paper presented at the Luce Conference on State Funding of the Arts, Berry Hill, Va., September 2002.

McLuhan, Marshall. *Understanding Media: The Extensions of Man.* New York: McGraw-Hill, 1964.

McNamara, Jo Ann, and John E. Halborg. *Sainted Women of the Dark Ages.* Durham, NC: Duke University Press, 1992.

Melion, Walter S. "Hendrick Goltzius's Project of Reproductive Engraving." *Art History* 13, no. 4 (1990): 458–87.

Mendels, Franklin F. "The Tasks of Economic History." *Journal of Economic History* 32, no. 1 (1972): 241–61.

Meneghin, Vittorino. "Bernardino da Feltre, i Monti di Pietà e i banchi ebraici." *Archivum franciscanum historicum* 73 (1980): 688–703.

Menning, Carol Bresnahan. *Charity and State in Late Renaissance Italy: The Monte di Pietà of Florence.* Ithaca, NY: Cornell University Press, 1993.

Metcalf, D. M. "The Templars as Bankers and Monetary Transfers between West and East in the Twelfth Century." In *Coinage in the Latin East,* edited by P. W. Edbury and D. M. Metcalf, 1–17. Oxford: B.A.R., 1980.

Mezzatesta, Michael P., ed. *Jerusalem and the Holy Land Rediscovered: The Prints of David Roberts (1796–1846).* Durham, NC: Duke University Museum of Art, 1996.

Michalowski, Roman. "Le don d'amitié dans la société carolingienne et les 'translationes sanctorum.'" In *Hagiographie: Cultures et sociétés, IV-XIIe siècles,* 399–416. Paris: Études augustiniennes, 1981.

Miedema, Nine. "Following in the Footsteps of Christ: Pilgrimage and Passion Devotion." In MacDonald, Ridderbos, and Schlusemann, *The Broken Body,* 73–92.

Miller, Angela. *The Empire of the Eye: Landscape Representation and American Cultural Politics, 1825–1875.* Ithaca, NY: Cornell University Press, 1993.

———. "The Moving Panorama, the Cinema, and the Emergence of the Spectacular." *Wide Angle: A Film Quarterly* 18, no. 2 (1996): 34–69.

Miller, D. "Consumption and Commodities." *Annual Review of Anthropology* 24 (1995): 141–61.

Miller, Marc H. *The Panorama of New York City: A History of the World's Largest Scale Model.* New York: Queens Museum, 1990.

Mitchell, W. J. T. "Holy Landscape: Israel, Palestine, and the American Wilderness." *Critical Inquiry* 26 (Winter 2000): 193–223.

———. *What Do Pictures Want? The Lives and Loves of Images.* Chicago: University of Chicago Press, 2005.

Monk, Daniel. *An Aesthetic Occupation: The Immediacy of Architecture and the Palestine Conflict.* Durham, NC: Duke University Press, 2002.

———. Review of Gilbert Herbert and Silvina Sosnovsky, *Bauhaus on the Carmel and the Crossroads of Empire*. *AA Files* 28 (1994): 94–99.

Moore, Derek. "Carlo Borromeo, Milano e i Sacri Monti." *Zodiac* (March–August 1993): 12–51.

Moore, G. Alexander. "Walt Disney World: Bounded Ritual Space and the Playful Pilgrimage Center." *Anthropological Quarterly* 53, no. 4 (1980): 207–18.

Moore, Robert Ian. *The Formation of a Persecuting Society*. New York: Blackwells, 1987.

Morey, Charles Rufus. "The Painted Panel from Sancta Sanctorum." In *Festschrift zum sechzigsten Geburtstag von Paul Clemen, 31. Oktober 1926*, 151–67. Bonn: F. Cohen, 1926.

Moscrop, John James. *Measuring Jerusalem: The Palestine Exploration Fund and British Interests in the Holy Land*. London: Leicester University Press, 2000.

Mosley, Leonard. *The Real Walt Disney: A Biography*. London: Grafton, 1986.

Muther, Richard. "Bruno Piglhein." *Zeitschrift für Bildende Kunst* 22 (1887): 170.

Nef, John U. "Prices and Industrial Capitalism in France and England, 1540–1640." *Economic History Review* 7, no. 2 (1937): 55–85.

Nelkin, Dorothy. "God Talk: Confusion between Science and Religion (Posthumous Essay)." *Science, Technology and Human Values* 29, no. 2 (2004): 139–52.

Neri, Damiano. *Il S. Sepolcro riprodotto in occidente*. Jerusalem: Franciscan Printing Press, 1971.

"The Newest Weeping Icons." *Sacred Art Journal* 9, no. 3 (1988): 72–77.

Nicholson, Helen. *The Knights Templar: A New History*. Stroud, UK: Sutton, 2001.

Noonan, John T., Jr. *The Scholastic Analysis of Usury*. Cambridge, MA: Harvard University Press, 1957.

Nova, Alessandro. "Popular Art in Renaissance Italy: Early Response to the Holy Mountain at Varallo." In *Reframing the Renaissance: Visual Culture in Europe and Latin America, 1450–1650*, edited by Claire Farago, 113–26. New Haven, CT: Yale University Press, 1995.

Oettermann, Stephan. *The Panorama: History of a Mass Medium*. Translated by Deborah Lucas Schneider. New York: Zone Books, 1997.

Onne, Eyal. *Photographic Heritage of the Holy Land 1839–1914*. Manchester: Institute of Advanced Studies, Manchester Polytechnic, 1980.

Ordoardo, Giovanni. "La custodia francescana di Terra Santa nel VI centenario della sua constituzione (1342–1942)." *Miscellanea francescana* 43 (1943): 217–56.

Os, Hank van. *Der Weg zum Himmel: Reliquienverehrung im Mittelalter*. Regensburg: Verlag Schnell & Steiner, 2001.

Ousterhout, Robert. "Rebuilding the Temple: Constantine Monomachus and the Holy Sepulchre." *Society of Architectural Historians Journal* 48, no. 1 (1989): 66–78.

———, ed. *The Blessings of Pilgrimage*. Illinois Byzantine Studies, vol. 1. Urbana: University of Illinois Press, 1990.

Oxford English Dictionary. Oxford University Press, 1989.

Pacciani, Riccardo. "L'archittetura delle cappelle di S. Vivaldo: Rapporti stilistici e iconografici." In Gensini, *La "Gerusalemme" di San Vivaldo e I Sacri Monti in Europa*, 299–331.

Pacciani, Riccardo, and Guido Vannini. *La "Gerusalemme" di S. Vivaldo in Valdelsa*. Commune di Montaione, Italy: Titivillus Edizioni, 1998.

Pamuk, Sevet. "The Ottoman Empire in Comparative Perspective." *Review* 11, no. 2 (1988): 127–49.

Pardi, Renzo. "L'architettura sacra degli ordini militari." In *Templari e Ospitalieri in Italia: La chiesa di San Bevignate a Perugia*, edited by Mario Roncetti, Pietro Scarpellini, and Francesco Tommasi, 27–38. Milan: Electa, 1987.

Parker, Thomas W. *The Knights Templars in England*. Tucson: University of Arizona Press, 1963.

Parsons, Anscar. "Bernadino of Feltre and the Montes Pietatis." *Franciscan Studies* 22 (March 1941): 11–32.

Peeters, Paul. *L'Orient et Byzance: Le tréfonds oriental de l'hagiographie byzantine*. Vol. 26. Brussels: Société des Bollandistes, 1950.

"Per il completamento del sacro monte de San Carlo ad Arona." *Zodiac* 9 (1993): 52–63.

Perelman, Michael. *The Invention of Capitalism: Classical Political Economy and the Secret History of Primitive Accumulation.* Durham, NC: Duke University Press, 2000.

Perkins, Clarence. "The Wealth of the Knights Templars in England." *American Historical Review* 15 (1909): 252–63.

Perrone, Stefania Stefani, ed. *Questi sono li Misteri che sono sopra el Monte de Varalle (in una 'Guida' poetica del 1514).* Varallo, Italy: Società per la conservazaione delle opere d'arte e dei monumenti in Valsesia, 1987.

Perry, Nicholas, and Loreto Echeverría. *Under the Heel of Mary.* London: Routledge, 1988.

Peters, F. E. *Jerusalem.* Princeton, NJ: Princeton University Press, 1985.

Petzet, Michael, ed. *Das Panorama in Altötting: Beiträge zu Geschichte und Restaurierung.* Munich: Karl M. Lipp Verlag, 1990.

Pieper, Jan. "The Garden of the Holy Sepulchre in Görlitz." *Daidalos* 58 (December 1955): 38–43.

Pietz, William. "Death of the Deodand: Accursed Objects and the Money Value of Human Life." *Res* 31 (Spring 1997): 97–108.

———. "The Fetish of Civilization: Sacrificial Blood and Monetary Debt." In *Colonial Subjects: Essays on the Practical History of Anthropology,* edited by Peter Pels and Oscar Saleminck, 53–81. Ann Arbor: University of Michigan Press, 1999.

Piquet, Jules. *Des banquiers au moyen âge: Les Templiers, étude de leurs opérations financières.* Paris: Hachette, 1939.

Plesch, Véronique. "A Pilgrim's Progress: Guidebooks to the New Jerusalem in Varallo." *Art on Paper* 6, no. 2 (2001): 50–57.

Polanyi, Karl. "Aristotle Discovers the Economy." In *Trade and Market in the Early Empires: Economies in History and Theory,* edited by Karl Polanyi, Conrad M. Arensberg, and Harry W. Pearson, 64–94. Glencoe IL: Free Press, 1957.

Postan, Michael. "The Rise of a Money Economy." *Economic History Review* 14, no. 2 (1944): 123–34.

Prawer, Joshua. *The Latin Kingdom of Jerusalem: European Colonialism in the Middle Ages.* London: Weidenfeld and Nicolson, 1972.

Pringle, Denys. "A Templar Inscription from the Haram al-Sharif in Jerusalem." *Levant* 21 (1989): 197–201.

Pullan, Brian. "Jewish Banks and Monti di Pietà." In *The Jews of Early Modern Venice,* edited by Robert C. Davis and Benjamin Ravid, 53–72. Baltimore: Johns Hopkins University Press, 2001.

Raby, R. Cornelius. *The Regulation of Pawnbroking.* New York: Russell Sage Foundation, 1924.

Ramsey, Peter. "The European Economy in the Sixteenth Century." *Economic History Review* 12, no. 3 (1960): 456–62.

Reid, Donald M. *Whose Pharaohs? Archaeology, Museums, and Egyptian National Identity from Napoleon to World War I.* Berkeley and Los Angeles: University of California Press, 2002.

"A Relief by Giovanni Della Robbia Given by Samuel Mather." *Bulletin of the Cleveland Museum of Art* 10, no. 1 (1923): 3–7.

Resnik, David B. *Owning the Genome: A Moral Analysis of DNA Patenting.* Albany: State University of New York Press, 2004.

Riant, Paul Edouard Didier. *Dépouilles religieuses à Constantinople au XIIIe siècle.* Vol. 4, ser. 6, *Mémoires de la Société nationale des antiquaires de France.* Paris: La Société, 1875.

Richardson, Joanna. *Zola.* London: Weidenfeld and Nicolson, 1978.

Riley-Smith, Jonathan. *Hospitallers: The History of the Order of St. John.* London: Hambledon Press, 1999.

Ritoók, Pál. "The Architecture of the Knights Templars in England." In *Military Orders: Fighting for the Faith and Caring for the Sick,* edited by Malcolm Barber, 167–78. Aldershot, UK: Variorum, 1994.

Roover, Raymond de. "New Interpretations of the History of Banking." In *Business, Banking, and Economic Thought in Late Medieval and Early Modern Europe: Selected Studies of Raymond de Roover,* edited by Julius Kirshner, 200–238. Chicago: University of Chicago Press, 1974.

———. *San Bernardino of Siena and Sant'Antonino of Florence: The Two Great Economic Thinkers of the Middle Ages.* Kress Library of Business and Economics, vol. 19. Cambridge, MA: Harvard University Printing Office, 1967.

———. "Scholastic Economics: Survival and Lasting Influence from the Sixteenth Century to Adam Smith." *Quarterly Journal of Economics* 69, no. 2 (1955): 161–90.

Rosenberg, Marc. *Niello bis zum Jahre 1000.* Vol. 4 of *Geschichte der Goldschmiedekunst auf technischer Grundlage.* Reprint, Osnabrück: Otto Zeller Verlag, 1972.

———. *Zellenschmelz. Die Frühdenkmäler.* Vol. 3 of *Geschichte der Goldschmiedekunst auf technischer Grundlage.* Reprint, Osnabrück: Otto Zeller Verlag, 1972.

Ross, Andrew. *The Celebration Chronicles: Life, Liberty & the Pursuit of Property Values in Disney's New Town.* New York: Ballantine Publishing Group, 1999.

Ross, Marvin Chauncey. *Metalwork, Ceramics, Glass, Glyptics, Painting.* Vol. 1 of *Catalogue of the Byzantine and Early Mediaeval Antiquities in the Dumbarton Oaks Collection.* 3 vols. Washington, DC: Dumbarton Oaks Center for Byzantine Studies, 1962.

Sabra, Adam Abdelhamid. *Poverty and Charity in Medieval Islam: Mamluk Egypt, 1250–1517.* Cambridge: Cambridge University Press, 2001.

Safdie, Moshe. *Jerusalem: The Future of the Past.* Boston: Houghton, Mifflin and Company, 1989.

Said, Edward W. "Invention, Memory, and Place." *Critical Inquiry* 26 (Winter 2000): 175–92.

———. *Orientalism.* New York: Vintage Books, 1979.

Samuel, Lawrence R. *Pledging Allegiance: American Identity and the Bond Drive of World War II.* Washington, DC: Smithsonian Institution Press, 1997.

Satorio, Giuseppina Pisani. "The Reconstruction of Rome in Bigot and Gismondi's Models." *Rassegna* 15, no. 55 (3) (1993): 82–88.

Satterlee, Herbert L. *J. Pierpont Morgan: An Intimate Portrait.* New York: MacMillan, 1939.

Sayyid-Marsot, Afaf Lutfi. *Egypt in the Reign of Muhammad Ali.* Cambridge: Cambridge University Press, 1984.

Schama, Simon. *Landscape and Memory.* New York: A. A. Knopf, 1995.

Schein, Sylvia. "Between Mount Moriah and the Holy Sepulchre: The Changing Traditions of the Temple Mount in the Central Middle Ages." *Traditio* 40 (1984): 175–95.

———. "La *Custodia Terrae Sanctae* franciscaine et les Juifs de Jérusalem à la fin du moyen-age." *Revue des études juives* 141, nos. 3–4 (1982): 369–77.

Schlumberger, Eveline. "Un théâtre de la foi: le Sacro Monte d'Orta." *Connaissance des arts* 305 (1977): 70–78.

Schreiner, Klaus. "'Discrimen veri ac falsi' Ansätze und Formen der Kritik in der Heiligen- und Reliquieverehrung des Mittelalters." *Archiv für Kulturgeschichte* 48, no. 1 (1966): 1–53.

Schütz, Christiane. *Preussen in Jerusalem (1800–1861): Karl Friedrich Schinkels Entwurf der Grabeskirche und die Jerusalempläne Friedrich Wilhelms IV.* Berlin: Mann, 1988.

Scriba, Friedemann. "Die Mostra Augustea della Romanità in Rom 1937/38." In *Mostra Augustea della Romanità: Faschismus und Gesellschaft in Italien; Staat—Wirtschaft—Kultur,* edited by Jens Petersen and Wolfgang Schieder, 133–57. Cologne: SH-Verlag, 1998.

Segal, Haggai. *Dear Brothers: The West Bank Jewish Underground.* Woodmere, NY: Beit-Shamai Publications, 1988.

Segal, Rafi, and Eyal Weizman. *A Civilian Occupation: The Politics of Israeli Architecture.* London: Verso, 2002.

Segre, Renata. "Bernardino da Feltre: I Monti di Pietà e i banchi ebraici." Review of *Bernadino da Feltre e i Monti di Pietà,* by Vittorio Meneghin. *Rivista storica italiana* 90 (1978): 818–33.

Shepstone, Harold J. "Restoring the Walls of Jerusalem." *Graphic* (April 19, 1924): 577.

Shiva, Vandana. *Protect or Plunder? Understanding Intellectual Property Rights.* London: Zed Books, 2001.

Silberman, Neil Asher. *Digging for God and Country: Exploration, Archaeology and the Secret Struggle for the Holy Land.* New York: A. A. Knopf, 1982.

Silver, Larry. "Mapped and Marginalized: Early Printed Images of Jerusalem." *Jewish Art* 23–24 (1997–98): 313–24.

Simonsohn, Shlomo. *History of the Jews in the Duchy of Mantua*. Publications of the Diaspora Institute, vol. 17. Jerusalem: Kiryath Sepher, 1977.

Skubiszewski, Piotr. "La staurothèque de Poitiers." *Cahiers de civilisation médiévale* 35, no. 3 (1992): 65–75.

Smith, Jonathan Z. *To Take Place*. Chicago: University of Chicago Press, 1987.

Solon, Leon V. "Suggestions and Models for Architectural Rendering: The Lithographic Work of David Roberts." *Architectural Record* 46 (1919): 211–20.

Sombart, Werner. *Luxury and Capitalism*. Translated by W. R. Dittmar. Ann Arbor: University of Michigan Press, 1967.

Southwell QC, Richard. "Challenges to the Inns." *Inner Temple Yearbook* (2002/2003): 5–6.

Spufford, Peter. *Money and Its Use in Medieval Europe*. London: Cambridge University Press, 1988.

Staudhamer, S. "Vom Panorama in Altötting." *Die christliche Kunst* 3 (1906–7): 57–60.

Stein, Siegfried. "The Development of the Jewish Law on Interest from the Biblical Period to the Expulsion of the Jews from England." *Historia Judaica* 17, no. 1 (1955): 3–40.

Stevens, Gorham P. "Plaster Model of the Acropolis of Athens: Restoration of the End of the First Century B.C." *Bulletin de correspondance hellénique* 70 (1946): 557–59.

Stewart, Susan. *On Longing: Narratives of the Miniature, the Gigantic, the Souvenir, the Collection*. Baltimore: Johns Hopkins University Press, 1984.

St. John Hope, W. H. "The Round Church of the Knights Templars at Temple Bruer, Lincolnshire." *Archaeologia* 61 (1908): 177–98.

Strachey, Lytton. *Eminent Victorians* [1918]. London: Penguin, 1986.

Stroumsa, Guy G. "Mystical Jerusalems." In Levine, *Jerusalem*, 15–40. New York: Continuum, 1999.

Strouse, Jean. "J. Pierpont Morgan: Financier and Collector." *Bulletin of the Metropolitan Museum of Art* 57, no. 3 (2000): 4–64.

———. "The Unknown J. P. Morgan." *New Yorker* 75, no. 5 (March 29, 1999): 65–79.

Sutton, Denys. "Discoveries." *Apollo* 122 (August 1985): 118–28.

Szövérffy, Joseph. "Venantius Fortunatus and the Earliest Hymns to the Holy Cross." *Classical Folia* 20, no. 2 (1966): 107–22.

Taussig, Michael. "History as Commodity in Some Recent American (Anthropological) Literature." *Critique of Anthropology* 9, no. 1 (1989): 7–23.

Tawney, R. H. *Religion and the Rise of Capitalism: A Historical Study; Holland Memorial Lectures, 1922*. New York: Harcourt Brace, 1926.

Testori, Giovanni. *Il gran teatro montano: Saggi su Gaudenzio Ferrari*. Milan: Giangiacomo Feltrinelli Editore, 1965.

Thiede, Carsten Peter, and Matthew D'Ancona. *The Quest for the True Cross*. London: Weidenfeld and Nicolson, 2000.

Thomas, Nicholas. *Entangled Objects: Exchange, Material Culture, and Colonialism in the Pacific*. Cambridge, MA: Harvard University Press, 1991.

Thompson, E. P. *The Making of the English Working Class*. New York: Pantheon Books, 1964.

Thurston, Herbert. *The Stations of the Cross: An Account of Their History and Devotional Purpose*. London: Burns and Oates, 1906.

Titmuss, Richard. *The Gift Relationship: From Human Blood to Social Policy*. Edited by Ann Oakley and John Ashton. 2nd ed. New York: New Press, 1997.

Tomlin, Graham S. "The Medieval Origins of Luther's Theology of the Cross." *Archiv für Reformationsgeschichte* 89 (1998): 22–40.

Trachtenberg, Marvin. "Qu'est-ce que 'le gothique'?" *Cahiers de la recherche architecturale et urbaine* 9–10 (January 2002): 41–52.

———. "Suger's Miracles, Branner's Bourges: Reflections on 'Gothic Architecture' as Medieval Modernism." *Gesta* 39, no. 2 (2000): 183–205.

Tsafrir, Yoram. "Byzantine Jerusalem: The Configuration of a Christian City." In Levine, *Jerusalem*, 133–50. New York: Continuum, 1999.

———. "Jerusalem." In *Reallexikon zur byzantinische Kunst*, 3:544–51. Stuttgart: Hiersemann, 1975.

Tuchman, Barbara W. *Bible and Sword: England and Palestine from the Bronze Age to Balfour*. New York: New York University Press, 1956.

Twyman, Michael. *Breaking the Mould: The First Hundred Years of Lithography*. London: British Library, 2001.

———. *Lithography, 1800–1850: The Techniques of Drawing on Stone in England and France and Their Application to Works of Topography*. London: Oxford University Press, 1970.

Vance, James E. "Land Assignment in the Precapitalist, Capitalist, and Postcapitalist City." *Economic Geography* 47, no. 2 (1971): 101–20.

Van Dam, Raymond. *Saints and Their Miracles in Late Antique Gaul*. Princeton, NJ: Princeton University Press, 1993.

Vanderlinder, S. "Revelatio Sancti Stephani." *Revue des études byzantines* 4 (1946): 178–217.

Vannini, Guido. "S. Vivaldo e la sua documentazione materiale: Lineamenti di una ricerca archeologica." In Gensini, *La "Gerusalemme" di San Vivaldo e I Sacri Monti in Europa*, 241–70.

Venturi, Robert, Denise Scott Brown, and Steven Izenour. *Learning from Las Vegas*. Cambridge, MA: MIT Press, 1972.

Vikan, Gary. *Byzantine Pilgrimage Art*. Washington, DC: Dumbarton Oaks, 1982.

———. "Early Byzantine Pilgrimage *Devotionalia* as Evidence of the Appearance of Pilgrimage Shrines." In *Jahrbuch für Antike und Christentum, Ergänzungsband; Studi di antichità cristiana, 52*, edited by Ernst Dassmann and Josef Engemann, 377–88. Münster: Aschendorff, 1995.

———. "Two Unpublished Pilgrim Tokens in the Benaki Museum and the Group to Which They Belong." In Andreade et al., *Thumíama ste mneme tes Laskarínas Mpoúra*, 341–46.

Vincent, Louis-Hugues, and M. Abel. *Jérusalem: Recherches de topographie, d'archéologie et d'histoire*. 2 vols. Paris: J. Gabalda for l'Académie des Inscriptions et Belles-Lettres, 1912–26.

Vincent, Nicholas. *The Holy Blood: King Henry III and the Blood Relics of Westminster and Hailes*. Cambridge: Cambridge University Press, 2001.

Voltz, Eugène. "La chapelle des Templiers de Metz." *Congrès archéologique de France 1991* 149 (1991): 517–24.

Ward-Perkins, Bryan. "Specialisation, Trade, and Prosperity: An Overview of the Economy of the Late Antique Eastern Mediterranean." In *Economy and Exchange in the East Mediterranean during Late Antiquity: Proceedings of a Conference at Somerville College, Oxford*, edited by Sean Kingsley and Michael Decker, 167–75. Oxford: Oxbow, 1999.

Warren, Hillary. "Southern Baptists as Audience and Public: A Cultural Analysis of the Disney Boycott." In *Religion and Popular Culture: Studies on the Interaction of Worldviews*, edited by Daniel A. Stout and Judith Mitchell Buddenbaum, 169–87. Ames: Iowa State University Press, 2001.

Wasserstein, Bernard. *The British in Palestine: The Mandatory Government and the Arab-Jerwish Conflict 1917–1929*. Oxford: Basil Blackwell, 1991.

Watson, Charles Moore. *The Life of Major-General Sir Charles William Wilson, Royal Engineers*. London: Murray, 1909.

Webb, Geoffrey. *Architecture in Britain: The Middle Ages*. Harmondsworth, UK: Penguin, 1956.

Weber, Max. *Economy and Society: An Outline of Interpretive Sociology* [1914]. Translated by Ephraim Fischoff, Hans Gerth, A. M. Henderson, Ferdinand Kolegar, C. Wright Mills, Talcott Parsons, Max Rheinstein, Guenther Roth, Edward Shils, and Claus Wittich. Edited by Guenther Roth and Claus Wittich. 2 vols. Berkeley and Los Angeles: University of California Press, 1978.

———. *Protestant Ethic and the Spirit of Capitalism*. Translated by Talcott Parsons. Los Angeles: Roxbury Publishers, 1998.

Weiner, Annette B. *Inalienable Possessions: The Paradox of Keeping-While-Giving.* Berkeley and Los Angeles: University of California Press, 1992.

Weiss, Daniel H. *Art and Crusade in the Age of Saint Louis.* Cambridge: Cambridge University Press, 1998.

Weitzmann, Kurt. "*Loca sancta* and the Representational Arts of Palestine." In *Studies in the Arts at Sinai,* 19–62. Princeton, NJ: Princeton University Press, 1982.

———, ed. *Age of Spirituality: Late Antique and Early Christian Art, Third to Seventh Century; Catalog of the Exhibition at the Metropolitan Museum of Art, November 19, 1977 through February 12, 1978.* New York: Metropolitan Museum of Art, 1979.

Weltecke, Dorothea. *Die "Beschreibung der Zeiten" von Mor Michael dem Grossen (1126–1199): Eine Studie zu ihrem historischen und historiographiegeschichtlichen Kontext.* Vol. 594, subsidia 110 of *Corpus scriptorum Christianorum Orientalium.* Louvain: Peeters, 2003.

———. "Contacts between Syriac Orthodox and Latin Military Orders." In *East and West in the Crusader States: Context, Contacts, Confrontations,* edited by Krijnie Ciggaar and Herman Teule, 53–77. Leuven, Belgium: Uitgeverij Peeters, 2003.

Wessel, Klaus, and Irene Rosalind Gibbons. *Byzantine Enamels from the Fifth to the Thirteenth Century.* Shannon: Irish University Press, 1968.

Wharton, Annabel. "Erasure: Eliminating the Space of Late Ancient Judaism." In *From Dura to Sepphoris: Studies in Jewish Art and Society in Late Antiquity,* edited by Lee L. Levine, 195–214. Ann Arbor: University of Michigan Press, 2000.

———. "Icon, Idol, Fetish and Totem." In *Icon and Word: The Power of Images in Byzantium,* edited by A. Eastmond and L. Hunt, 12–23. London: Ashgate, 2003.

———. *Refiguring the Post Classical City: Dura Europos, Jerash, Jerusalem and Ravenna.* Cambridge: Cambridge University Press, 1995.

———. "Westminster Cathedral: Medieval Architectures and Religious Difference." *Journal of Medieval and Early Modern Studies* 26, no. 3 (1996): 523–55.

Wilcox, Scott B. "Introduction: Unlimiting the Bounds of Painting." In Hyde, *Panoramania!,* 13–43.

Wilkinson, John. *Jerusalem Pilgrims before the Crusades.* Warminster, UK: Aris and Phillips, 1977.

Williams, Raymond. *Keywords: A Vocabulary of Culture and Society.* Rev. American ed. New York: Oxford University Press, 1985.

Williamson, G. C. "The Oppenheim Reliquary and Its Contents." *Burlington Magazine* 23 (1913): 296–301.

Williamson, John Bruce. *The History of the Temple, London: From the Institution of the Order of the Knights of the Temple to the Close of the Stuart Period.* New York: Dutton, 1924.

Williamson, Paul. "The West Doorway of the Temple Church, London." *Burlington Magazine* 127 (October 1985): 716.

Wilson, Alexander. "The Betrayal of the Future: Walt Disney's EPCOT Center." In *Disney Discourse: Producing the Magic Kingdom,* edited by Eric Loren Smoodin, 118–30. London: Routledge, 1994.

Wilson, Ian. *The Turin Shroud.* New York: Doubleday, 1979.

Winner, Laurer. "Praise at Celebration." *Christian Century,* January 19, 2000, 3.

Wittkower, Rudolf. "'Sacri Monti' in the Italian Alps." In *Idea and Image: Studies in the Italian Renaissance,* 175–84. London: Thames and Hudson, 1978.

Wixom, William D. "Morgan: The Man and the Collector." In K. Brown, Kid, and Little, *From Attila to Charlemagne,* 2–7.

Wolf, Kenneth Baxter. *The Poverty of Riches: St. Francis of Assisi Reconsidered.* Oxford: Oxford University Press, 2003.

Wolfe, Tom. *The Painted Word.* New York: Farrar, Straus and Giroux, 1975.

Wood, Diana. *Medieval Economic Thought.* Cambridge: Cambridge University Press, 2002.

Wood, R. Derek. "The Diorama in Great Britain in the 1820s." *History of Photography* 17, no. 3 (1993): 284–95.

Woolf, Virginia. *Roger Fry: A Biography*. New York: Harcourt, Brace and Company, 1940.

Worringer, Wilhelm. *Abstraction and Empathy: A Contribution to the Psychology of Style*. Translated by Michael Bullock. New York: International Universities Press, 1953.

Yamey, B. S. "Scientific Bookkeeping and the Rise of Capitalism." *Economic History Review* 1 (1949): 99–113.

Yarden, Leon. *The Spoils of Jerusalem on the Arch of Titus: A Re-Investigation*. Skrifter utgivna av Svenska institutet i Rom, vol. 16. Stockholm: Paul Åströms, 1991.

Zanzi, Luigi. "Peak of the Most High: Varese." *FMR Magazine of Franco Maria Ricci* 20 (1998): 37–46.

Zarnecki, George. "The West Doorway of the Temple Church in London." In *Beiträge zur Kunst des Mittelalters: Festschrift für Hans Wentzel zum 60. Geburtstag*, edited by Hans Wentzel, Rüdiger Beckmann, Ulf-Dietrich Korn, and Johannes Zahlten, 245–53. Berlin: Bebr. Mann Verlag, 1975.

Žižek, Slavoj. *Welcome to the Desert of the Real! Five Essays on September 11 and Related Dates*. London: Verso, 2002.

INDEX

Note: Italicized page numbers indicate illustrations.